Social Media for Seniors

Studio Visual Steps

Social Media for Seniors

Personal and business communication through social networking

This book has been written using the Visual Steps™ method.
Cover design by Studio Willemien Haagsma bNO

With the assistance of Yvette Huijsman
Edited by Jolanda Ligthart, Rilana Groot and Mara Kok
Translated by Irene Venditti, *i-write* translation services and Chris Hollingsworth, *1st Resources*.

First printing: April 2012
ISBN 978 90 5905 018 1

Do you have questions or suggestions?
E-mail: info@visualsteps.com

Would you like more information?
www.visualsteps.com

Website for this book:
www.visualsteps.com/socialmedia
Here you can register your book.

Subscribe to the free Visual Steps Newsletter:
www.visualsteps.com/newsletter

Table of Contents

Appendices

Foreword

Dear readers,

Nowadays, social media websites have become part of our daily lives and are used by a growing number of people. These sites are used for both private purposes as well as commercial activities. Worldwide, there are more than 845 million active *Facebook* users, as of December 2011. The social network or microblogging service called *Twitter* also has millions of users. You can hardly find a company, club, newspaper or television program that does not have its own page on *Facebook* or *Twitter*. For many sports organizations, clubs and hobbies, such a page has proved to be indispensable for communicating with their members,

In this book you will get to know *Facebook*, *LinkedIn, Twitter* and *WordPress*. Besides creating an account, you will learn how to fill your account with personal information. You will also learn how to add blogs and photos. The next step is to add friends or contacts. Finally, we will discuss some of the important elements to consider when dealing with the various privacy settings.

Do you own a company, or are you involved in a club organization? Then you will get valuable commercial tips about using your page for communicating with your customers and members. These days, social media pages can play a major part in your business!

I wish you lots of luck in your networking career!

Yvette Huijsman

PS We welcome your comments and suggestions.
Our e-mail address is: info@visualsteps.com

Newsletter

All Visual Steps books follow the same methodology: clear and concise step-by-step instructions with screen shots to demonstrate each task. A complete list of all our books can be found on our website **www.visualsteps.com.** You can also sign up to receive our **free Visual Steps Newsletter**.

In this Newsletter you will receive periodic information by e-mail regarding:
- the latest titles and previously released books;
- special offers, supplemental chapters and free informative booklets.
Our Newsletter subscribers may also download any of the documents listed on the web pages **www.visualsteps.com/info_downloads**
When you subscribe to our Newsletter you can be assured that we will never use your e-mail address for any purpose other than sending you the information as previously described. We will not share this address with any third-party.
Each Newsletter also contains a one-click link to unsubscribe.

Introduction to Visual Steps™

The Visual Steps handbooks and manuals are the best instructional materials available for learning how to work with computers and computer programs. Nowhere else will you find better support for getting to know the computer, Internet, *Windows*, *Mac*, the iPad or related software.

Key components in every Visual Steps book:

- **Comprehensible contents**
  Addresses the needs of the beginner or intermediate computer user for a manual written in simple, straight-forward English.
- **Clear structure**
  Precise, easy to follow instructions. The material is broken down into small enough segments to allow for easy absorption.
- **Screen shots of every step**
  Quickly compare what you see on your own computer screen with the screen shots in the book. Pointers and tips guide you when new windows are opened so you always know what to do next.
- **Get started right away**
  All you have to do is turn on your computer or tablet, place the book next to your device or keyboard and carry out each action as directed.

In short, I believe these manuals will be excellent guides for you.

dr. H. van der Meij
Faculty of Applied Education, Department of Instruction Technology, University of Twente, the Netherlands

Register Your Book

When you can register your book, you will be kept informed of any important changes that are necessary to you as a user of the book. You can also take advantage of our periodic Newsletter informing you of our product releases, company news, special offers, etcetera.

What You Will Need

In order to work through this book, you will need to have a number of things installed on your computer:

The main requirement is a computer that is installed with *Windows 7*, *Vista* or *XP*.

You can also use this book if you are working with a *Mac OS X* computer. Occasionally, you may see some differences between your own screen and the screen shots in this book, but you can solve the problem by searching for a similar button or function.

Internet Explorer — *Internet Explorer 9* (or any other Internet browser).

An active Internet connection.

How to Use This Book

This book has been written using the Visual Steps™ method. The method is simple: just place the book next to your computer and execute all the tasks step by step, directly on your computer. With the clear instructions and the multitude of screenshots, you will always know exactly what to do. This way, you will quickly learn how to use the various programs or services, without any problems.

In this Visual Steps™ book, you will see various icons. This is what they mean:

Techniques

These icons indicate an action to be carried out:

The mouse icon means you need to do something with the mouse.

The keyboard icon means you should type something on your keyboard.

 The hand icon means you should do something else, for example, turn on the computer or carry out a task previously learned.

In addition to these icons, in some areas of this book extra assistance is provided to help you successfully work through each chapter.

Help

These icons indicate that extra help is available:

 The arrow icon warns you about something.

 The bandage icon will help you if something has gone wrong.

 Have you forgotten how to do something? The number next to the footsteps tells you where to look it up at the end of the book in the appendix *How Do I Do That Again?*

In this book you will also find a lot of general information, and tips. This information is displayed in separate boxes.

Extra information

Information boxes are denoted by these icons:

 The book icon gives you extra background information that you can read at your convenience. This extra information is not necessary for working through the book.

 The light bulb icon indicates an extra tip for using the program or service.

Prior Computer Experience

This book has been written for users who possess some basic computer skills.

The Website Accompanying This Book

There is a website accompanying this book: **www.visualsteps.com/socialmedia**
Be sure to check this website regularly, to see if we have added any additional information, supplements or errata for this book.

Test Your Knowledge

After you have worked through this book, you can test your knowledge online, on the **www.ccforseniors.com** website.

By answering a number of multiple choice questions you will be able to test your knowledge about social media as well as other topics regarding computing. After you have finished the test, your *Computer Certificate* will be sent to the e-mail address you have entered.
Participating in the test is **free of charge**. The computer certificate website is a free service from Visual Steps.

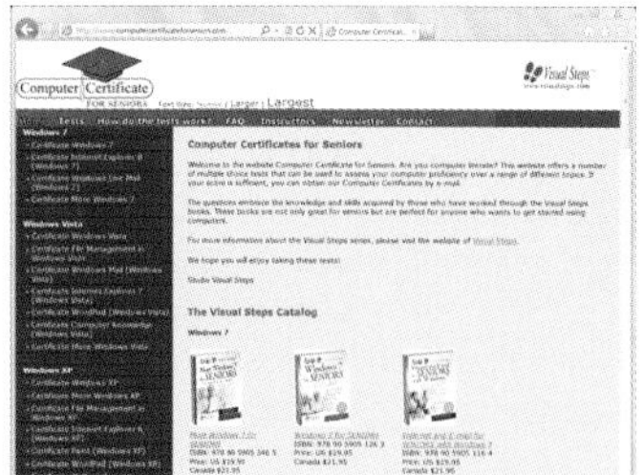

For Teachers

This book is designed as a self-study guide. It is also well suited for use in groups or a classroom setting. For this purpose, we offer a free teacher's manual containing information about how to prepare for the course (including didactic teaching methods) and testing materials. You can download this teacher's manual (PDF file) from the website that accompanies this book: **www.visualsteps.com/socialmedia**

The Screen Shots

The screen shots in this book were made on a computer running *Windows 7 Ultimate* edition. The screen shots used in this book indicate which button, folder, file or hyperlink you need to click on your computer screen. In the instruction text (in **bold** letters) you will see a small image of the item you need to click. The black line will point you to the right place on your screen.
The small screen shots that are printed in this book are not meant to be completely legible all the time. This is not necessary, as you will see these images on your own computer screen in real size and fully legible.

Here you see an example of an instruction text and a screen shot. The black line indicates where to find this item on your own computer screen:

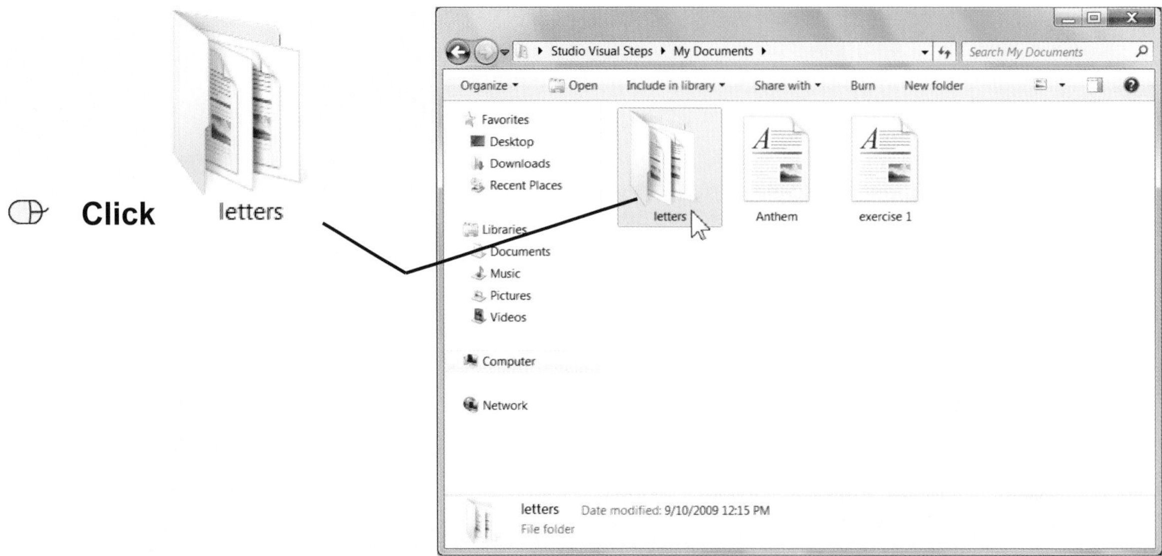

Sometimes the screen shot shows only a portion of a window. Here is an example:

In the top left of the window:

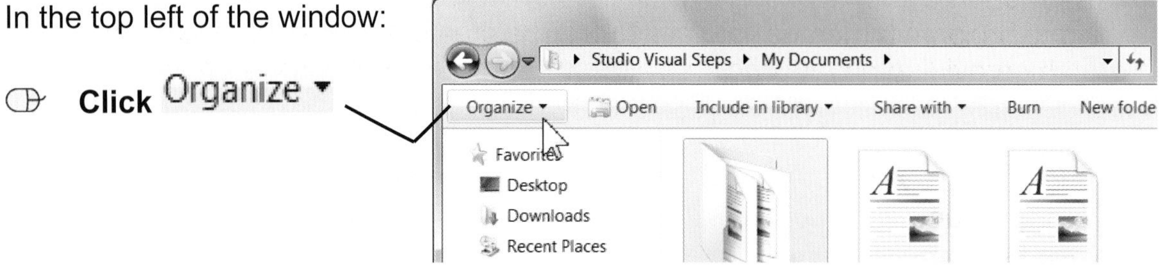

We would like to emphasize that we **do not intend you** to read the information in all of the screenshots in this book. Always use the screen shots in combination with the image you see on your own screen.

1. Facebook

Facebook is a free online social network site, specifically developed to allow users to connect and stay connected with friends and acquaintances in a simple way. The network can also be used for getting to know new people. Through *Facebook* you can connect to people who have the same interests as you, you can maintain a blog, and share photos and videos with friends. The name *Facebook* is derived from the paper 'face books' that are distributed among new American college students and staff workers, so they can quickly get to know each other.

Facebook is a very inviting website. Anyone can view the website and search for people who have created a *Facebook* profile. When you first visit the website and are not signed up, you will see very little information. Only after you have created your own *Facebook* profile, will you be able to fully participate in the social network. Then you can build a group of friends, view their profiles and interact with them.

Facebook began in 2004 and since then, the network has drawn more than 845 million users, from all over the world (data from December 2011). It does not cost anything to become a member of *Facebook*. The creators of *Facebook* earn their revenue by providing advertising space. This means you will have to endure the various advertisements, if you want to use the networking site.

In this chapter you will learn how to sign in, create a profile, manage your *Facebook* page and build up a group of friends. We also include information about using groups and official pages for companies, clubs and organizations.

In this chapter you will learn how to:

- sign in with *Facebook*;
- view and edit your profile;
- view and change your privacy settings;
- look for friends with the Friend Finder;
- look for friends, add them and confirm this action;
- write and publish notes;
- add a photo album;
- write a note on a friend's Timeline;
- deactivate your account;
- use groups and official pages.

 **Please note:**

The developers of the *Facebook* website are constantly adding new options to the program. As a result, the screenshots in this chapter may differ from the windows you see on your own screen. This does not need to be a problem as most of the time the existing options will not be removed. Buttons and hyperlinks may have a new location. If your screen differs from the examples in this book, it is best to look for a similar button or option.

1.1 Creating a Facebook Account

In this chapter you will learn how to create and maintain your own group of friends on the *Facebook* website. First, you need to surf to the *Facebook* website:

Open the www.facebook.com website [1]

You will see the *Facebook* home page:

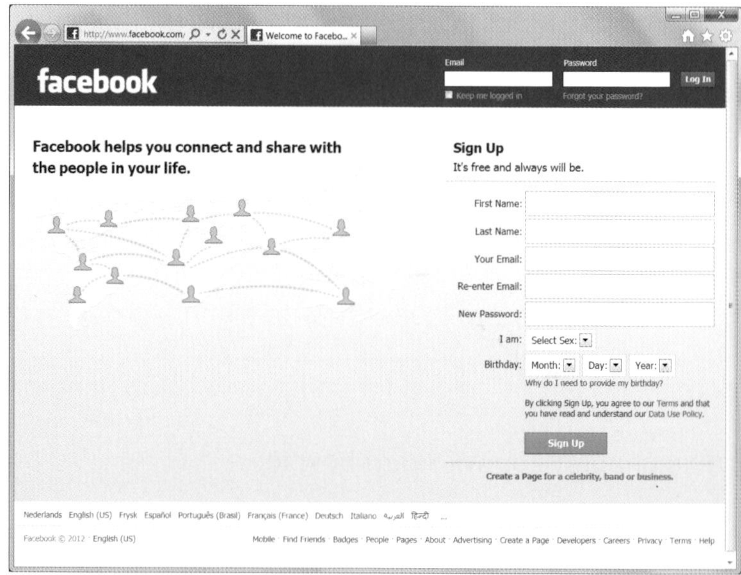

In order to use the services of the *Facebook* social media site, you need to sign in with a free *Facebook* account. This account will give you access to *Facebook*, and you will be able to start your own group of friends.

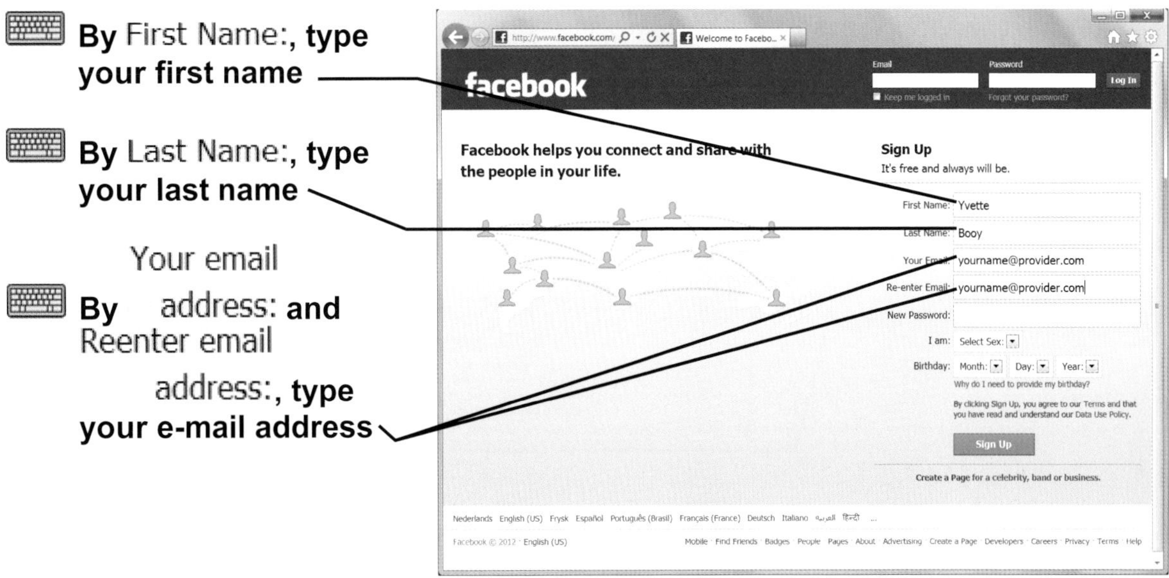

- By First Name:, type your first name
- By Last Name:, type your last name
- By Your email address: and Reenter email address:, type your e-mail address

You can choose your own password. This password needs to consist of at least six characters, and can contain letters, numbers and special characters.

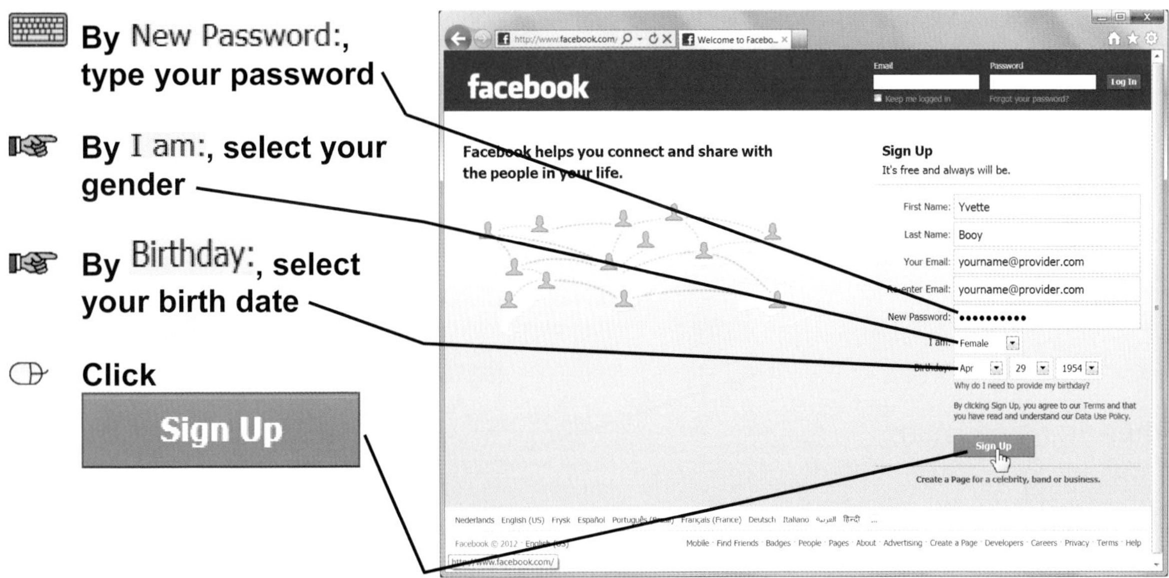

- By New Password:, type your password
- By I am:, select your gender
- By Birthday:, select your birth date
- Click **Sign Up**

Write down your password on a piece of paper and store it in a safe place

Now the next window appears:

Facebook offers to help you find your friends by using your e-mail address book. For now, this will not be necessary:

Click Skip this step

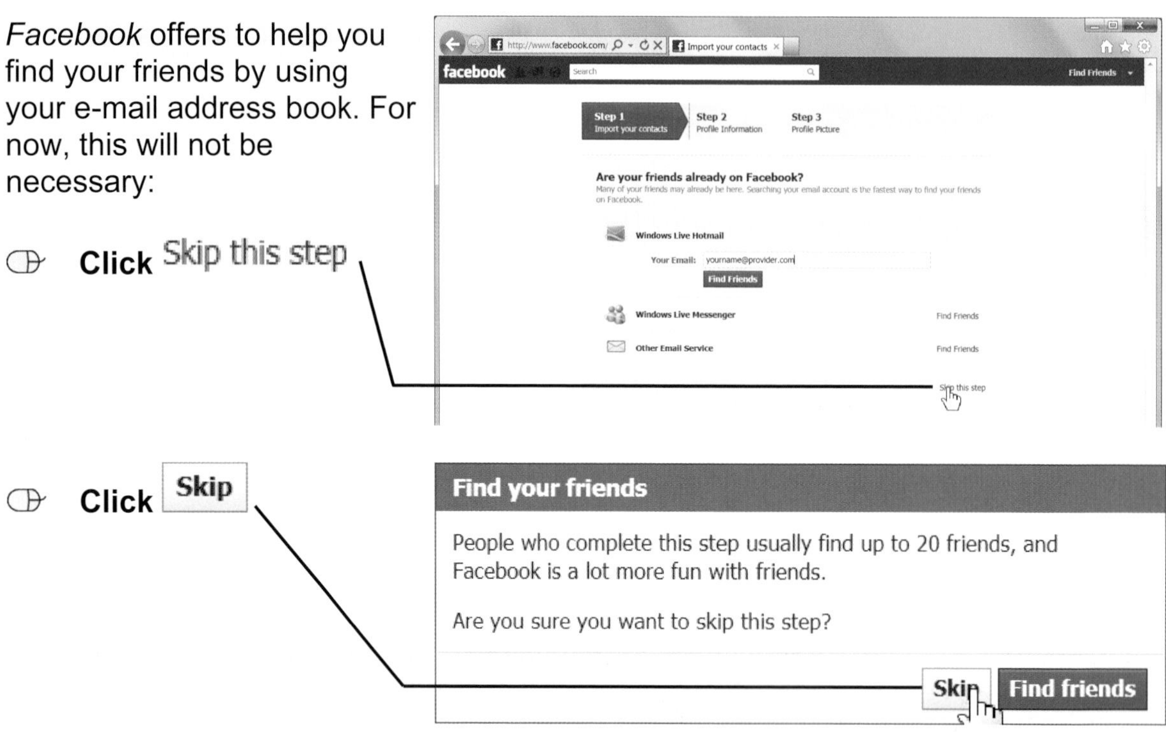

Click Skip

In the next window you can enter the name of your secondary school, a high school, college or university or your employer. This information will help you find your friends on *Facebook*. Of course, you can skip any data that is not relevant to you.

By High School:, type the name of your school

When you start typing, immediately a list of school names will appear. You can choose one of these:

Click your high school

If you cannot find the name of your school, just type in the full name.

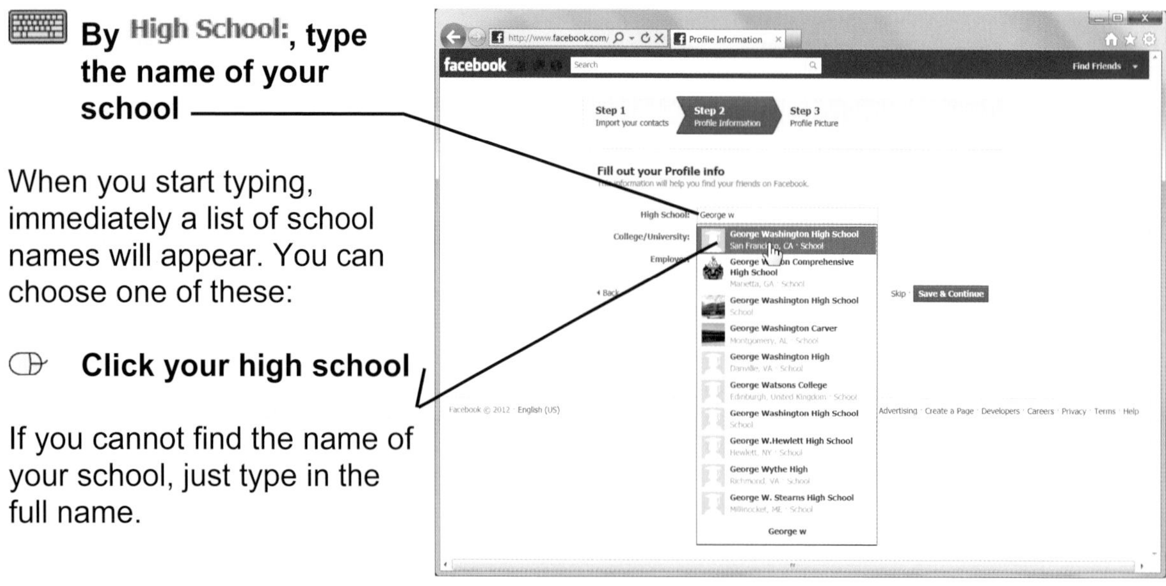

Select the time period by Class End Year:

If applicable:

By College/University, type the name of the college or university where you studied

Select the time period by Class End Year:

By Employer, type the name of your employer

Click Save & Continue

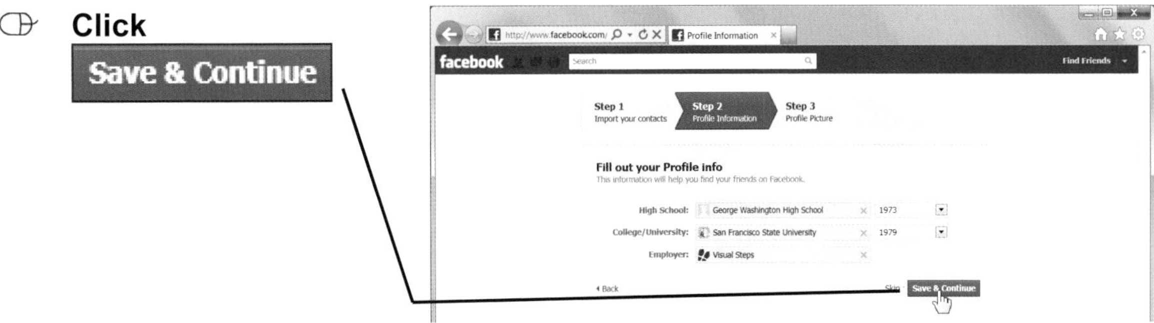

You might see the next window about adding people. With the help of the information you have added to your profile, *Facebook* has selected a number of people you might know. These could be people who graduated from high school in the same year as you, or people who work for the same company. You can skip this step:

If necessary, drag the scroll bar downwards

Click, if necessary, Skip

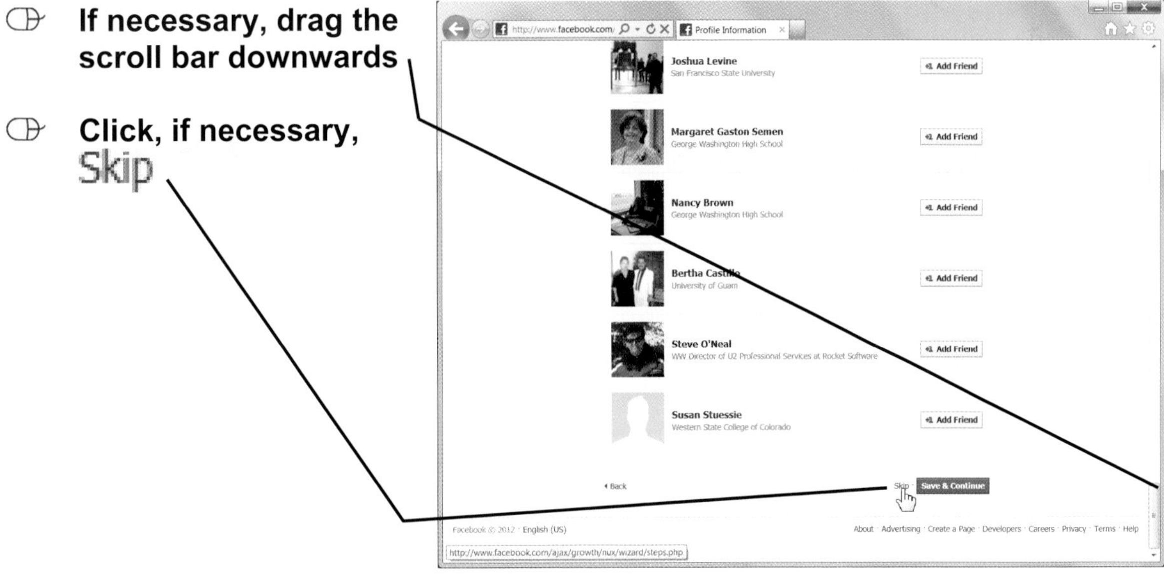

As a last step you can add a photo to your profile. This will make it easier for your friends to recognize you when they try to find you on *Facebook*.

If you have a photo of yourself on your computer, you can add the photo like this:

Click **Upload a photo**

If you do not yet wish to add a profile photo, you can click Skip:

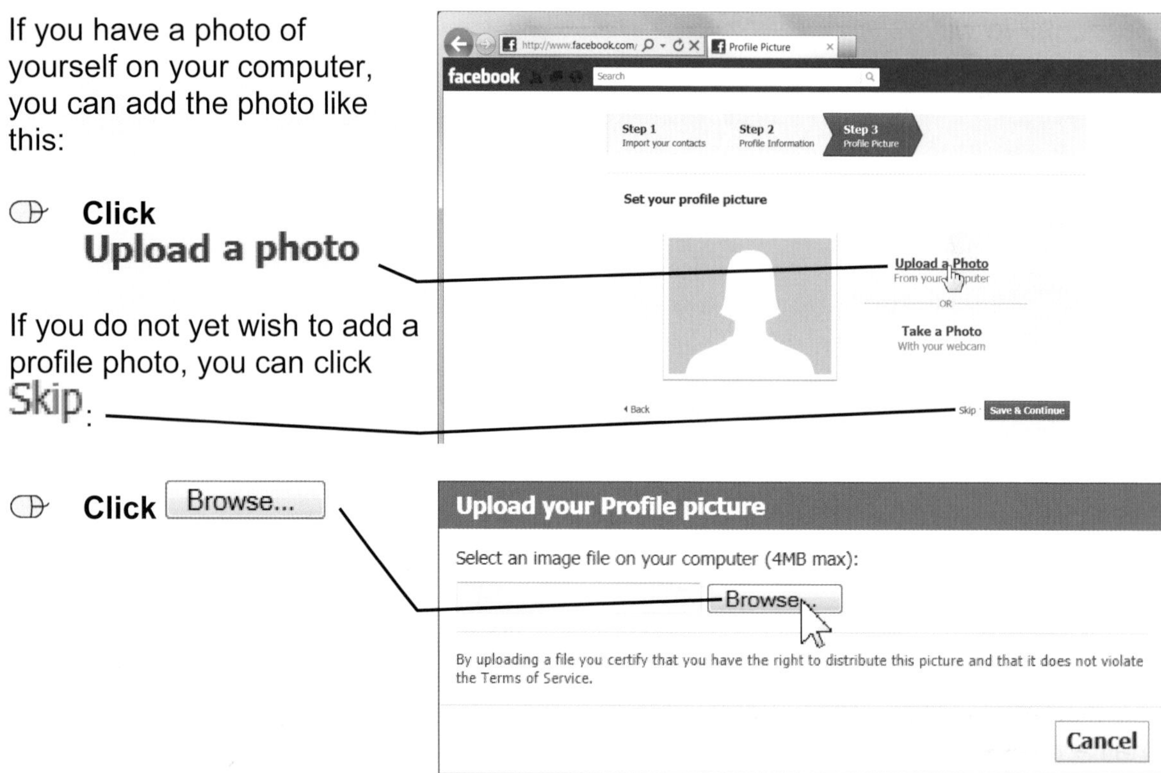

Click Browse...

Upload your Profile picture

Select an image file on your computer (4MB max):

Browse...

By uploading a file you certify that you have the right to distribute this picture and that it does not violate the Terms of Service.

Cancel

Open the folder in which the photo has been stored:

Open the folder with the pictures, for example Pictures

Click the desired photo

Click Open

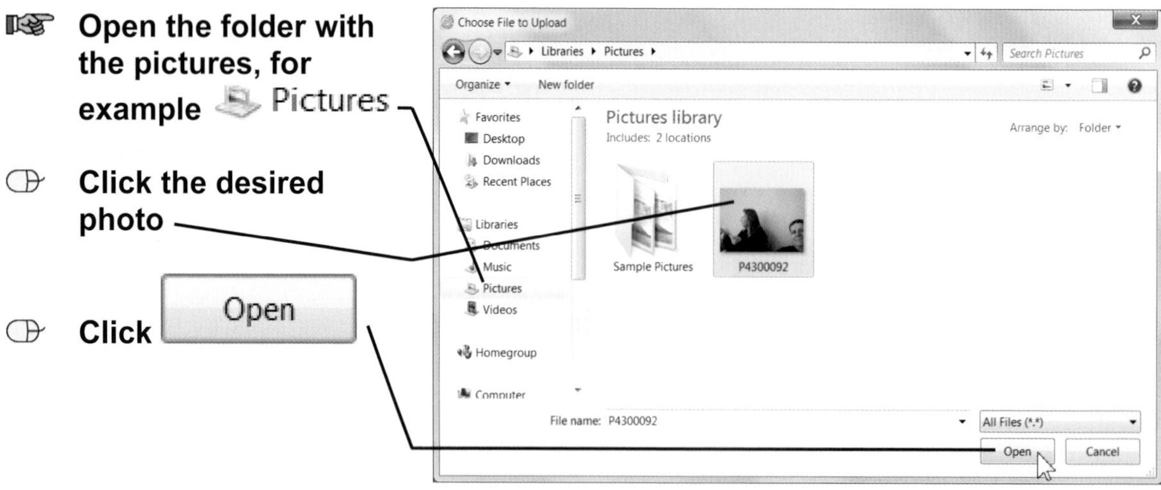

Now the photo will be uploaded to *Facebook*. After a while you will see this window:

Click

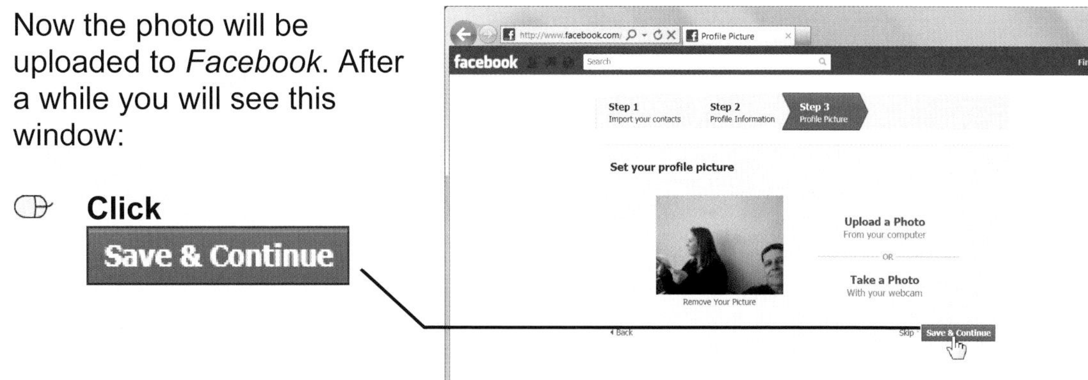

The registration procedure is nearly completed. You will see a message telling you to open the e-mail message that *Facebook* has sent to your e-mail address:

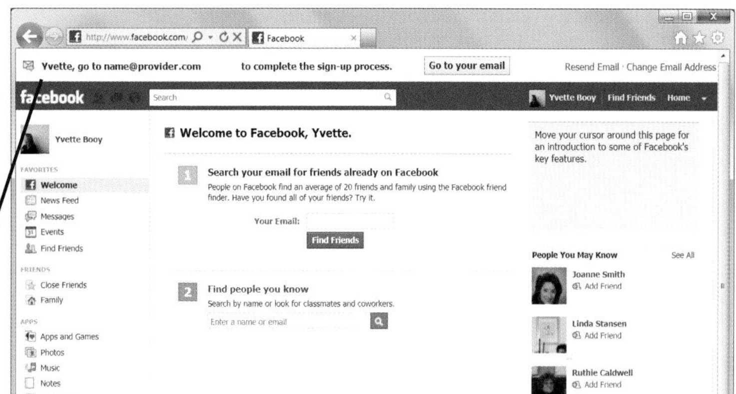

Close the *Facebook* window 4

Open the e-mail message from *Facebook* in your e-mail program; this message is called *Just one more step to get started on Facebook*

Inside the message:

Click

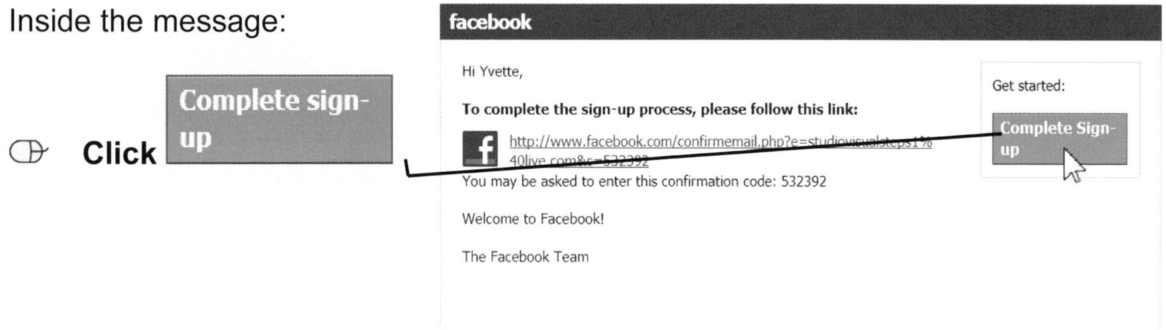

You may need to log on again. Use the same username and password that you filled in when you created your account.

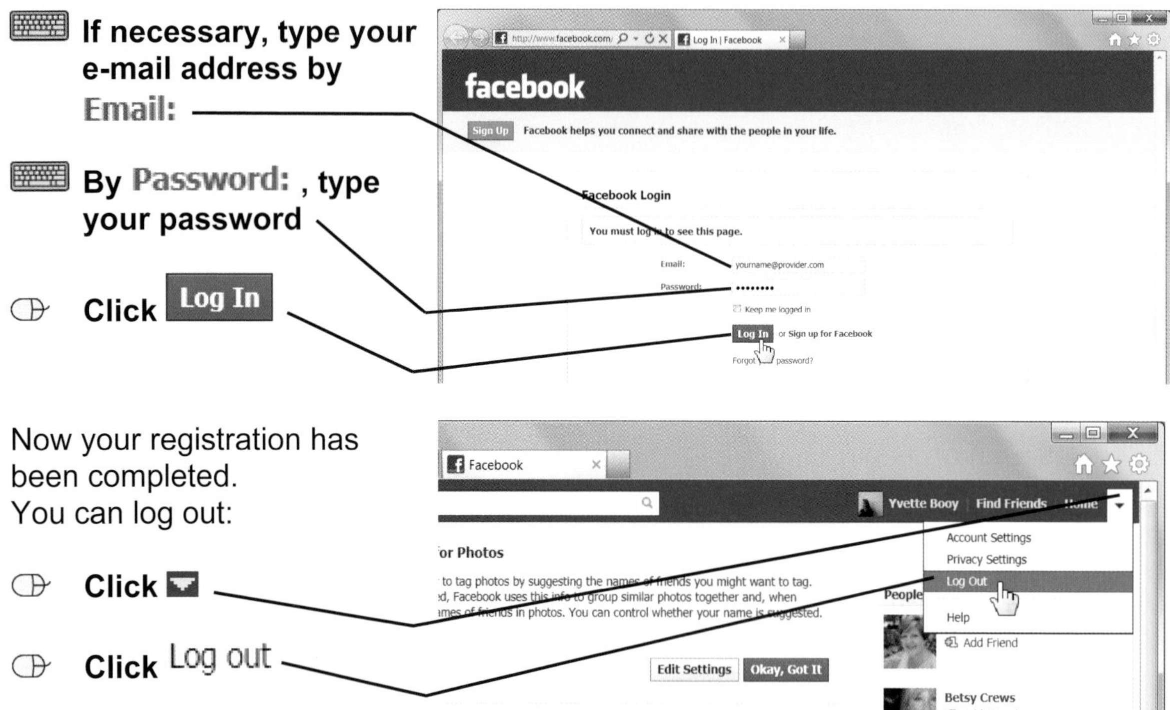

If necessary, type your e-mail address by Email:

By Password: , type your password

Click Log In

Now your registration has been completed.
You can log out:

Click ▾

Click Log out

Close the window with the e-mail message 4

1.2 View and Edit Your Profile

In the previous section you have logged out from *Facebook*. To edit your profile, you need to log in again, with your e-mail address and your password:

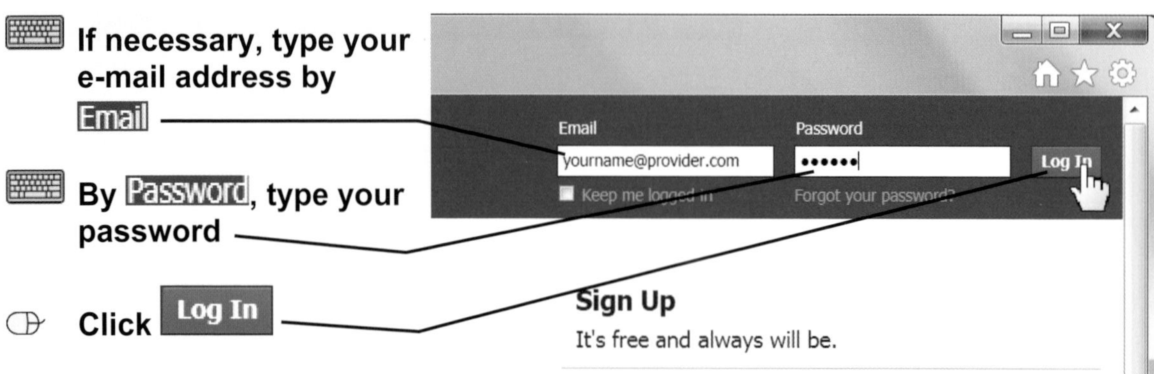

If necessary, type your e-mail address by Email

By Password, type your password

Click Log In

Tip

Stay logged in

Do you want to avoid having to log in each time you open *Facebook*? Then check the box next to Keep me logged in.

It is possible that you will see a message alert at the bottom of the window, where you can choose to save your password:

In this example we will not save the password:

- **Click** No

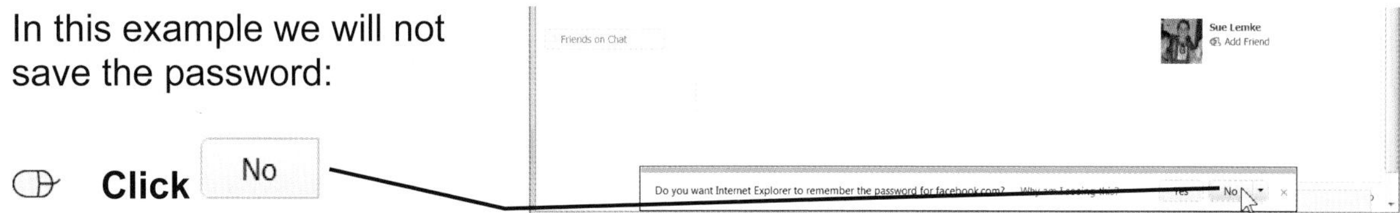

This is how you view your profile:

In the top right of the window:

- **Click your name. In this example it is Yvette Booy**

Your profile contains personal information, which will be visible to your friends. You can modify your profile like this:

- **Click** About

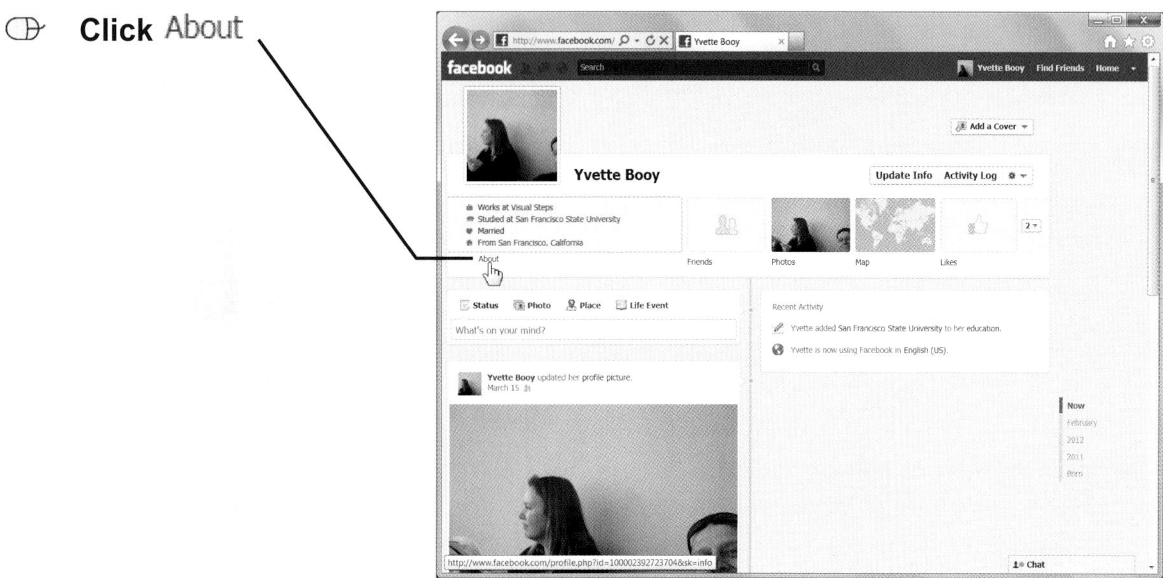

The page with your profile data will be opened. You will see a number of categories for the data you can add or edit:

For example, you can enter your home town in the *Living* category, or write a short story about yourself in the *About you* category:

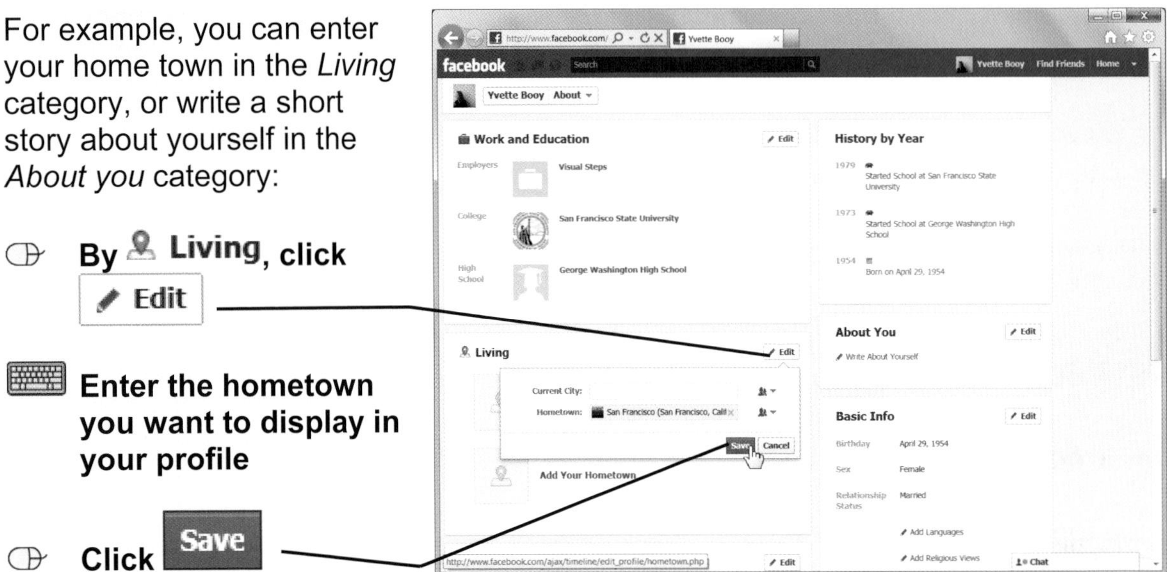

- By **Living**, click **Edit**
- **Enter the hometown you want to display in your profile**
- **Click** **Save**

In the Profile picture category you can add a profile photo, if you have not done this yet. This is also where you can change a picture that was previously added.

Go to the **Relationships and Family** category. In this category you can enter your current relationship status and if relevant, your partner's name. You can also enter the names of other family members and state how you are related to them.

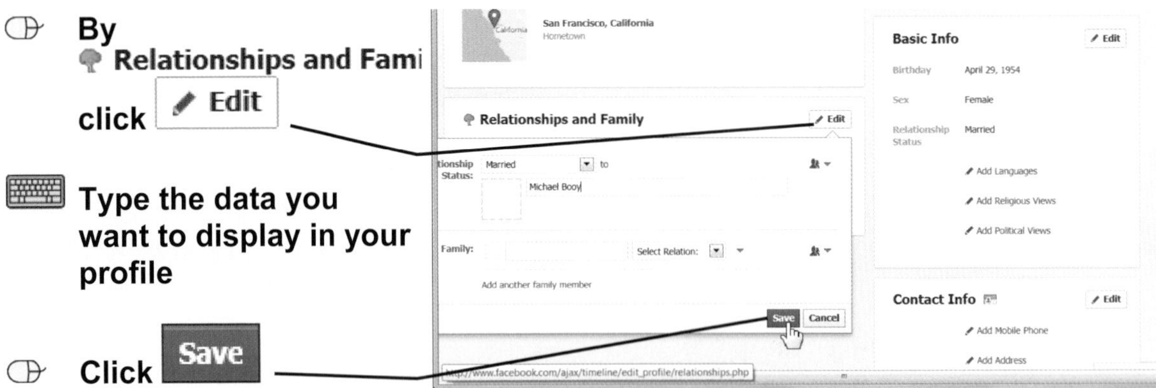

- **By Relationships and Family click** **Edit**
- **Type the data you want to display in your profile**
- **Click** **Save**

Tip

Family members in list of friends

If you have added your family members to your list of friends, you can select them in this window, and state in which way you are related to them. When your brother confirms that he actually is your brother, this relationship will also be displayed in his profile.

Work and Education: here you can add further information about your education, and your current and previous employer(s).
Basic Info: here you can add information about your religious beliefs and political preferences.
Contact Info: here you can type your address, phone number, website address, and other e-mail addresses.

It is up to you to decide which categories to use and not to use.

Add information to the categories you want to use in your profile

Other information such as your favorite music, hobbies and interests can also be added to your profile page. This is how you do that:

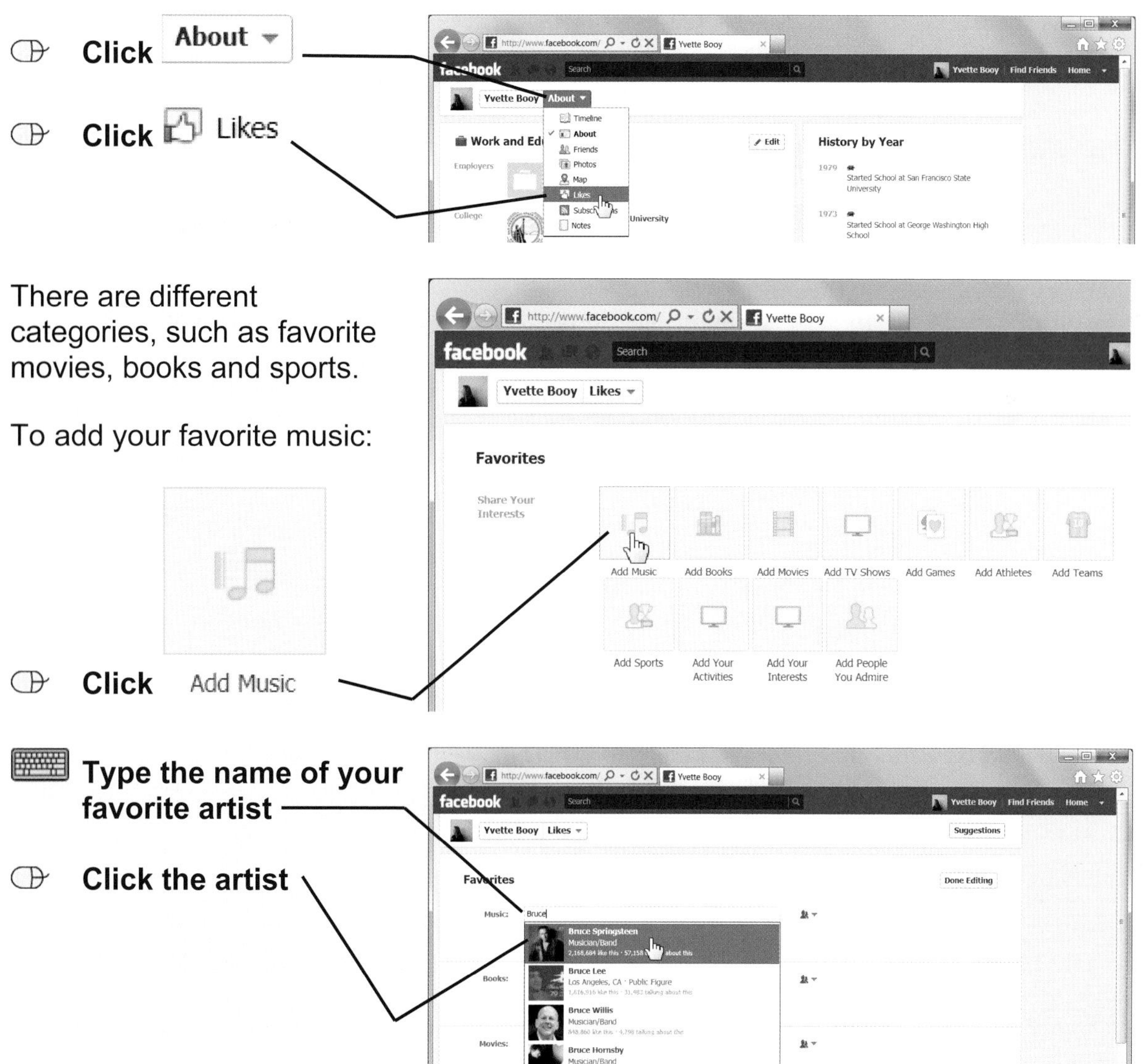

The artist has been added to your favorites:

Click **Save Changes**

It is up to you to decide which information you would like to add.

Add the favorites you would like to add to your profile

After you have added the information by a category:

Click 

Now you can take a look at your profile page:

Click your profile name

You will see that the information that you have added by Favorites is now included in the Timeline:

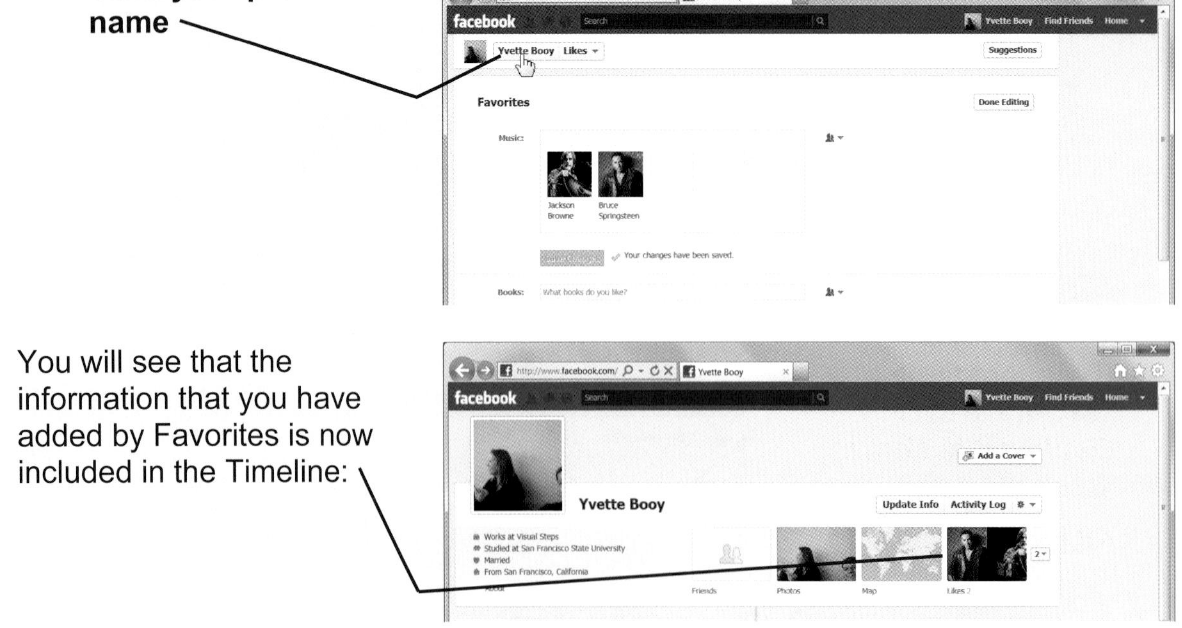

You can personalize you profile by adding a cover. A cover is a large photo shown at the top of your Timeline that can be viewed by everyone. You can add a cover photo like this:

- Click Add a Cover

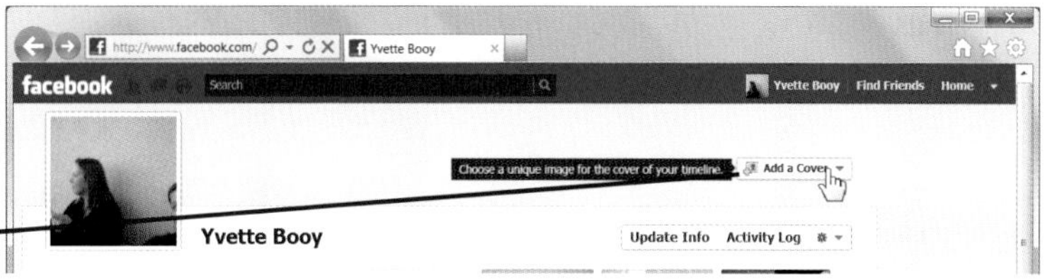

- Click Okay

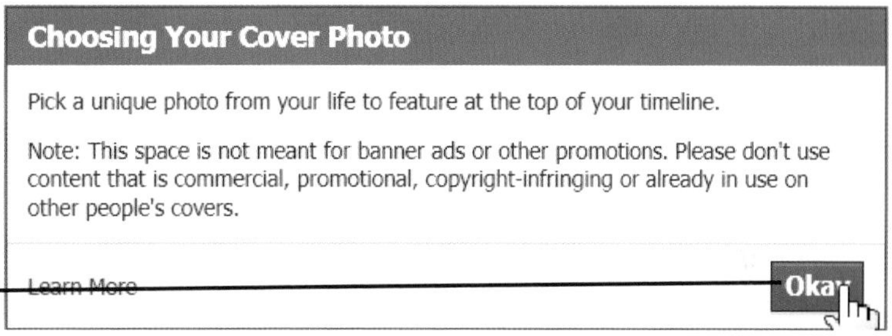

To upload a new photo:

- Click Upload Photo...

- **Add the desired picture** 5

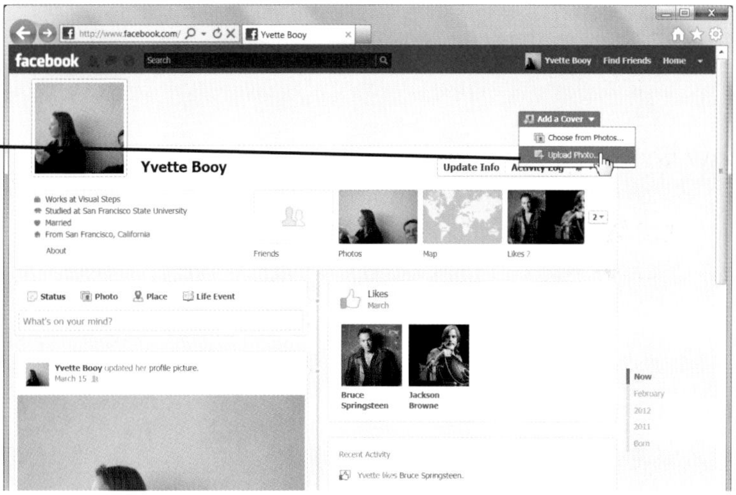

- **Drag the photo, if desired, until the portion of the photo that you want to be displayed is shown**

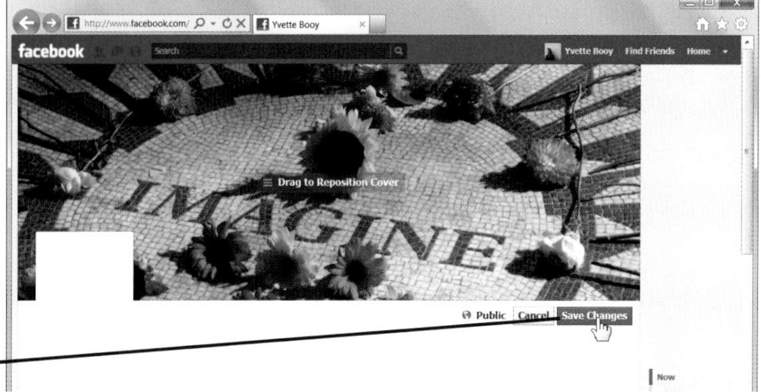

- Click Save Changes

You can see what your profile will look like to your friends:

Naturally, your own profile will look different from the profile in this example.

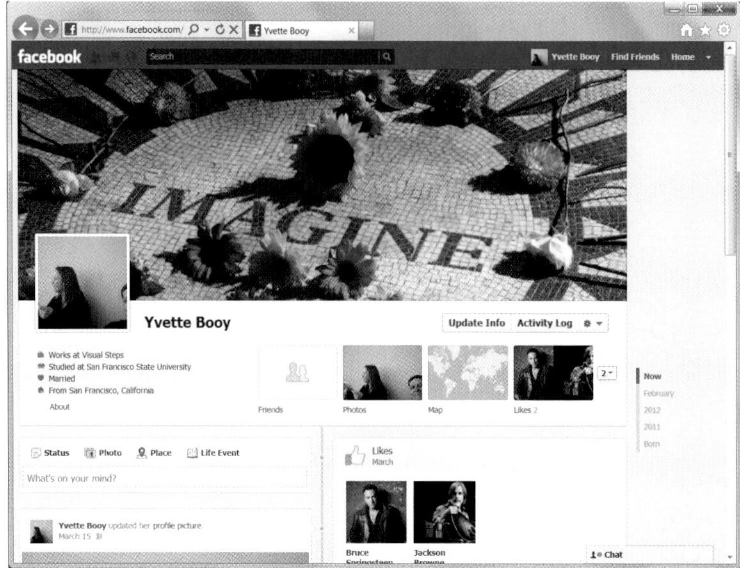

In the following section you can read how to change your privacy settings. This way, you can prevent other people, with the exception of your friends from viewing your profile.

Tip

Edit Profile Picture

There are a couple of options you can use to edit your profile picture. Here's how to access the options:

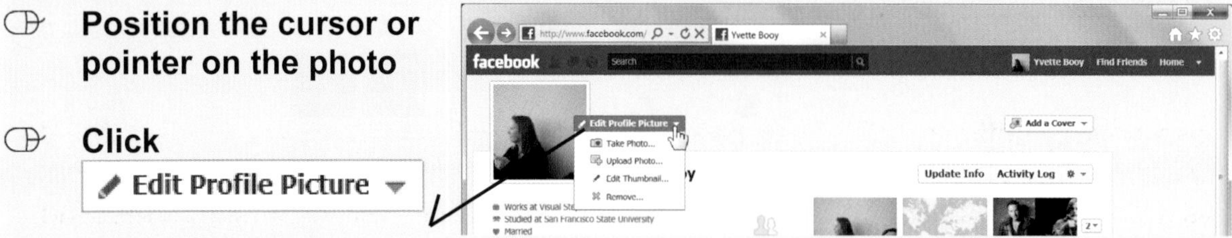

- **Position the cursor or pointer on the photo**
- **Click** Edit Profile Picture

There are different options:

Take Photo...: Take a photo by using your webcam.

Upload Photo...: upload a new photo.

Edit Thumbnail...: edit the thumbnail of your profile picture.

Remove...: remove your current photo.

1.3 View and Edit Your Privacy Settings

Here is how to view the privacy settings for your *Facebook* account:

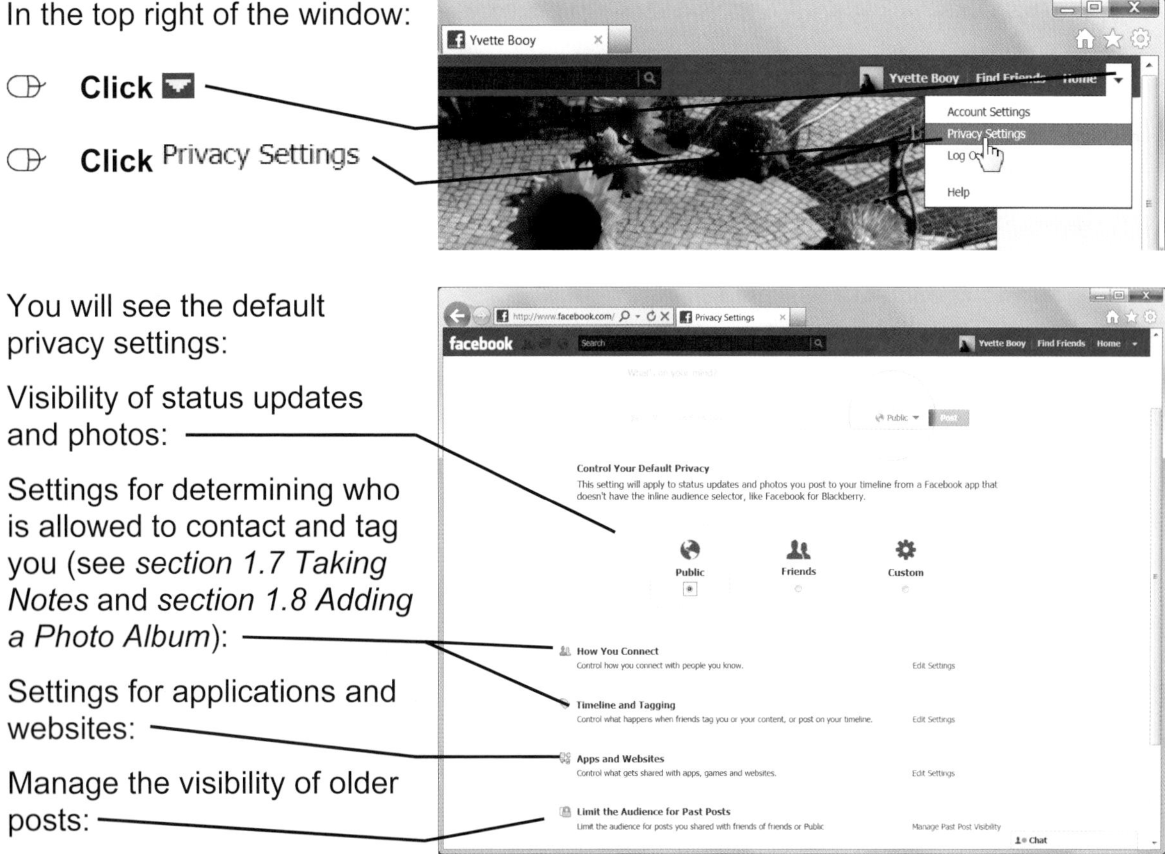

In the top right of the window:

- **Click** ▼
- **Click** Privacy Settings

You will see the default privacy settings:

Visibility of status updates and photos:

Settings for determining who is allowed to contact and tag you (see *section 1.7 Taking Notes* and *section 1.8 Adding a Photo Album*):

Settings for applications and websites:

Manage the visibility of older posts:

These privacy settings will let you determine who is allowed to view various activities and sections of your profile. The default setting for most *Facebook* options is *Public*. This means that everybody can view this information. This will stimulate connecting with others and allows you to quickly build your own extensive social network.

But you can decide to limit your account to be viewed only by a select group of people, such as *Friends*. These are people who have logged in to *Facebook* first, and have been added to your connections as a friend. Another category is *Friends of Friends*. These are the people who have been added to your own *Facebook* friends, as a friend.

For instance, you can determine that *status updates* can only be read by your friends. Status updates are brief messages you add to your profile, in which you tell people what you are currently doing (see *section 1.9 Using the Timeline*).

If you only want to display these status updates to your friends:

- By Control Your Default Privacy click Friends

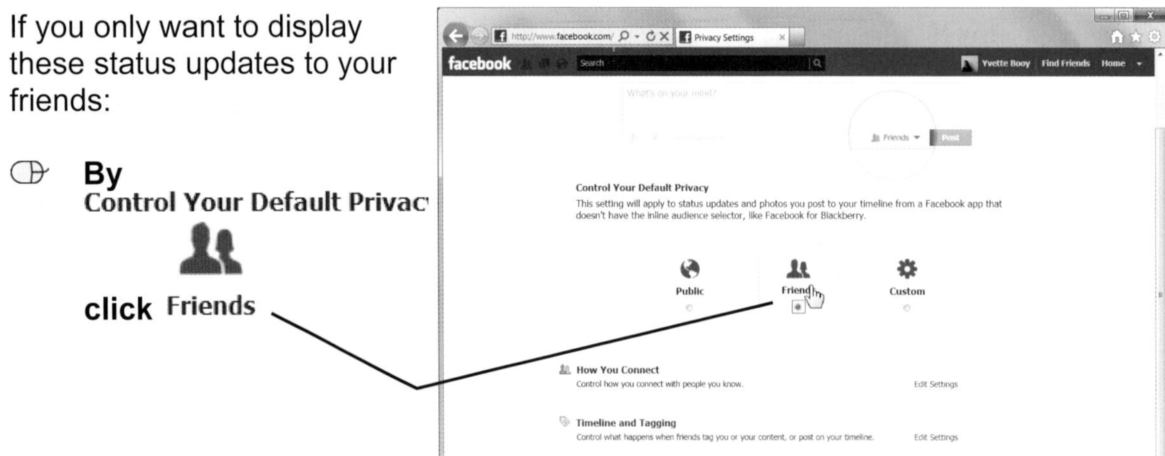

In this window you can also enter the privacy settings for various other activities. At the moment, most sections will not mean much to you, but you can always modify the settings at a later stage.

The settings for connecting to others form an important part of the privacy settings. Among other things, this is the place where you can determine who is allowed to look up your profile by name, and who is allowed to send you a friend request.

- By How you connect, click Edit Settings

For example, if you do not want anyone to send you *Facebook* messages except those persons you have designated as friends:

- By Who can send you Facebook messages? click Everyone
- Click Friends
- Click Done

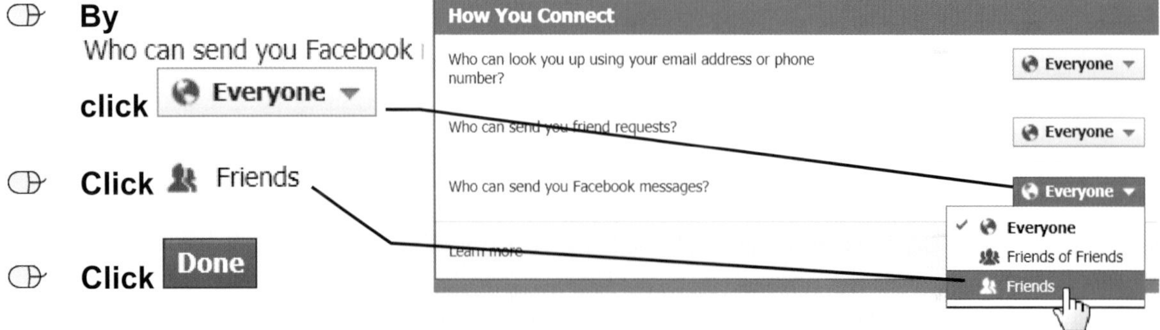

In the same way you can modify the other privacy settings:

Read the descriptions and modify the other privacy settings as desired

Click your name

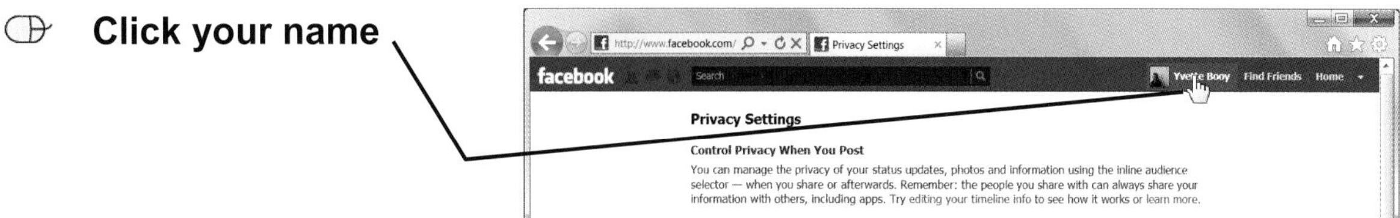

There are even more privacy settings. For instance, you can determine who is allowed to view specific profile information:

Click About

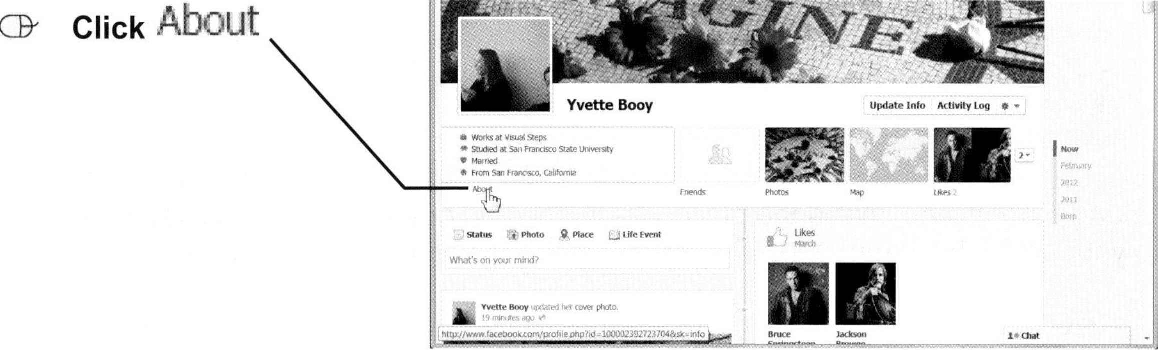

You will see the page with your profile information:

Nearly every item comes with a privacy icon:

For example, if you want to change the privacy settings for your home town:

By Living, click Edit

Click

Click the desired setting

Click Save

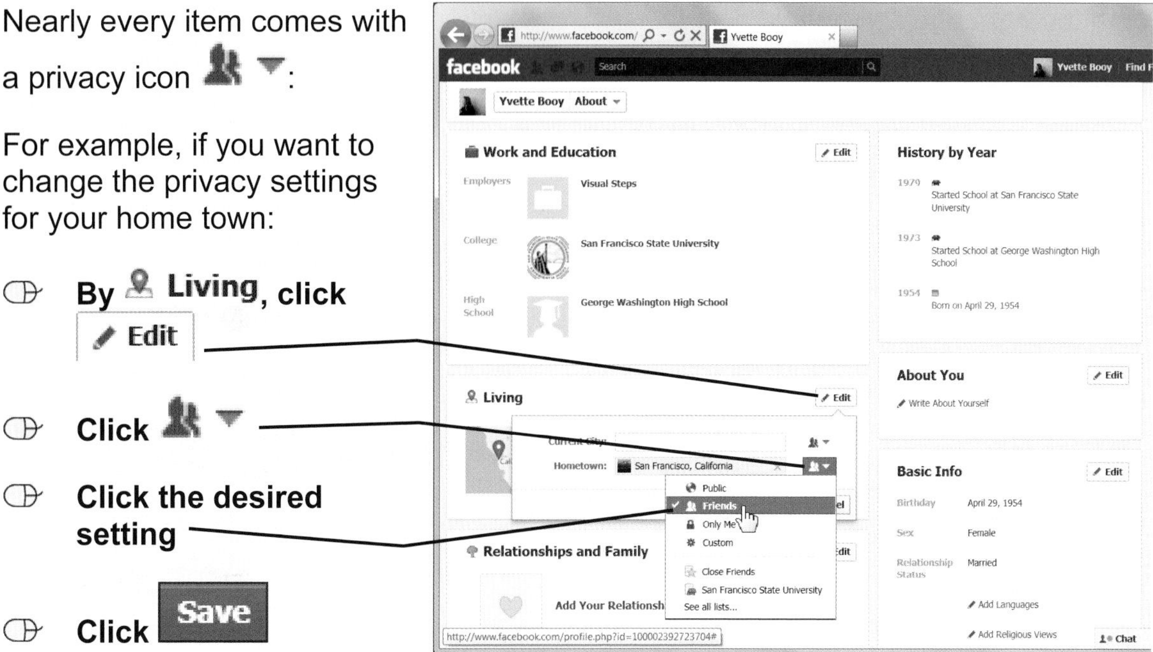

Tip

Custom settings

With the Custom privacy setting you will have even more options to determine who is and who is not allowed to view a certain section of your profile. For example, you will be able to determine this for individual persons:

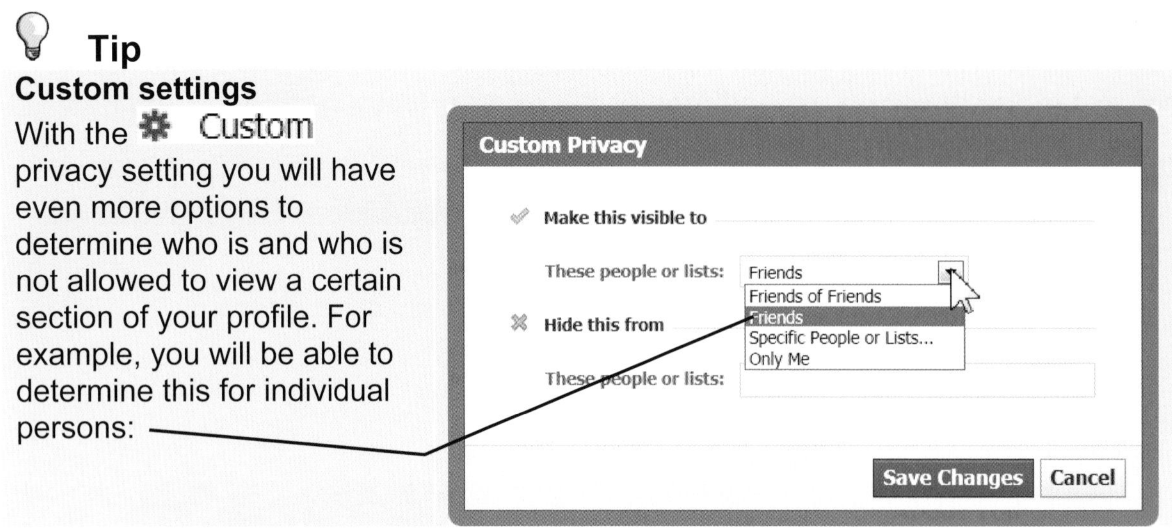

In this way you can define exactly which information will be visible to the people who visit your profile.

1.4 Looking for Friends with the Friend Finder

Facebook has a useful function that allows you to check whether any of the contacts from your e-mail address book are already active on *Facebook*. This is how you start the Friend Finder:

In the top right of the window:

Click Find friends

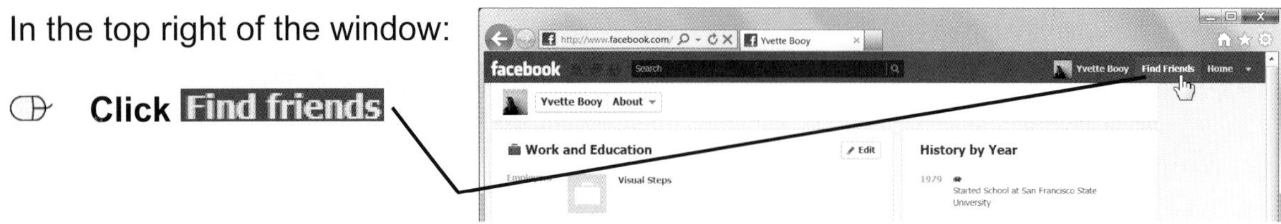

While executing this feature, *Facebook* cooperates with other services such as *Windows Live Messenger*, *Windows Live Hotmail*, *Yahoo* and *Skype*. In this example, the e-mail address with which the *Facebook* account has been created is used:

The e-mail address has already been entered:

Click Find friends

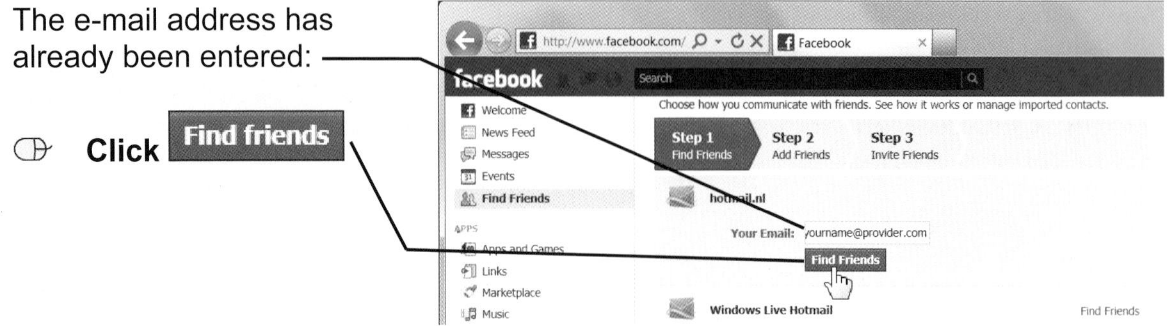

You may need to sign in with your e-mail account first, or sign in with the service you use. In this example, a *Windows Live Hotmail* account is used, which requires you to sign in a separate window with your *Windows Live ID*:

Type your password in the text box

Click Sign in

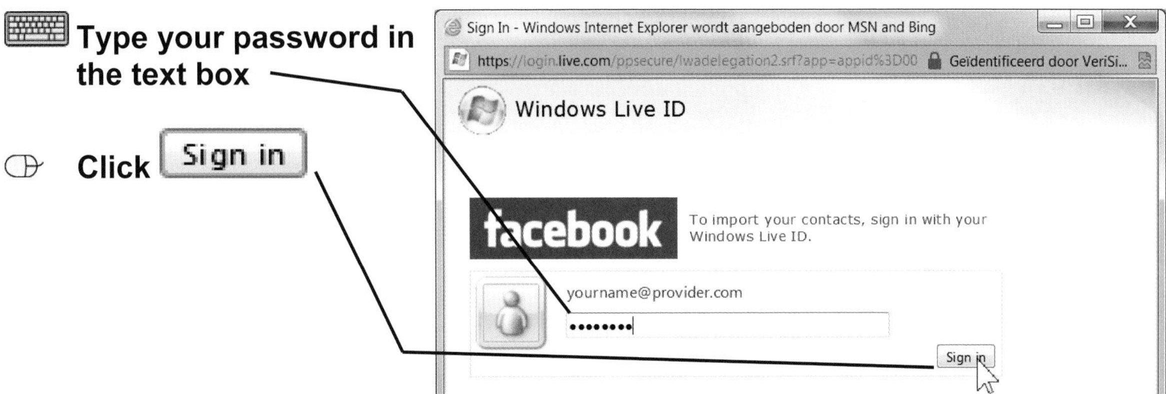

Do you use a different e-mail provider, e-mail program or a different service, such as *Yahoo* or *Skype*, to look up your friends?

Then click Find friends **in the relevant windows of that service**

Follow the onscreen instructions

In this example we have found a person who is also on *Facebook*. This is how you can add this person as a friend:

If necessary, check the box ☑ next to the person or persons you want to add

Click Add Friends

Please note:

These persons will not be added directly to your list of friends. They will receive your friend request. Only after they have confirmed they want to become your friend, will they appear in your list of friends.

Your own address book may contain people who do not yet have a *Facebook* page. You can invite these people per e-mail and ask them to create a *Facebook* account as well:

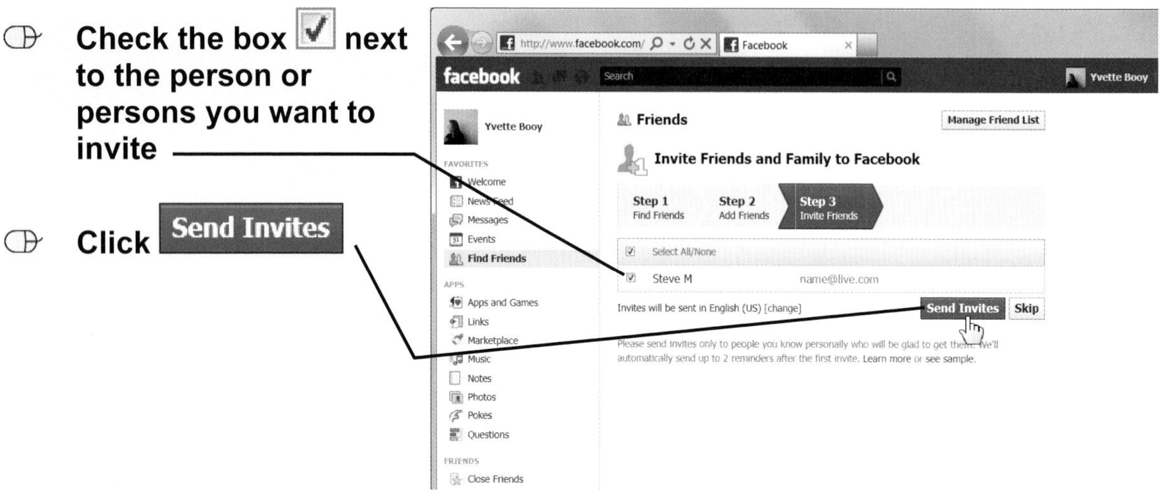

Check the box ☑ next to the person or persons you want to invite

Click Send Invites

Now the invitation will be sent. After the first invitation, two reminders will be sent, in case the recipient does not react.

1.5 Directly Finding Friends on Facebook

You can also start a direct search for friends who already have a *Facebook* page and send them a friend request:

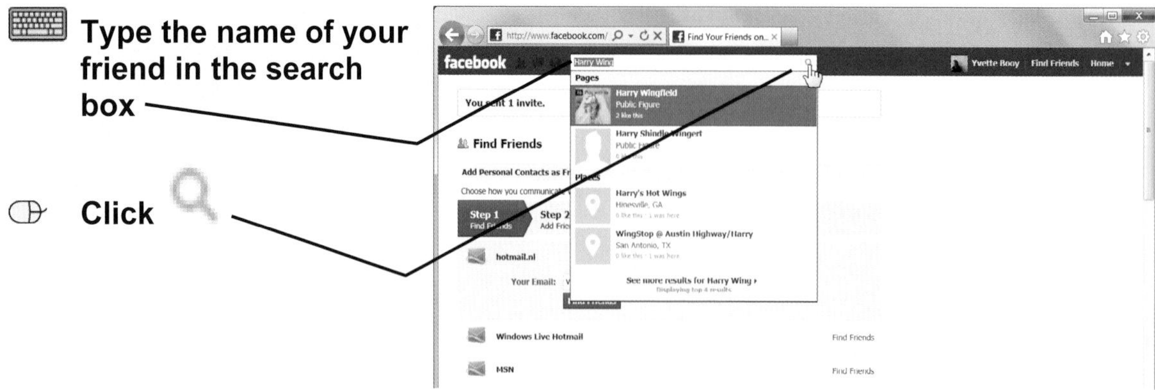

Type the name of your friend in the search box

Click 🔍

You will see a list of *Facebook* users with names that are similar to the name you are looking for. If the person you are searching for is in the list, you can send him or her a friend request:

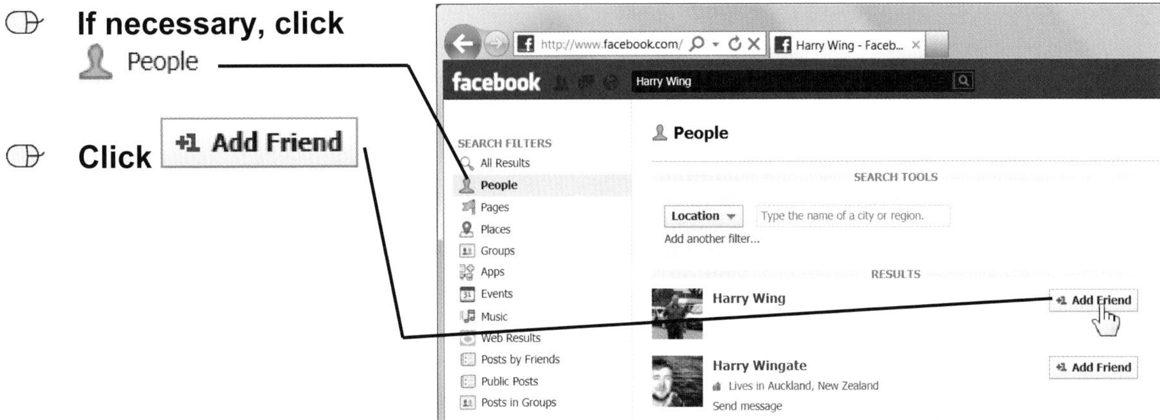

Tip

Whom do I need to contact?

Are you not sure about selecting the right person from the list? Just click a few names. You will see the data shared by these people with others who are looking for them on *Facebook*. It may help you pick the right person.

You will see that the **+1 Add Friend** button has turned into **+1 Friend request sent**.

This way, you can add other friends who already have a *Facebook* page. After you have finished sending the friend requests, you can open your *Facebook* home page:

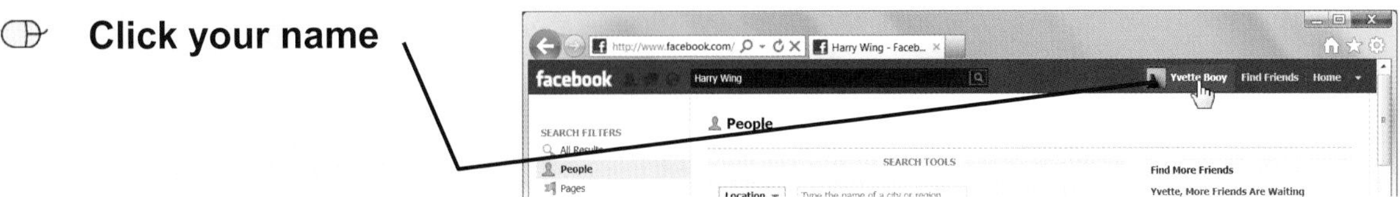

1.6 Confirm Friends

The people you have sent a friend request, will need to confirm that they really are your friends. But they can also decide to ignore your request.

You need to do the same thing when someone tries to add you as a friend. When this happens you will receive an e-mail message, if your settings require this. You will also see a friend request on your *Facebook* page. If you have not yet received any friend requests you can just read through this section, up to the next page.

You can recognize a friend request by the icon in the top left of the window. To accept the request:

Click

Click **Confirm**

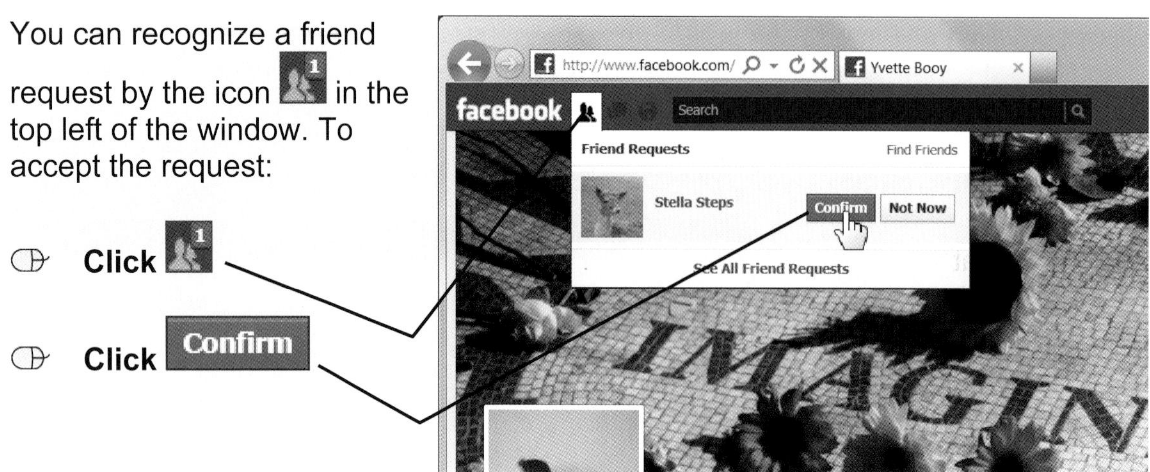

Of course, you can also turn down the request by clicking **Not Now**.

Almost immediately, you will see that you have become friends with this person:

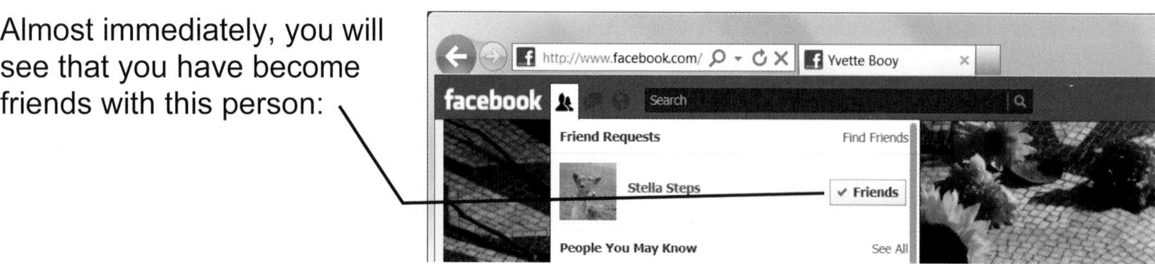

Tip

Friend requests

Friend requests can also appear in other places besides the top left of the window. Here you see an example of a friend request, as it is displayed on the home page. To accept the request:

Click **Confirm**

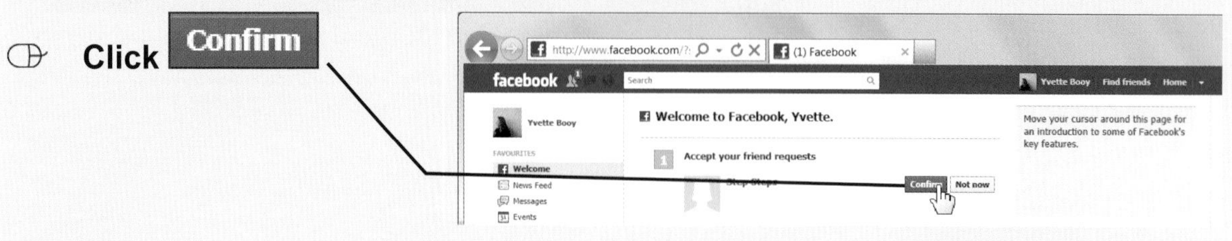

Right away, you will see a confirmation that you are now friends with this person.

Now you are going to take a look at your list of friends. In the top right of the window:

Click your name

You will see the page which contains your profile. This page also displays your friends:

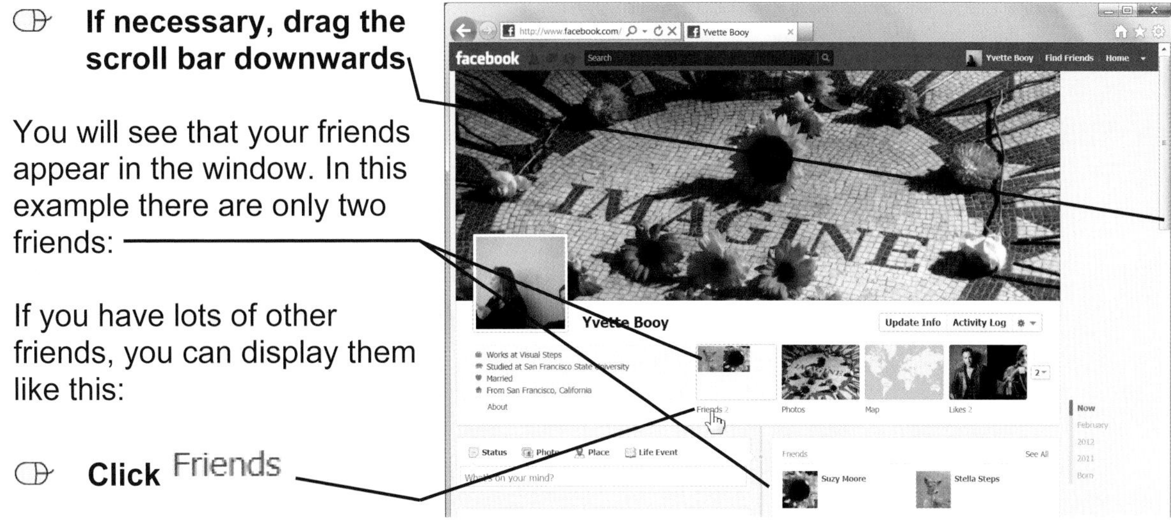

If necessary, drag the scroll bar downwards

You will see that your friends appear in the window. In this example there are only two friends:

If you have lots of other friends, you can display them like this:

Click Friends

You will see a page with a summary of all your friends:

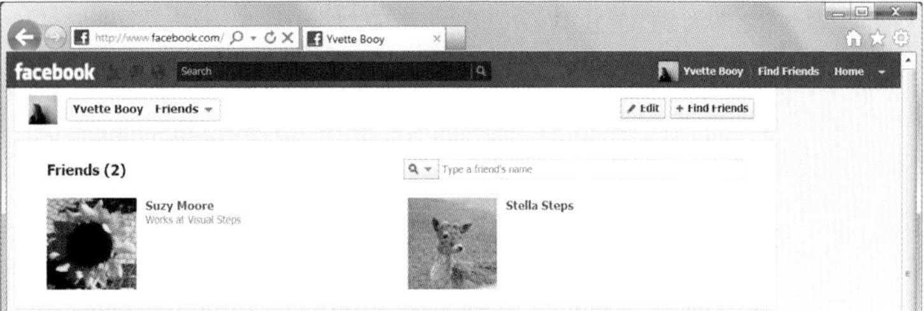

1.7 Taking Notes

On *Facebook* you can also maintain a *blog*. A blog is an online diary or journal, also known as a *weblog*. If your friends like to read about your daily adventures, you can keep them posted through your blog. For this you can use the *Notes* function. Each update of your blog consists of a separate note. This is how you add a note:

In the top left of the window:

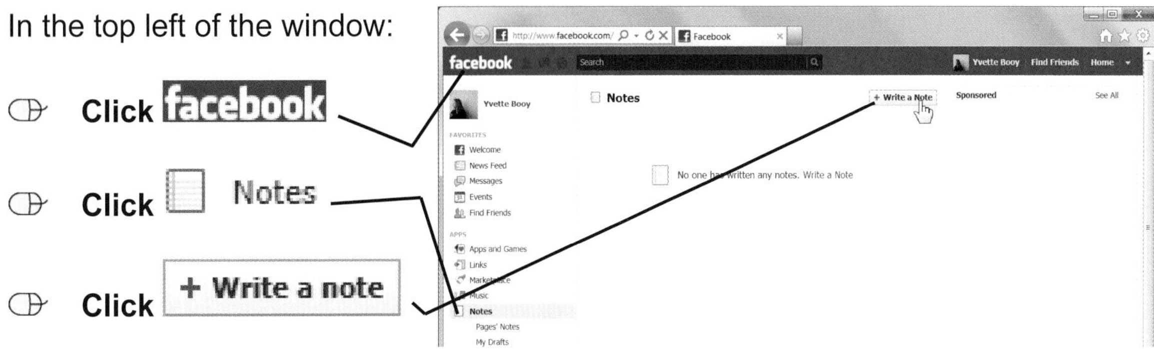

Click facebook

Click Notes

Click + Write a note

HELP! I do not see Notes.

If Notes is not visible, you can open it like this:

- **Place the mouse pointer on APPS**
- **Click MORE**
- **Click Notes**

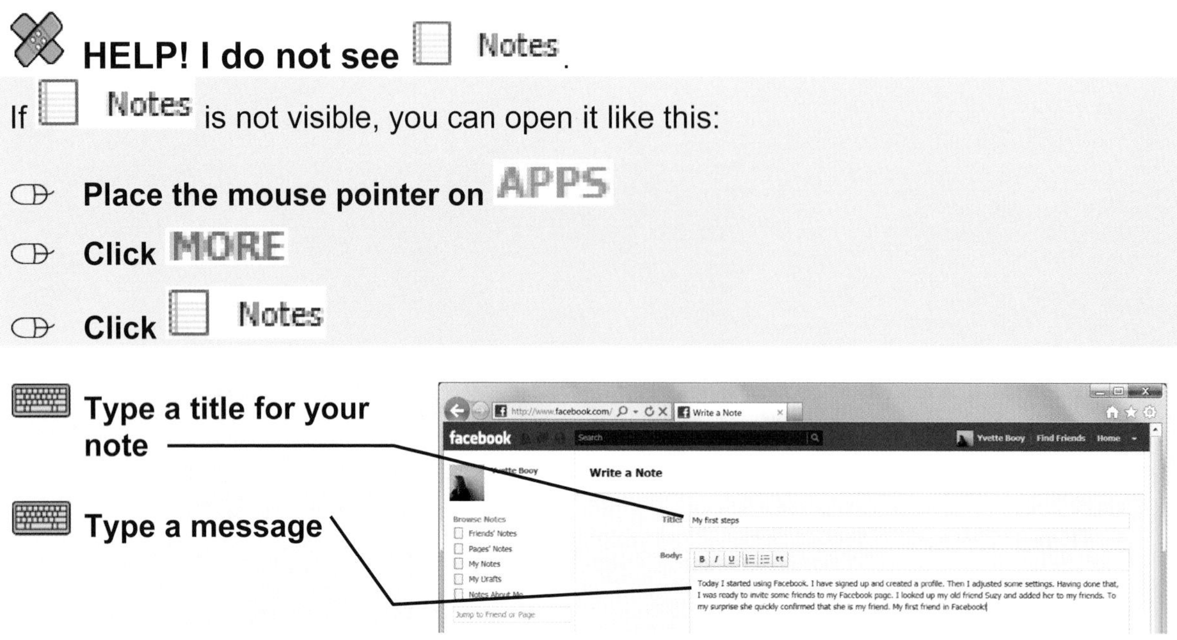

- **Type a title for your note**
- **Type a message**

The nice thing about the *Notes* feature in *Facebook* is that you can *tag* your friends in your notes. A *tag* is a keyword that describes a file, or a note, in this case. In this way, your friends can easily look up the notes in which they are featured, and you can find the notes in which they have written about you. Although, if you want to tag a friend, this friend needs to have confirmed that you actually are his or her friend. This is how you add a tag:

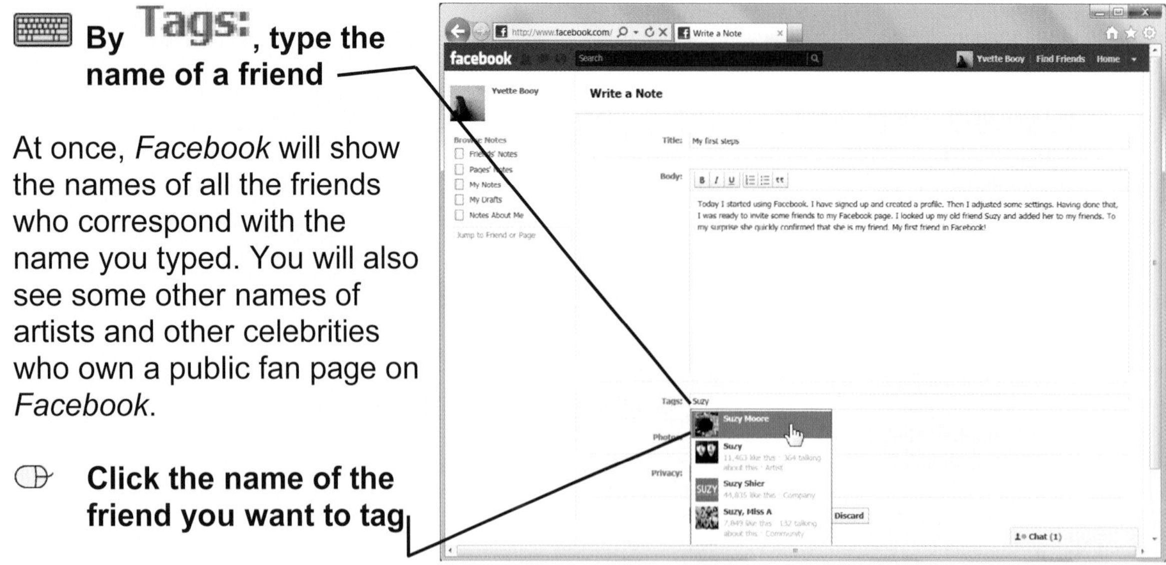

- **By Tags:, type the name of a friend**

At once, *Facebook* will show the names of all the friends who correspond with the name you typed. You will also see some other names of artists and other celebrities who own a public fan page on *Facebook*.

- **Click the name of the friend you want to tag**

You can add as many tags as you want. Now you can publish your note:

- **If necessary, drag the scroll bar downwards**
- **Click** Publish

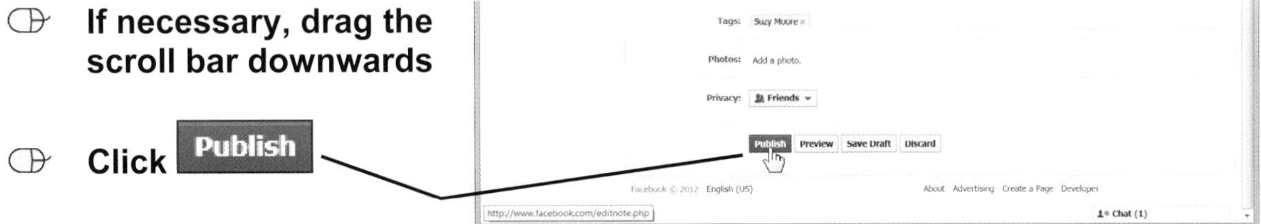

Your note has been published:

Now you can take a look at the note on your Timeline:

- **Click your name**

- **If necessary, drag the scroll bar downwards**

Your note has been posted on your Timeline:

Your friends will see the same message in their News Feed.

- **Click the title of your note**

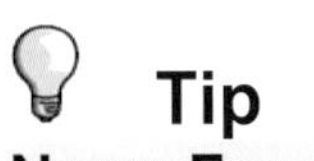

Tip

News Feed

The News Feed is the list of messages on your *Facebook* home page, containing the most recent news from the people or *Pages* that you follow. The News Feed is constantly updated. For example, if one of your friends updates his profile, or posts a note, you will see a message appear in the News Feed. The other way round, your friends will also see messages from you when you update your status on *Facebook*. The News Feed does not contain information about which profile or photo you are viewing, which notes you read, which friend requests you have ignored, or anything about the friends you have removed from your group of friends.

You will see your note and the friend you tagged in this note:

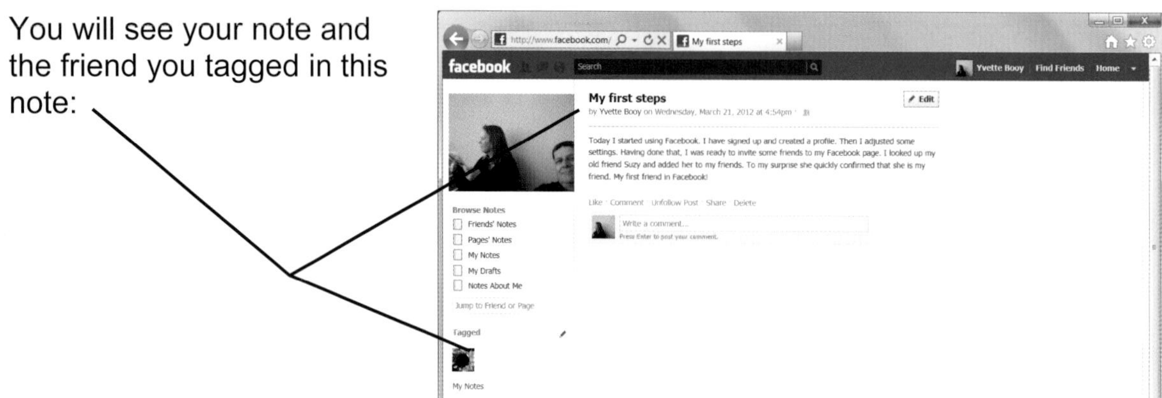

Tip

Message when you are tagged

When one of your friends posts a note, you will see a message in the News Feed. If your friend has tagged you in a note, you will receive a message.

This is how you can view the message and after that, the note. In the top left of the window:

Click

Click the message

The note will be opened. This is another way of finding the notes in which you are tagged:

Click Notes, Notes about me

Tip

Messages

You will also see the messages by when somebody accepts your friend request, not just when you are tagged.

1.8 Adding a Photo Album

Another way to let friends know about something you have recently experienced is by adding one or more photos to your *Facebook* page:

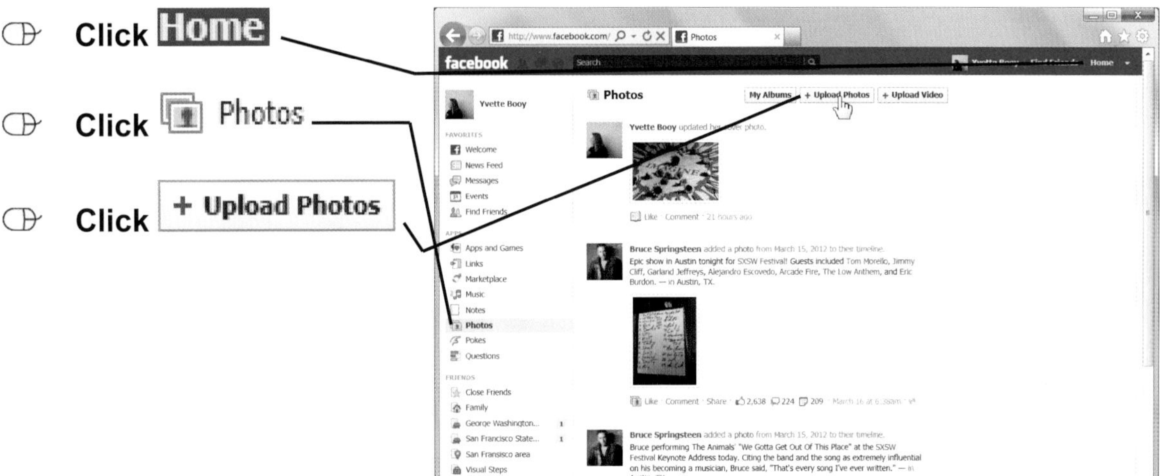

In this example, we will create a new photo album and select photos that are stored in the *Pictures* folder. Your photos may of course be stored in a folder with another name. Open the folder that contains the photos you want to use:

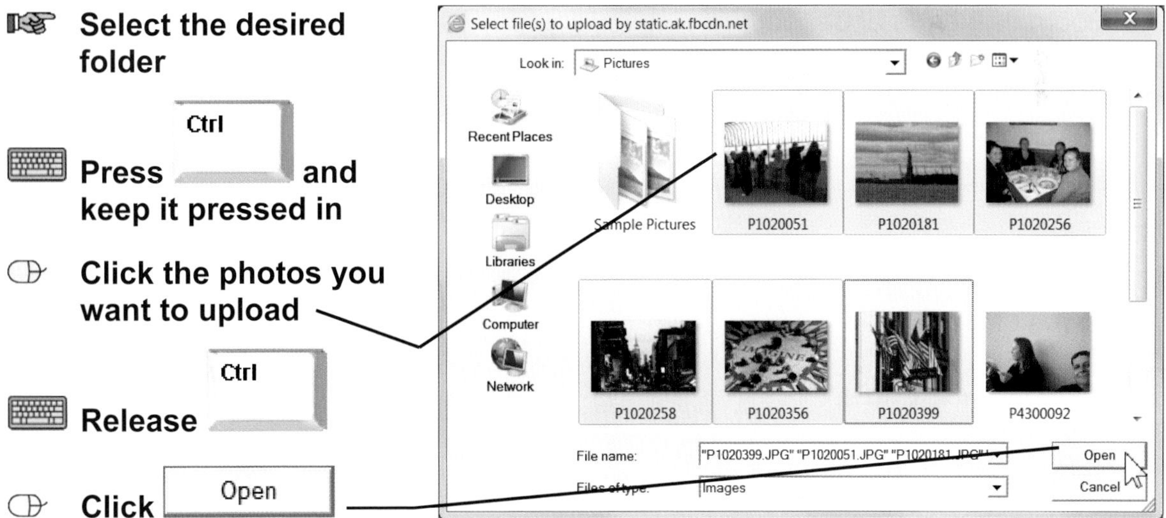

The photos will be uploaded. In the meantime you can enter a name and a description for the photo album:

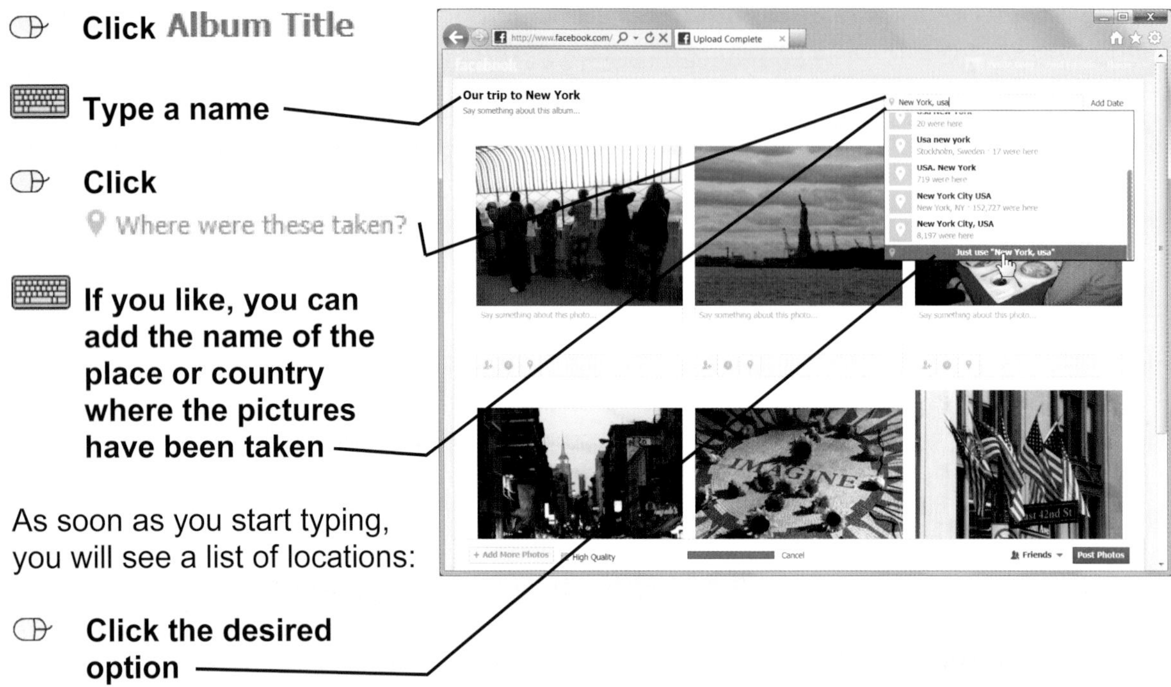

Click Album Title

Type a name

Click
Where were these taken?

If you like, you can add the name of the place or country where the pictures have been taken

As soon as you start typing, you will see a list of locations:

Click the desired option

Facebook now offers face recognition and can recognize the faces in the pictures of your album. If friends appear in the picture, you can immediately add a tag to their faces. You can also add a tag to yourself, if you appear in a picture. This is how you add tags:

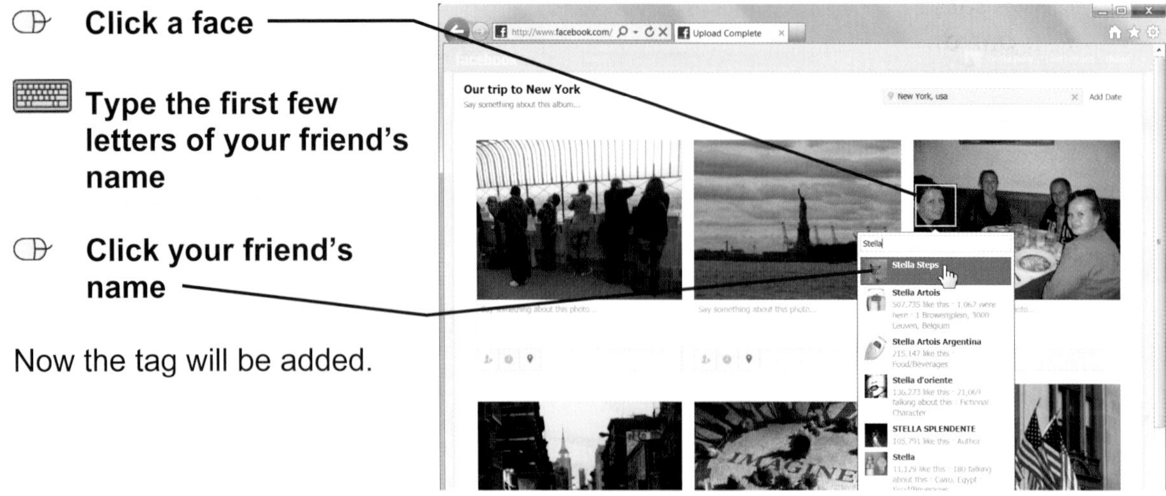

Click a face

Type the first few letters of your friend's name

Click your friend's name

Now the tag will be added.

If your own folder contains more pictures with people in it, you can add tags for all these photos. If you do not want to tag persons, just skip this step.

Tip

Removing a tag from a photo

If you have added a wrong tag, you can remove it. Here is how you do this when the album has not yet been posted:

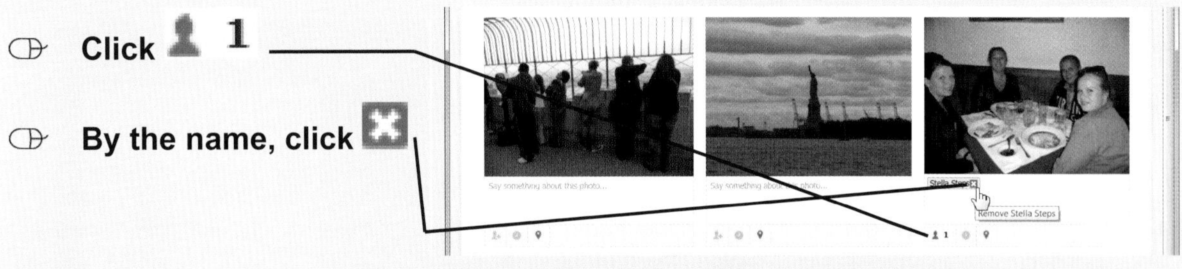

- **Click** 1
- **By the name, click**

When the album already has been posted, you can remove it like this:

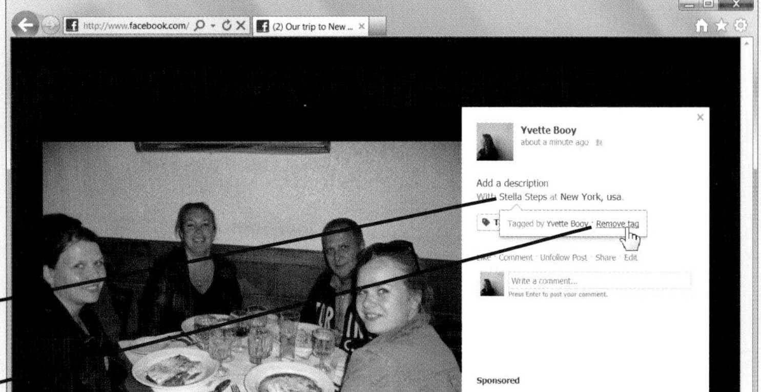

- **Click the photo**
- **Place the mouse pointer on the name**
- **Click** Remove tag

After all the photos have been uploaded, you can create an album:

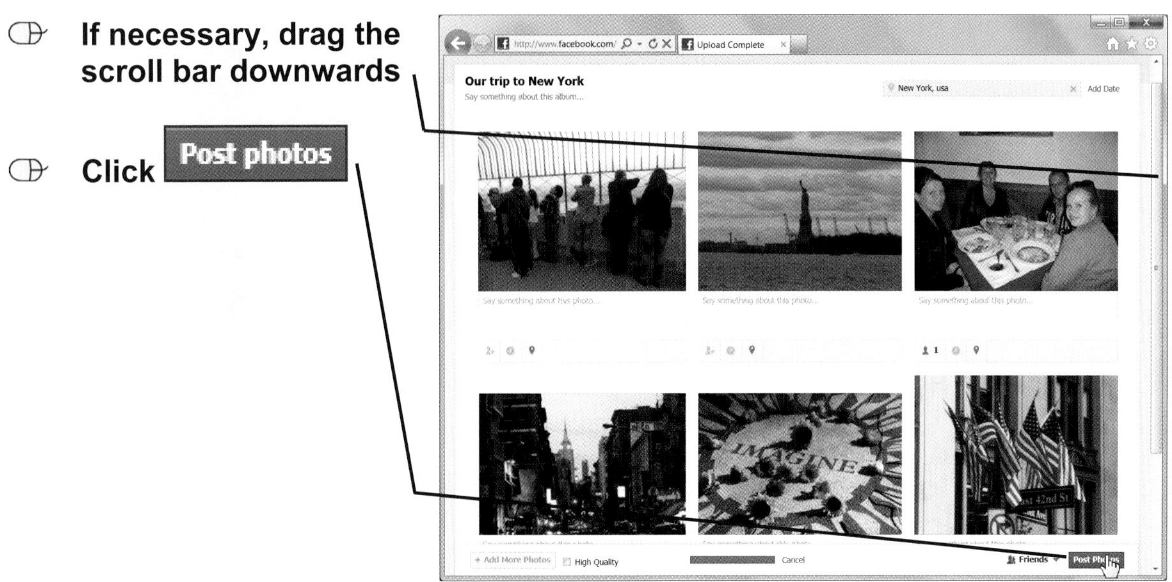

- **If necessary, drag the scroll bar downwards**
- **Click** Post photos

Now you can start editing your photo album. This is how to add captions to your photos:

Click a photo

Now you will see a larger image of the photo:

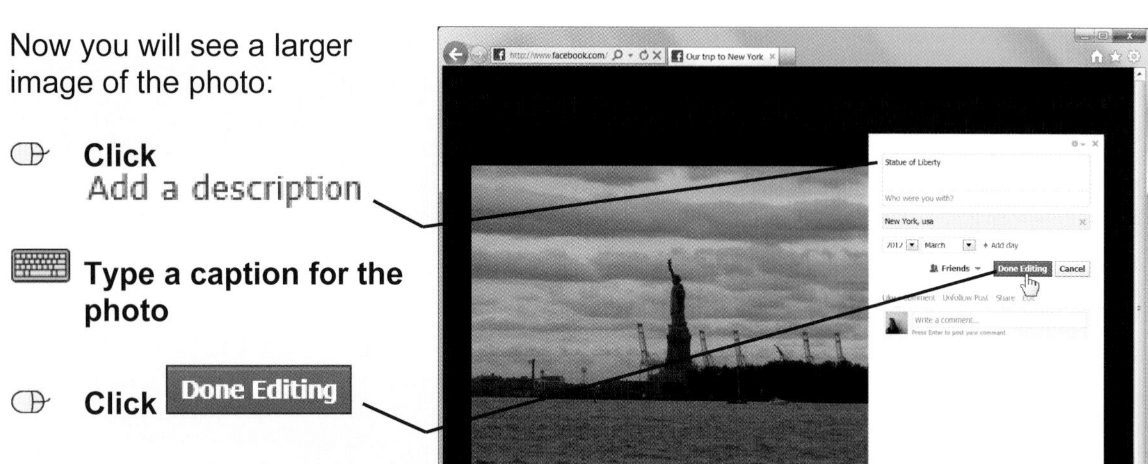

Click Add a description

Type a caption for the photo

Click Done Editing

With the and buttons to the left and right of the photos, you can display the other photos in the album and add captions to these photos too. After you have finished, click the button at the top right of the photo and return to the home page:

Click

Click your name

If necessary, drag the scroll bar downwards

You will see a new message about your photo album:

Your friends will see this message in their News Feed.

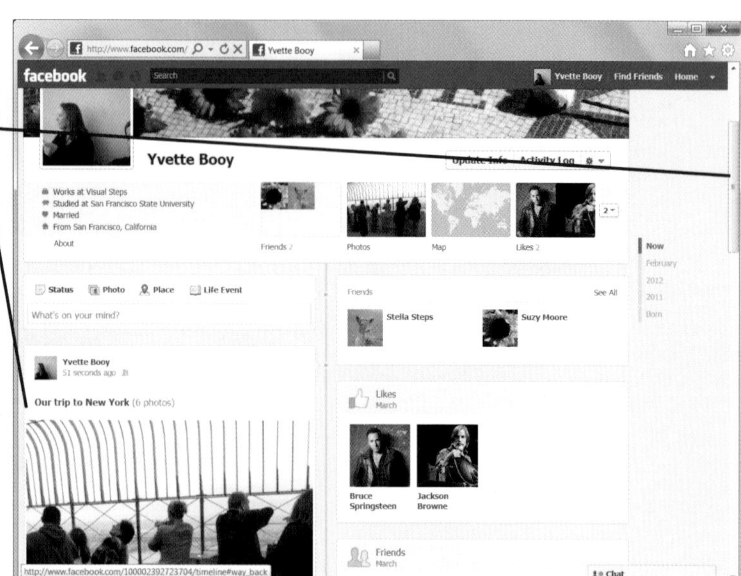

1.9 Using the Timeline

By now, you have engaged in several activities on *Facebook*. You can see how other people see your profile. Here is how you do that:

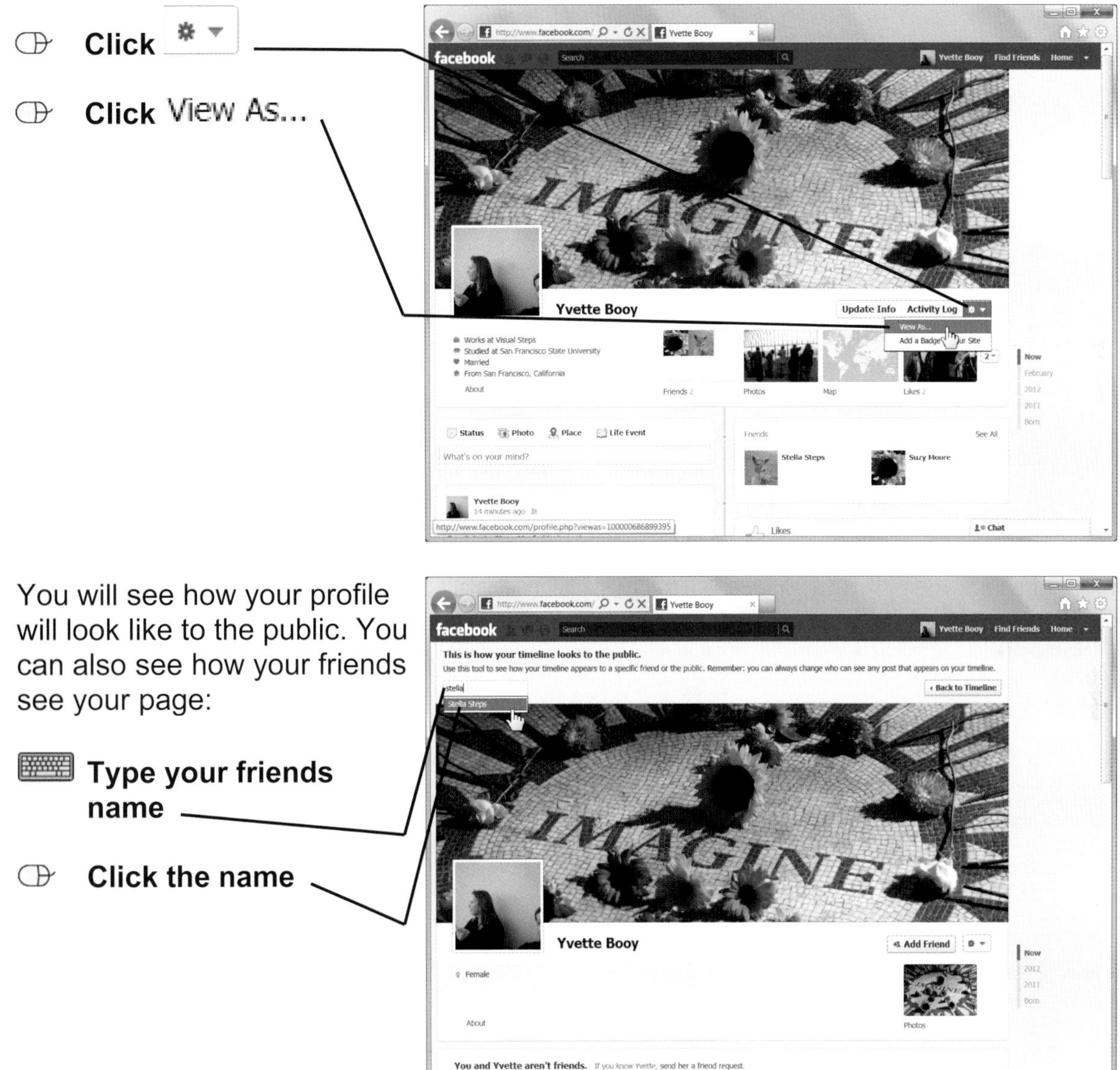

- Click ✱ ▾
- Click View As...

You will see how your profile will look like to the public. You can also see how your friends see your page:

- **Type your friends name**
- **Click the name**

This is how your friends see the page:

You can go back to the Timeline:

Click **Back to Timeline**

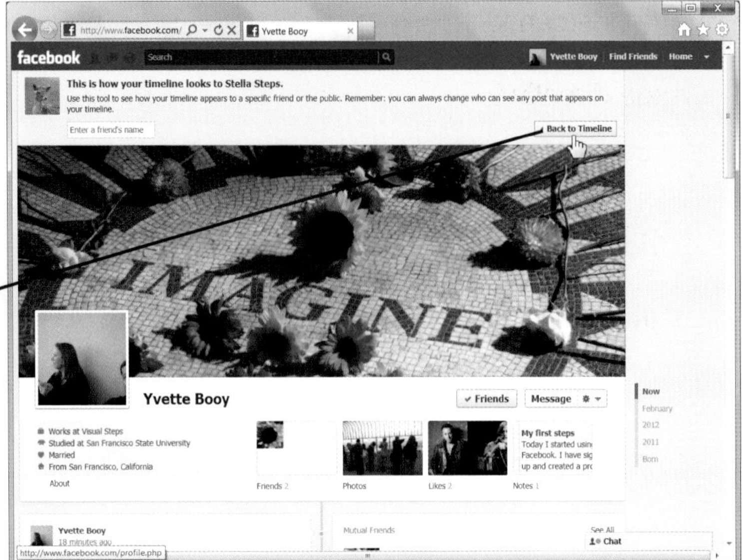

Your profile consists of these sections: About, Friends, Photos, Notes, Likes, Map and Subscriptions.

If necessary, drag the scroll bar downwards

Notice that a menu appears:

On the Timeline you will see a summary of your most recent activities on *Facebook*:

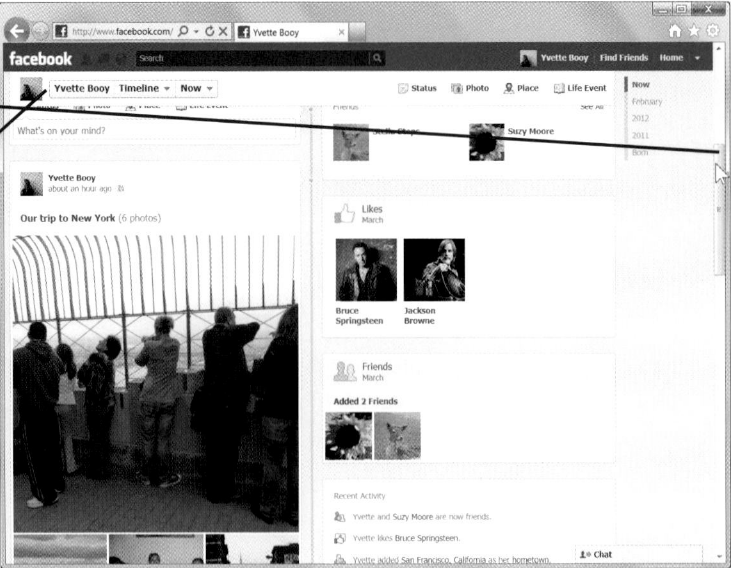

Your friends can write messages and add photos, video clips and links to your Timeline. These messages are also visible to your other friends. You can also post a message directly to the Timelines of your own friends. If you do not yet have any friends, you can just read through this section.

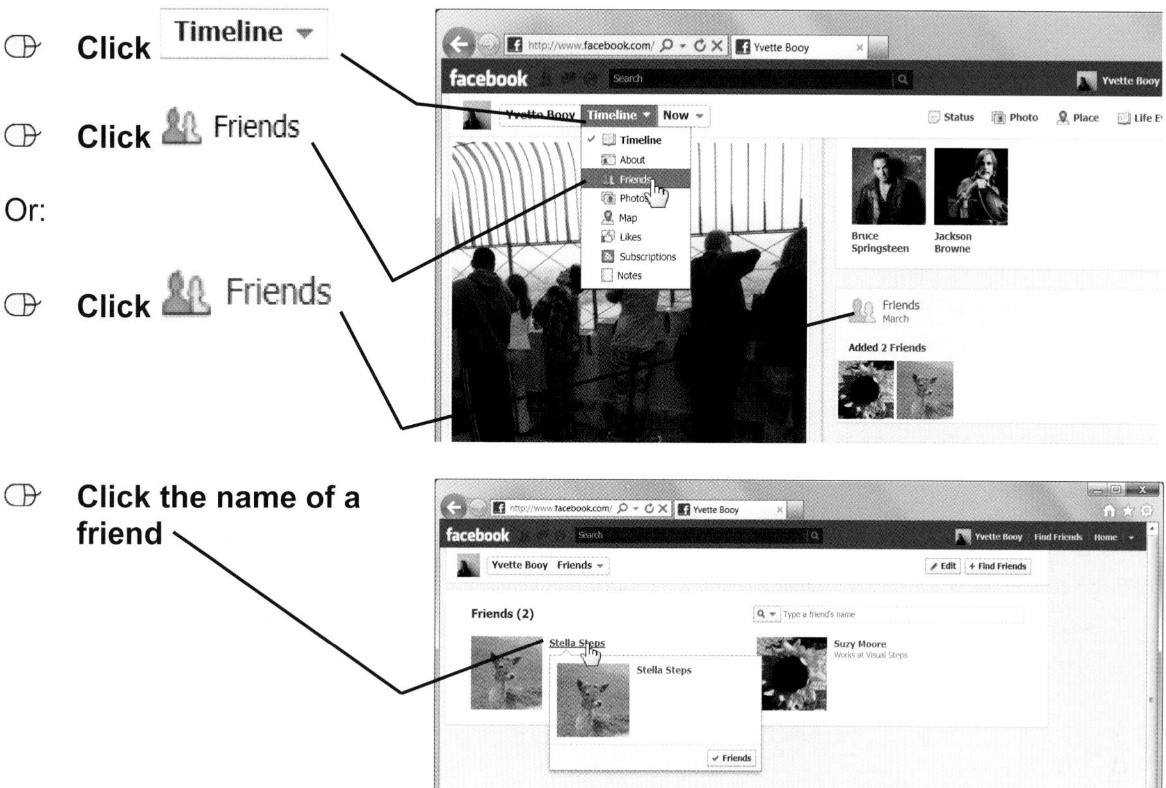

Click Timeline

Click Friends

Or:

Click Friends

Click the name of a friend

Your friend's profile will be opened.

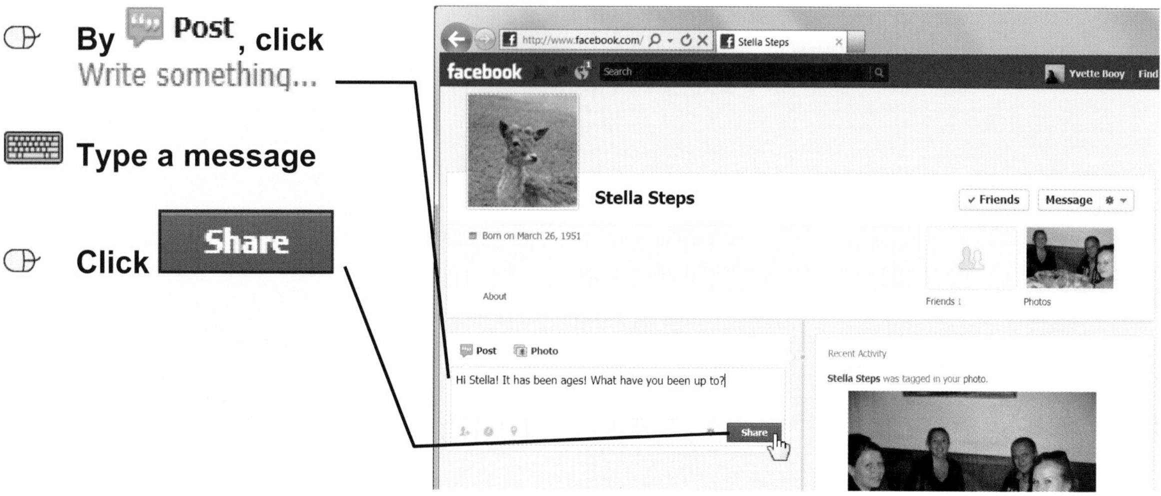

By Post**, click** Write something...

Type a message

Click Share

Now your message is posted on your friend's Timeline:

Mutual friends will see this message appear in their News Feed.

If you want to delete the message anyway, you can use the button:

This button will appear when you move the pointer over your message.

Please note: your friend can also delete your message.

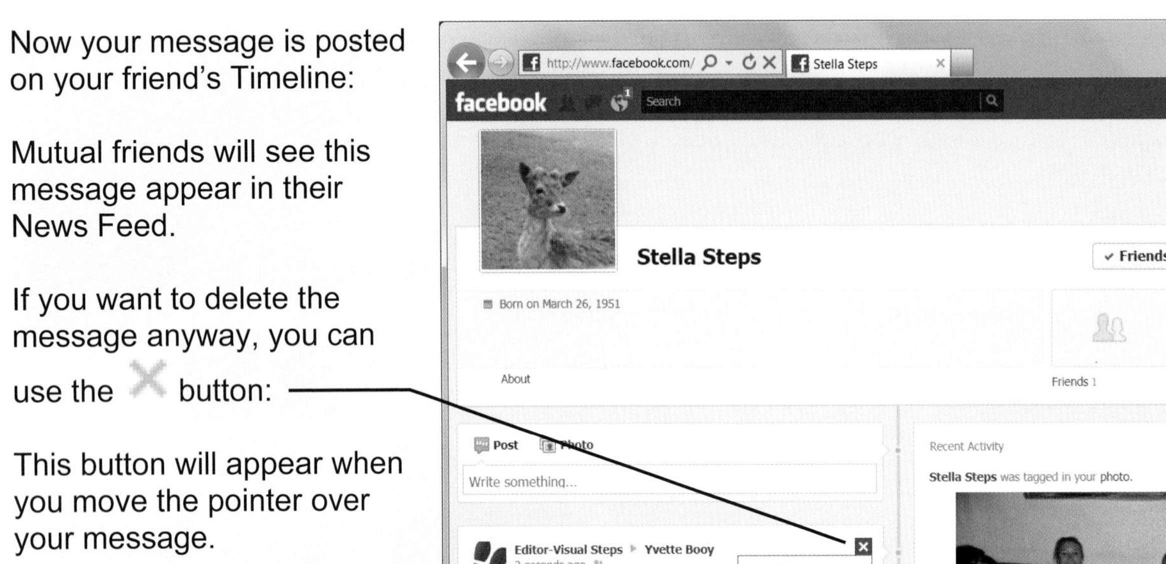

In the privacy settings, you can determine the way in which your Timeline can be used by others. In the top right of the window:

- **Click** ▼, Privacy Settings
- **By** How you connect, **click** Edit Settings

Here you see that the settings allow your friends to send Facebook messages:

These settings at the top of the window can be modified according to your own wishes. If you do not remember how to do this, go back to *section 1.3 View and Edit Your Privacy Settings*.

Click 

Tip

Share photos and links

Besides messages, you can also share a photo, a website link or a video clip with your friends. To do this, you need to return to your friend's Timeline:

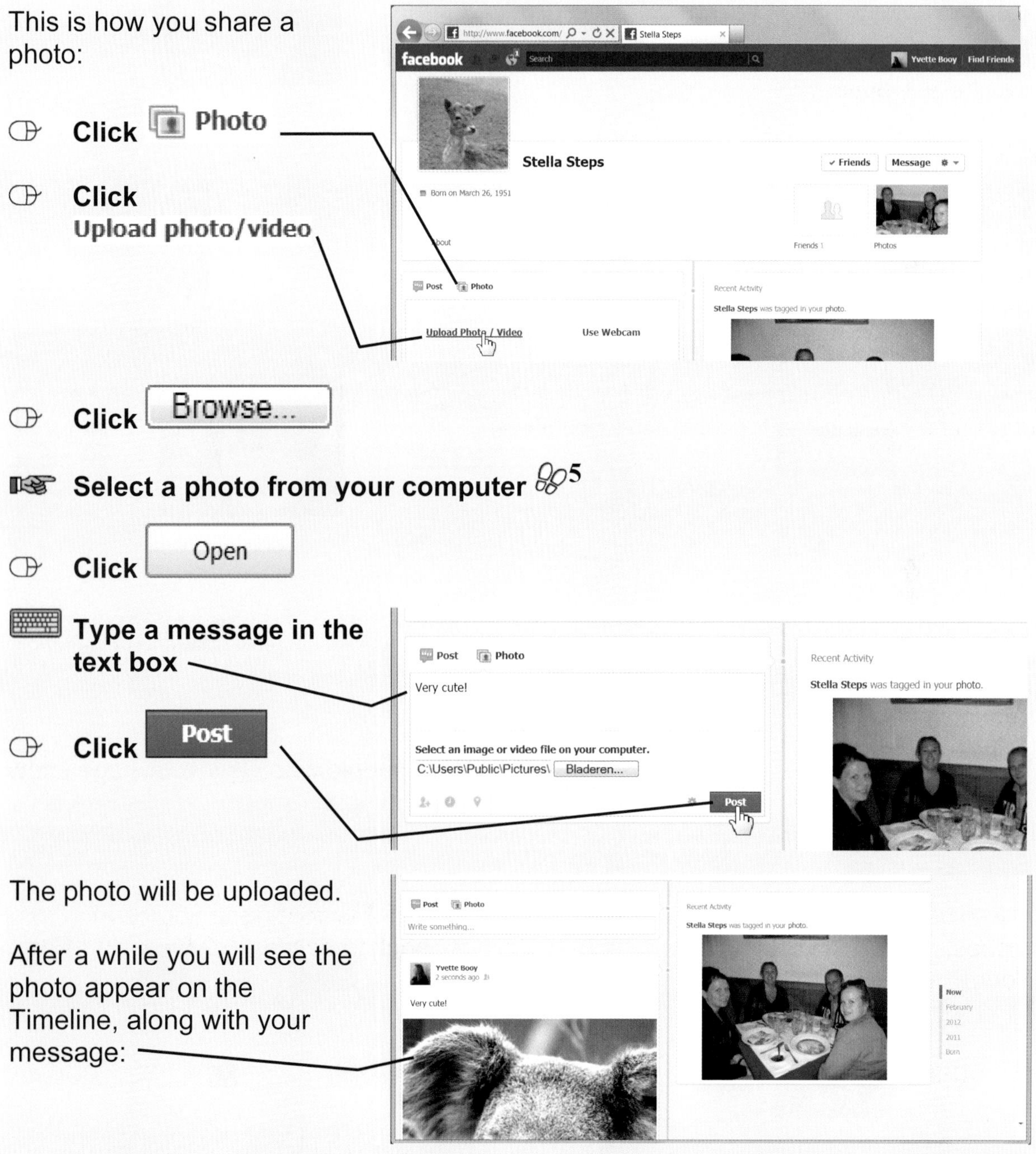

By Friends, click the name of a friend

This is how you share a photo:

Click Photo

Click Upload photo/video

Click Browse...

Select a photo from your computer 5

Click Open

Type a message in the text box

Click Post

The photo will be uploaded.

After a while you will see the photo appear on the Timeline, along with your message:

- Continue on the next page -

This is how you share a link to a specific website:

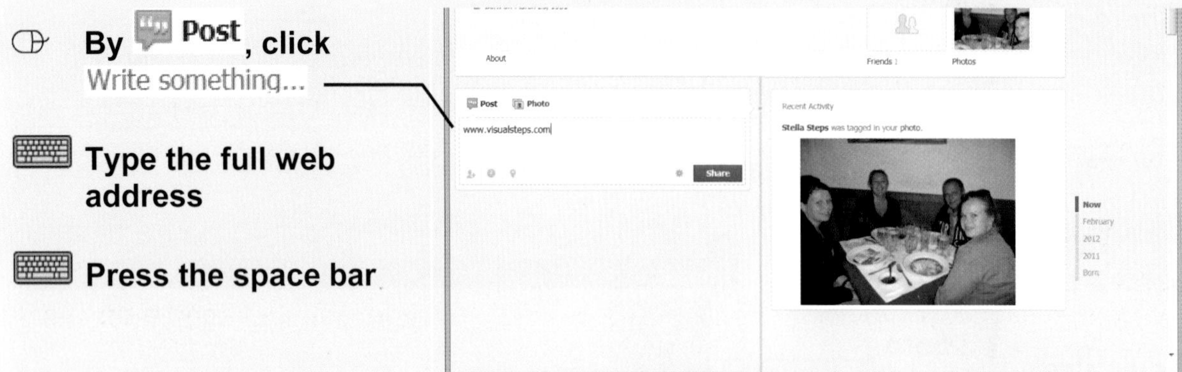

By Post, click Write something...

Type the full web address

Press the space bar

Facebook will display information about this website:

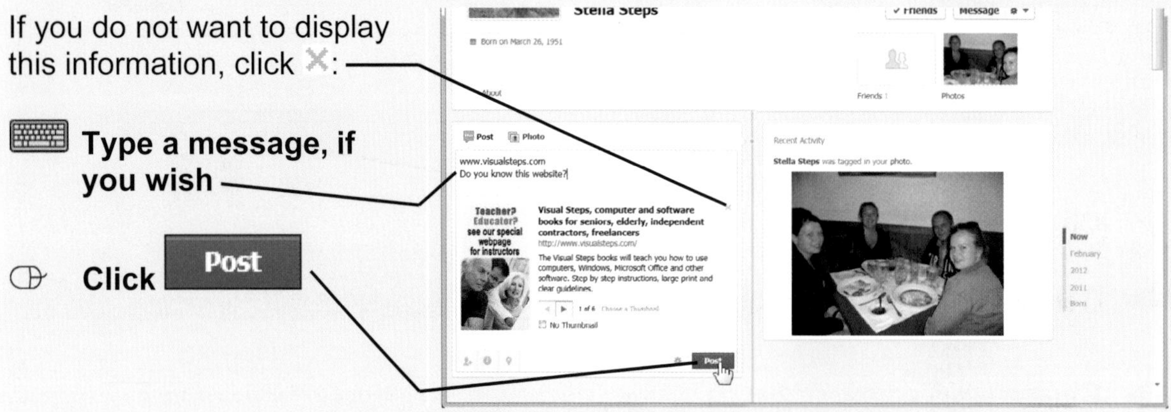

If you do not want to display this information, click ×:

Type a message, if you wish

Click Post

The link to the website will be posted on the Timeline.

Tip

What are you doing?

You can post a status message on *Facebook*, to let people who view your page know what you are doing. Your status updates will appear in your Timeline, News Feeds and in your friends' News Feeds. You can enter your status update on your profile page as well as on your News Feed page:

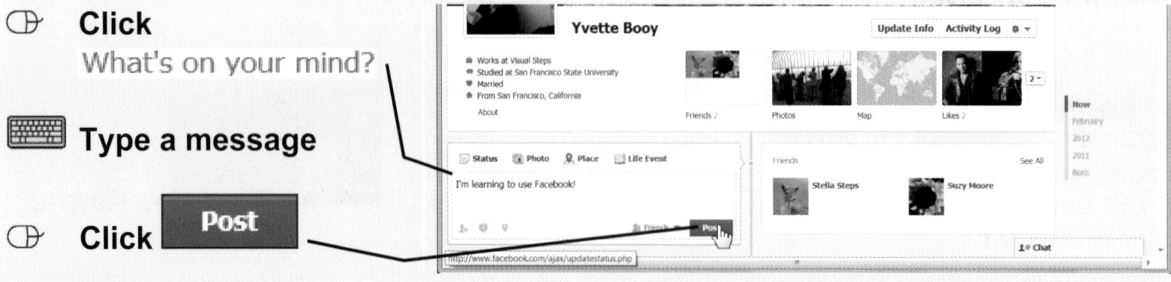

Click What's on your mind?

Type a message

Click Post

- *Continue on the next page* -

You can also add a photo or a link to your status update. In the previous *Tip* you learned how to do this.

Facebook may try to help while you are typing your message by displaying windows with tips. For example, tips for adding the location and the people you contact to your message. You can just read these tips and close the window, if they do not apply.

Tip

Send a private message

If you do not want all your friends to read a certain message, you can send a private message to a friend. *Facebook* uses a type of internal e-mail service for such messages. This is how you send such a message to a specific friend:

- **Click the name of your friend**

You will see your friend's profile page:

- **Click** Message
- **Type a message**
- **Click** Send

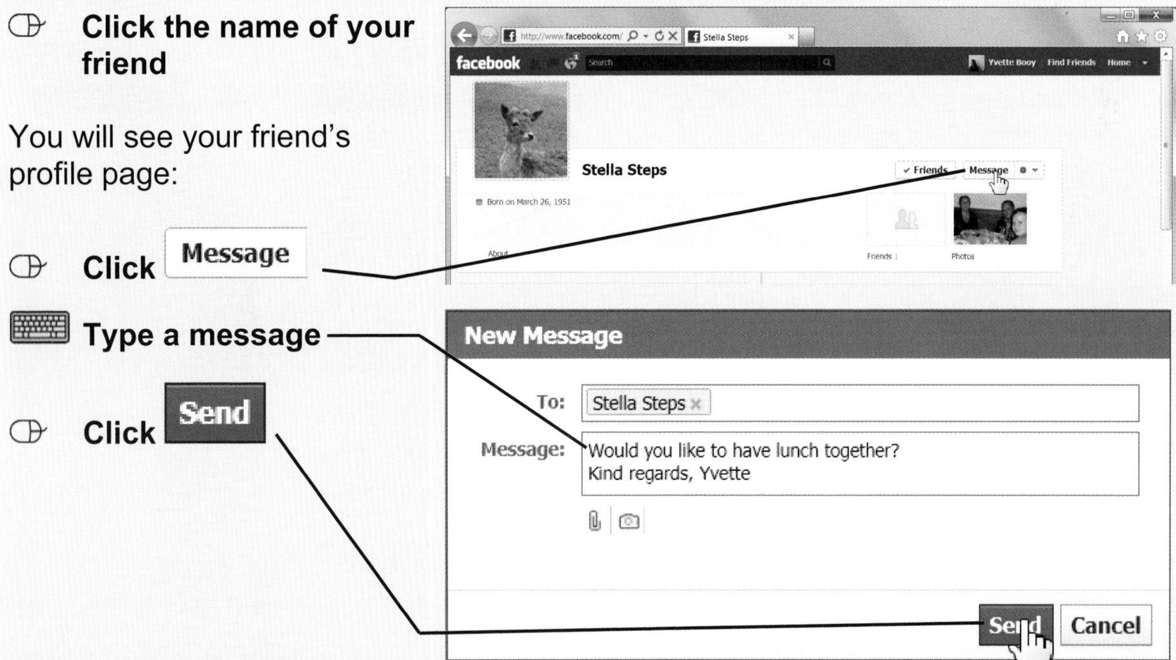

Your friend will notice this message by the change to the icon shown in the top left: . If you click , an extra window opens with a list of the most recent posts in your mailbox. If you click a link, the message will be opened.

1.10 Deactivate Your Account

If you ever decide to stop using *Facebook*, you can deactivate your account. Here is how to do that:

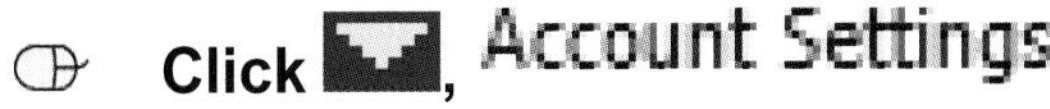

Click Security

Click
Deactivate your account.

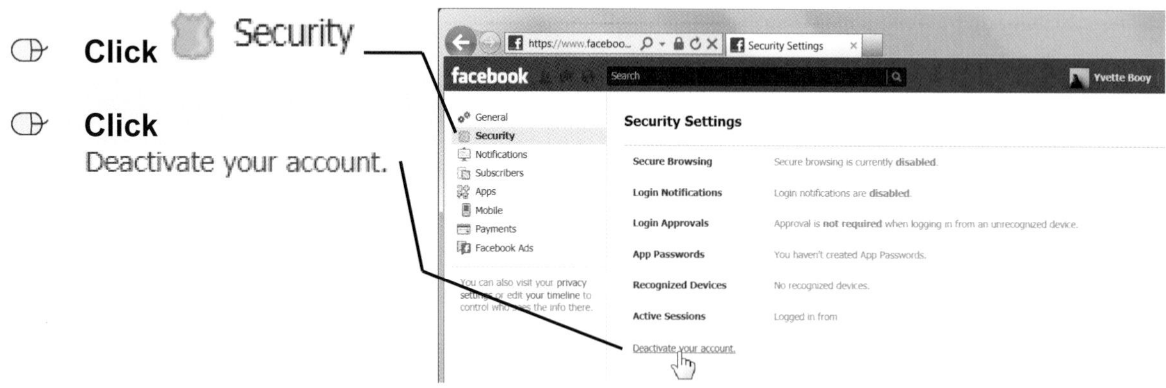

Facebook will ask you why you want to deactivate your account. You can select a reason from the list:

Click the radio button next to a relevant reason

You will see a yellow area with an explanation by *Facebook*.

Check the box at Email opt out:

Click Confirm

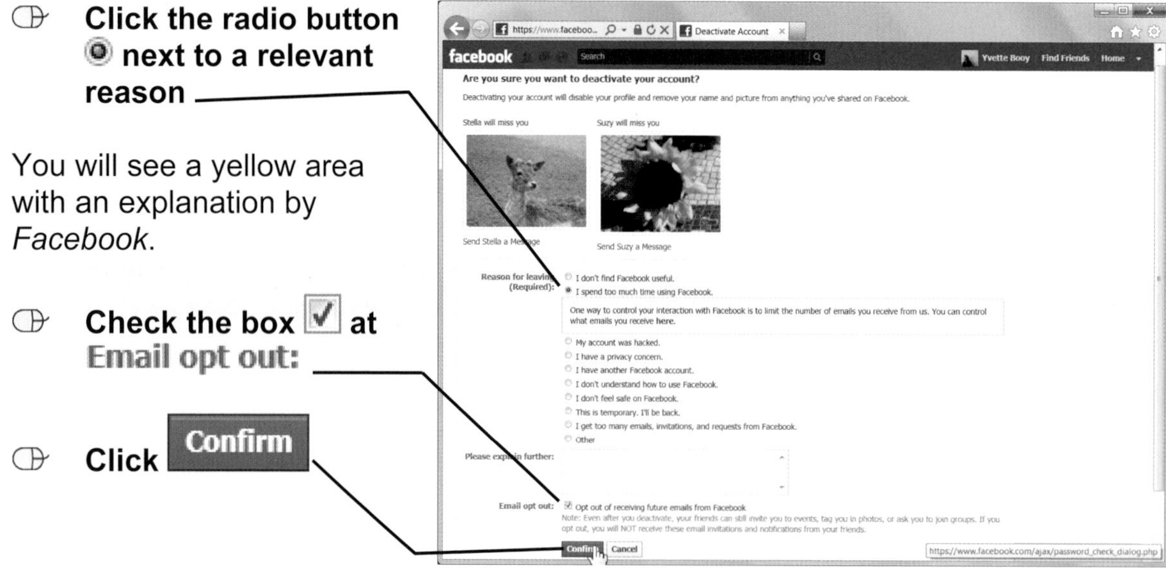

Facebook will ask you to confirm this action by entering your password:

Type your password

Click Deactivate now

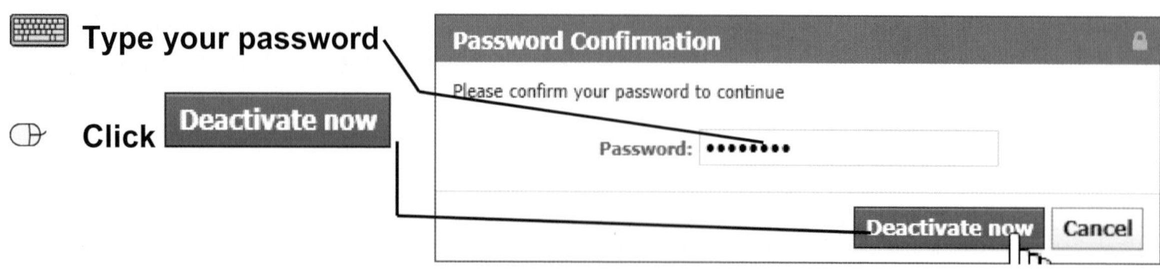

For an extra security check you might need to copy the characters from the text box:

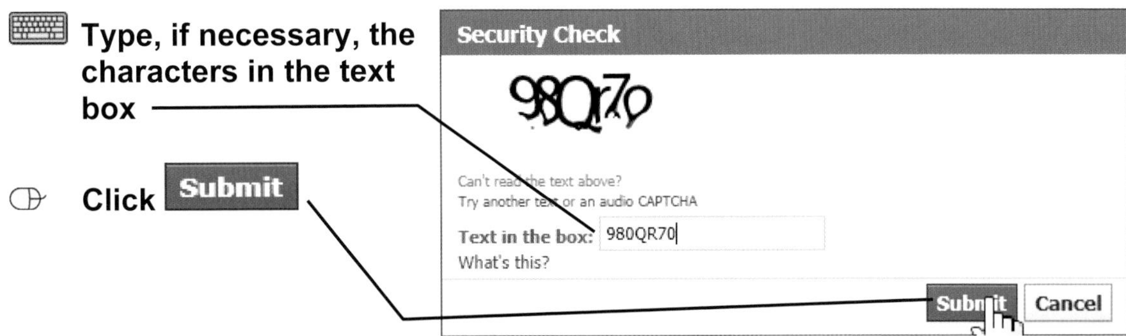

Now your account has been deactivated and you will no longer receive e-mails from *Facebook*. Your profile and all other information stored along with your account are no longer accessible to other *Facebook* users. They will not be able to find you on *Facebook* anymore. If you ever want to activate your *Facebook* account again, you can log in with your e-mail address and password.

Close *Internet Explorer* 4

In this chapter you have been introduced to the main functions of the *Facebook* social networking site. *Facebook* also offers many possibilities for commercial use by businesses, brands, organizations and clubs. With the knowledge you have acquired you can set up an account for these purposes. You can read more about this topic in the next sections.

1.11 Using Facebook for Commercial Purposes

Facebook is the biggest online social network in the world. By the end of 2011 there were more than 845 million active users, worldwide. Daily, tens of thousands of new users are registered. This means that *Facebook* has become an interesting medium for companies and organizations. Through a modern platform such as *Facebook*, messages can spread like wildfire. This can be a powerful tool for things such as getting feedback about a new product; allowing your followers be the first ones to know about an important event or by posting a well-thought out response to a frequently asked question.

Facebook offers various methods for promoting your company, product, organization or club:

- the official page (also called the 'fan page');
- the group;
- advertising on *Facebook*.

We will only discuss the first two options, which are completely free. On the www.facebook.com/advertising web page, you can find additional information about advertising on *Facebook*.

The main difference between official pages and groups on *Facebook* is that an official page can only be created by a formal representative of a company, brand, product, organization, artist or celebrity. Whereas groups can be created by any user, regarding any subject. A group is a place where users can share their opinions and interests regarding a certain topic.

Please note:

It is not permitted to use a personal profile for promoting your company or business. But you will need to have a personal profile before you can create an official page or a group.

Here are some of the similarities and differences between official pages and groups:

Official page	**Group**
• an official page is always a public page and it can also be found by people who do not have a *Facebook* account.	• a group may be **open** (members and content visible to everyone), **closed** (members visible, content not visible) or **secret** (members and content not visible to non-members).
• an official page will be indexed, so it can also be found by search engines such as *Google*.	• a group is not indexed, so it is not visible to search engines.
• *Facebook* users can become a **fan** by clicking the Like button.	• *Facebook* users can become a **member** by using the +1 Ask to join button. With closed groups, permission to join needs to be given by the administrator or you need to be invited by a group member. Joining a secret group is only possible if you are invited.
• unlimited number of fans possible.	• unlimited number of members possible.
• the name of the page's administrator is **not** visible.	• the name of the group administrator **is visible**.
• a *Facebook* user can be a fan of up to 500 pages (maximum).	• a *Facebook* user can be a member of up to 300 groups (maximum).

- Continue on the next page -

• apps may be used.	• apps may not be used.
• the administrator cannot send messages to the fans' inboxes.	• the administrator can send personal messages to the members' inboxes directly (groups can consist of up to 5000 members).
• a recognizable web address can be used, in which the company name is included.	• a recognizable web address cannot be used.

 **Please note:**

If you create an official page, you will not be able to convert such a page to a different type of page later on. Neither can an official page be converted to a group. So think carefully for which purpose you want to use such a page, before creating an official page.

1.12 A Group or a Page?

Are you having difficulty deciding which form is the best for your company, organization or club? Official pages are a good way of building long-term relationships with your fans, customers or members. There are various types of official pages for local companies, brands, products or organizations, as well as for artists, bands and celebrities. An official page can be found by search engines, such as *Google.* If you are the administrator, you will remain anonymous.

With groups you can choose to create an open, closed or secret group. Anyone can become a member of an open group. The names of the group members and the messages will be visible to everybody else on *Facebook*.

In a closed group, new members can be added by the current members. If a non-member wants to become a member by using the **+1 Ask to join** button, the administrator will need to approve this application. The messages on the group page are only visible to group members.

A secret group is not at all visible on *Facebook* and new members can only join if they are invited by current members.

An open group can be used to quickly attract attention to a specific subject. In their turn, group members can invite all their friends at once to join the group, so the message will spread extremely quickly among the *Facebook* community.

Since it is possible to send messages directly to the members' inboxes, a group would be a good alternative for a sports or hobby club. In such a case, it is best to create a closed or secret group.

Tip
Official page or group?

- brand → official page for a brand, product or organization
- national chains of shops, restaurants, gyms, etc. → official page for a brand, product, or organization
- restaurant → official page for a local business
- shop → official page for a local business
- sport school, gym → official page for a local business
- sports club, tennis club → closed or secret group
- group for a specific cause… → open group

1.13 Creating a Group

You can create a group on your own *Facebook* page:

Open your home page 2

In the left-hand side of the window:

Click Create group

Type a name for your group

To invite a friend to join the group:

By Members:, type the first few letters of the friend's name

Click the name

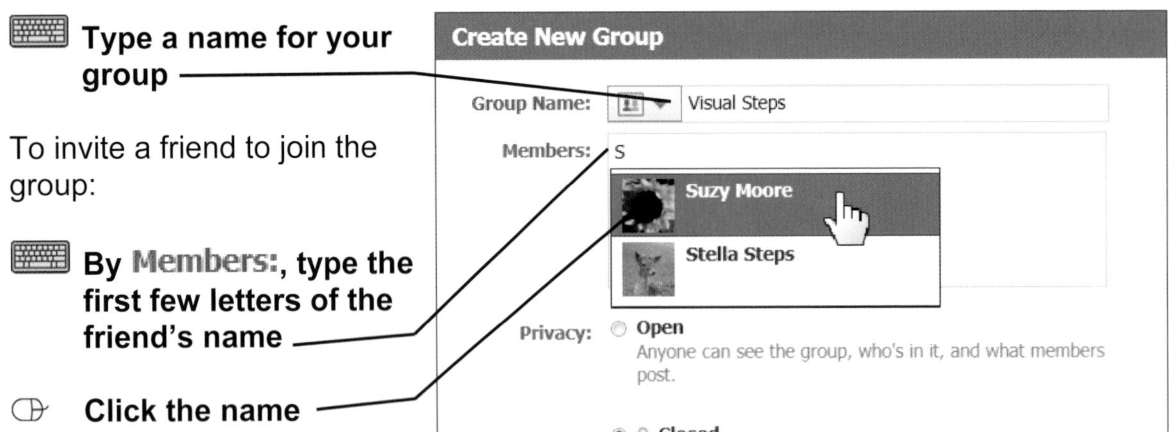

Repeat this operation for all the friends you want to invite

By Privacy:, click the desired privacy settings (closed, open or secret)

Click Create

Now the group has been created.

At the top you will see the photos of the members of the group:

Here you see the name of the group:

On the right-hand side you see how many members there are:

If you want to add more friends, you can use the **+ Add friends to group** button:

You will see a News Feed regarding the group activities:

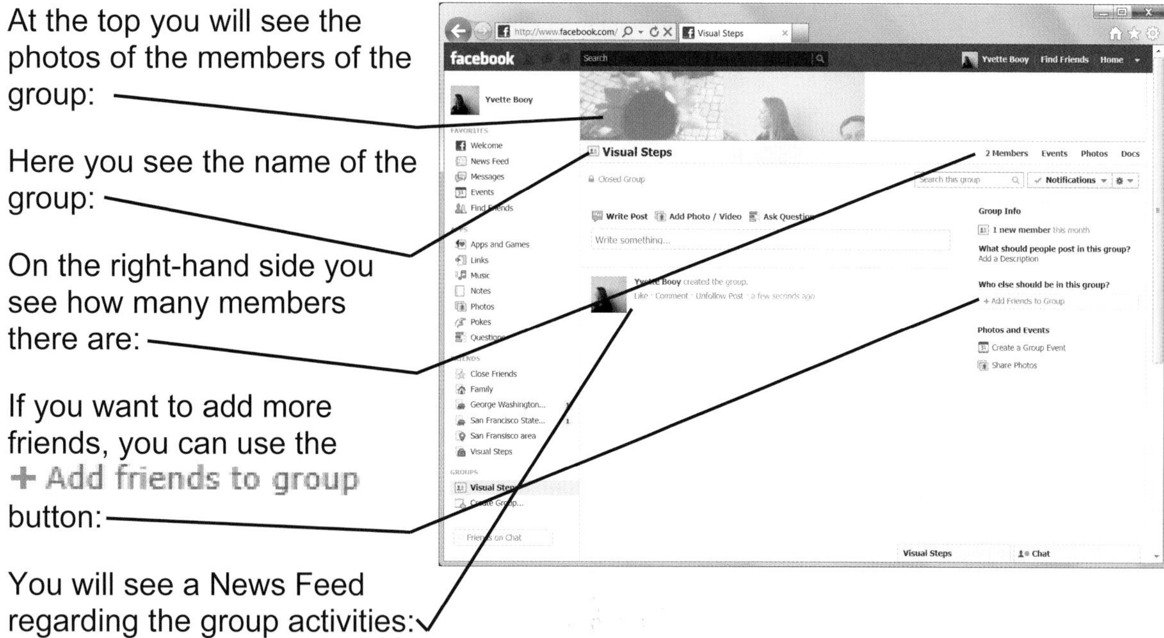

Tip

Where can I find this group?

If you have joined a group or if you are the group's administrator, you need to click the link to the Visual Steps group on the left-hand side of your home page.

You can replace the photo strip with profile pictures of members by a group picture. Here's how to do that:

Place the pointer on the photo strip

Click

Click Upload a Photo

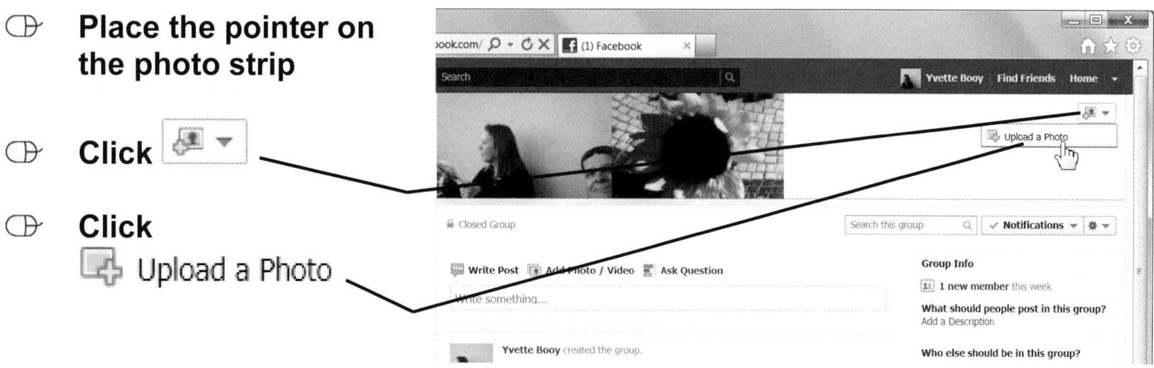

Select an image from your computer and add this image 5

The photo appears. You can drag the photo to reposition it.

If you want to save the changes:

- Click **Save Changes**

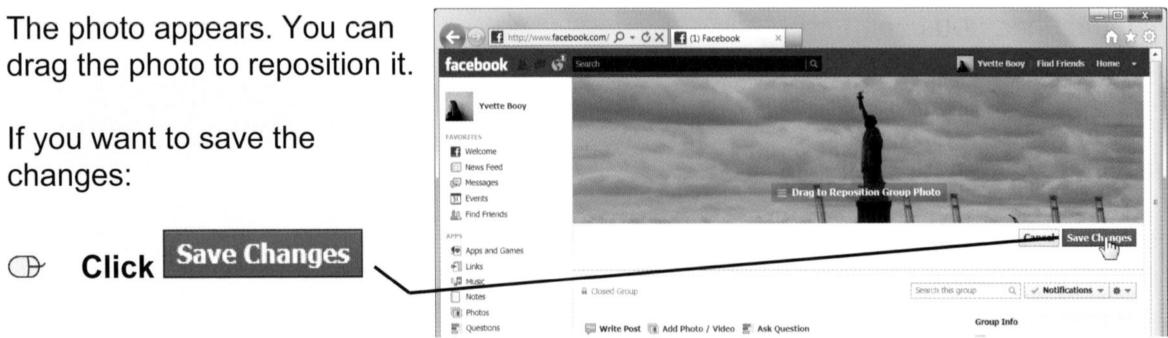

The photo has been added:

Tip

Remove group picture

You can also remove the group picture. By doing this the photos of your members will appear at the top of the window. Here is how to remove the group photo:

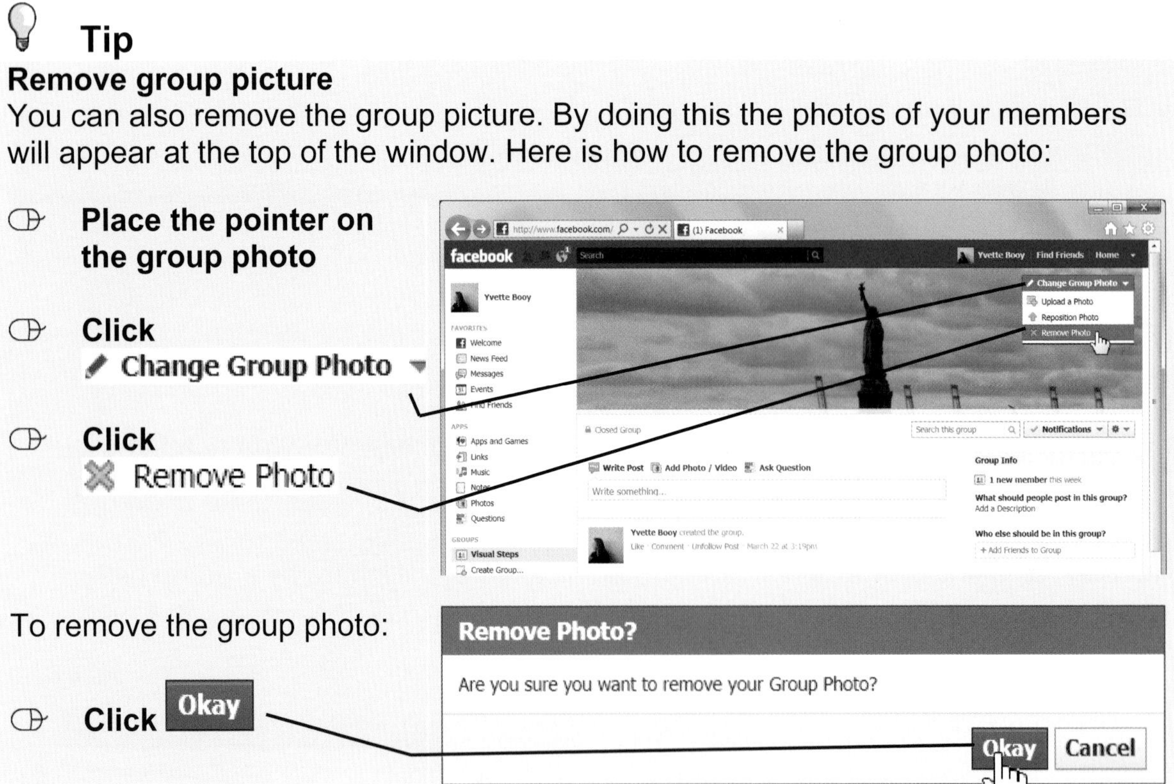

- **Place the pointer on the group photo**
- **Click** Change Group Photo
- **Click** Remove Photo

To remove the group photo:

- **Click** Okay

Now you can modify the general settings for this group. In the top right of the window:

- **Click** , Edit Group

On this page you can change the group name and the privacy settings:

You can also enter an e-mail address for the group.
An e-mail message sent to this address will be forwarded to all the group members' inboxes.

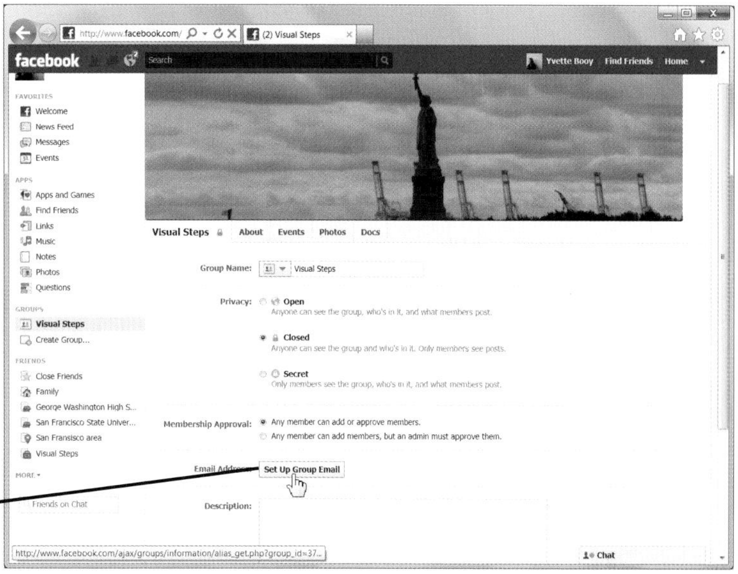

Click Set Up Group Email

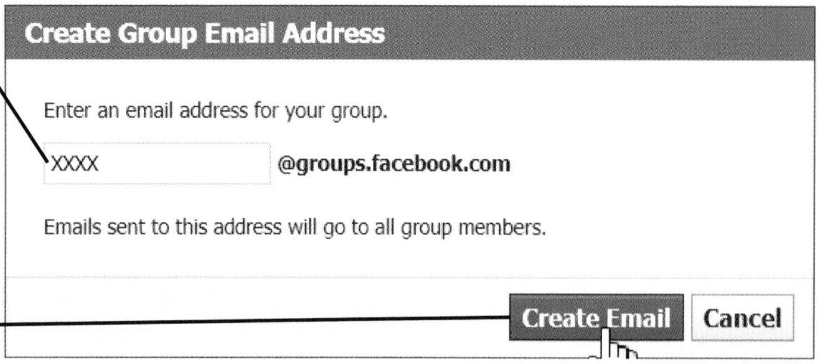

Type an e-mail address

Click Create Email

By Description:**, type a description for the group**

For open and closed groups, all potential members will see this description.

Click 

Tip

Share

On the group page, you and your members can share messages, links and photos. You can do this in the same way as on your personal profile page. These messages will appear in the News Feeds as updates.

Both the administrator and the group members can announce events.
An event can be anything: a meeting, a concert, a clearance sale, a lecture, etc. Click the button in the top right of the window, and then click Create Event. In the next window you can enter the information about the event, after which you click Create.

All group members will be invited to this event through a personal message.

With the Docs button you can start a new document. In a document you can start a discussion. You could ask members to add their ideas to the document, for example. A document can be read, modified and completed by all the members of the group. If a document has been edited by multiple members, you can use the ◄ ► buttons to flip through the various versions of the document. For each version you will see the names of the members who have most recently edited this version.

Tip

Change group settings

As a group administrator or member you can determine if and when you want to receive e-mail messages concerning the activities in the group. You can also select whether you want to display the group updates in the News Feed on your home page:

- **Click the group name**
- **In the top right, click** ✓ Notifications ▾, Settings...

With the edit your notifications settings. link, you will jump to a page where you can change the *Facebook* notification settings.

Notification settings

Notify me about: All posts ▾

☑ Also send an email to:

To turn off all group emails, edit your notifications settings.

Save Changes Cancel

After you have changed a setting:

- **Click** Save Changes

Tip

Delete a group

Facebook will automatically delete a group when the group does not have members anymore. If you want to delete a group as an administrator, you will need to delete all the members first:

- **Click the name of the group**
- **At the right-hand side of the window click** Members

Now the *Members* window will be opened. For the members you want to delete:

- **Click** ×
- **Click** Confirm

If you are the only remaining member, this is how you can delete the group:

- **Click the name of the group**
- **Click** , Leave Group
- **Click** Delete group

1.14 Creating an Official Page

You can find the link for creating an official *Facebook* page on the official page of any random company or product. Just take a look at the official page of Internet store Amazon.com:

Open the webpage www.facebook.com/#!/Amazon [1]

Now you will see Amazon's official page. Take your time to view the contents of this page. After you have finished:

- **Drag the scroll bar upwards**

In the top right of the window:

- **Click** Create a Page

Please note:

An official page can only be created by the official representative of the company, brand, product, organization, artist or celebrity.

First, you need to select the type of page you want to create. In this example we will create an official page for a local company.

Click Local business or place

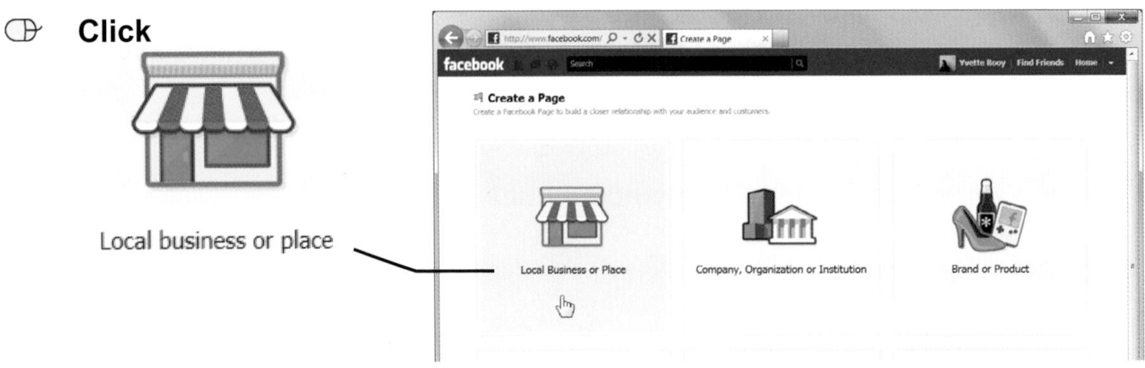

By Choose a category, **click** ▼

Click the appropriate category in the list

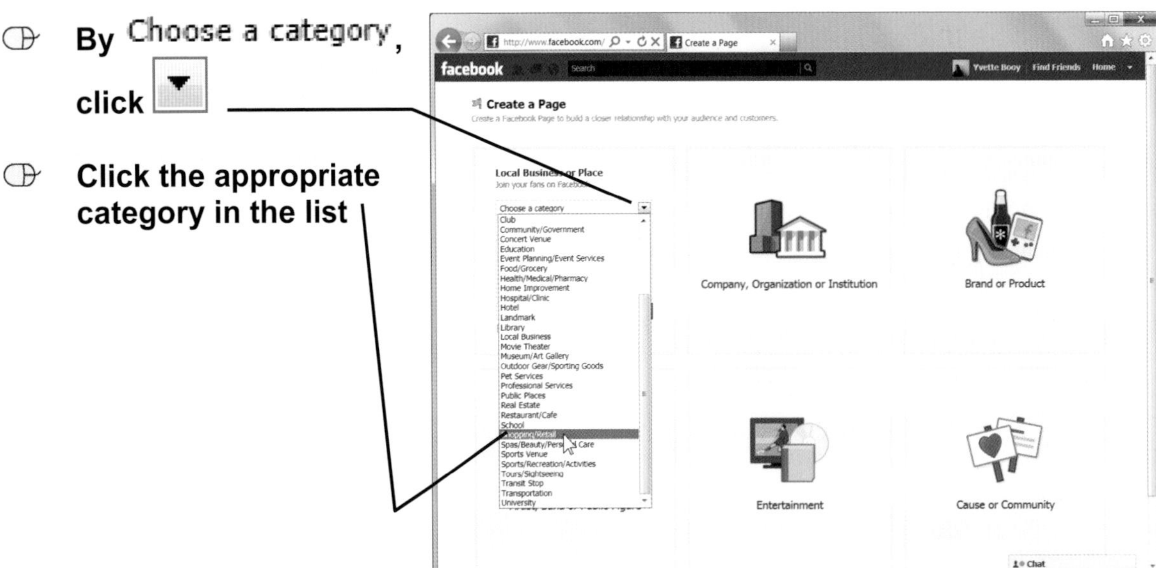

Type the name and address of the company

Check the box ☑ **next to** I agree to Facebook Pag

Click Get started

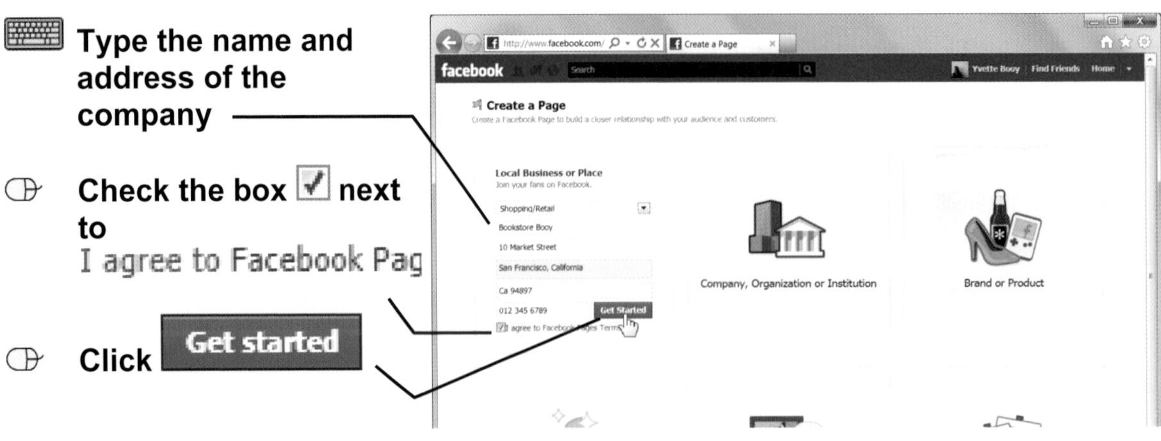

Now the page will be created. You can start editing the page right away. You can begin by adding a photo for example:

Click **Upload From Computer**

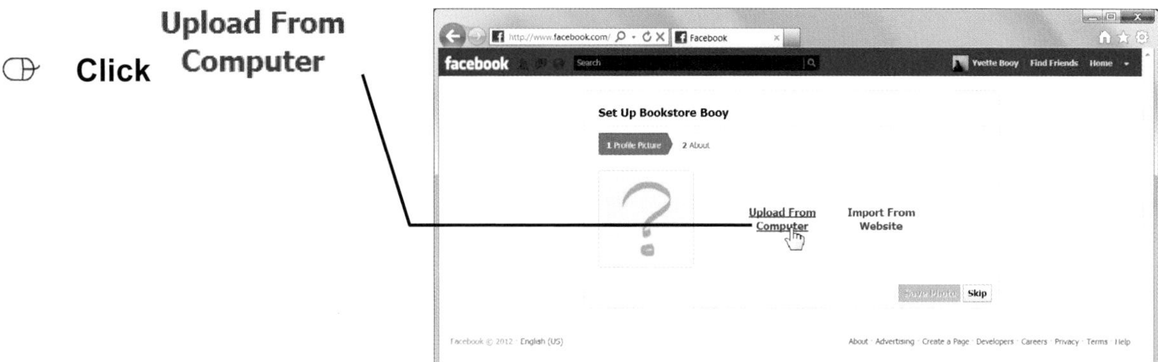

Locate a photo that will effectively represent this page:

Click **Browse...**

Select an image on your computer and add this image 5

Click **Next**

Now you can add some basic information about the company, organization, artist or brand:

Click Please provide some basic inf

Type the desired information

You can also add a link to a website:

Click **Save Info**

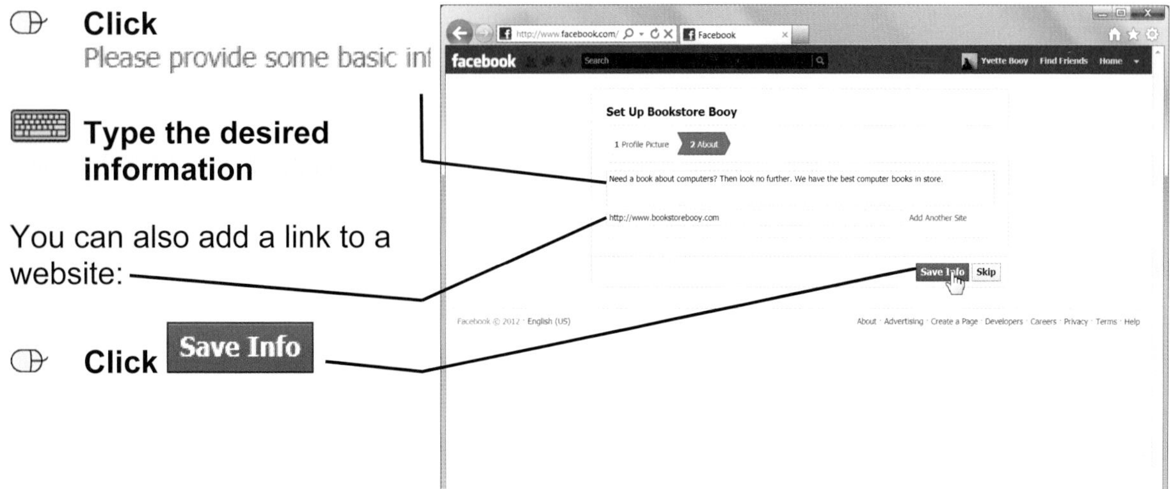

You will see a window with information about liking your page:

Click, if necessary, **Like**

You will see another window with information about inviting friends to visit your page:

Click, if necessary, **Next**

You can also invite your e-mail contacts:

Click, if necessary, **Next**

You can share something on your page. For now you can skip this step:

Click Skip

You are going to add more detailed information:

Click Manage

Click Edit Page

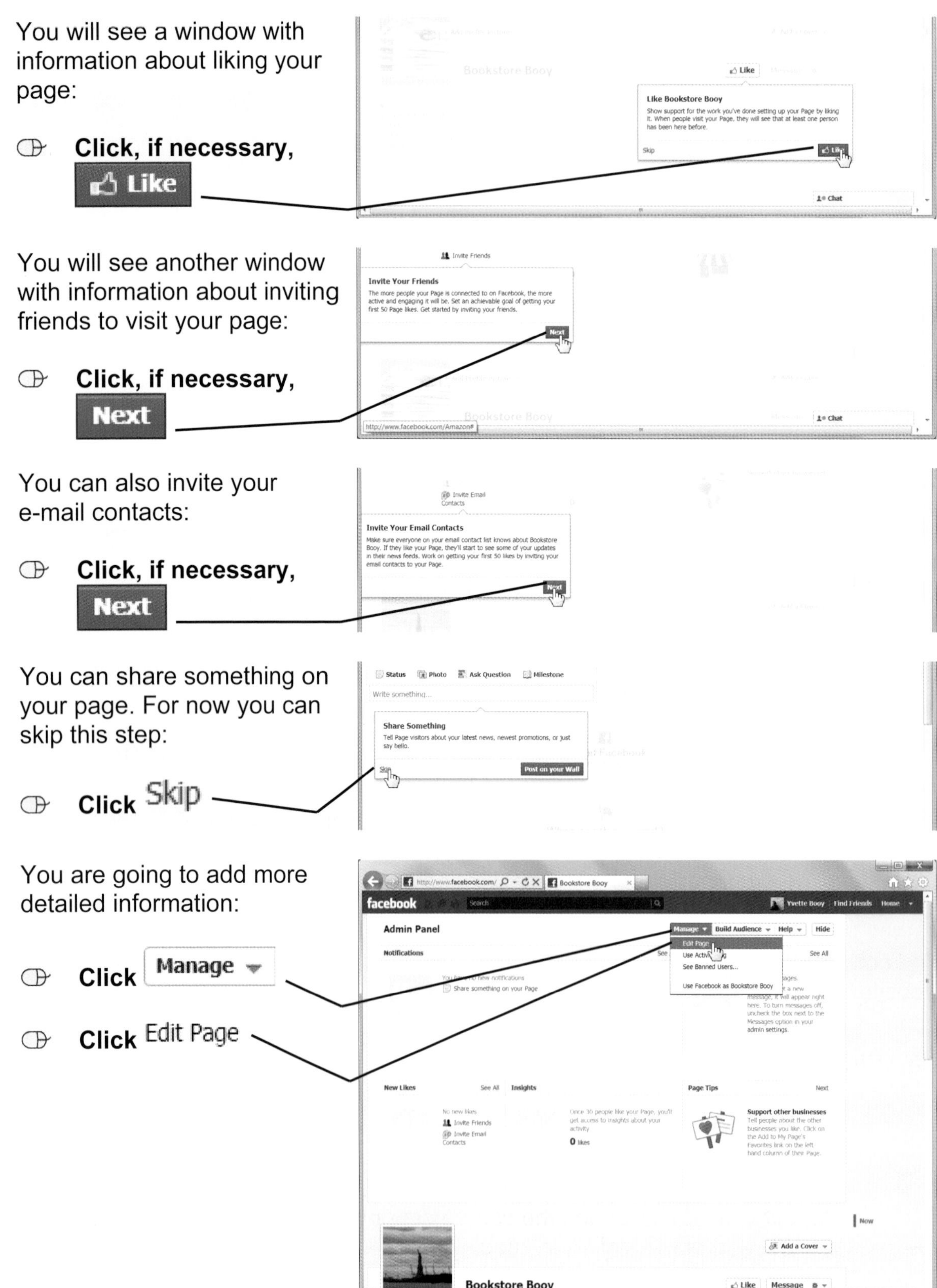

You will see a page where you can enter more detailed information.

Please note:

If you have selected a different category than a 'local business or place' while creating your official page, you will be able to add other types of information than what is shown in this example.

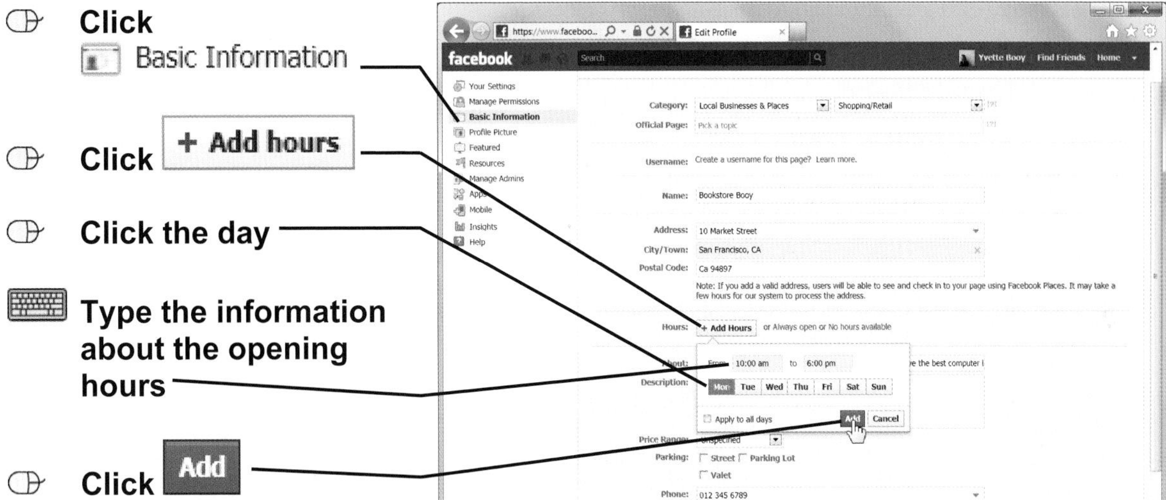

Repeat the same steps for all the hours of operation

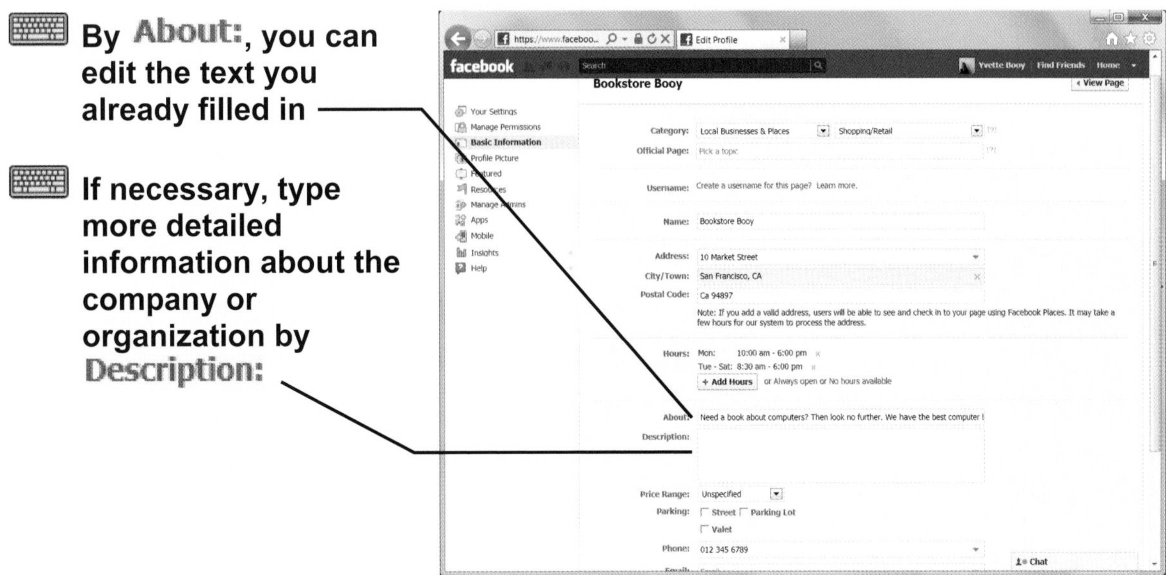

In the profile text you can introduce the company or organization. You can update this text regularly and call attention to special offers or activities.

You can also provide useful information such as parking facilities within the nearby vicinity. Most important, don't forget to mention your website and e-mail address.

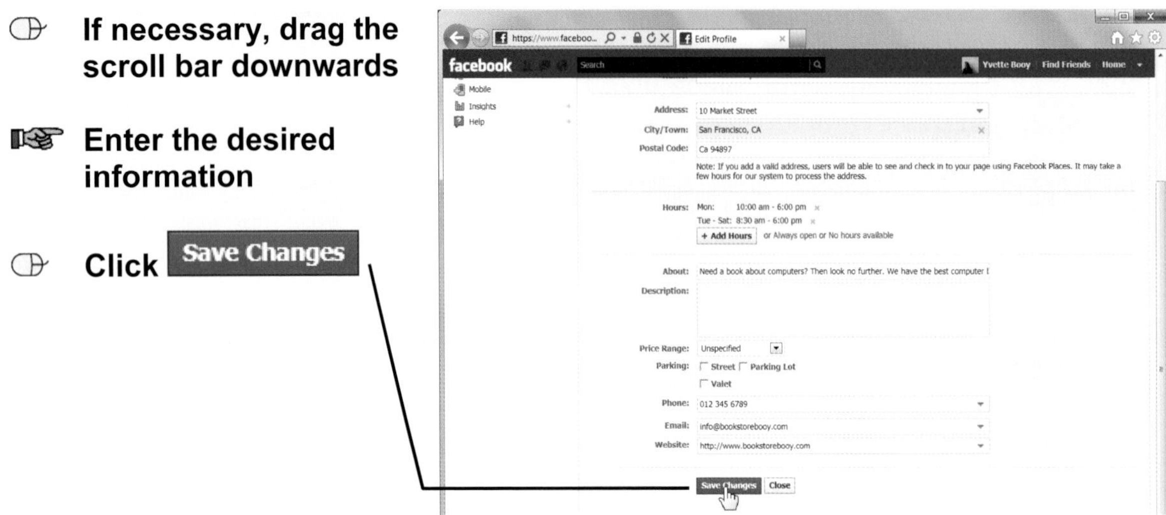

If necessary, drag the scroll bar downwards

Enter the desired information

Click **Save Changes**

In the top right of the page:

Click **View Page**

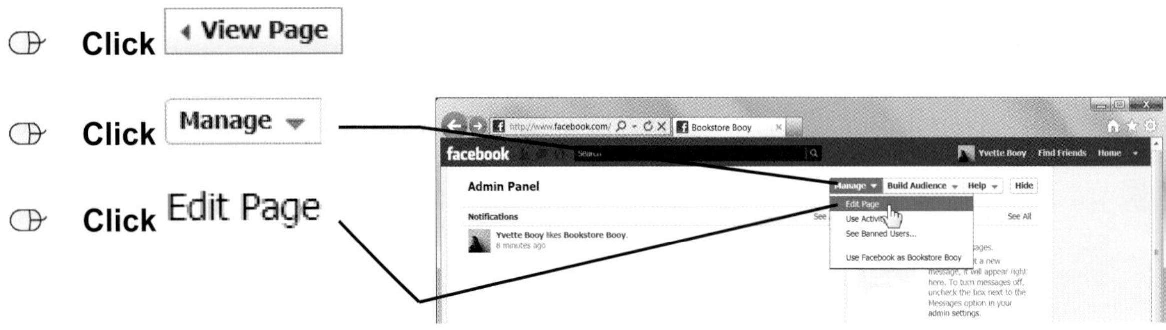

Click **Manage**

Click **Edit Page**

Now you can start editing the official page of the company or organization. To do this, first select the elements you want to use for this page:

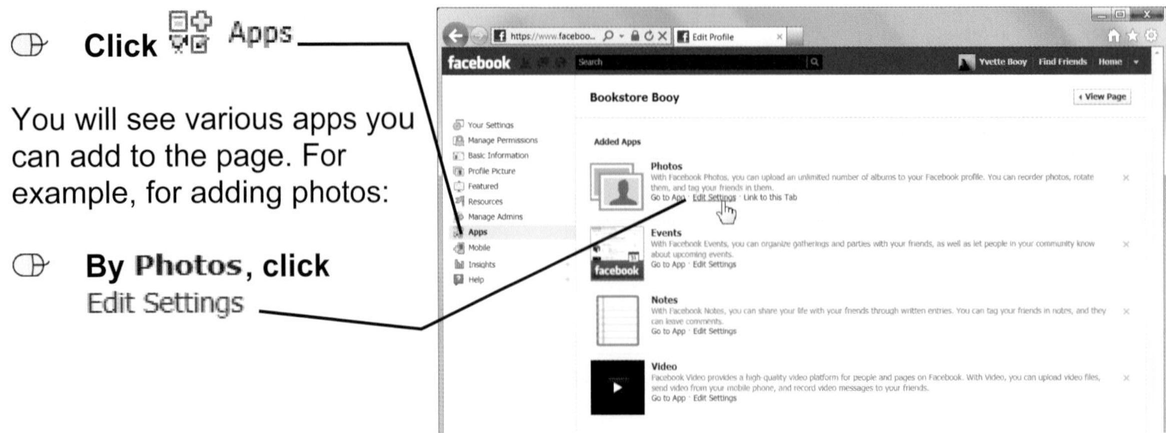

Click **Apps**

You will see various apps you can add to the page. For example, for adding photos:

By Photos, click Edit Settings

Here you can determine whether fans of the page will be allowed to upload photos:

- **Click** Additional Permissions

If you do not want to give fans the ability to upload photos, you need to uncheck the box ✔ by Publish content to my Wall.

By default, the *Photos* page will be displayed on the page. If you do not want this to happen, then follow these steps:

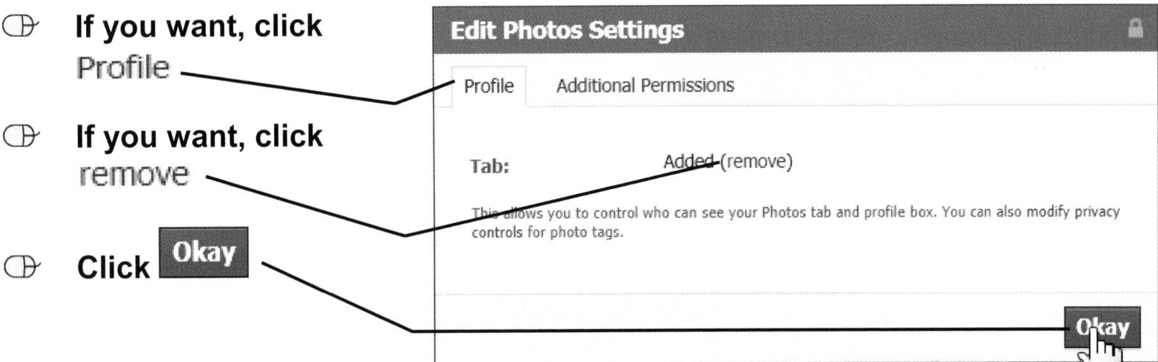

- **If you want, click** Profile
- **If you want, click** remove
- **Click** Okay

In the top right of the page:

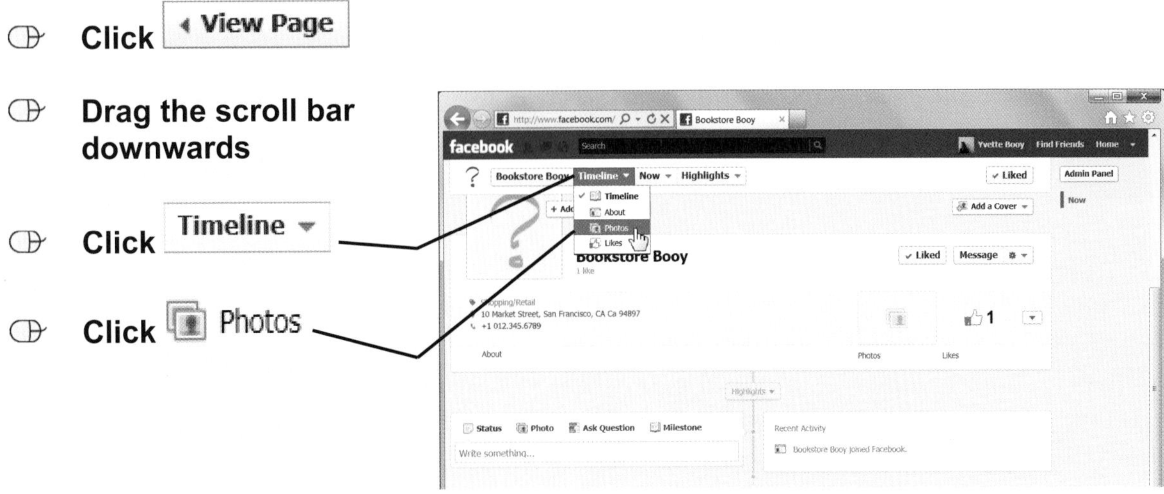

- **Click** ◂ View Page
- **Drag the scroll bar downwards**
- **Click** Timeline ▾
- **Click** Photos

Now you can add photo albums featuring the company, events, products, employees, etcetera. You can do this in the same way as on your personal *Facebook* page. Do not forget to add captions.

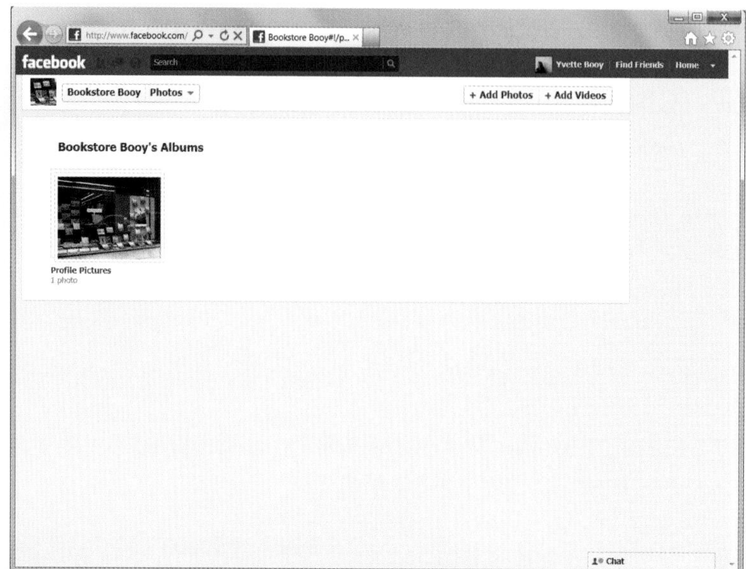

Tip

Additional apps

Apart from Photos, you can also add several other additional apps to the page:

With *Events* you can organize and announce events. An event can be anything: a meeting, a concert, clearance sale, lecture, etcetera.

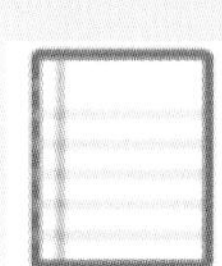

With *Notes* you can add a blog message to your page.

With *Video* you can upload videos, forward videos from your smartphone and record video messages to send to friends.

Tip

The Timeline

Share information through status updates posted on the Timeline. This can be anything: a bit of news about a particular product, opening of a new location, a job opening, or the launch of a brand new product. A message may contain up to 365 characters. You can easily add a link, photo or video to the message as well.

You can set your own preferences regarding the way fans are allowed to react to the messages on the Timeline.

Please note:

The Timeline is the main area where fans can make direct contact. *Facebook* users will expect that they can comment on posts and be able to publish messages themselves.

In the top left of the page:

Click the name of your page

This is how you can check the settings for the Timeline:

Click 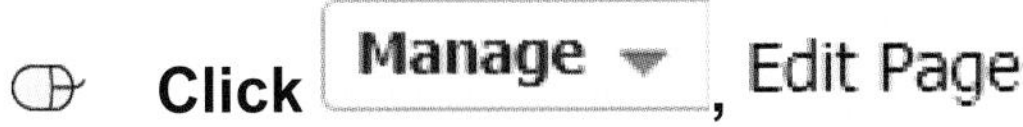

Click 

If necessary, you can set restrictions as to the country of origin and age of the visitors of your page:

By default, fans will be able to post messages, photos and videos:

If you have changed a setting:

Click Save Changes

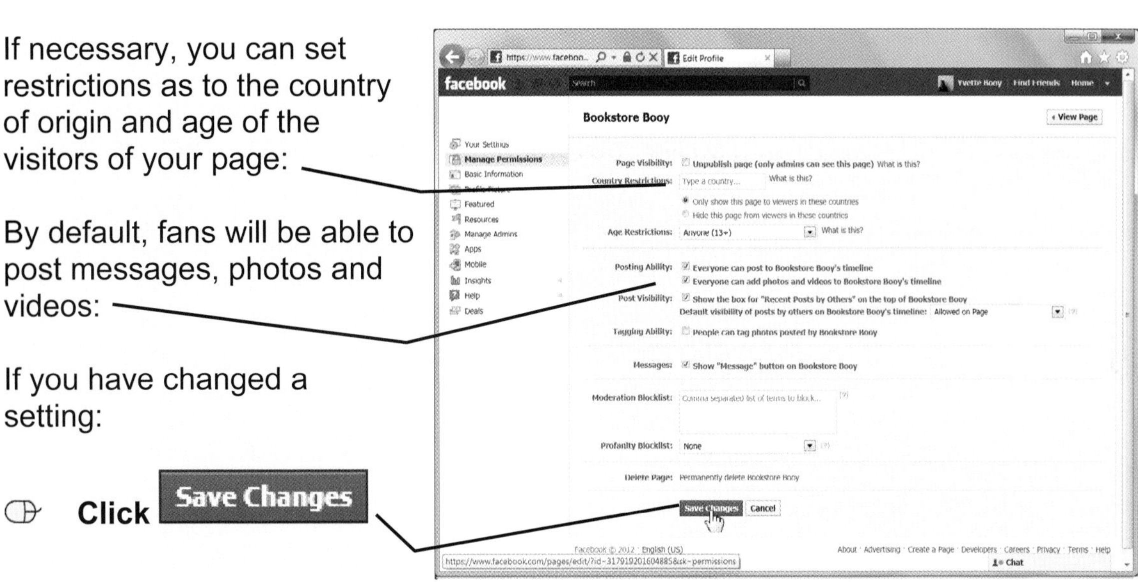

Tip

Change settings

You can always change these settings later on if you want. But if you want to create a page that will build traffic the quickest, it is better not to change anything.

Tip

Call attention to your page

Underneath the option Build Audience you will find various methods for calling attention to the page, and pointing out the page to friends, customers and other contacts:

Invite Email Contacts...	Import contacts from a file or from your webmail account and invite them to your page. If your contacts already have a *Facebook* account, they will see this link on their page: Recommended Pages / Book Trade Booy / Yvette Booy has suggested you take a look at her page. / Like.
Invite Friends...	Introduce the page to the friends you have gathered on your personal *Facebook* page. When you send an invitation, your friend will see a link appear on his or her home page.
Share Page...	With this option you can share the page on your own Timeline, on a friend's Timeline, in a group, on your page or in a private message.
Create An Ad	You can promote a *Facebook* page on your own website. You can specify a custom message and a call-to-action. Please note: a *Facebook* ad is not free, you will need to pay a fee for it.

Tip

Other settings

There are a many other settings you can modify for this page:

- **Click** Manage, Edit Page

Basic Information	Here you can edit the general profile information about this page. This is the information that is displayed on the About page.
Profile Picture	Here you can change/edit the profile photo for the page.

- Continue on the next page -

Featured — Here you can add a selection of *Likes*. To do this, you will need to use *Facebook* as the 'Bookstore Booy' page instead of as 'Yvette Booy'. In the next *Tip* you can read how to do this.
The pages you like will be displayed on the left-hand side of the page. You can choose which alternating pages you want to display here, by selecting them as 'Featured'.

Resources — Here you will find various methods for attracting attention to your page. Along with the methods you have seen earlier on with Build Audience, you will also find a link for sending an update to all of the fans of the page.

Manage Admins — Here you can add one or more additional admins for the page. This can be useful when you are on vacation or otherwise unable to attend to the page administration.

Apps — Here you can change the settings for the *Events*, *Photos*, *Video* and *Notes* pages. If on second thought, you decide not to display a certain app on the page, you can click Edit Settings and then remove. You can also add additional apps to the page here.

Mobile — Here you will find an assortment of settings that can be used with your smartphone.

Insights — Here you will find some interesting (or perhaps uninteresting) statistics concerning the use of the page.

Tip

Use Facebook as a page

By default, the first thing you see after you have logged in is your personal *Facebook* page. If you do not use your personal page for other purposes, you can also use *Facebook* as a page. Here is how to do that:

In the top right of the window, click

By Use Facebook as:**, click your page**

- Continue on the next page -

For more information:

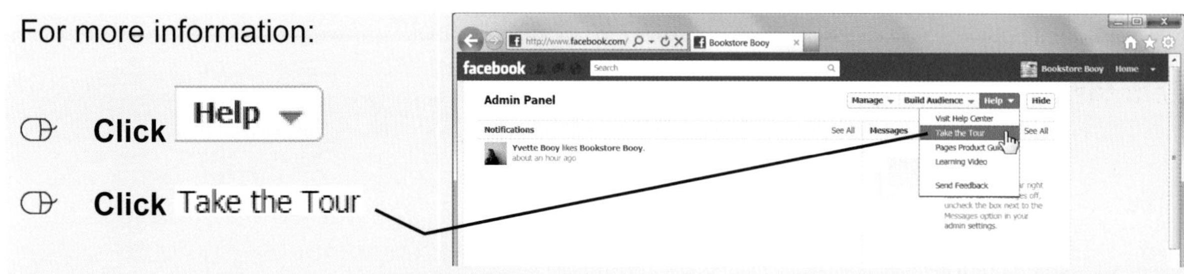

- **Click** Help
- **Click** Take the Tour

This is how you go back the old situation:

- **In the top right of the window, click**
- **By** Use Facebook as:**, click your name**

Tip

Where is that page?

If you are the administrator of an official page and you are using *Facebook* 'as yourself', you will sometimes need to search your personal *Facebook* page for a while before you have find the official page again. Here is how to quickly retrieve the official page:

- **Click** Home

In the left-hand side of the window:

- **By** PAGES**, click the page**

Tip

Request a recognizable URL

As soon as you have gathered 25 fans or more, you can apply for a recognizable URL (for example, www.facebook.com/nikefootball). For more information:

- **Click** Manage, Edit Page
- **Click** Basic Information
- **By** Username:**, click** Learn more.

 **Tip**

Updates

Unfortunately, you cannot send messages directly to the inbox of your fans from an official page. You can only send *updates*.
These will appear in the *Updates* folder in the inbox on your fans' *Facebook* page.

Your fans will *not* see a message to warn them they have received an update and they will not see a message in their News Feed. That is why these updates are not very effective. You will probably have a better chance of reaching more people if you post a new status message on the Timeline. This message will appear in most of your fans' News Feeds, at least, if they have not changed their settings. If some of your fans are very active on *Facebook*, however, you will run the risk that your status message is buried under the large pile of messages in their News Feed.

 **Tip**

Delete a page

If you do not want to use the page any longer, it is best to delete the page at once. A page that is not maintained and updated will make a bad impression on potential new customers or members. Here is how to delete the page:

- **Click** Manage ▾, Edit Page
- **Click** Manage Permissions
- **By** Delete Page:, **click** Permanently delete
- **Click** Delete

1.15 Do's and Don'ts

Lots of companies, organizations and clubs are already active on *Facebook*, in one form or another. Unfortunately, they are not always easy to find. One of the reasons may be that they use multiple group pages. These pages often include pages created by customers or members, which means that the company or club cannot control the content of such a page. Because of this, the members are scattered all over the Internet and it becomes quite difficult for the company to reach all of these members at once.

The biggest pitfall for many companies and organizations is creating a page or group, and then not actively doing anything with such a page or group. This is not very wise; a *Facebook* page presents a great opportunity for contacting your target group.

Below you will find a number of tips regarding the things you should and should not do with your official page or group page:

Tip

Do this!

1. Use the Timeline

The Timeline is the most important part of the page. Fans or members can post messages here. These messages are visible to all visitors of the official page and to all members of the group (depending on the group settings). You can also leave messages, links and photos on the Timeline yourself. It is not recommended to close the Timeline. Your fans or members will expect the Timeline to be available.

2. React to comments on the Timeline

Try to answer questions posted on the Timeline within 24 hours. Do this in a professional and positive way. If necessary, react to comments and other reactions, even if it is just to say thank you. Or click the Like button. Always react if somebody takes the time to post a photo or a link to the Timeline. The more you actively post messages and react to others, the more your members or fans will feel that you take them seriously. You will increase your chances of your fans becoming your ambassador and telling others about your product or service.

3. Actively post status updates, photos, events and notes

If you do not post any messages yourself, the activity on your page will slowly come to an end.

4. Post a few good bargains or special offers for your fans every once in a while

If you manage an official page, it is a good idea to post an attractive or enticing offer once in a while to reward your fans. This will attract even more fans to your page.

5. Use the birthday notifications

Just like on your personal *Facebook* page, you will be able to see the dates of your members' and fans' birthdays. It will not be much trouble to send a birthday card. If you own a local business, you can even send a greeting card with a small gift. For instance, a free dessert in your restaurant or a discount for a purchase in your shop.

6. Link your Facebook page to your company or club website

Display the Like button on the company, organization, club or artist's regular website. If they click this button, *Facebook* users will automatically become a fan of your *Facebook* page.

 **Tip**

Do not do this!

1. Post text-only messages

If you keep posting messages that contain nothing else but text, your fans or members will quickly lose interest. Make sure you also post links, photos and videos. Pose a question every now and then; this will provoke reactions (and therefore activity). Remember: the updates of your official or group page will also appear in your fans' or members' News Feeds.

2. Post too many messages

If you post messages several times a day, this may irritate your fans or members. As a consequence, they might decide to hide your page or group updates in their News Feed.

3. Delete messages

If you do not like a question or comment on the Timeline, or somebody is not telling the truth, it is always better to react to such a message than to simply delete it. Keep in mind that lots of people will be following you and will read these messages. If a discussion with a customer or a member threatens to get out of hand, it is better to pick up the phone and have a conversation with this person and solve the problem.

4. Only offer ads

People did not become a fan of your page to receive nothing but advertising messages in their News Feeds. They will quickly stop visiting you. Alternate such commercial messages with interesting news flashes, tips, information, links and photos.

1.16 Background Information

Dictionary

Account	An account provides a user access to a service. In order to use *Facebook*, you will need to have an e-mail address and a password.
Administrator	A person who maintains an official page or a group page. The administrator of a group page is clearly visible, but you cannot see who the administrator of an official page is.
App	Users can add apps (applications) to their profile, page, or group. A well-know app is the popular game called *Farmville*. There are lots of applications, most of them developed by external programmers. Visit the www.facebook.com/apps/directory.php page to see an overview of various apps.
Application	A different name for a software program.
Deactivate	If you deactivate your account, all at once, your profile and all accompanying information will no longer be accessible to other *Facebook* users. This action will remove your account from *Facebook*, but you will always have the possibility to activate your account again at a later stage.
Document	A function on a group page, where group members can write and edit notes together. A document can only be read or edited by group members.
Event	A function that lets you announce a meeting, conference, action, or some other event to your friends, fans or group members. Group members will automatically receive an invitation for an event.
Facebook	Free social network site where you can easily make contact with friends and acquaintances and get to know new people.
Fan	A person who has indicated that he or she likes the official page of a company, organization, brand, celebrity, band or artist.
Fan page	A different name for an official page.

- Continue on the next page -

Forum	A discussion forum where fans can engage in discussions and post new topics.
Friend Finder	A feature in *Facebook* that helps you find friends in your e-mail address book, or in other programs, such as *Skype* and *Windows Live Messenger*.
Friendship request	A message you will receive when another *Facebook* user wants to add you as a friend. You can accept or ignore the request.
Index	An official *Facebook* page will be indexed, so search engines such as *Google* will be able to find this page.
News Feed	An element on your *Facebook's* home page. In the News Feed you can see what your friends are up to on *Facebook*. If you are a fan of a page, or a member of a group, you will also receive updates on the activities on these other pages.
Notes	A function that helps you maintain a *blog* (online diary). Each issue of your blog consists of a separate note.
Official page	A *Facebook* page intended for use by companies, organizations, brands, artists and celebrities. *Facebook* users can become a fan of an official page. Only the official representative of a company, organization, brand, artist or celebrity is allowed to create and edit an official page.
Profile	Your profile contains information about yourself and is visible to your friends. By using the *Privacy Settings* page, you can determine which parts of your profile will be displayed to various categories of *Facebook* users.
Status update	An element on your *Facebook* page which you can use to let your friends know what you are currently doing or thinking.
Tag	A keyword or a name you can add to a note, photo or video.
Timeline	An element on your *Facebook* page. Here, your friends, fans or members can post a message which becomes visible to others.

Source: Facebook Help

1.17 Tips

Tip

Finding a group or an official page

Groups and official pages can be found in the same way as friends. You can use the search box to find these pages:

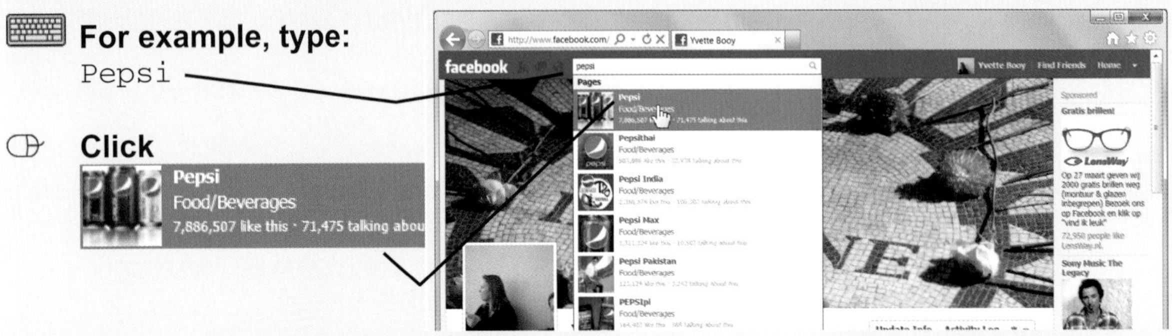

For example, type: `Pepsi`

Click

By the statement 7,886,507 like this you can tell that this is an official page.

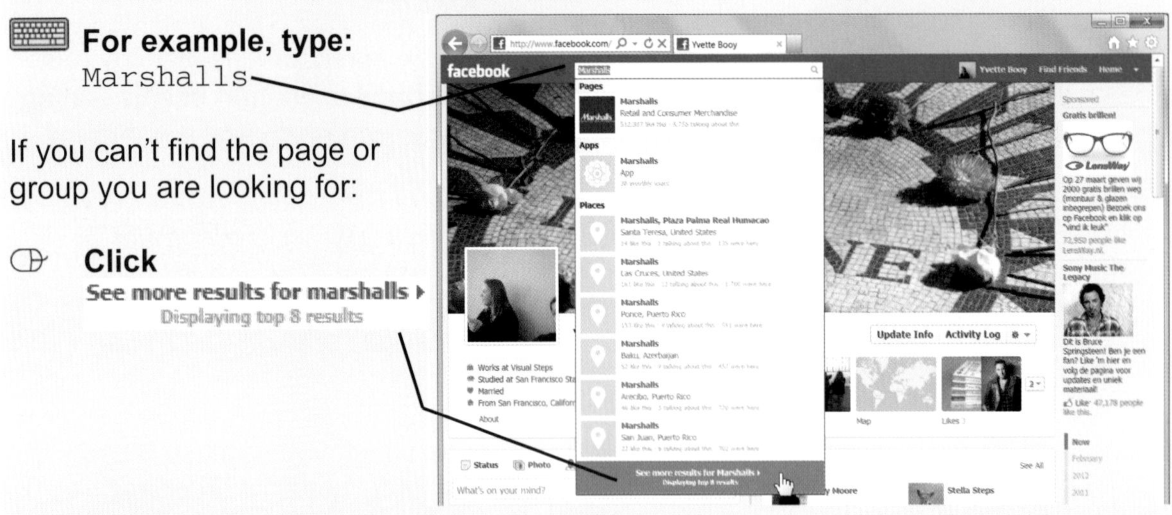

For example, type: `Marshalls`

If you can't find the page or group you are looking for:

Click

You will see more pages. You can use the Like button to become a fan of the page. To view the application, click Go to App ▸.

Please note: if you see the +1 Add Friend button on a company or club page, the administrator has mistakenly used a personal profile instead of a group or page.

2. LinkedIn

LinkedIn is a social network site directed at professionals who want to strengthen and expand their network, by publishing their resume or CV and other professional information online. In the last few years, *LinkedIn* has grown enormously. As of 2012, there are now over 150 million registered members worldwide.

The main objective of *LinkedIn* is to let the members benefit from each other's business network and contacts. For instance, you can use this network if you are looking for a new job or new business opportunities. Jobseekers can take a look at the profile of future or potential employers and find out which one of their current contacts may be able to introduce them to such employers. Employers can publish job openings, look for possible candidates and check the job applicants' work history and education.

If you sign up for one of the groups in *LinkedIn*, you will get to know even more people. A large number of groups have formed around a vast array of topics and specialist issues. You can also follow the company where you are currently employed or where you have previously worked. This enables you to stay up to date about new job openings and other information about this company.

In this chapter you will find a number of tips which will help you make efficient use of your *LinkedIn* membership and benefit as much as possible from your network contacts. This will not only help you find the right contacts, but will also make it easier for others to find you.

In this chapter you will learn how to:

- create a *LinkedIn* account;
- edit and view your profile;
- add a photo to your profile;
- view and change settings;
- find, add and confirm contacts in *LinkedIn*;
- use introductions;
- search for a group and become a member of this group;
- search for a company and follow this company;
- delete your account.

Please note:

LinkedIn is subject to regular changes. It is possible that the windows on your own screen may look different from the examples in this chapter. If you cannot find a specific button, you might find it somewhere else, in the same window.

2.1 Creating an Account

In order to use *LinkedIn*, you will need to have an account. First, you are going to visit the website:

Open the www.linkedin.com website 1

Now you will see the *LinkedIn* home page. You can start creating your account, straightaway:

By First Name: , type your first name

By Last Name: , type your last name

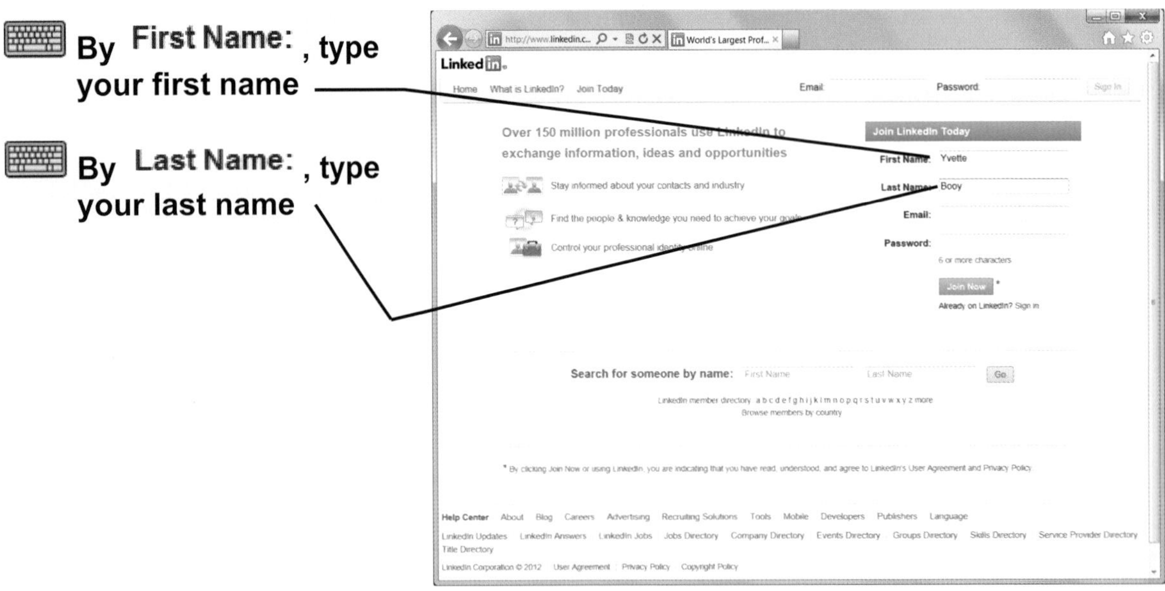

Tip

Which e-mail address?

You may be inclined to enter your professional e-mail address. If you are the owner of the company, this will be okay. But if you are an employee, you may decide to change jobs, at a certain point in time. This means you will no longer be able to use your former company's e-mail address. So it is better to use your personal e-mail address, or create a new *Hotmail* or *Gmail* address for this purpose. *LinkedIn* allows you to link multiple e-mail addresses to your profile. You can always add your professional e-mail address as a secondary address later on.

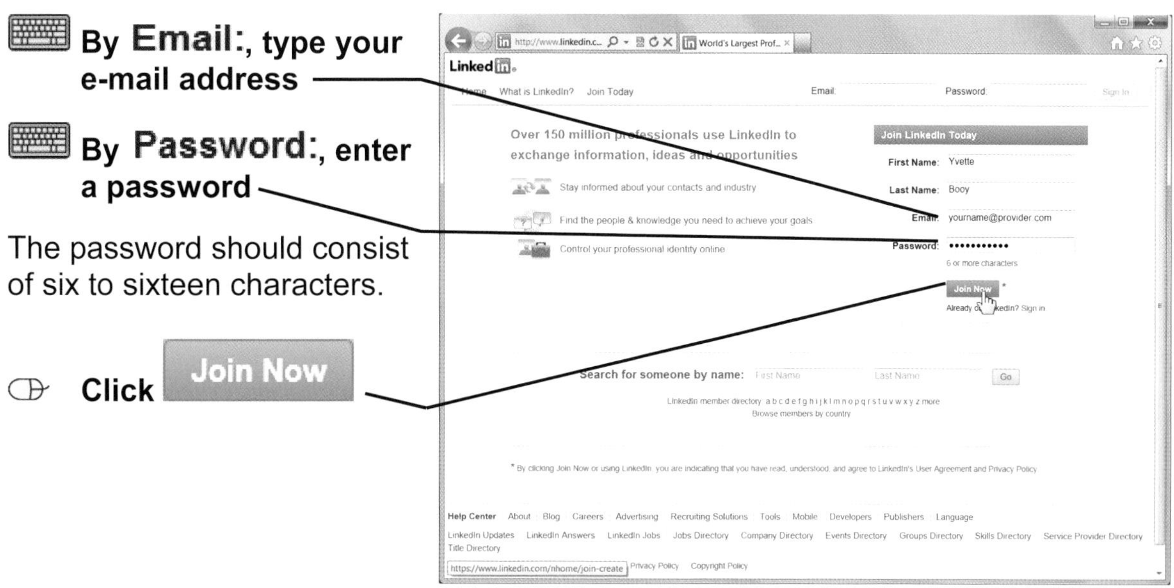

By Email:, type your e-mail address

By Password:, enter a password

The password should consist of six to sixteen characters.

Click Join Now

Write down your e-mail address and password on paper and store this in a safe place.

You can immediately start creating your professional profile on *LinkedIn*.

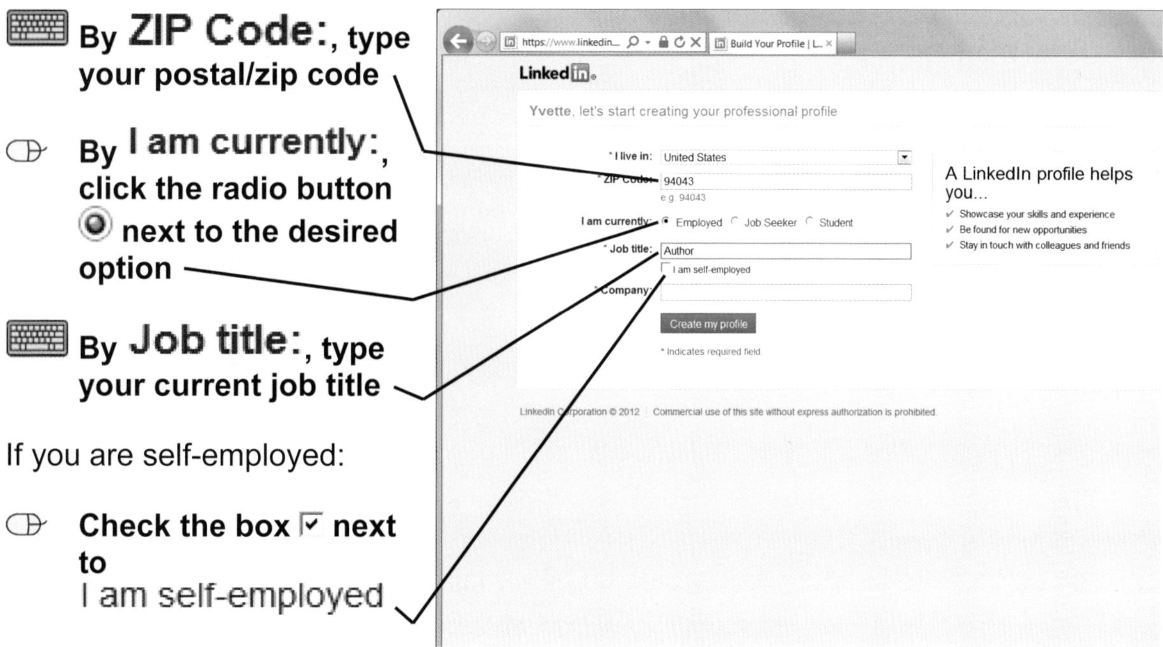

By ZIP Code:, type your postal/zip code

By I am currently:, click the radio button next to the desired option

By Job title:, type your current job title

If you are self-employed:

Check the box ☑ next to I am self-employed

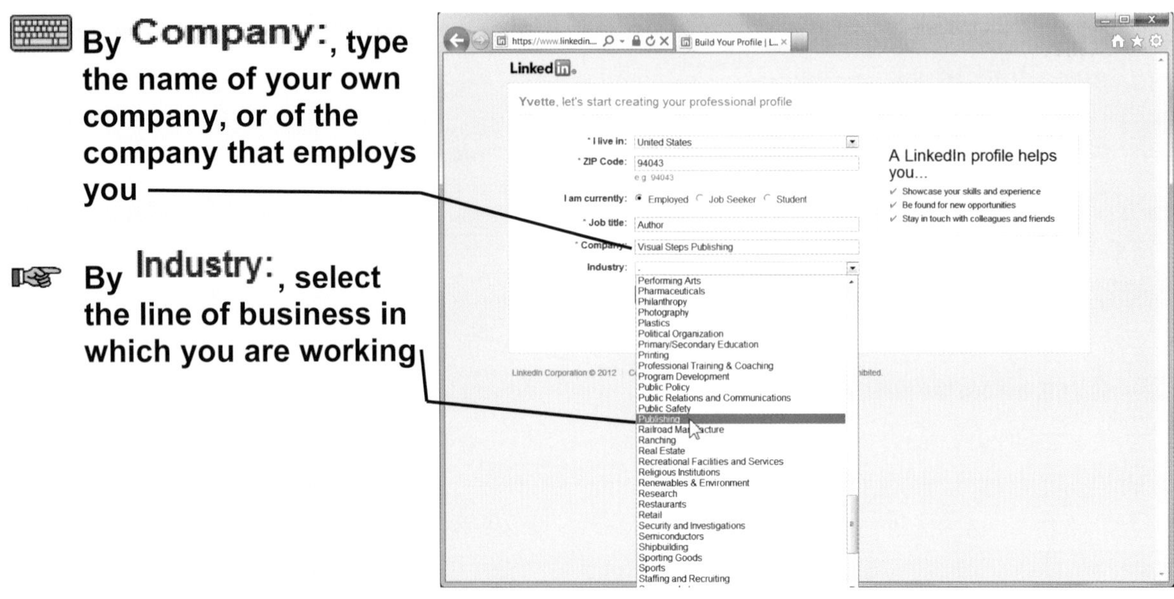

By Company:, type the name of your own company, or of the company that employs you

By Industry:, select the line of business in which you are working

Click Create my profile

LinkedIn will now suggest searching for other *LinkedIn* users in your e-mail address book. For now, you are going to skip this step:

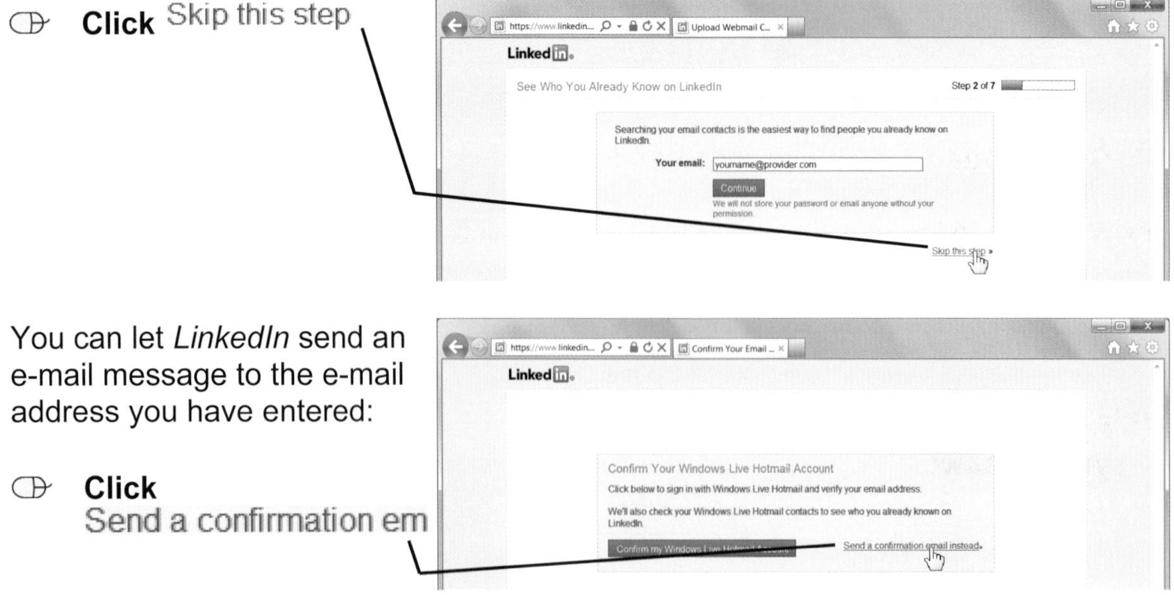

Click Skip this step

You can let *LinkedIn* send an e-mail message to the e-mail address you have entered:

Click Send a confirmation em

In this e-mail message you will find a hyperlink with which you can confirm your e-mail address and activate your account:

Open your e-mail program and open the message sent by *LinkedIn*

Click **Click here**

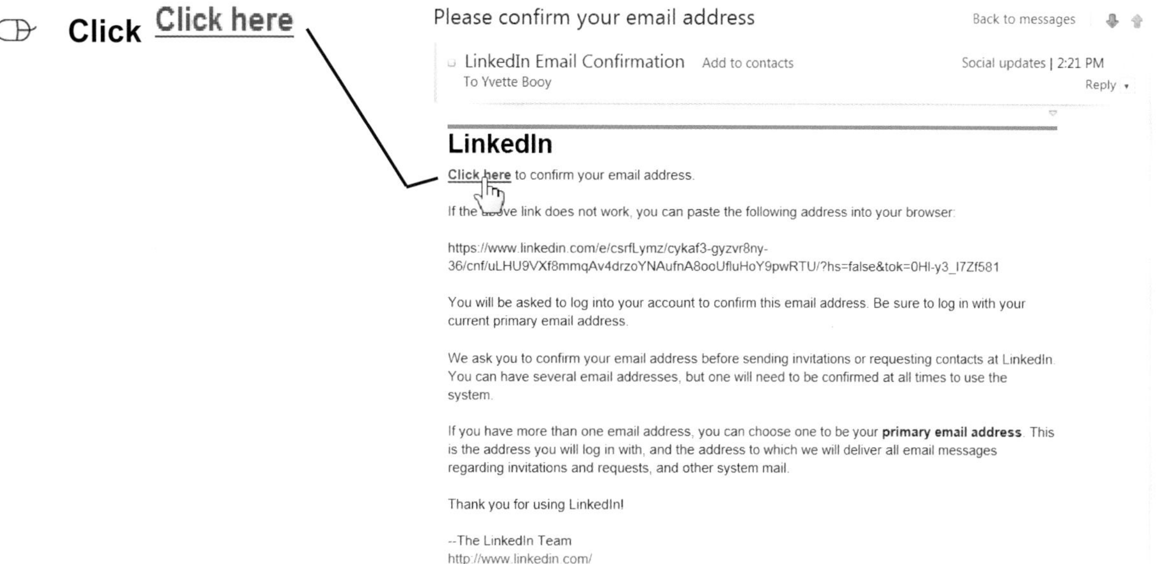

A new window will be opened, where you will be asked to confirm your e-mail address:

Click **Confirm**

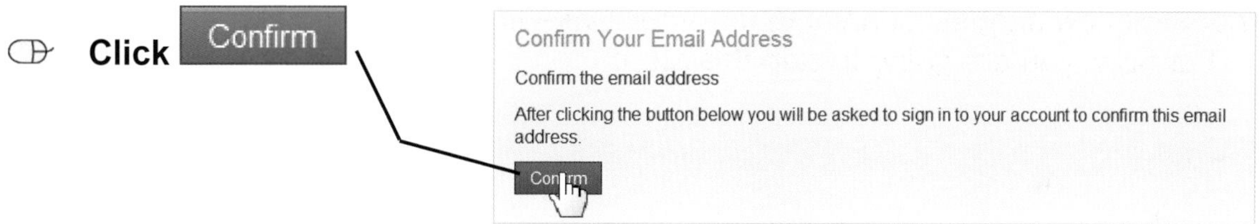

Close your e-mail program's window

Now you need to log on with your e-mail address and password:

Your e-mail address has already been entered:

By Password:, type your password

Click **Sign In**

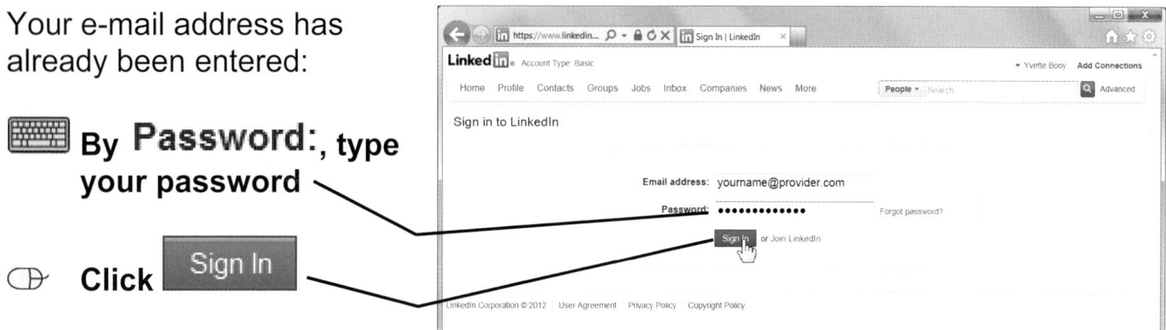

You may see a window where you are asked whether you want to save your password. In this example we have decided not to save the password. We have also decided not to display this type of window alert again. If you are using *Internet Explorer version 8*, you will see a similar window.

By No**, click** ▾

Click Don't Ask Again

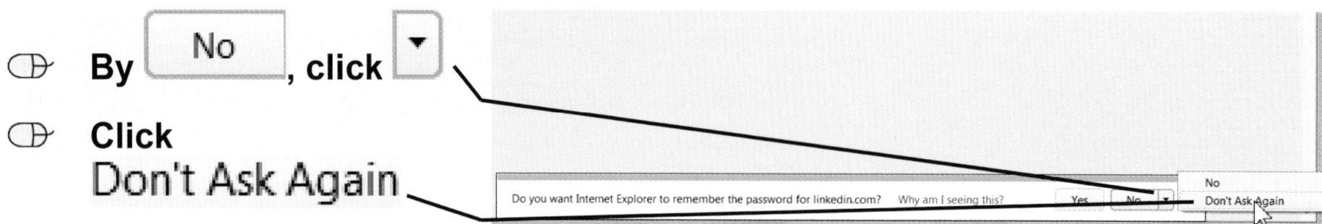

Now you will see the next step in the registration process. *LinkedIn* allows you to use *Facebook* and *Twitter* to communicate to the world that you are now registered with *LinkedIn*. But you can skip this step:

Click Skip this step

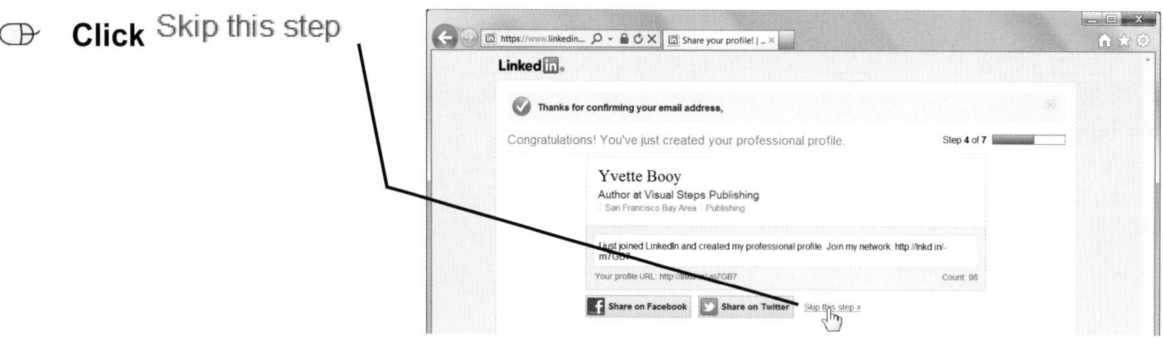

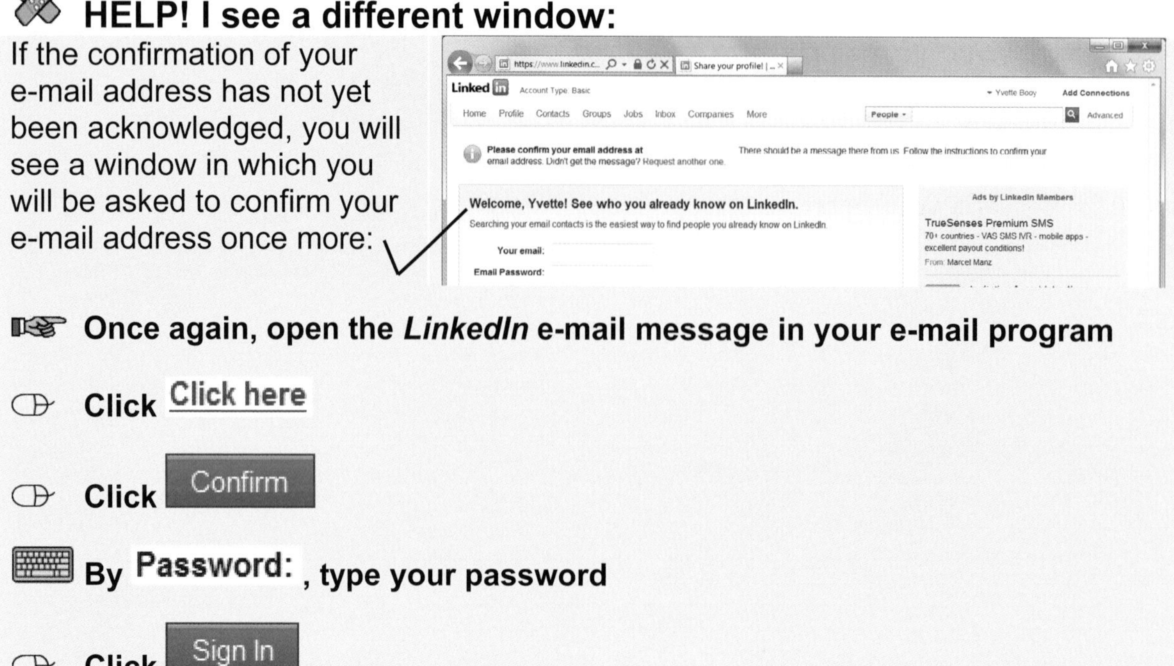

HELP! I see a different window:

If the confirmation of your e-mail address has not yet been acknowledged, you will see a window in which you will be asked to confirm your e-mail address once more:

Once again, open the *LinkedIn* e-mail message in your e-mail program

Click Click here

Click Confirm

By Password:**, type your password**

Click Sign In

In the next window you will be asked whether you want to use the free (*Basic*) version of *LinkedIn*, or the paid (*Premium*) version. The paid version offers more and extensive options. For instance, you have an unlimited view of all sorts of profiles, including the profiles of members who do not belong to your own network. And you can check which persons have viewed your profile. In this example we have chosen to use the free version:

Click

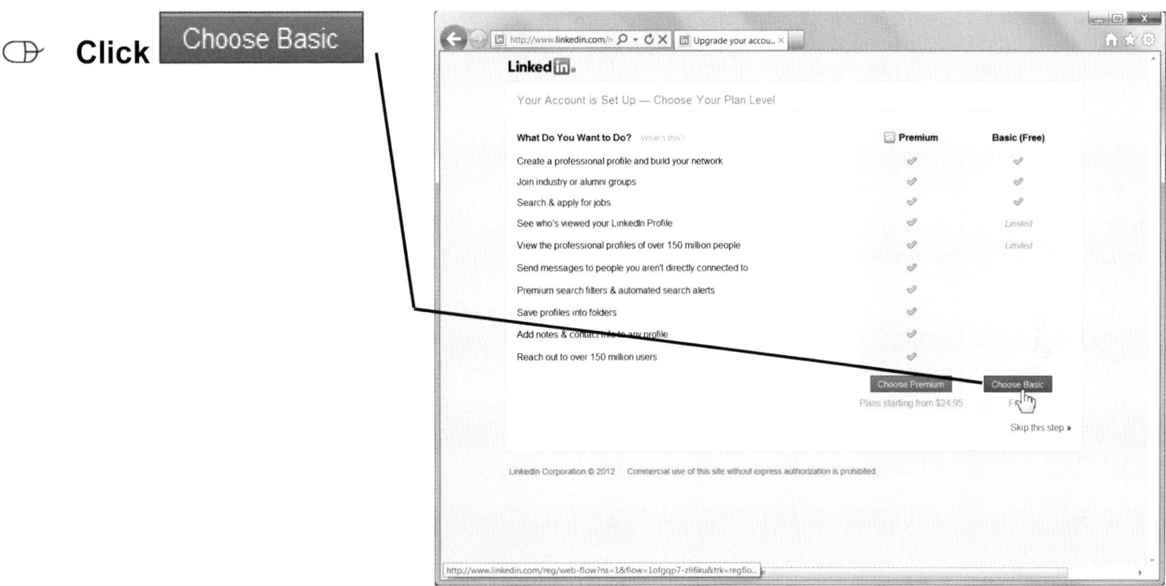

Now your *LinkedIn* home page will be opened:

There is not a whole lot to see on this page, as it is still quite empty:

In the next section you will learn how to edit your profile.

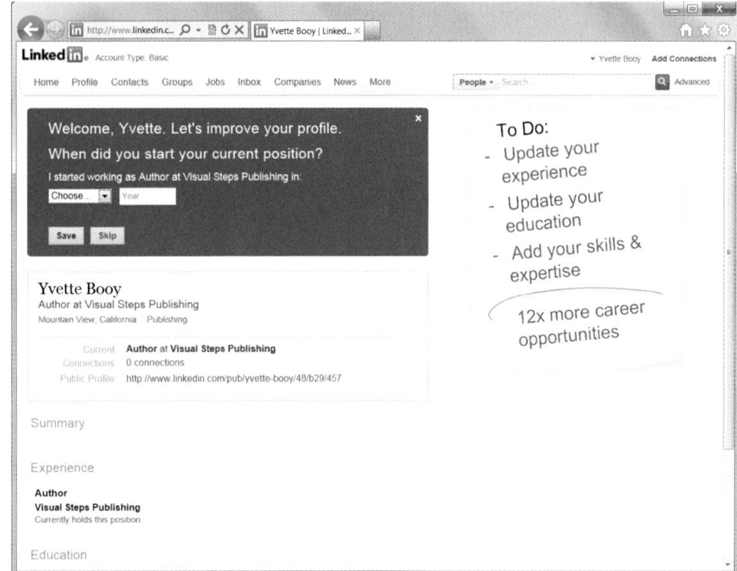

You are going to sign out from *LinkedIn*:

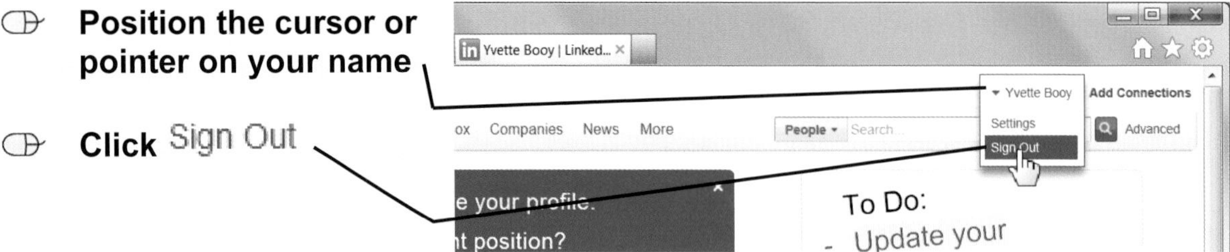

Position the cursor or pointer on your name

Click Sign Out

You may see a warning message:

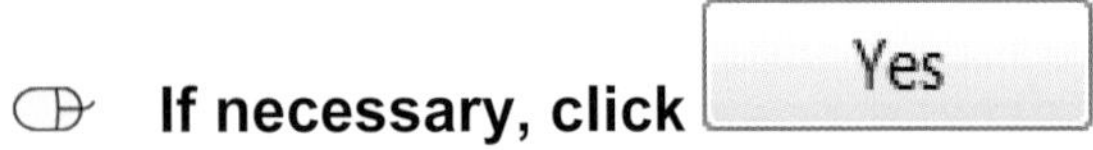

If necessary, click Yes

Now you will see this message: You have signed out.

2.2 Editing Your Profile

In the previous section you signed out from the *LinkedIn* website. If you want to edit your profile, you need to sign in again:

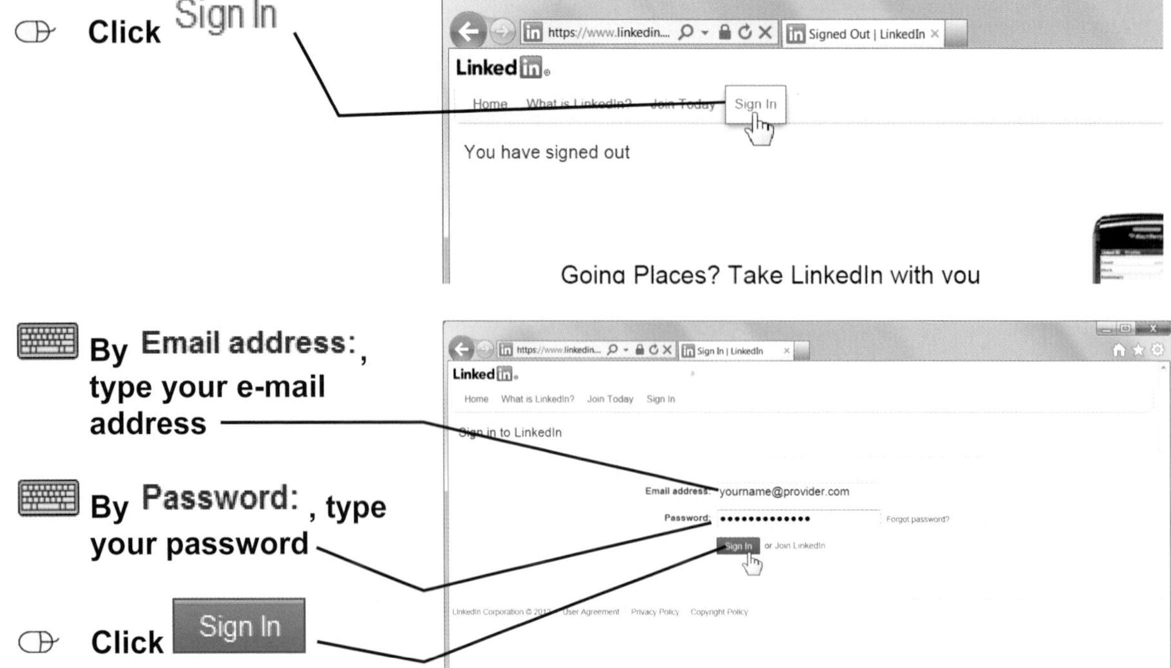

Click Sign In

By Email address:**, type your e-mail address**

By Password:**, type your password**

Click Sign In

Now you need to open the page where you can edit your profile:

Click Profile

Click Edit Profile

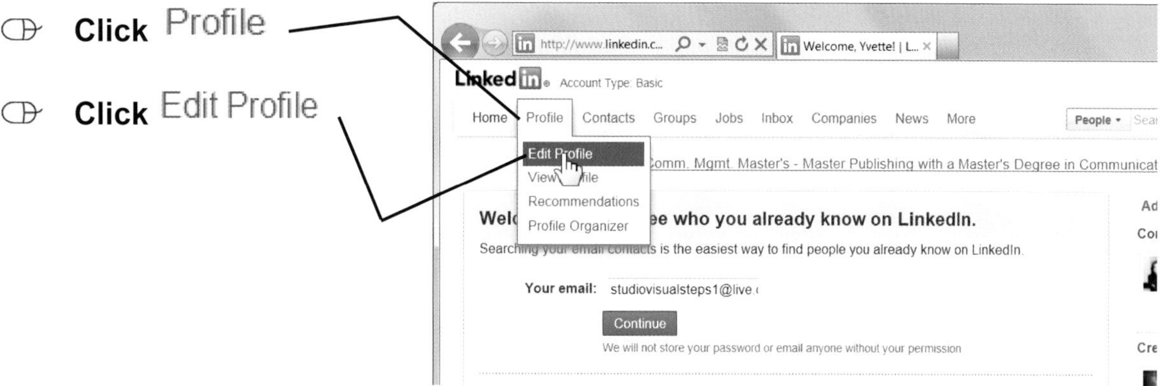

You are going to start by adding a photo of yourself:

Click + Add Photo

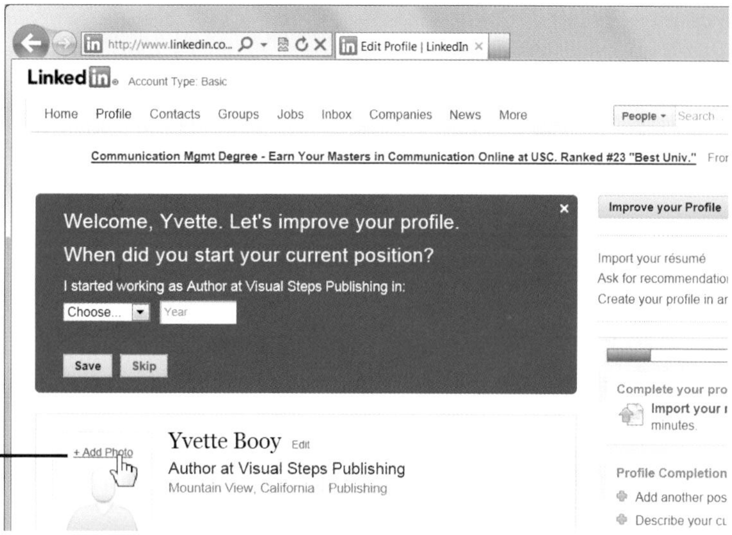

Click Browse...

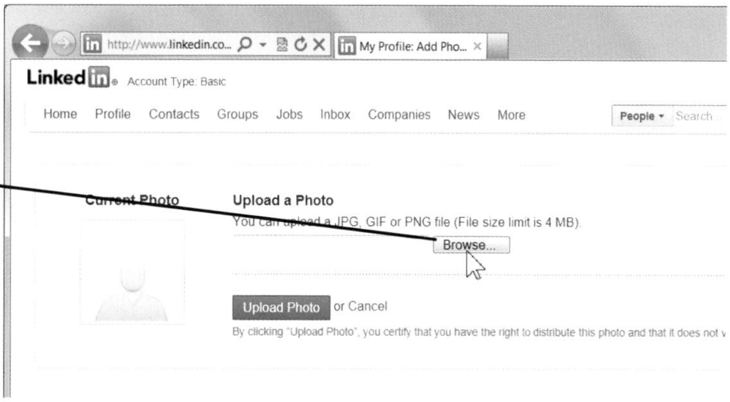

Tip

Add your own portrait photo

It is a good idea to add a photo where your face is clearly visible. This will make your online profile more personal and will encourage people to contact you.

- **Open the desired folder**
- **Click the desired photo**
- **Click** Open

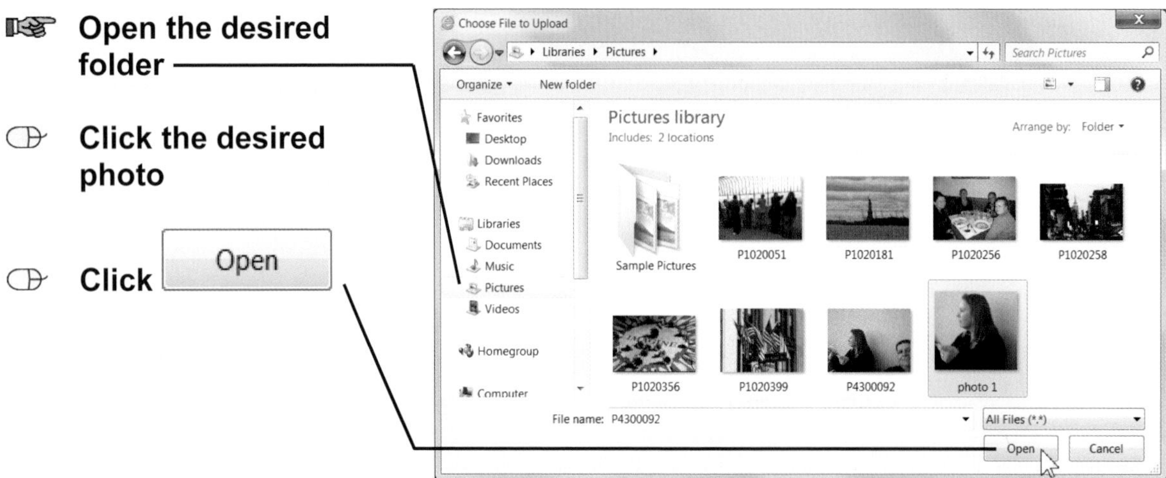

Afterwards, you can upload the photo:

- **Click** 

On *LinkedIn*, the photo will be cropped and displayed in a square frame. You can modify the photo yourself and decide which part of it will be cropped:

- **Drag the yellow square across the photo**

If you want, you can drag the yellow block inwards to make the square smaller:

In the top left of the window, you can see a live rendering of what the photo will look like in *LinkedIn*:

If you are satisfied:

- **Click** Save Photo

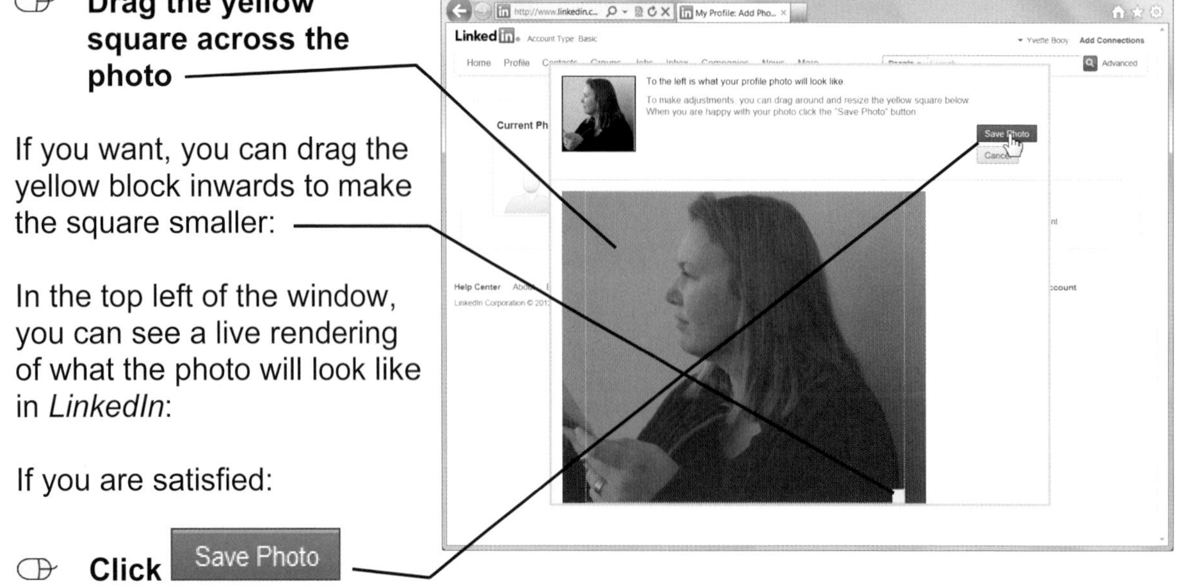

You will see the message **Your picture has been saved.**. Now you still need to decide who is allowed to view this picture. You can select your own contacts (*my connections*), the people in your network (*my network*) or publish the photo for everyone to see (*everyone*):

Click the radio button next to the desired option

Click Save Settings

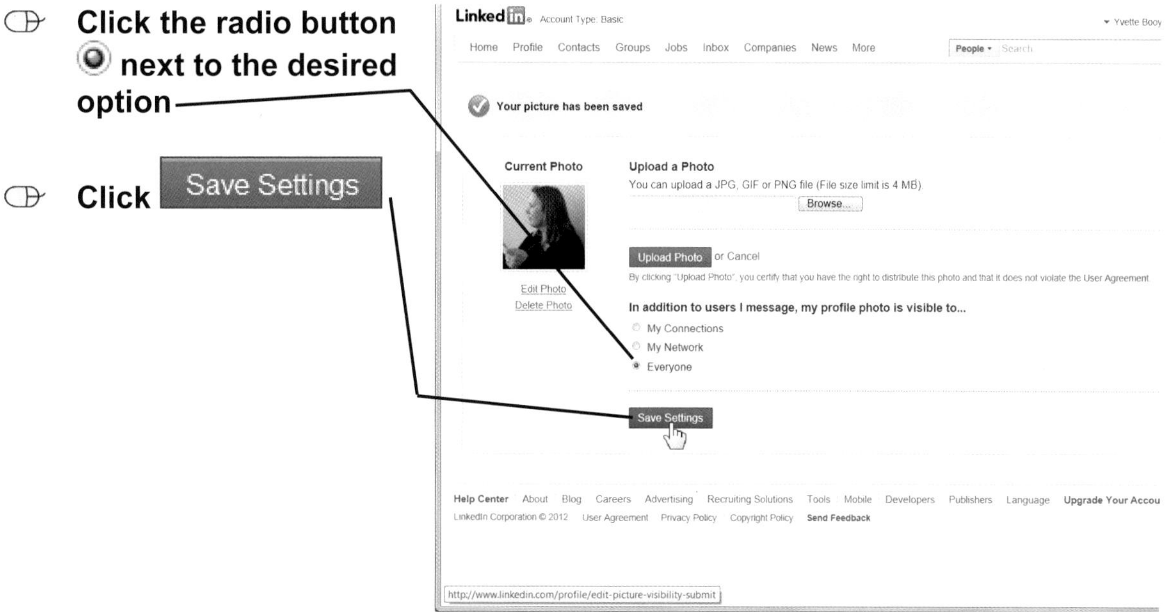

Now you can enter some career information. You have already entered information about your current job (*current position*). First, you are going to edit this information:

By Current**, click** Edit

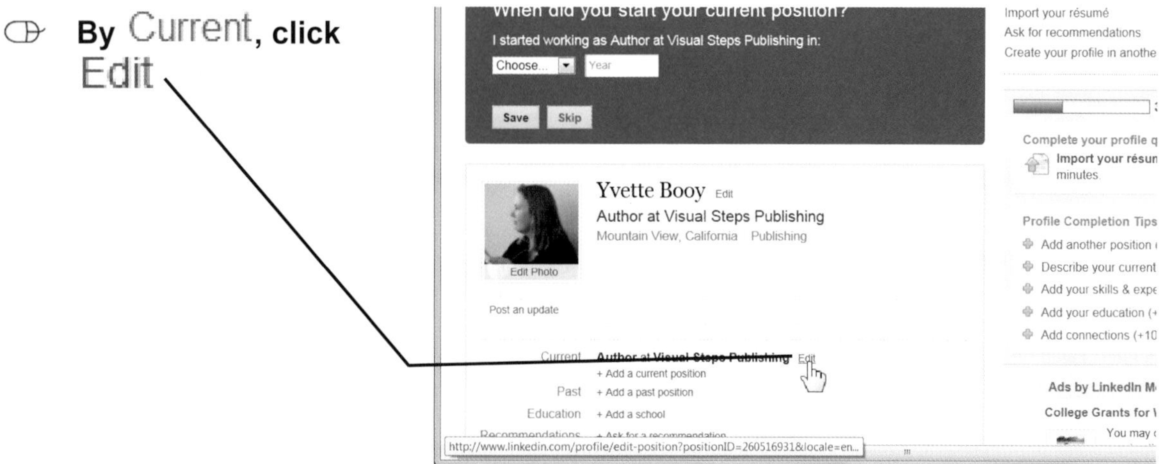

By Website:, type the web address of your company

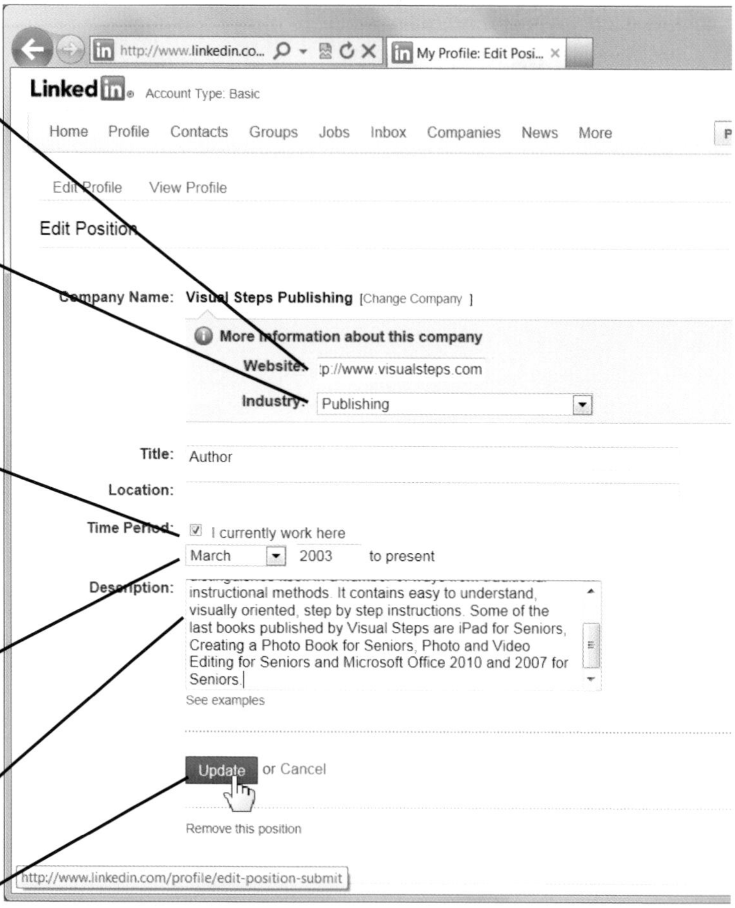

If you want, you can also change the branch of industry by **Industry:**.

If you are still holding this job:

Check the box ☑ next to I currently work here

Select the month and year in which you started work in this job

By Description:, type a job description

Click Update

Now you can enter additional information about your professional career, in the same way as described above. You can start by entering the previous position you had:

Click + Add a past position

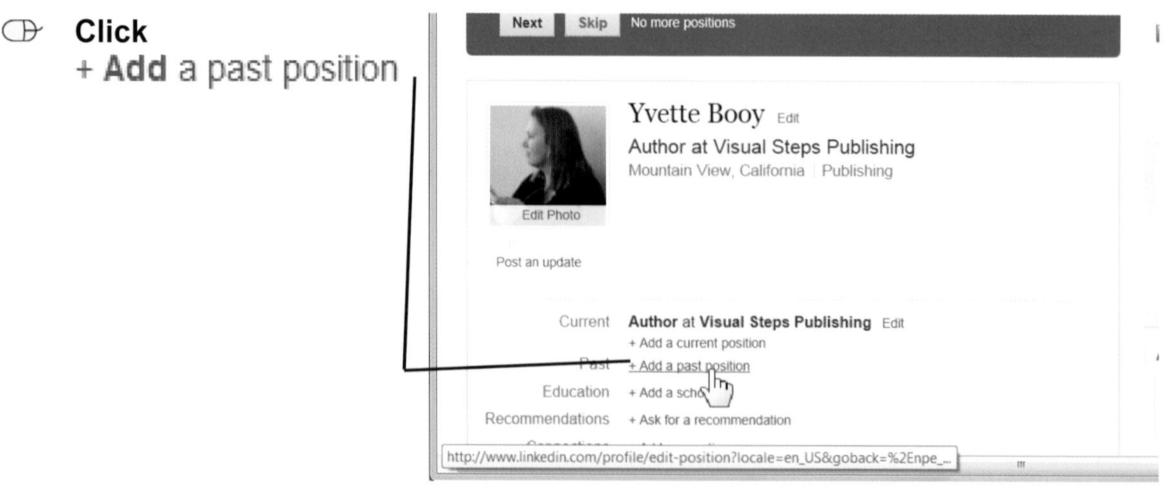

Enter all the data regarding your past position

Click 

Tip

Previous positions

If you no longer hold a specific job, you do not need to check the box next to I currently work here. Instead, you enter the time period for your previous job:

If you have entered just one previous position and you want to add additional work history information:

Drag the scroll bar downwards

You will see your current and your previous position:

By Experience, **click** + Add a position

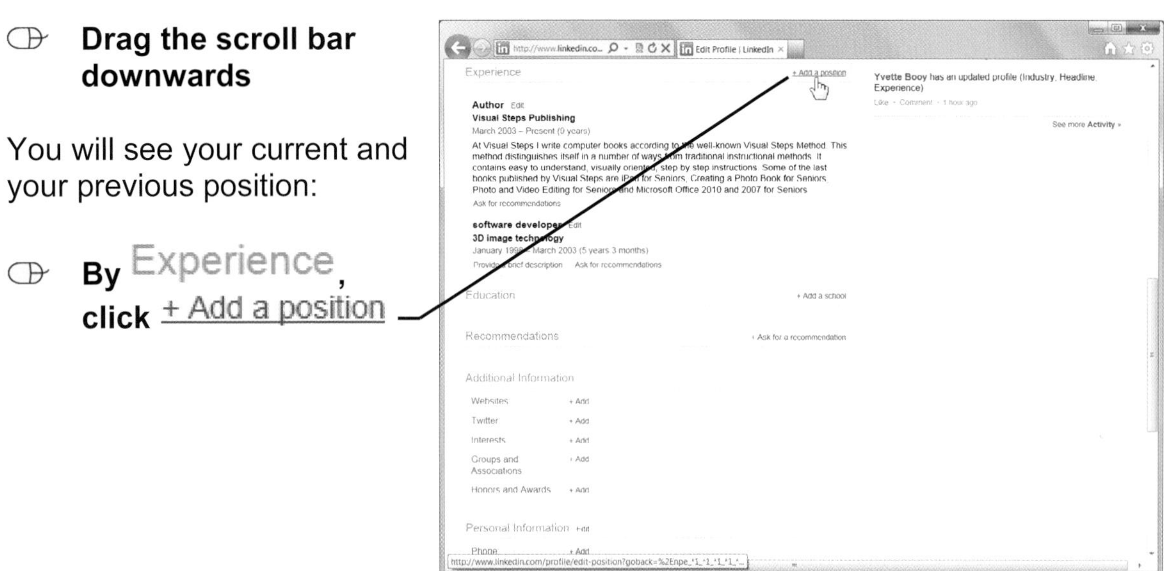

Now you can type the information about another position you held.

Enter the data for all the jobs you have held

Besides your professional career, you can also describe your education. It is a good idea to start with your most recent education:

By Education, **click** + Add a school

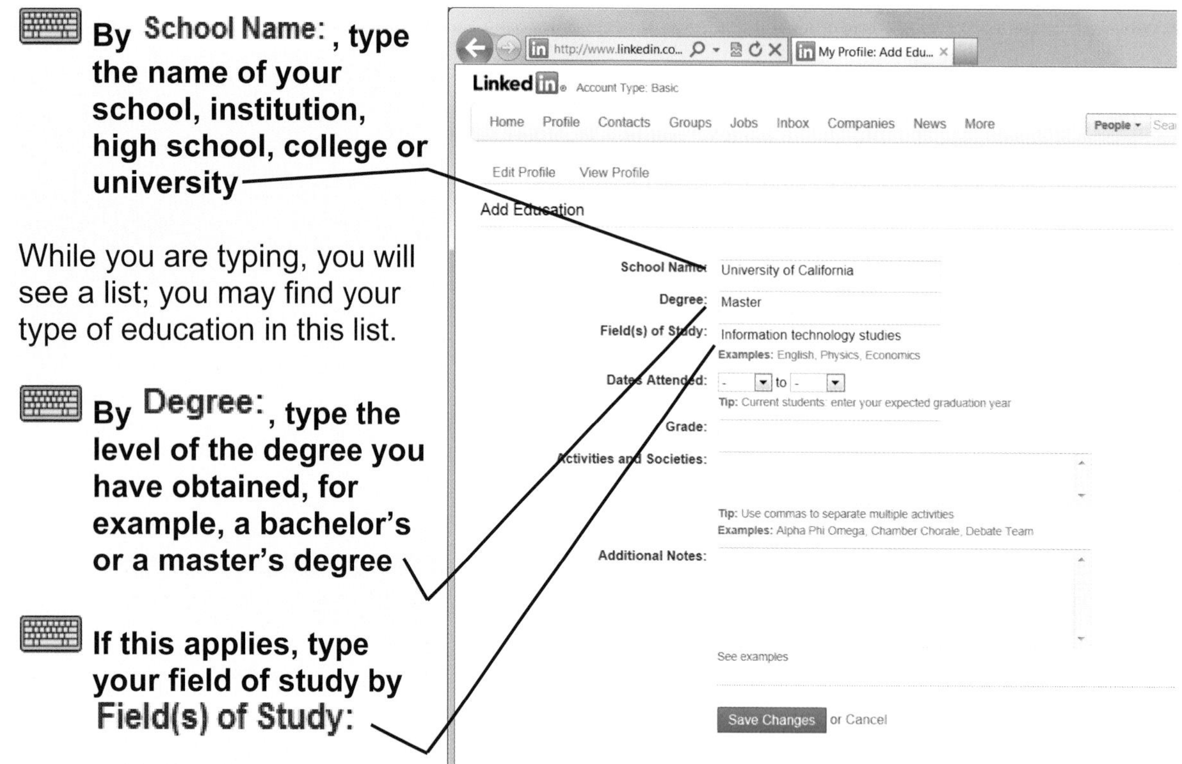

By School Name:, type the name of your school, institution, high school, college or university

While you are typing, you will see a list; you may find your type of education in this list.

By Degree:, type the level of the degree you have obtained, for example, a bachelor's or a master's degree

If this applies, type your field of study by Field(s) of Study:

By Dates Attended:, select the dates for the beginning and end of your studies

By **Activities and Societies:** you can add further activities you have engaged in, for instance, the membership of various committees, student organizations, sports teams or clubs. By **Additional Notes:** you can add additional comments.

After you have entered all the data:

Click 

To enter more information about your education:

By Education, click + Add a school

Enter the data for all the schools you have attended

You can also add some websites to your profile.

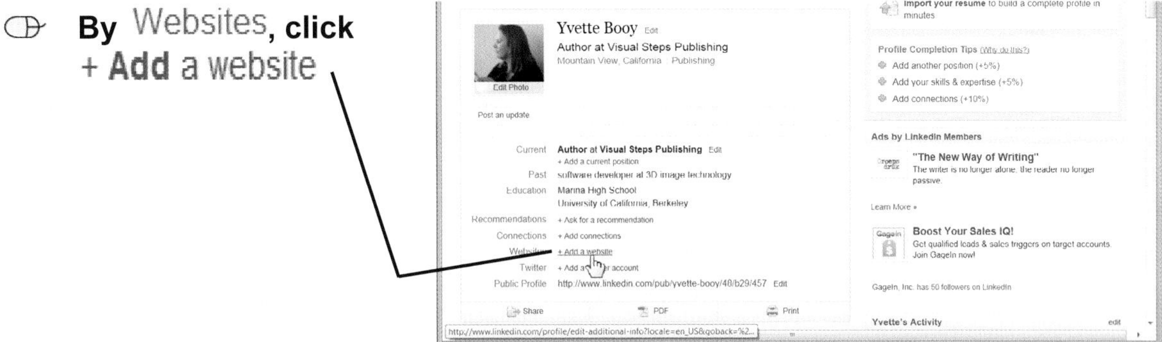

For instance, add your company's commercial website (*company website*), and your personal website (*personal website*). If you are maintaining a blog, you can also mention this website. This way, a visitor can gather more information about you, along with the information listed with *LinkedIn*.

Tip

WordPress

In *Chapter 4 WordPress* of this book you can read how to maintain a free blog with *WordPress*.

This is how you add websites on the Additional Information page:

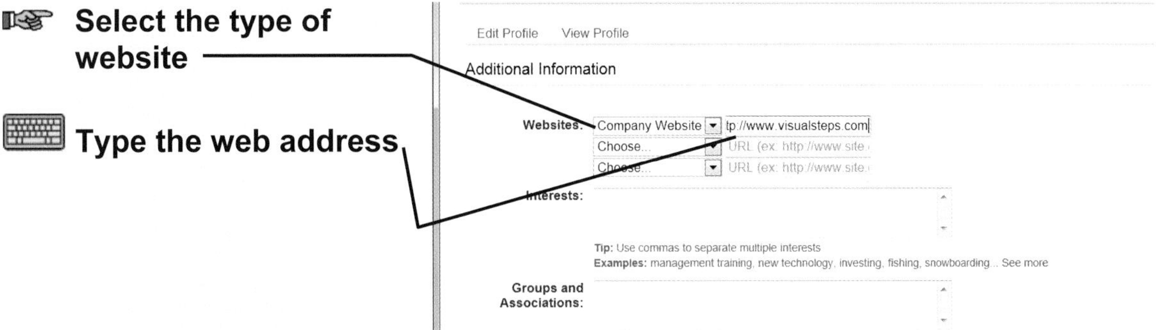

You can enter the names of up to three websites

On this page you can enter even more information, about yourself or your activities.

Interests: : here you can state your interests. These can be work-related (presentation skills, computers, technology) or your personal hobbies (football, skiing, photography).

Groups and Associations: : here you can list your membership with professional organizations, or sports clubs or other types of organizations.

Honors and Awards: : here you can list the (relevant) honors or awards you have received, or describe the patents that have been granted to you.

Enter the information you want to share with your visitors

Click 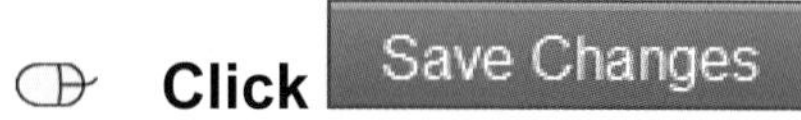

Tip

Summary and specialties

By Summary you will see a button called + Add Summary. If you click this button, you can add the following information:

Professional Experience & Goals: Here you can add a summary of all your experiences, which will be placed at the top of your profile. Briefly state your activities and what you have to offer your clients. What are your main motives, goals, and interests? Think about the things you would tell a new employer, if he would ask you to summarize what you have to offer. Focus on the results you have achieved, not on the work you have done.

Specialties Here you can briefly tell a story about your specialties and strengths. This way, you will relate to your target group more quickly. For instance, if you hold specific certificates or diplomas, you should mention them here.

Drag the scroll bar all the way downwards

By Personal Information you can enter your contact information:

For instance, your phone number, home address, your address for instant messaging, birthday, and your marital status:

Click + Add

Now a window is opened where you can enter all this information at once.

Type all the data

Click Save Changes

Tip

Visibility

The data you have entered by Personal Information will only be visible to your own contacts.

Drag the scroll bar downwards

By Contact Yvette for: you can choose the items for which you want to be addressed through *LinkedIn*:

Contact Yvette for: Change contact preferences

- career opportunities
- new ventures
- expertise requests
- reference requests
- consulting offers
- job inquiries
- business deals
- getting back in touch

Applications + Add an application

- career opportunities : jobs, career moves.
- new ventures : new business propositions.
- expertise requests : requests for your expertise.
- reference requests : requests for references.
- consulting offers : consultancy.
- job inquiries : job offers.
- business deals : business deals.
- getting back in touch : getting back in touch with old friends.

By Contact Yvette for:, **click** Change contact preferences

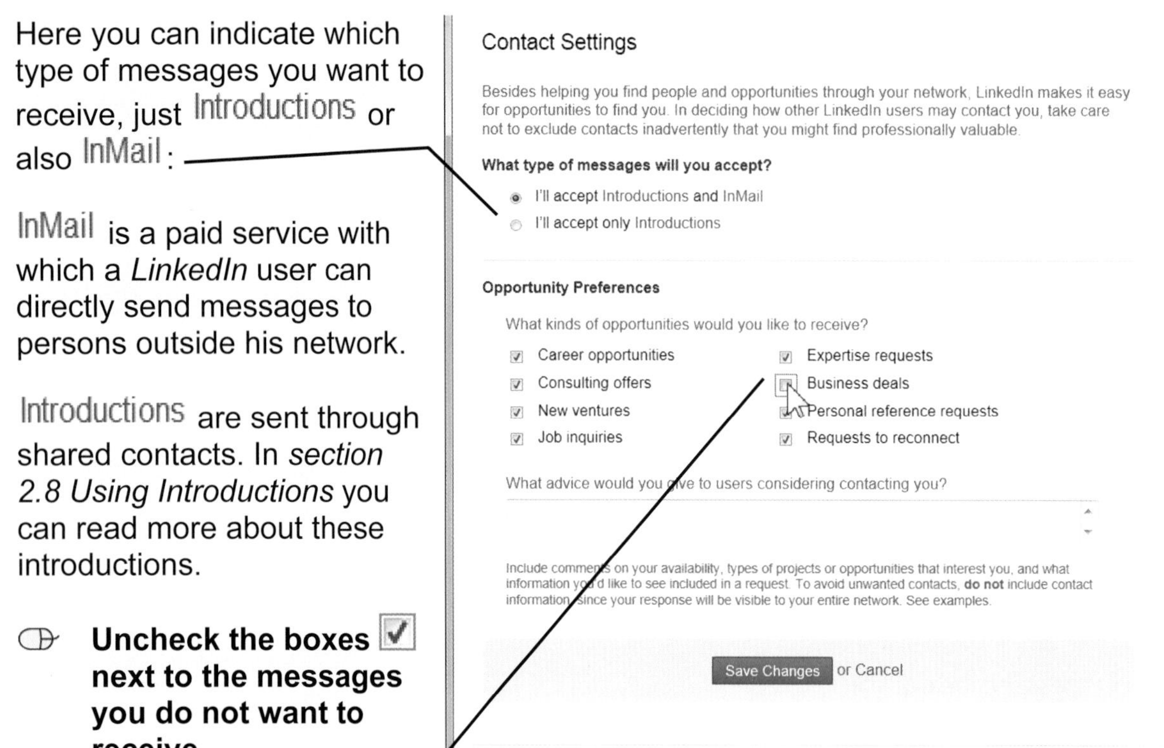

Here you can indicate which type of messages you want to receive, just Introductions or also InMail:

InMail is a paid service with which a *LinkedIn* user can directly send messages to persons outside his network.

Introductions are sent through shared contacts. In *section 2.8 Using Introductions* you can read more about these introductions.

Uncheck the boxes ☑ next to the messages you do not want to receive

Tip

Advice

In the box next to What advice would you give to users considering contacting you? you can enter some advice for the people who want to contact you. Do not enter contact information in this field, in order to prevent you from receiving unwanted messages. In this field you can list the type of project that interests you, or the type of information you would like to receive if somebody sends you a request, for example.

If you have changed anything:

 **Click** Save Changes

Please note:

You may be asked repeatedly to sign in again with your password. This is done in order to protect your profile.

Now you are going to view the result of your work:

Click View profile

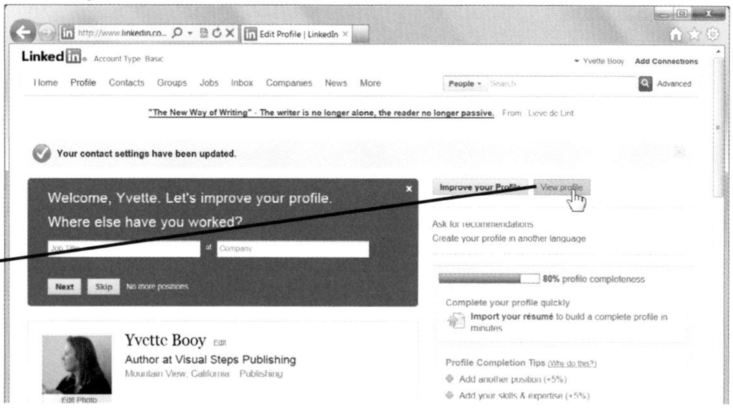

You will see your profile in the same way your visitors will view this page:

Drag the scroll bar downwards

Carefully check the data you have entered

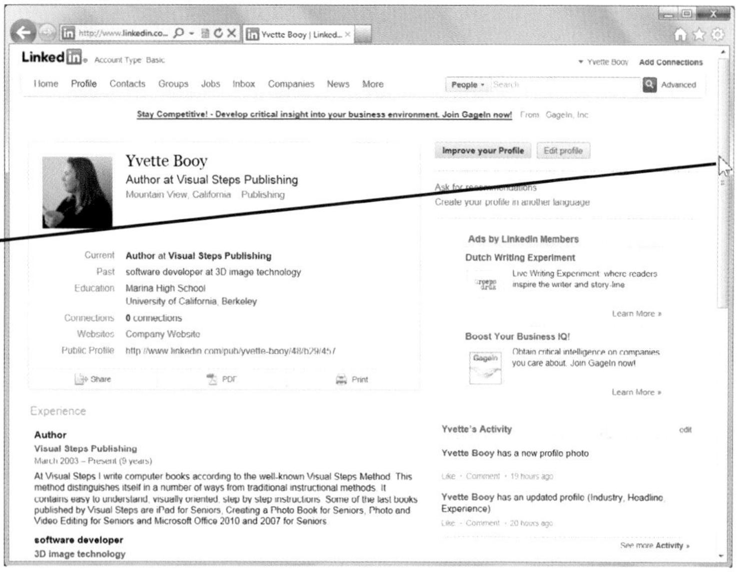

If you want to add or change anything, you need to go back to editing your profile:

Click Edit profile

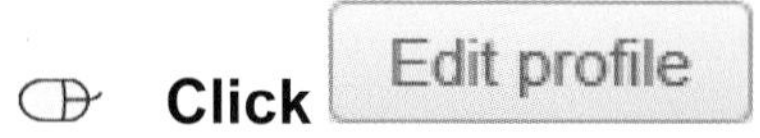

 **Tip**

Professional headline

Beneath you name you will see the title 'professional headline'; this is the professional 'header' of your profile.

This is the standard description of your current position, along with the name of your employer:

Yvette Booy

Author at Visual Steps Publishing

Mountain View, California | Publishing

This header is the first item people will see when they find your profile. Instead of your current position, you can also add some keywords that clarify who you are and what you can do for your target group. But you can also indicate that you are free to accept a new position. Here are some examples:

- *(Passionate) acquisition consultant, negotiator with good people skills, enthusiastic speaker & organizer in the field of small business and retail, in South Carolina.*
- *Marketing consultant, internet & printed media | director of the Johnson Media Group.*
- *Marketing communication specialist, looking for a new challenge.*

This is how you change your professional headline:

Click Edit profile

Click the Edit **button next to your name**

By Professional "Headline":**, type your new description**

Click Save Changes

Click View profile

Here you see the result:

Yvette Booy

Author at Visual Steps Publishing, also available for lectures!

Mountain View, California | Publishing

2.3 Adjusting the Settings

LinkedIn has a large number of settings you can change. This is how you open the settings page:

Position the cursor or pointer on your name

Click Settings

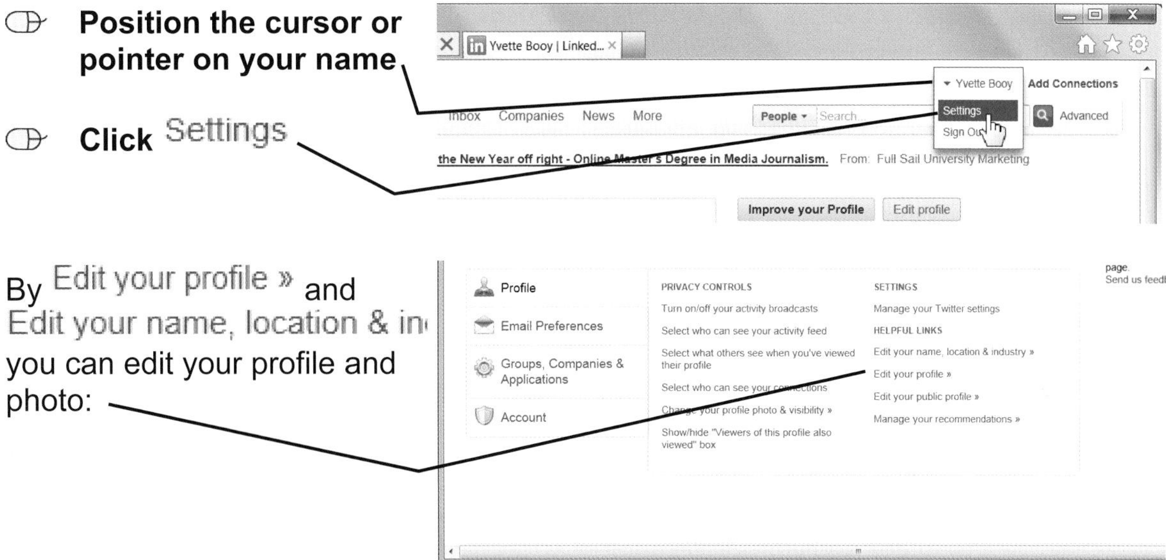

By Edit your profile » and Edit your name, location & in you can edit your profile and photo:

Take a look now and review the settings of your public profile:

Click Edit your public profile »

Tip

Public profile

Your public profile can be viewed by all Internet users and will also be found by search engines, such as *Google*.

On the first part of the page you can change the web address (URL) of your public profile. Instead of http://usa.linkedin.com.pub/yourname/1b2a3c you can use http://www.linkedin.com/in/yourname, for example. This way, your profile will be easier to find:

By Your current URL, **click** Customize your public profile URL

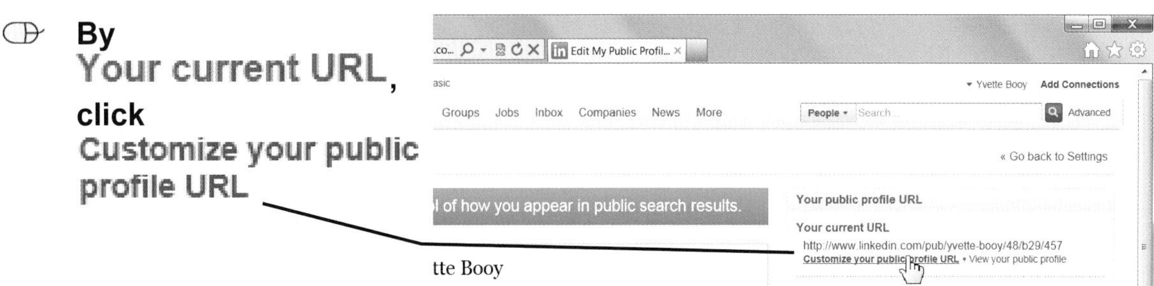

Type the desired notation for your name

You can only use letters and numbers:

Click Set Custom URL

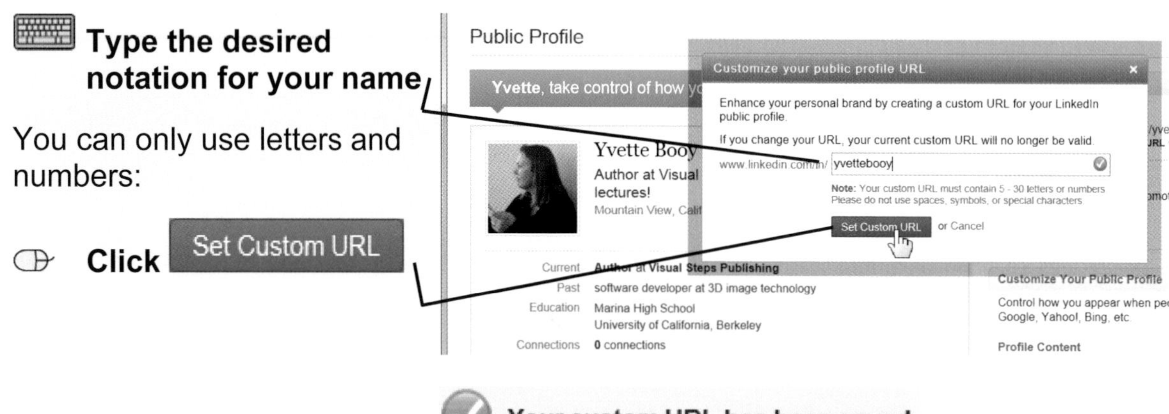

You will see this conformation: **Your custom URL has been saved.**

By **Customize Your Public Profile** you can indicate which parts of your public profile can be viewed by everybody on the Internet:

It is recommended to leave the option Make my public profile visible to **everyone** enabled. If you select Make my public profile visible to **no one**, your profile will not be found by the Internet search engines:

But you can choose which parts of your profile will be visible:

Uncheck the box ☑ next to the sections you do not want to display

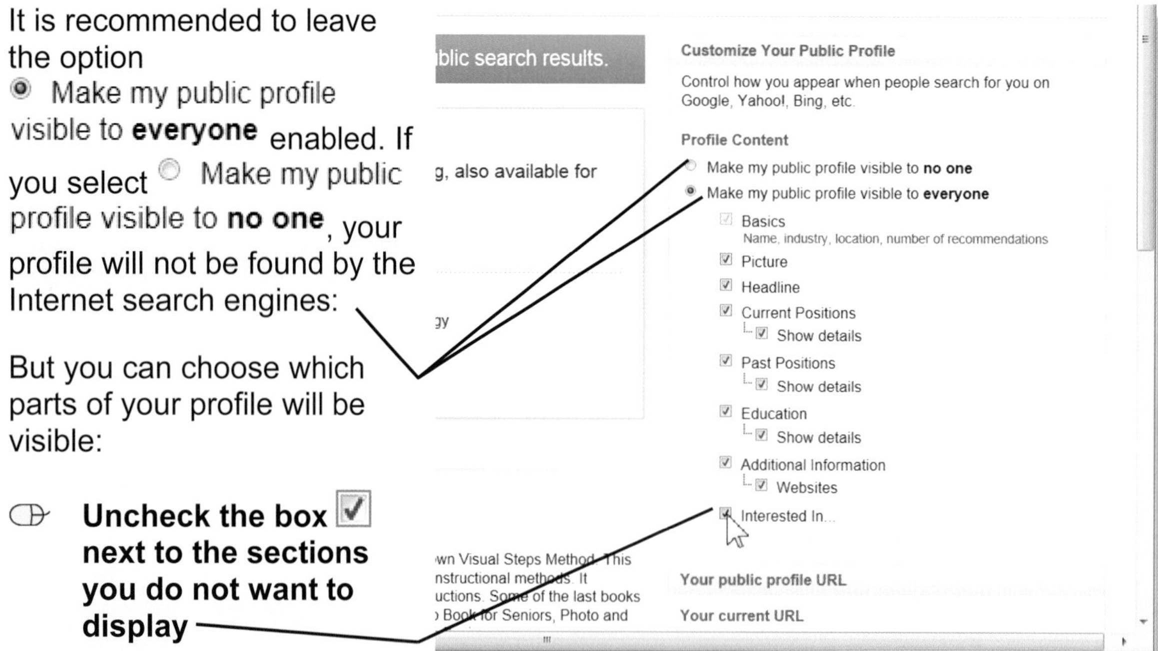

Now you can view your public profile:

By Your public profile click View your public profile

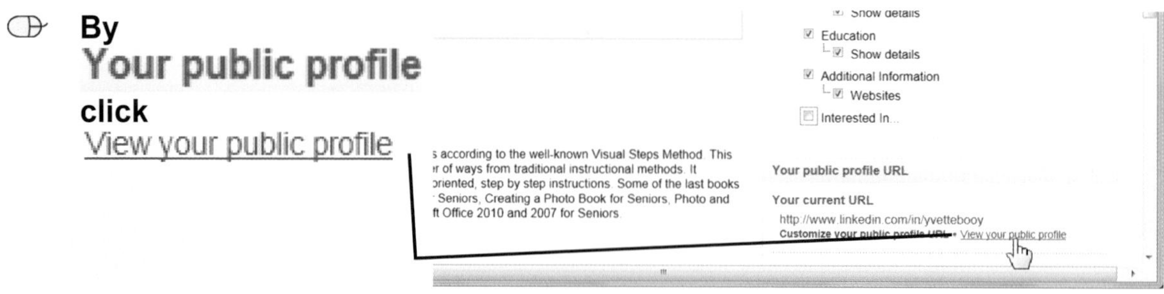

Now you will see your public profile on a new tab:

Please note: your public profile does not contain any contact information.

Through the hyperlinks
➜ Contact Yvette Booy

➜ Add Yvette Booy to your network
visitors can make contact with a (paid) *InMail* message, via a shared contact, or they can send you a request to add you to their network:

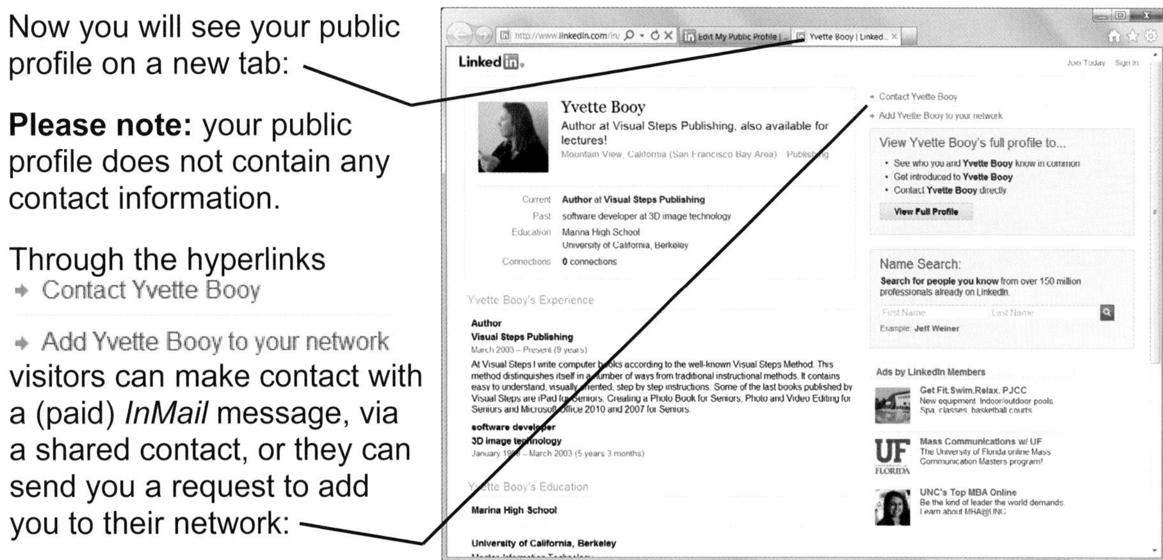

☞ **Close the new tab** 👣4

☞ **Open the** Settings **page** 👣7

By PASSWORD Change you can change your password.

You are allowed to use multiple e-mail addresses. This can be useful, if you expect to receive invitations of your new contacts through different e-mail addresses. For example, this is how you can add your professional e-mail address:

Here is your primary e-mail address:

- **By** PRIMARY EMAIL**, click** Change/Add

- **Type an extra e-mail address**

- **Click** Add email address

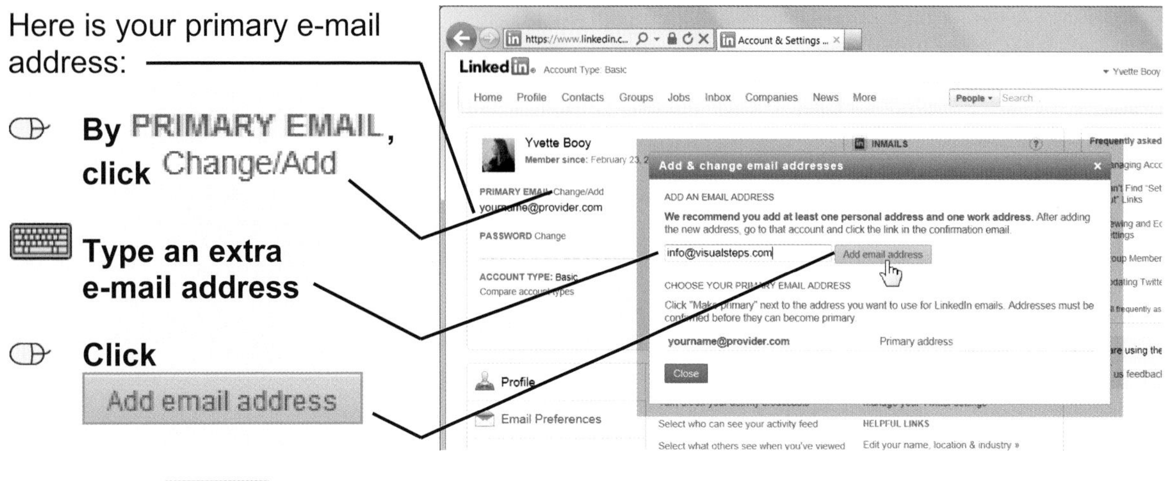

- **Click** Done

Repeat this operation for all the other e-mail addresses you want to add

Open your e-mail program and click the link(s) in the e-mail message(s) you have received from *LinkedIn*, in order to confirm the e-mail address(es)

Click Confirm

Close your e-mail program's window and close the new *Internet Explorer* window

Click Close

2.4 Finding Contacts through Your E-mail Address Book

LinkedIn has a useful function for checking whether some of the contacts from your e-mail address book are already active on *LinkedIn*.

Open the home page 8

Position the pointer on Contacts

Click Add Connections

If you are making use of a webmail service, such as *Hotmail*, *Yahoo Mail* or *Gmail*, then you can check for contacts like this:

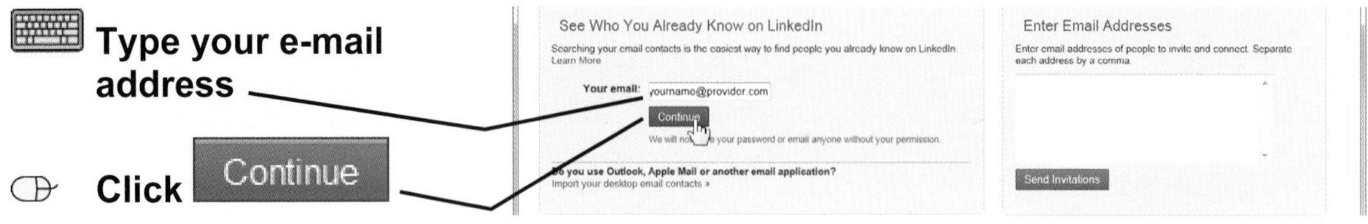

First, you will need to sign in with your e-mail account. In this example we have used a *Hotmail* account, where the user needs to sign in with his *Windows Live ID*, in a separate window:

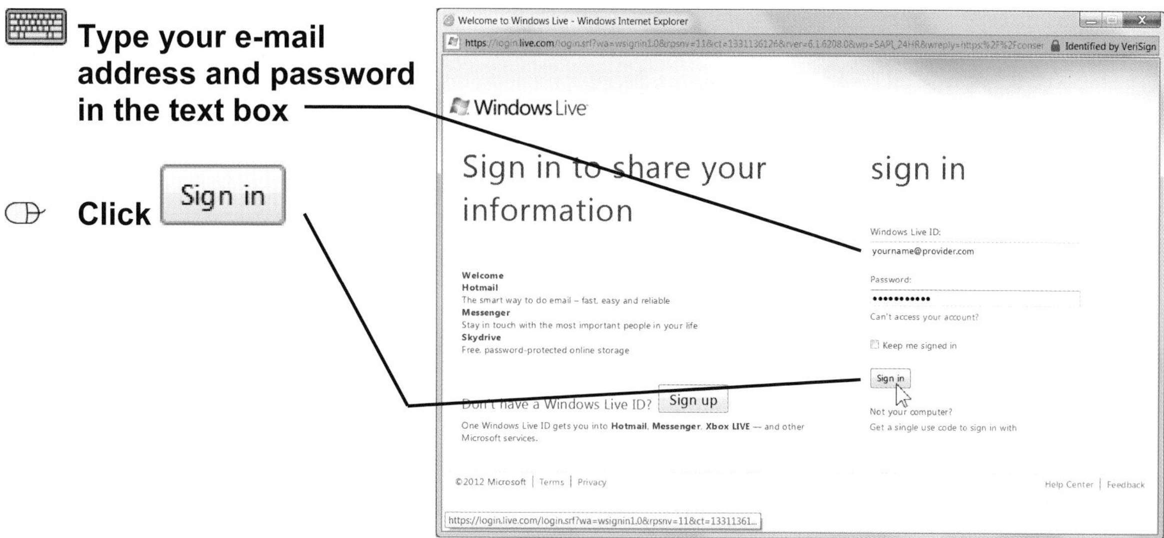

Type your e-mail address and password in the text box

Click Sign in

Now you will need to give permission to share your *Windows Live* contacts with *LinkedIn*. Just to be on the safe side, you will confine this permission to a single day:

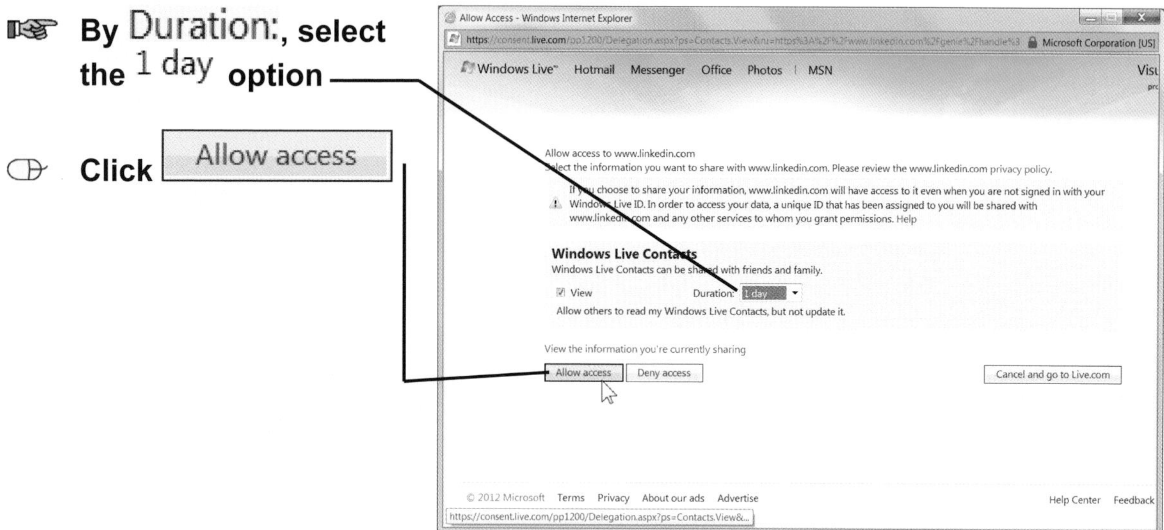

By Duration:, **select the** 1 day **option**

Click Allow access

Now the contacts will be looked up, and then the window will be closed. In this example, the first contact found has a *LinkedIn* account. After that, some persons are found who do not have a *LinkedIn* account. This is how you can invite people to become a connection of yours:

First, you see the contacts with a *LinkedIn* account:

Click Add Connection(s)

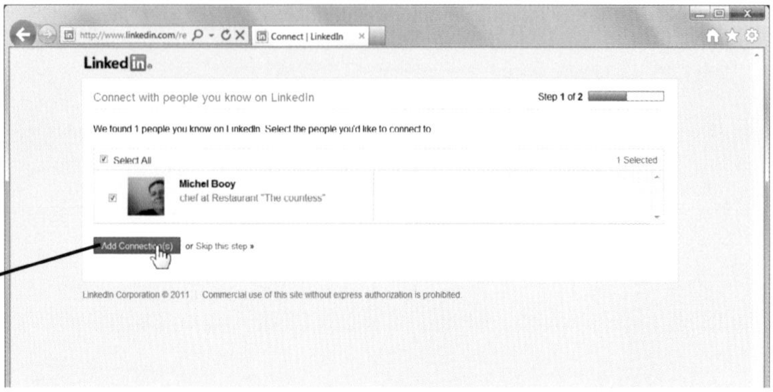

If necessary, uncheck the box ☑ next to the person or persons whom you do not want to invite

Click Invite to Connect

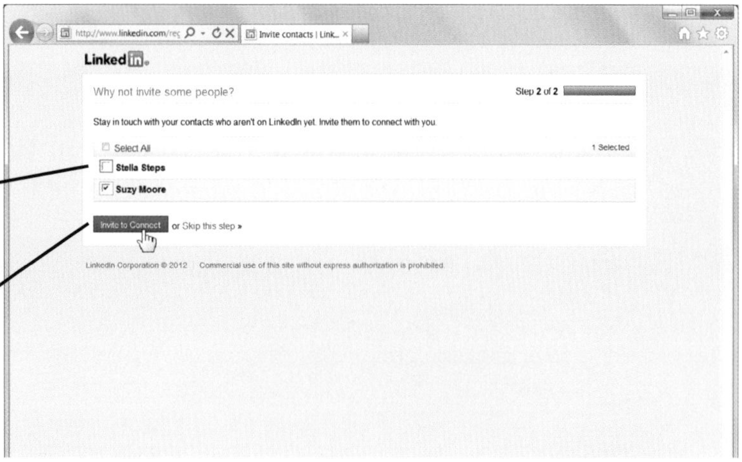

Please note:

These persons will not be added to your connections right away. First, they will receive your invitation. If they do not yet have a *LinkedIn* account, they will receive this invitation as a regular e-mail message. Once they have created their own account and have accepted your invitation, they will be connected to you and appear in your network.

Tip

Contacts from *Outlook*

If you use *Outlook*, or one of the other e-mail programs, you can import your contacts with a .CSV, .TXT or .VCF file. First, you need to create an export file in *Outlook*. But you can also create your own .TXT file, listing all the e-mail addresses, separated by a Tab.

This is how you import the file with your contacts:

Click Import your desktop email contacts.

Click Browse...

A folder window will be opened:

Select the file 5

Click Upload File

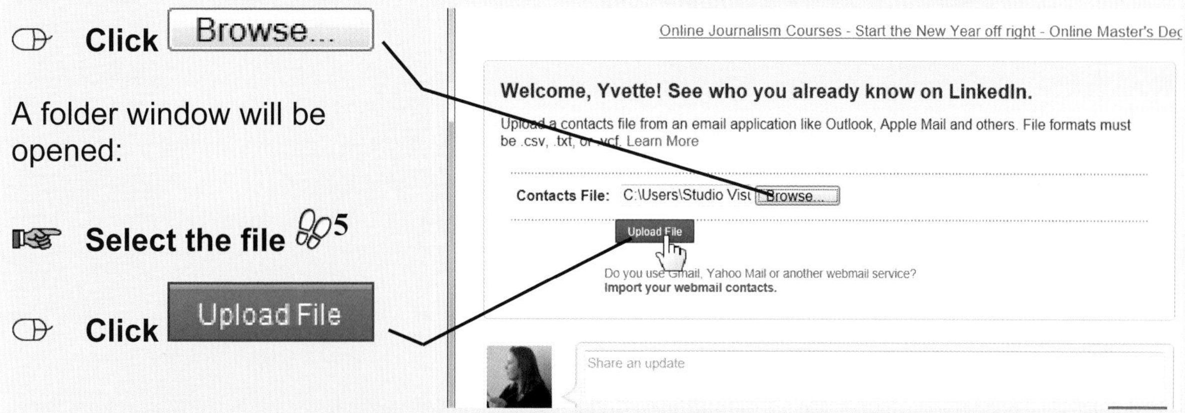

Afterwards, you will see which contacts have been found and you can choose the people you want to invite.

2.5 Searching for Contacts Directly with LinkedIn

You can look up and invite colleagues, former colleagues, fellow students, friends, and family members who are already active on *LinkedIn*:

Type the name in the search box

Click

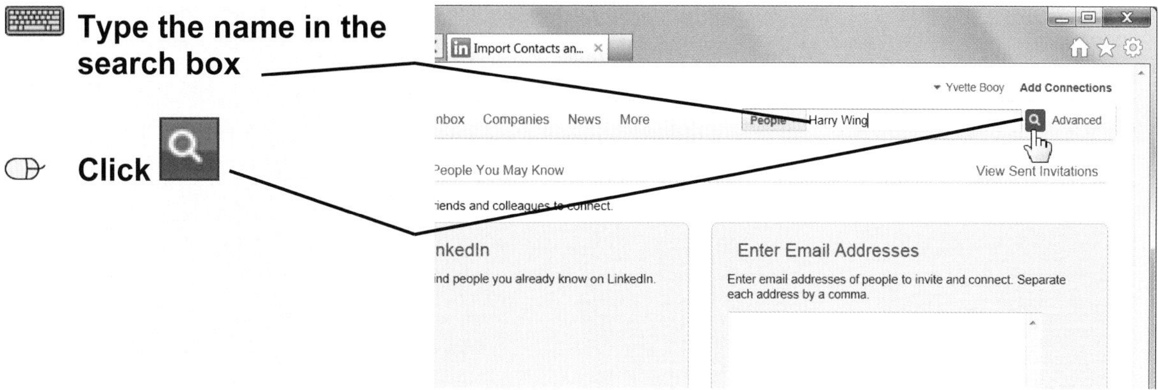

You will see one or more search results. If you have found the right person:

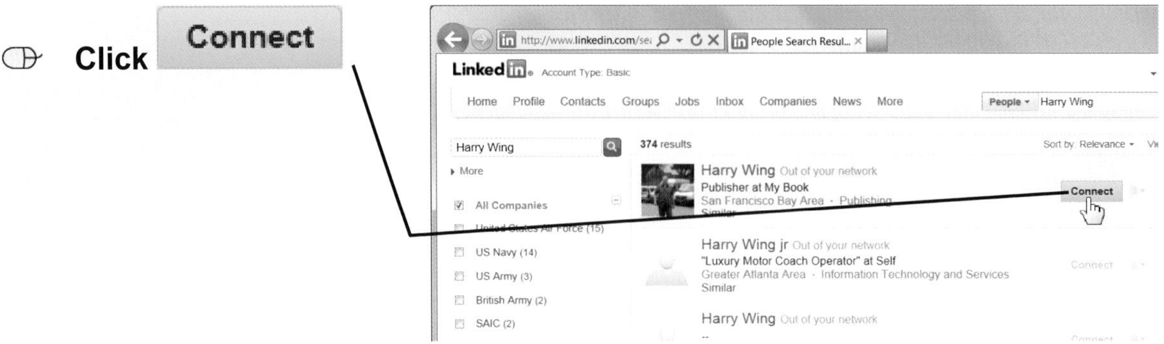

Tip

Who is who?

If you are not sure about the identity of a certain person on the list, then click some of the names. Then you will see the profile data shared by these persons with the people looking for them via *LinkedIn*. This may help you find the right person.

LinkedIn will ask you how you know this person:

Colleague : through work.
Classmate : because he or she is a fellow student or classmate.
We've done business together : through shared business.
Friend : a friend or a girlfriend.
Other : from something different.
I don't know (name): I do not know this person at all.

If you want to invite a colleague or business partner, you will need to state the name of the company where you have worked together. If you want to invite a classmate, you will be asked to enter the name of your old school. You can directly invite your personal friends. If you have chosen the 'Other' option, you will be asked to enter the person's e-mail address.

Please note:

If you have invited multiple contacts and all of them indicate that they do not know you, your account will be limited and you will need to enter an e-mail address for each new person you want to invite.

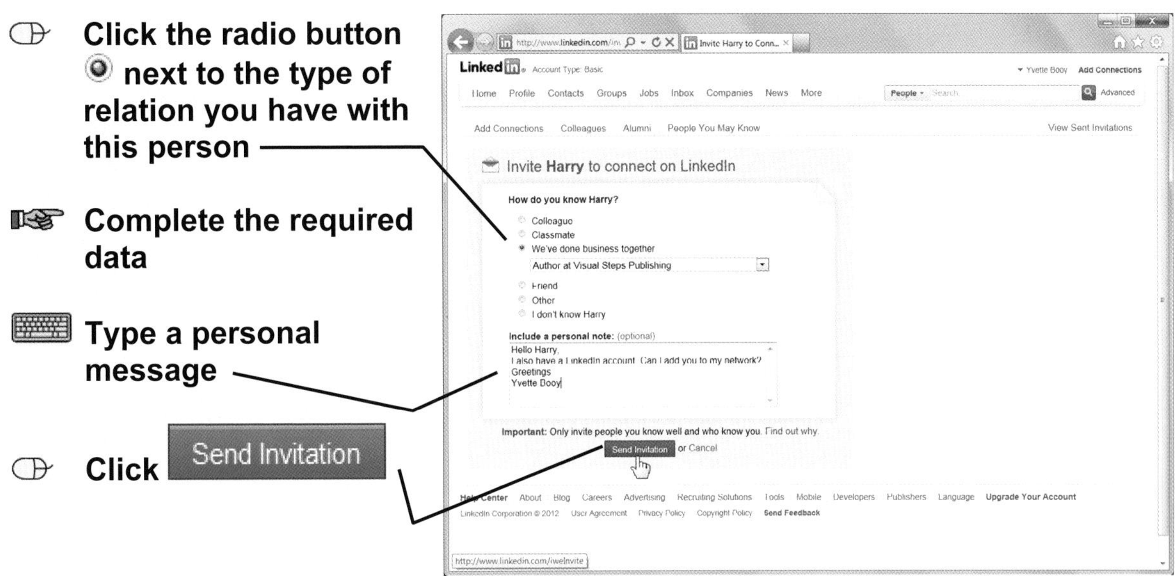

Click the radio button next to the type of relation you have with this person

Complete the required data

Type a personal message

Click Send Invitation

Now you will see a notification telling you that your invitation has been sent.

Repeat this operation for all the people you want to invite

After you have invited all of them, you can return to your home page:

Open your home page 8

Tip

Quickly find (former) colleagues or fellow students

LinkedIn has a useful function for quickly looking up (former) colleagues, classmates and fellow students. If you want to use this function however, you need to have entered accurate and correct information about your professional and school career in your profile.

For example, this is how you can search for and invite (former) colleagues:

Position the pointer on Contacts

Click Add Connections

- Continue on the next page -

- Click the **Colleagues** tab

In this example, a single colleague has been found at the address of a (former) employer:

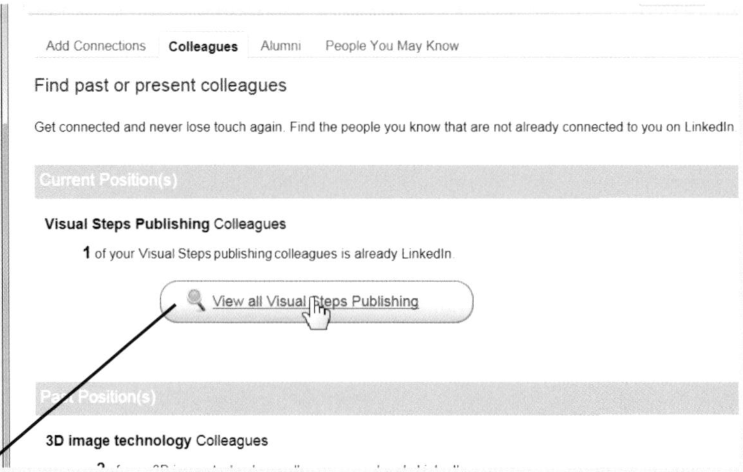

- Click **View all Visual Steps Publishing**

- Check the box next to the person you want to invite

- Check the box next to Add a personal note with your invitation?

- Type a personal message

- Click **Send Invitations**

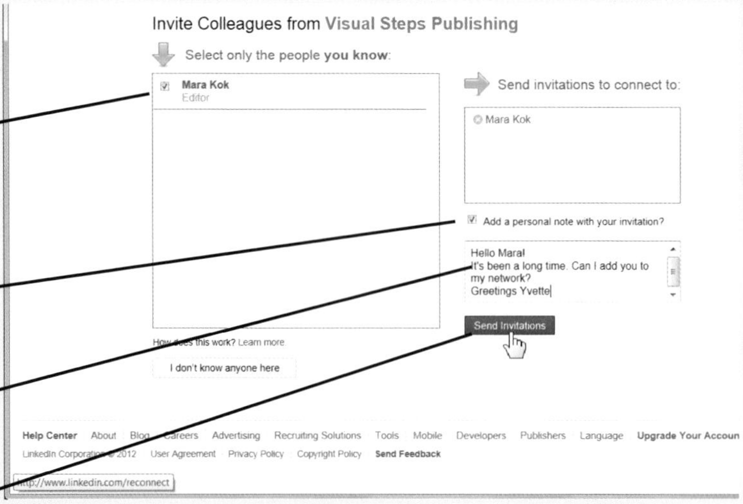

In the same way, you can use the **Alumni** tab to look for and invite classmates and fellow students.

2.6 Confirming Your Contacts

Every person you invite needs to confirm that they want to become part of your network. They can also decide to ignore your invitation.
You can do the same thing, when somebody tries to include you in his or her network. When this happens, you will receive an e-mail and a message in your *LinkedIn* inbox.

Please note:

If you have not yet received any invitations from other contacts, you can just read through this section.

LinkedIn uses a kind of internal e-mail service, where you can receive private messages.

Here you can see if your inbox contains a message:

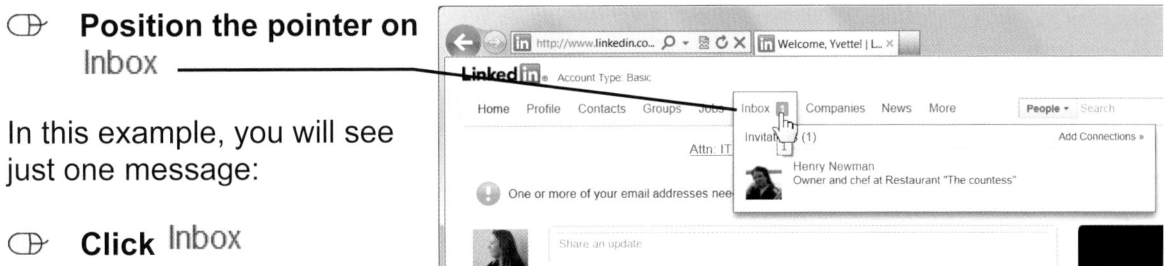

If you point at the inbox, you will see a summary of your messages immediately:

- **Position the pointer on** Inbox

In this example, you will see just one message:

- **Click** Inbox

Your inbox will be opened. There are separate tabs for Messages and Invitations:

You will see the Messages tab:

Just like in your e-mail program, you can read, answer and delete messages. In this example there are no messages.

- **Click the** Invitations 1 **tab**

This is how you accept an invitation:

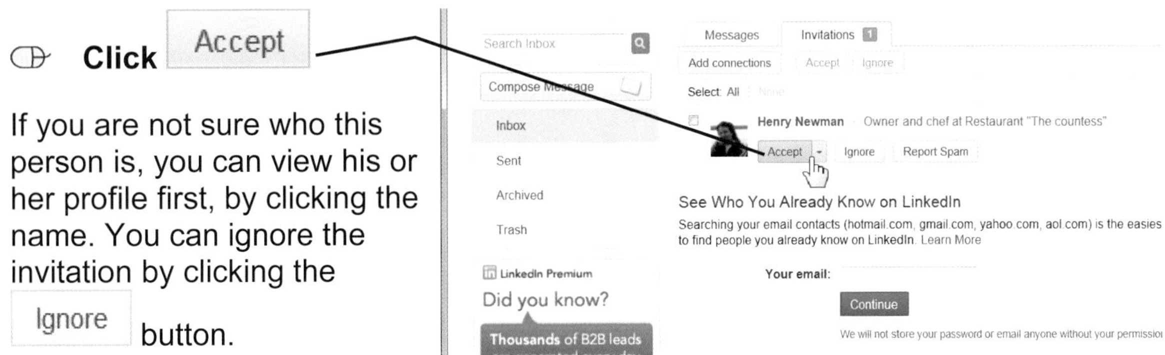

- **Click** Accept

If you are not sure who this person is, you can view his or her profile first, by clicking the name. You can ignore the invitation by clicking the Ignore button.

If you accept the invitation you will see this message:

You and Henry Newman are now connected.
See Henry Newman's 1 connection · View profile · Send a message.

2.7 Your Network on LinkedIn

In the previous sections you have read about how to build your own network by using *LinkedIn* to connect to your current and former business contacts, colleagues, fellow students as well as family members. This network is called your *1st degree network.* The persons in this network are directly connected to you.

But all these people have their own network too, and the persons in those networks make up your *2nd degree network*. In their turn, the contacts of your *2nd degree* network make up your *3rd degree network*.

The nice thing about *LinkedIn* is that your connections are not limited to the people in your 1st degree network. You can approach the persons in your 2nd degree network through an introduction of one of the contacts in your 1st degree network. If you want to connect wi th someone in your 3rd degree network, you will need to have two consecutive introductions. Because of this system of introducing others through a contact in your own network, mutual trust is ensured between all the members of these networks.

This is how you view the people in your own network:

Click Contacts

In this example you can see that there are two connections at the moment:

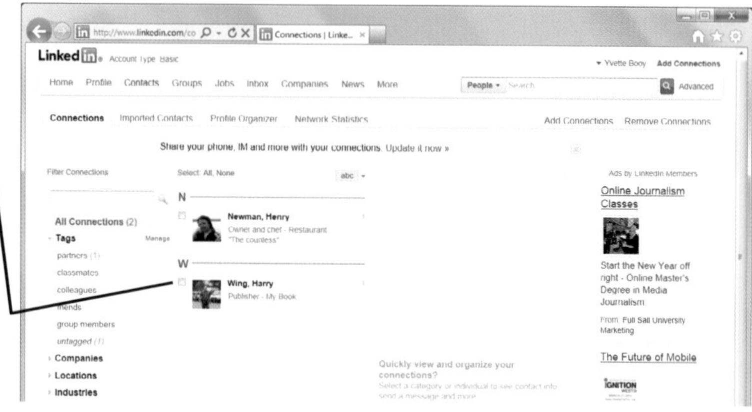

Your entire network will most likely be much larger. That is because the persons in your 2nd degree and 3rd degree network are also included in your overall network:

Position the pointer on Contacts

Click Network Statistics

In this example, the 1st degree network consists of two persons:

In total, there are 350 persons who can be invited through one of your connections:

The 3rd degree network consists of 375,300 persons. You can approach these persons through the connections of one of your own connections:

The overall *LinkedIn* network consists of more than 150 million people:

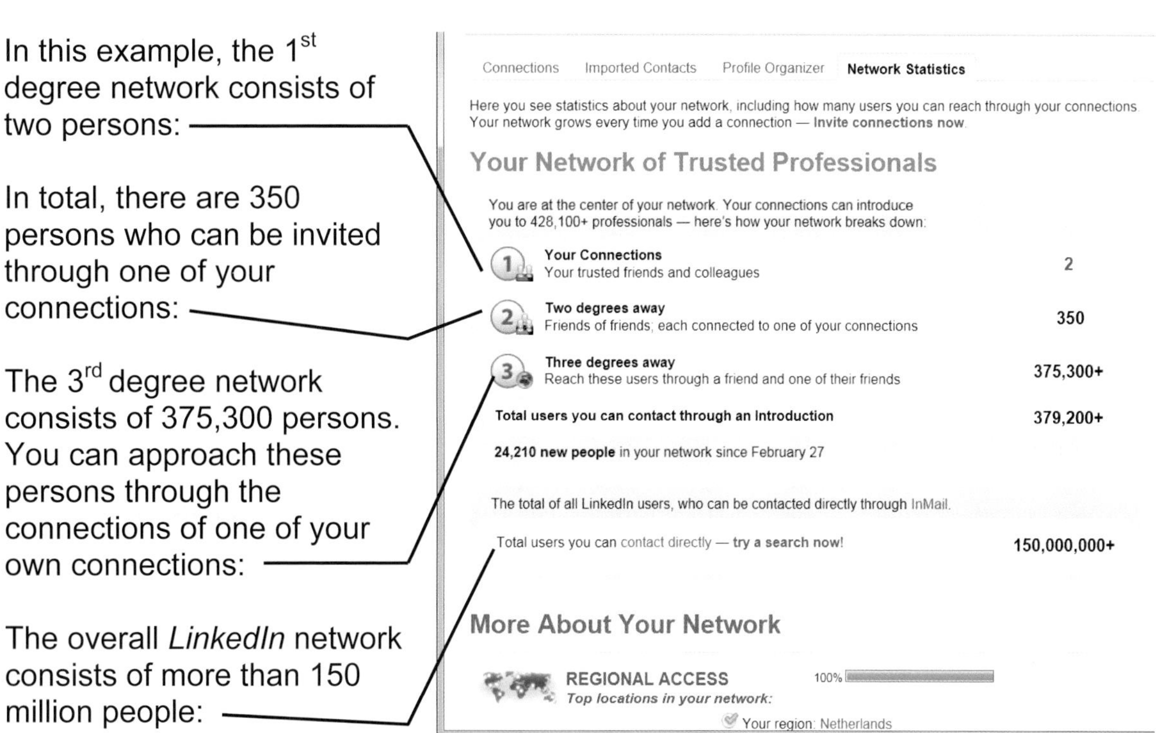

As you add more and more connections to your 1st degree network, your overall network of people you can approach through others will grow expansively. For that matter, through the paid *InMail* service offered by *LinkedIn* you can directly contact all 150 million members.

2.8 Using Introductions

It is quite possible that one of your own connections has a network contact with someone with whom you would like to connect yourself. Of course, you can try to add this person to your network. But there is a big chance that this person will ignore your invitation because he does not know you personally. It is better to ask your own contact to introduce you to such a person.

This is how you can view the connections of one of your own contacts:

- **Click** Contacts

- **Click the name of a contact**

You will see this contact's profile. In this profile you will also see the number of connections of this person:

- **Click** 2 connections

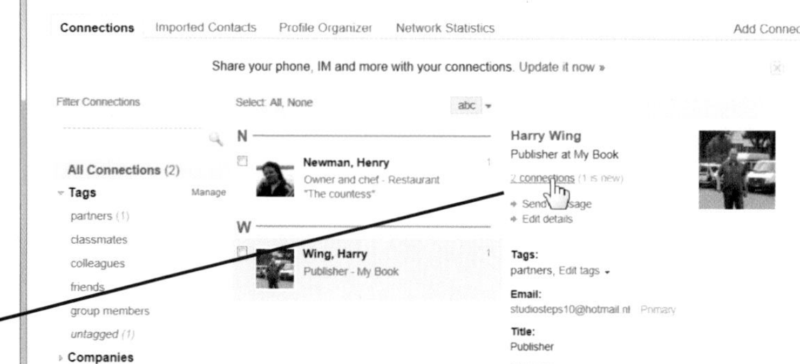

Now you will see an overview of all the connections:

(1st) indicates that this person belongs to your 1st degree network:

If you want to be introduced to a person from his network:

- **Position the mouse pointer on the name of this person**

- **Click** Connect

Now you can write a message to the person to whom you want to be introduced:

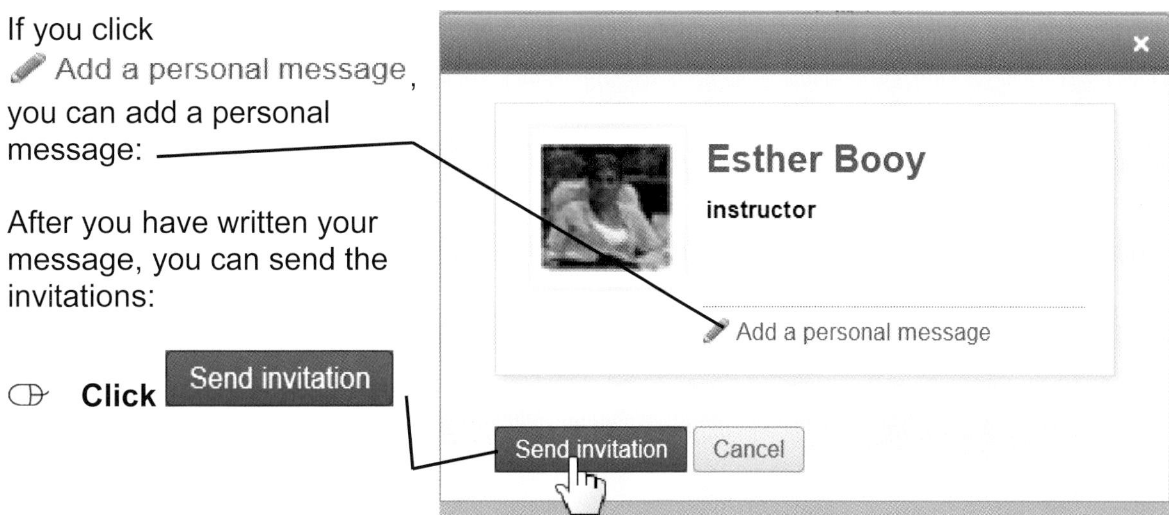

If you click Add a personal message, you can add a personal message:

After you have written your message, you can send the invitations:

Click **Send invitation**

Please note:

If you use this method to send a message to a person in your 3rd degree network, the message will be sent to your own contact first. This contact will decide whether to forward the message to a connection he or she shares with the person you want to approach. If the message is forwarded, the 'shared' connection will need to decide whether to forward this message and send it on to the final recipient. This means it may take a while before you receive a reply.

Please note:

All persons in the chain will be able to read your message in full. In other words: the person you want to contact will also see the message you have sent to your own connection.

Tip

A maximum of five

The free *LinkedIn* account allows you to use up to a maximum of five simultaneous requests for an introduction at any given time.

Tip

Outside your network

Whenever you view a random profile, you will see the text **Get introduced through a connection** at the top right of the window.

If you try to get introduced to a person who is not part of your 1st, 2nd or 3rd degree network, you will see this message:

Introductions ? How do Introductions work?

You cannot send this InMail because the recipient is not part of your network and is not currently open to receiving InMail.

You will not be able to send a message, because this person is not part of your network and also does not wish to receive *InMail* messages.

2.9 Searching For Groups and Using Groups

You can also connect to people in your own line of business by joining Groups. In these groups, people discuss certain specific topics with each other. For instance, 'Safety precautions in several branches of industry', or 'ICT Education'. Apart from these very specific groups, there are numerous groups of former students (alumni) and employees (former colleagues). It may be possible to find a group for your own company, line of business, specialism or hobby. This is how you look for a group:

Click Groups

Type a keyword, for instance: `first aid`

Click [search button]

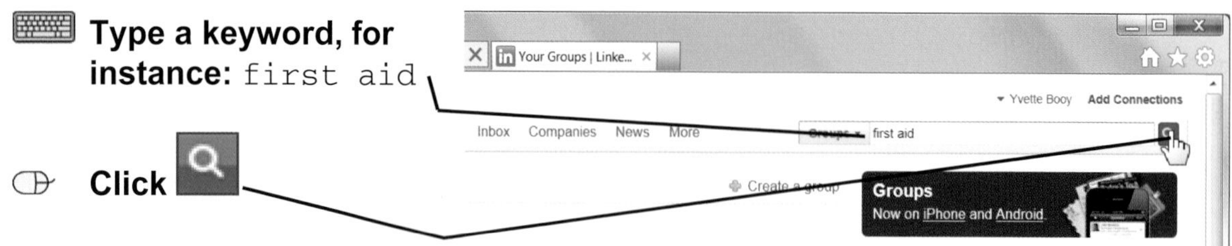

You will see a list of groups. To view additional information on a group:

Click the name of the group

If you decide to join the group:

Click

Click **here**

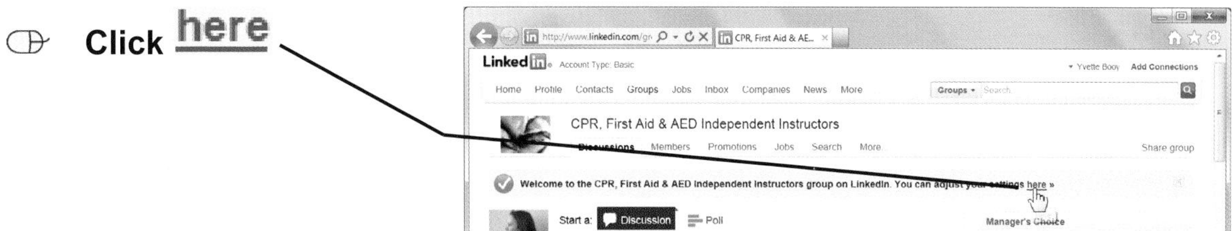

Now you will see a page with all the group settings:

By **Group Logo:** you can select whether you want to display the group logo in your own profile:
By **Contact Email:** you will see which e-mail address is used for messages addressed to the group:
You can also enter a new e-mail address.
A **Digest Email:** is an e-mail that contains a summary of all the group's activities: You can choose to receive such an e-mail on a *daily* or *weekly* basis:

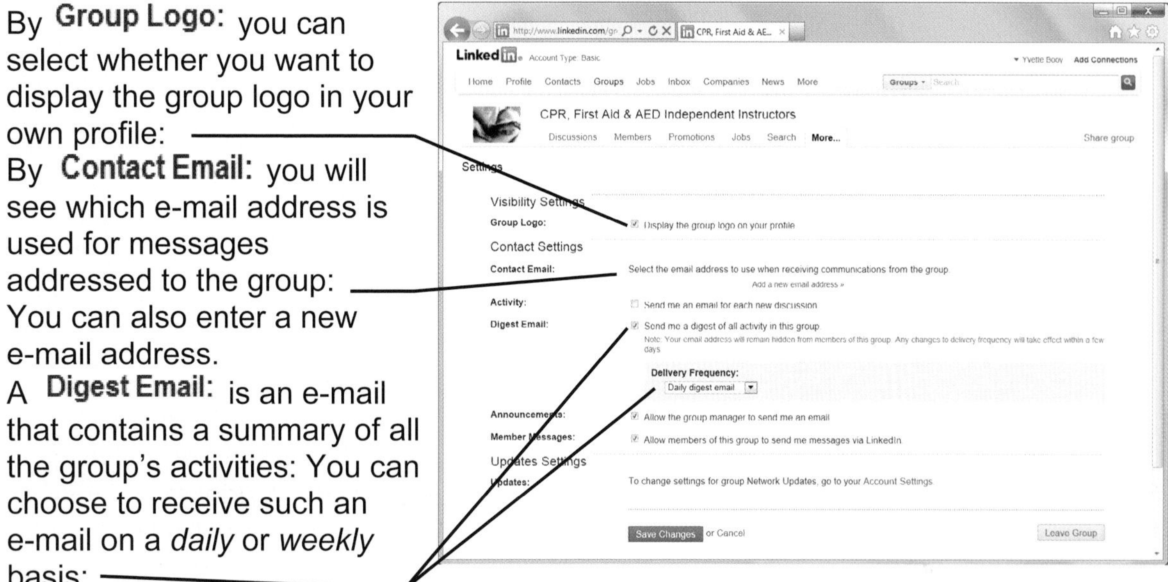

Announcements:: here you can choose if you want to receive group announcements.
Member Messages:: here you can determine whether the group members will be allowed to directly send messages to your e-mail address.

To save the data:

Click 

You may see this message: Your membership is pending approval. Send message · Withdraw request.
This means that your membership application needs to be approved by the group manager. You can use the Withdraw request link to withdraw your membership request, if you decide not to join the group.

After your request has been approved, you can easily find the groups of which you are a member:

Click Groups

You will see a list with the groups to which you belong. To open a group:

Click the name of a group

Discussions
If you want to take part in a discussion on the group page:

Click Comment **by the discussion group you want to join**

If you want to start up a discussion yourself:

Type a message of 200 characters, at the most

Click Share

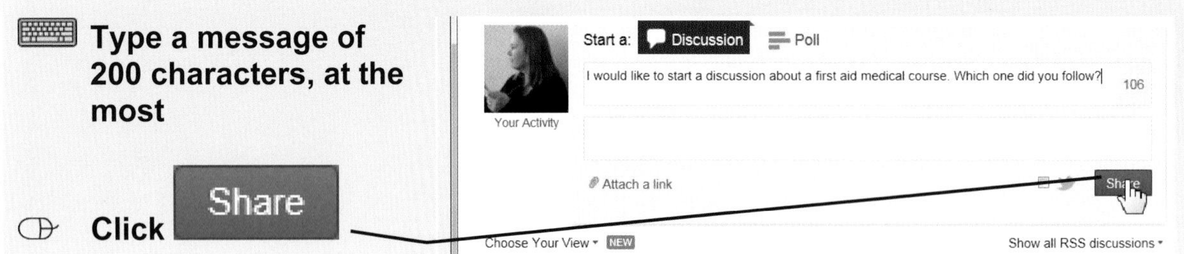

Leave a group
If you want to leave a group:

Click Groups

By the relevant group:

Click More...

Click Your Settings

Click Leave Group

2.10 Following Companies

By following a company you can keep up with the latest news about the company. This is how you can find a company:

Click Companies

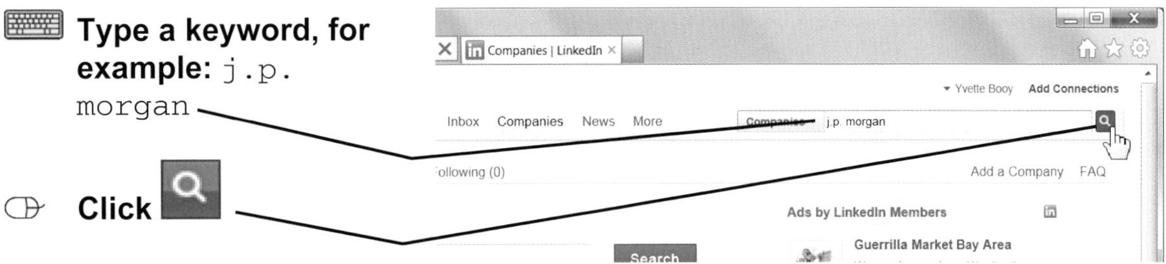

Type a keyword, for example: `j.p. morgan`

Click

You will see a list of companies. If you want to view additional information on a company:

Click the company name

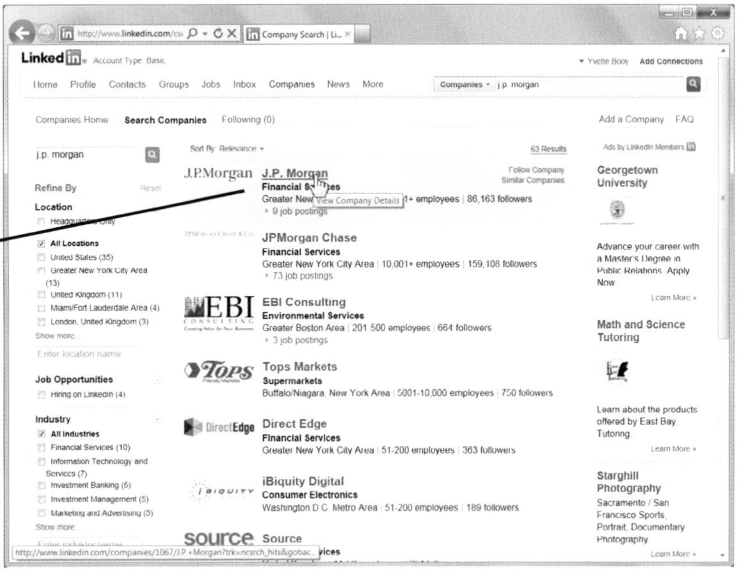

Now you will see an Overview page about the company:

Here you can see how many company employees are part of this network:

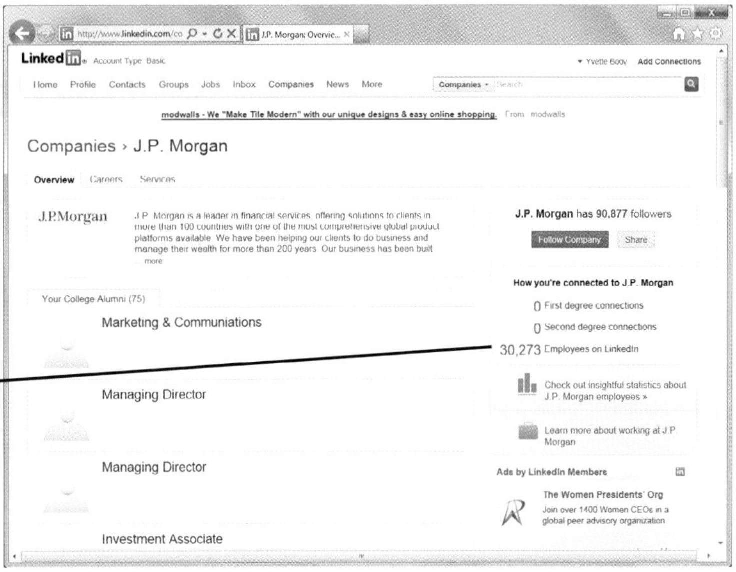

If you want to follow the changes in this company:

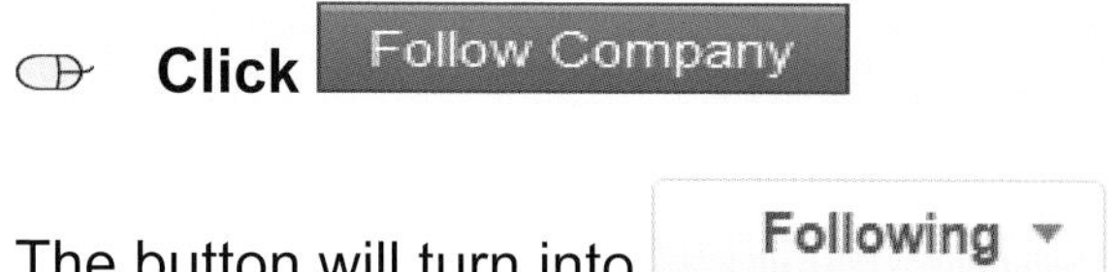

- **Click** Follow Company

The button will turn into Following.

This is how you can see which companies you are currently following:

- **Click** Companies

Here you can see the updates of the followed companies:

In this example there are currently no updates.

- **Click** Following (1)

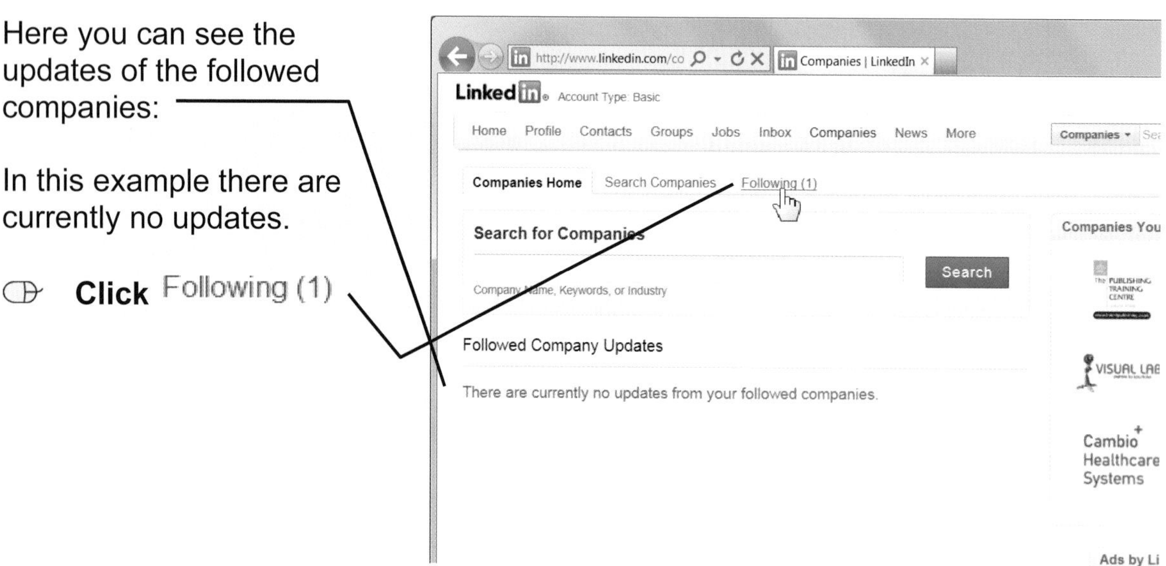

You will see an overview of the companies you follow.

If you no longer want to follow a company, you can click Stop following:

You can change the settings for the notifications you get regarding this company:

- **Click** Notification settings

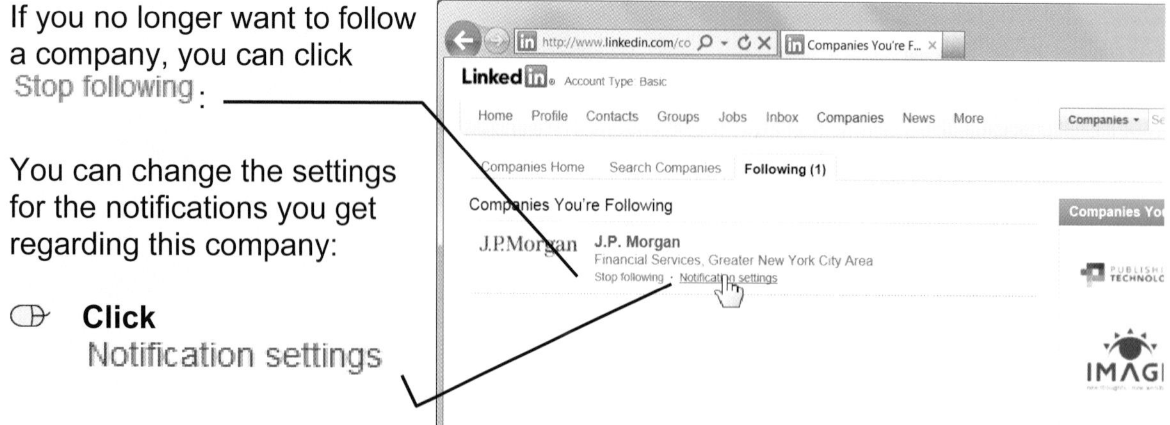

By default, you will receive a message when one of the persons in your network join or leave this company, or are promoted to a better position:

You will also receive a message when new job opportunities arise or when the company profile is updated:

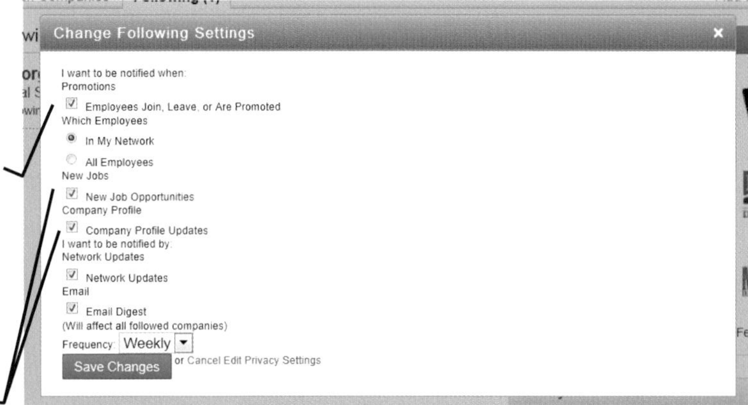

By **I want to be notified by:** you can indicate if you want to be notified by network updates on your home page and/or through a weekly or daily e-mail which contains all the latest news (*e-mail digest*).

After you have changed a setting:

2.11 Looking for a Job

LinkedIn has a very useful function for searching for job openings.

Click Jobs

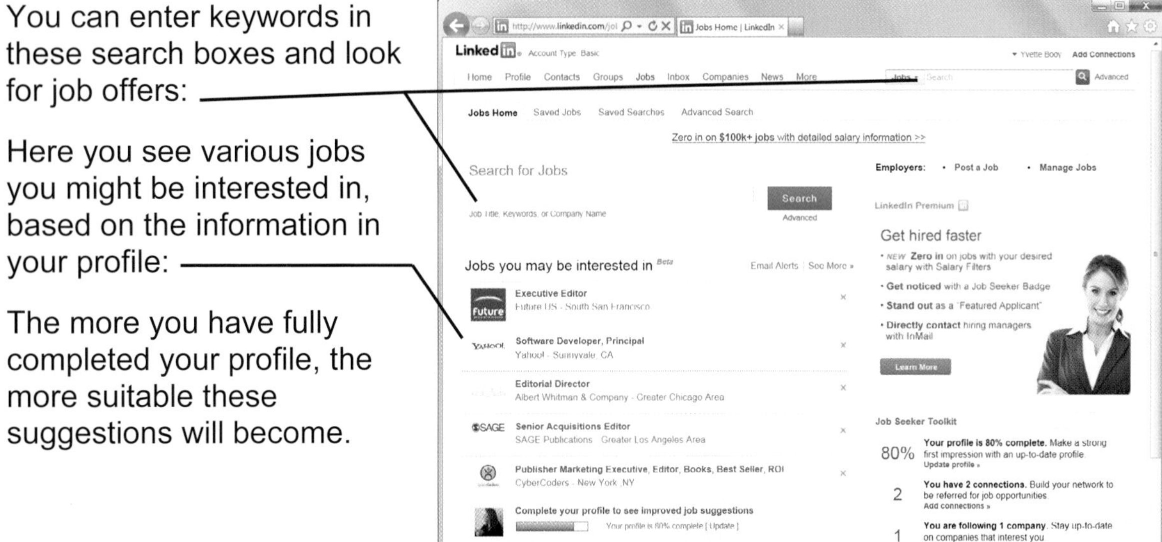

You can enter keywords in these search boxes and look for job offers:

Here you see various jobs you might be interested in, based on the information in your profile:

The more you have fully completed your profile, the more suitable these suggestions will become.

If you have found an interesting job offer, you can immediately check whether you are connected to the company in question, through your 1st degree or 2nd degree network:

Here you see the person who has published the job opening on *LinkedIn*:

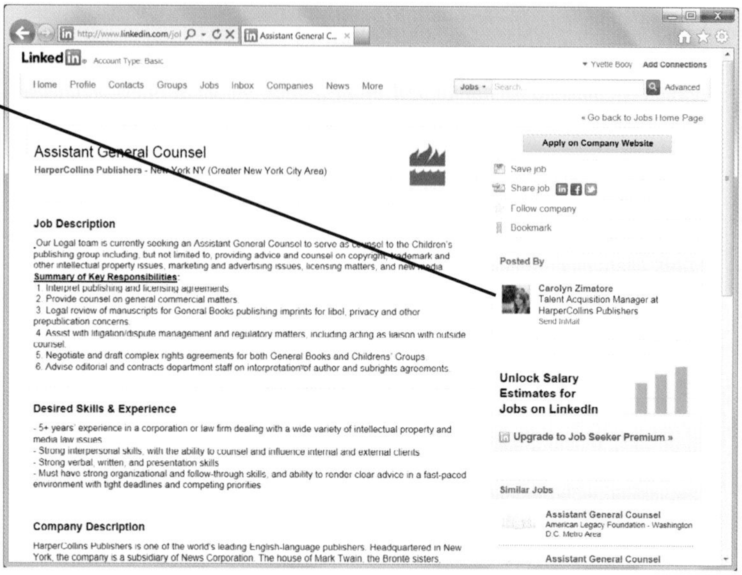

With the **Apply on Company Website** button you can open the company website, directly on the page where you can apply for this job. If you are connected to this company through a single person in your network, you can ask your connection for an introduction by clicking **Request Introduction**. If this button is not visible, you can also open your connection's profile and use the **Get introduced through a connection** link.

2.12 Closing an Account

If you do not wish to use *LinkedIn* anymore, it is recommended that you close your account. This will prevent others from trying to contact you in vain.

Open the Settings **page** 7

Please note:

You may be asked to use your password to sign in again. This is done in order to protect your profile.

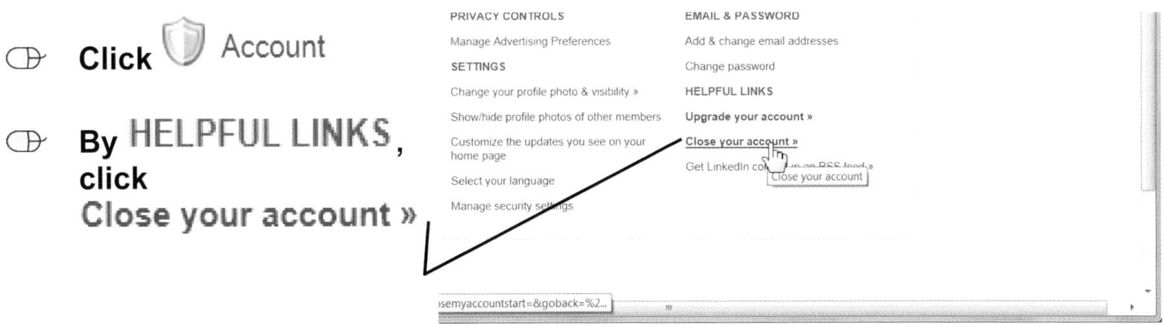

LinkedIn would like to know why you want to close your account:

- I have a duplicate account : I have another account I want to use.
- I am getting too many emails : I am receiving too many e-mails.
- I am not getting any value from my membership : my membership is not very useful to me.
- I am using a different professional networking service : I am using a different service.
- Other : any other reason.

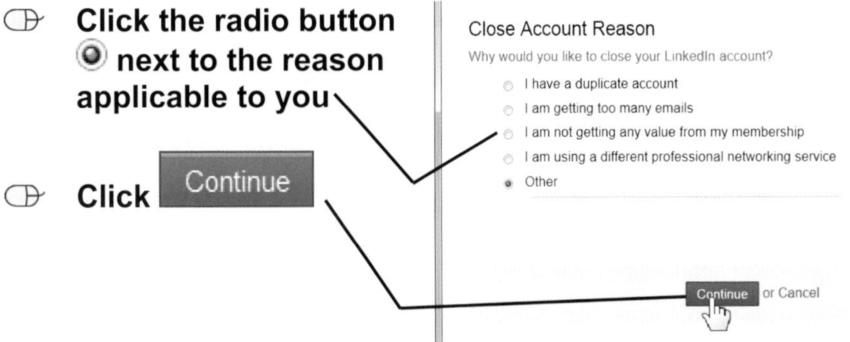

Now you will be asked to check whether you really want to close this account:

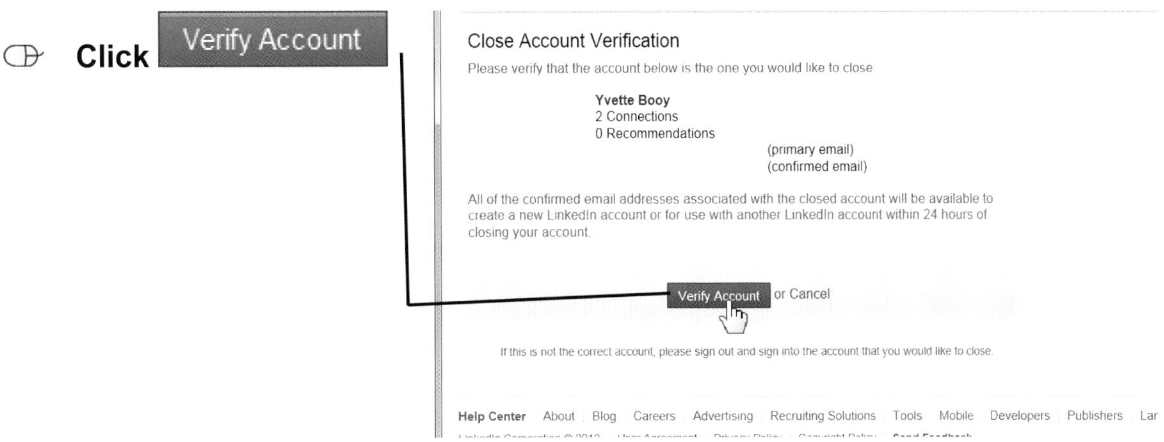

LinkedIn will let you know what the consequences are when you close your account. You will no longer have access to your profile, your contacts or messages. All of your recommendations will also be deleted. If you change your mind, you can use the same e-mail address you used previously to create a new account within 24 hours after closing your old account. Although your *LinkedIn* account will disappear at once, it will take a bit longer for your public profile to disappear from the search results of various search engines.

If you really want to delete your account:

Click

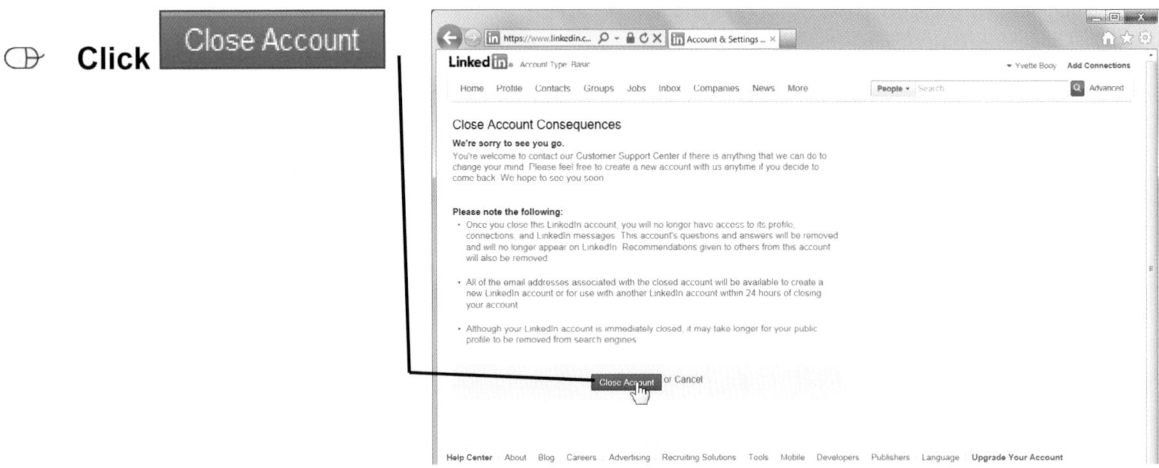

You will see a confirmation:

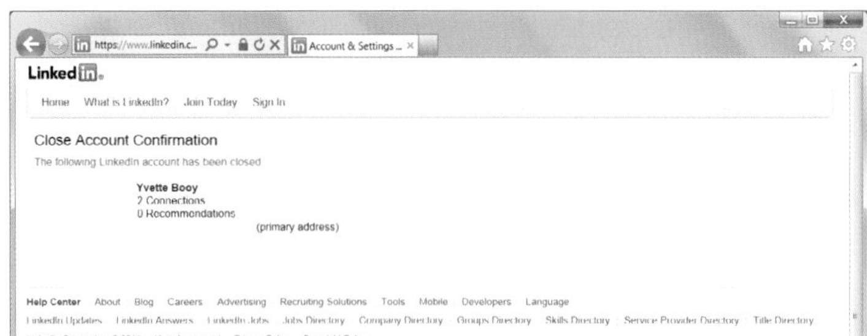

Your account has been closed and you will no longer receive e-mail messages from *LinkedIn*.

Close *Internet Explorer* 4

In this chapter you have made your acquaintance with the main functions in *LinkedIn*. In the next section you will find additional tips that will help you use *LinkedIn* in a more effective way.

2.13 Using LinkedIn Effectively

Here you will find a number of tips regarding the things you should and should not do while using *LinkedIn*. If you follow this advice, you will be able to make use of all the *LinkedIn* functions much more effectively.

 **Tip**

Do it!

1. Fully complete your profile and be truthful
Your profile will be viewed by colleagues, former colleagues, former classmates, etc. If you start embellishing things, people will notice.

2. Enter your professional headline
This header is the first thing people will see when they have found your profile. For instance, the header might say Author at Visual Steps Publishing: your current position and your current employer. But you can also add some keywords instead, to tell people a bit more about yourself and about the things you can do for your target group. If you want, you can add a web address. And you can also make it clear that you are open to suggestions and job offers.
If you just want to display your position and your employer, you will not need to do a lot of editing.

3. Type a summary and write about your specialties
Many people do not take the time to thoroughly read a profile. In your summary you can write about your activities and about your significance to your target group. In regard to your specialties, try to accurately describe as well as promote your specialties and strengths. This way, your profile will attract attention more quickly.

3. Search for former classmates or fellow students
These contacts constitute a valuable addition to your network.

4. Write a personal invitation
If you invite a known contact to join your network, you will be presented by the default invitation: I'd like to add you to my professional network on LinkedIn.
- Yvette Booy.
It will not cost you any trouble to type a personal message instead of this default text. This will increase the chances of your invitation being accepted. Invitations that only contain the default text are very impersonal.

- Continue on the next page -

5. Update your status once a week, at minimum
This will increase your visibility in the news overviews of your connections, and they will be sooner reminded of you, whenever they need someone with your expertise.

6. Write recommendations
Writing recommendations is the best way of making sure you also receive recommendations in return. You will need to have recommendations, if you want to complete your profile for the full 100%. This will ensure a higher ranking in the search results.

7. Join groups and engage in lively discussions
Look for groups that are related to your company, line of business, research area or specialism, and join these groups. This is a great way of getting to know people. Also, take a look at some local groups, such as other businesses who operate in your own neighborhood.
Start up a discussion, ask questions, and help others by answering their questions. All these activities will increase your visibility on *LinkedIn*.

A big advantage of joining groups is the fact that you can directly send e-mail messages to other group members, even if they do not belong to your network. This option can be disabled, but most people do not know how to do this. You can join up to 50 groups, at maximum.

8. Start your own group
Do you have an idea for a new group that does not yet exist on *LinkedIn*? Then start your own group and invite your contacts. In the *Tip* at the end of this chapter you can read how to start a group.

9. Take a look at your home page every day
This way, you will keep abreast of any changes in your network and will be able to react to these changes when needed. Perhaps one of your connections has started working on a new project to which you think you can contribute, or someone else has found a new job. You will always need to stay active and regularly check your profile, especially if you do not want to receive updates through your e-mail.

Tip

Do not do this!

1. Use a vacation snapshot as a profile photo
Your photo will tell people who you are. Using a full body vacation snapshot is not a good idea. It is better to use a photo that clearly shows your face. You can crop the photo yourself. Sometimes, people do not remember your name. A clear and distinct picture may help them remember you.

- Continue on the next page -

2. Invite people you do not know
It is not wise to start inviting people like mad. If the person does not know you, there is a good chance he will refuse your invitation and indicate he does not know you. If this happens a few times, your account will be limited and afterwards you will only be allowed to invite people whose e-mail address is known to you.

3. Invite people you do not know very well
There may come a time when you are asked to recommend one of your contacts, or introduce someone else to them. It will seem very strange if you do not really know much about such a contact. Remember this: the quality of your connections is much more important than the quantity.

4. Update your status multiple times a day
If you post several messages a day, this may irritate your connections. They might decide to hide your status updates and also the messages relating to your activities on *LinkedIn*.

5. Reply to a recommendation on the same day
If you have received a recommendation, then do not reply with your own recommendation on the very same day. This will stand out in the news overview of all shared connections. Wait at least a month before sending reciprocal recommendations.

6. Only use LinkedIn for advertising
Your connections will not be amused if your status updates contain nothing but advertising messages. This also goes for independent entrepreneurs, who want to make propaganda for their own business. Alternate these types of messages with news about your own activities or achievements and try adding interesting links to these messages.

Tip

Create a group
Do you have a good idea for a group that does not yet exist on *LinkedIn*? Then you can create and manage such a group yourself.

- **Position the pointer on** Groups
- **Click** Create a Group

- Continue on the next page -

By **Logo:** you can add a logo:

By ☐ * I acknowledge you can state that you are authorized to use this image:

By **Group Name:** you can type an identifiable name for the group:

By **Group Type:** you can select a category for your group:

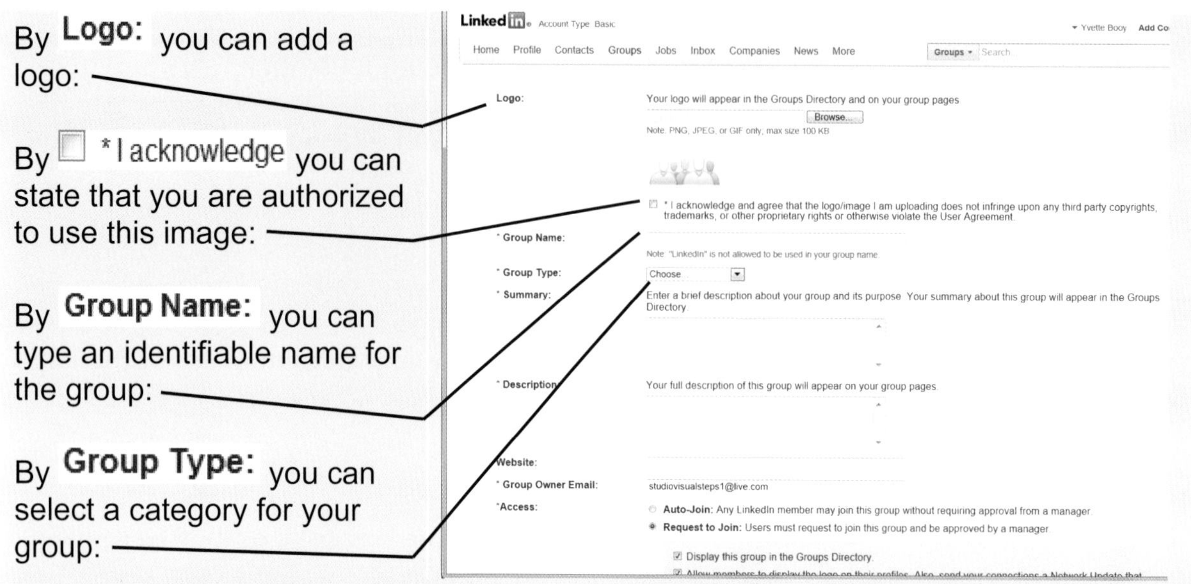

These are the options:
Alumni Group : this group is meant for former classmates or students who know each other from school, a college or university, or from a students' fraternity.
Corporate Group : a company group, for current and former employees of a specific company.
Conference Group : a group for people who visit the same conferences or meetings.
Networking Group : a group for people who want to broaden their network.
Non-Profit Group : a group for people who support the same non-profit cause.
Professional Group : a group for professionals with the same specialism, or in the same line of business.
Other... : all other groups that do not belong to one of the categories mentioned above.

By **Summary:** you can enter a brief description of the group and the goal of the group if applicable. This summary will be visible to all the people with a *LinkedIn* account.
By **Description:** you can enter a full description.
By **Website:** you can add a website for your group (optional).
By **Group Owner Email:** you need to type your own e-mail address, since you are the manager of the group.

- Continue on the next page -

Here you can choose the method for joining this group:

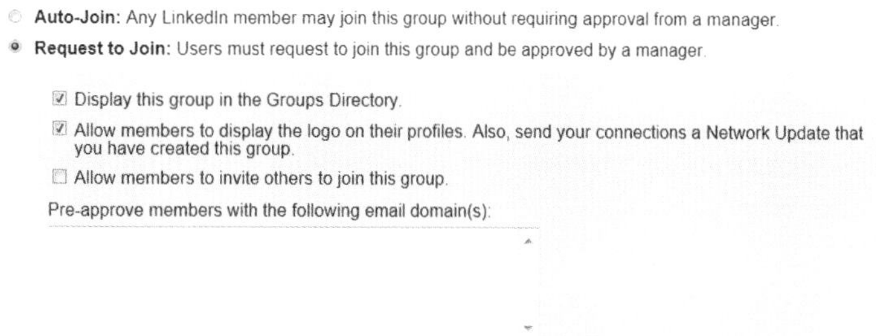

Auto-Join: Any LinkedIn member may join this group without requiring approval from a manager.
Request to Join: Users must request to join this group and be approved by a manager.

Display this group in the Groups Directory.
Allow members to display the logo on their profiles. Also, send your connections a Network Update that you have created this group.
Allow members to invite others to join this group.
Pre-approve members with the following email domain(s):

Auto-Join:: everyone can join at once.
Request to Join:: potential members need to apply first; it may be up to a manager to accept the application.

These are the other options you can select:

Display this group in the Groups Directory.: the group will be displayed in the *LinkedIn* group directory.
Allow members to display the logo on their profiles.: members are allowed to display their personal logo.
Allow members to invite others to join this group.: members are allowed to invite others to join the group.

In the box below Pre-approve members with the following email domain(s): you can enter the e-mail domains whose applications will automatically be accepted, for instance, @visualsteps.com

By **Language:** you can choose the official language of the group.
By **Location:** you can enter a specific geographic location for the group. If you check the box next to this option, you can enter a country and a postal (zip) code.
By **Twitter Announcement:** you can authorize LinkedIn to use your Twitter account.

After you have completed the entire page:

Check the box by
Check to confirm you have read and accept the Terms of Service.

Click Create an Open Group **or** Create a Members-Only Group

- Continue on the next page -

In the next window you can invite your contacts to join the group:

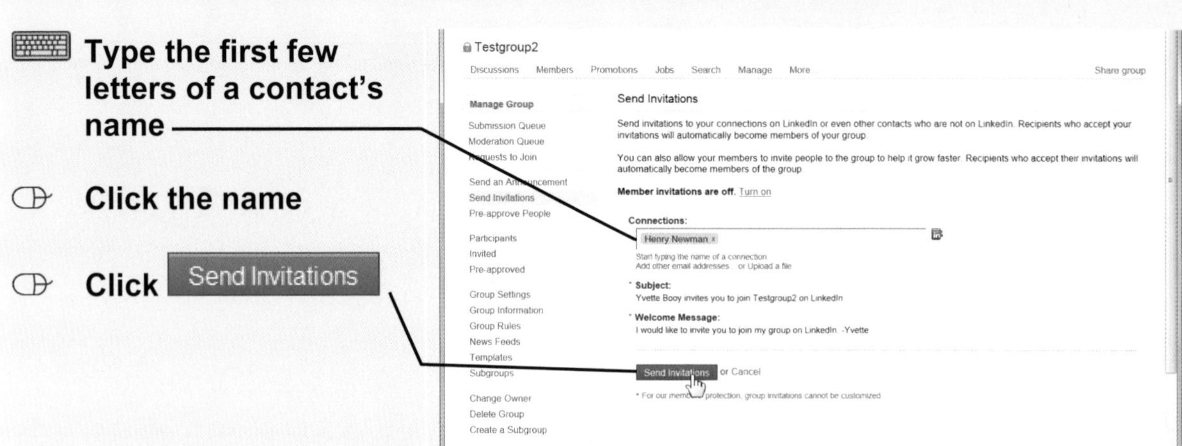

Type the first few letters of a contact's name

Click the name

Click Send Invitations

The invitation will be sent and your group will be created.

Now you can start your first discussion, using the method explained earlier in this chapter. Your connections will know that you have created a group, because they can see this in their news overviews, so applications may start appearing very soon. You can also make a short announcement about the group in your status update and ask your connections to join it.

If you want to delete the group:

Position the pointer on Groups

Click Your Groups

By the group you want to delete:

Click the group

Click Manage

In the left-hand side of the window, in the **Manage Group** column:

Click Delete Group

Click **Yes, delete this group**

Now you will see the confirmation:  **Group has been removed.**

2.14 Background Information

Dictionary

Account	An account provides access to a service. All users of such a service need to have an account; you will need to have an e-mail address and a password, to use *LinkedIn*.
Connections	Contacts that have been connected to you through *LinkedIn*.
Digest e-mail	An e-mail message that contains an overview of the activity within a group or a company, over the past day or week.
InMail	A paid service in *LinkedIn*, which lets you directly send messages to all of the 150 million members.
LinkedIn	A social network aimed at professionals, which enables them to strengthen and broaden their network by creating a profile and posting their resume or CV online, along with other business information.
Outlook	An e-mail program that is part of the *Microsoft Office* suite.
Professional headline	The professional 'header' at the top of your profile. This header is the first thing people see when they have found your profile. Instead of your current position you can also add keywords, to tell people about yourself and the things you can do for your target group.
1st degree network	Your own connections on *LinkedIn*, for example, current and former business contacts, colleagues, fellow students as well as family members. The persons in this network are directly connected to you.
2nd degree network	The connections of your own connections.
3rd degree network	The connections of the persons in your 2nd degree network.

Source: LinkedIn Help

2.15 Tips

Tip

Completeness of your profile

When you take a look at your profile, you will see the percentage for the completeness of this profile. This information is not available to the people in your network.

Click Profile

In this example, the profile has been completed for 80%:

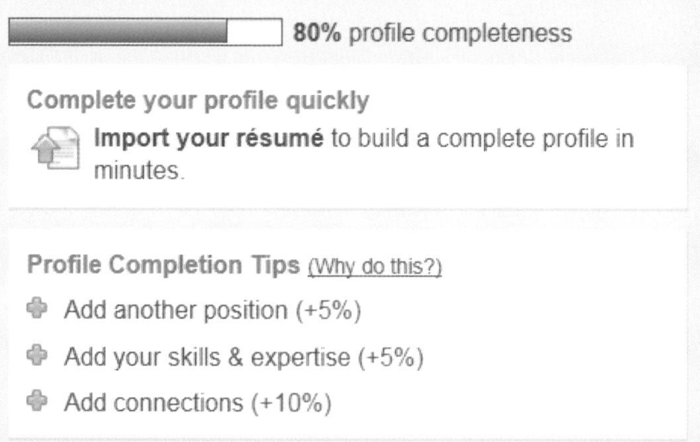

Here are four tips for completing your profile:

- add another job or position.
- add a summary of your activities.
- add your special skills.
- ask for a recommendation.

As the *LinkedIn* system is based on introductions and links from various connections, a recommendation is a good method for developing people's trust in your profile. When you receive a recommendation from one of your contacts, you will not be able to change anything in the text. Recommendations by higher ranking officials or clients and customers will inhance your profile's status.

You will need recommendations, if you want to complete your profile for the full 100%. You will be rewarded by a higher ranking in the search results.

Tip

Disable e-mail

Do you think you are getting too many e-mail messages through *LinkedIn*? You can determine the amount of e-mail you want to receive by changing the settings:

Open the *Settings* page 7

By , **click** Set the frequency of emails

- Continue on the next page -

Now an overview is opened of all the types of messages you can receive through *LinkedIn*. For each type you can choose to receive the e-mail messages directly (*individual e-mail*), or receive them grouped into a single e-mail message with an overview of the weekly messages (*weekly digest e-mail*) and finally you can choose not to receive any mail at all (*no e-mail*). Some of the message options will not be available.

For instance, if you do not wish to receive any e-mails and just want to view all the messages online, on the *LinkedIn* website:

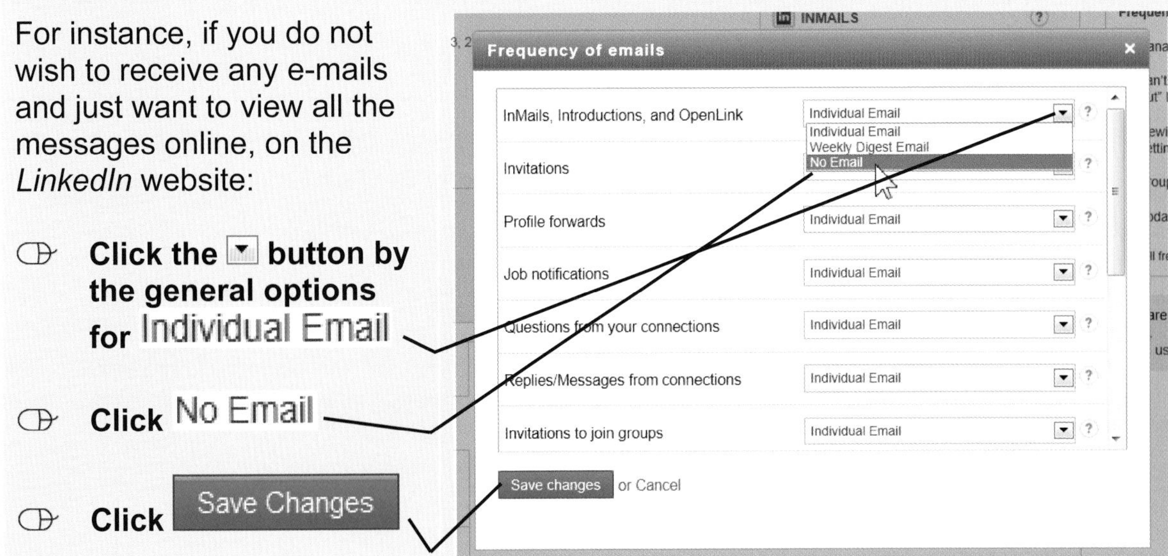

- **Click the ▼ button by the general options for** Individual Email
- **Click** No Email
- **Click** Save Changes

Tip

Recommendations

Naturally, you can ask your connections for a recommendation, but it is better to recommend someone else. Usually, this person will reciprocate the recommendation. For example, if you are very satisfied about a supplier who is also a member of *LinkedIn*, you can write a recommendation. You will find a link for such a recommendation in your contact's profile:

- **Click** **Recommend** Henry's work at Restaurant "The countess"

- Continue on the next page -

In the window below you will need to indicate in which role you recommend this person:

- as a (former) colleague;
- as a service provider;
- as a business partner;
- as a (fellow) student or classmate;

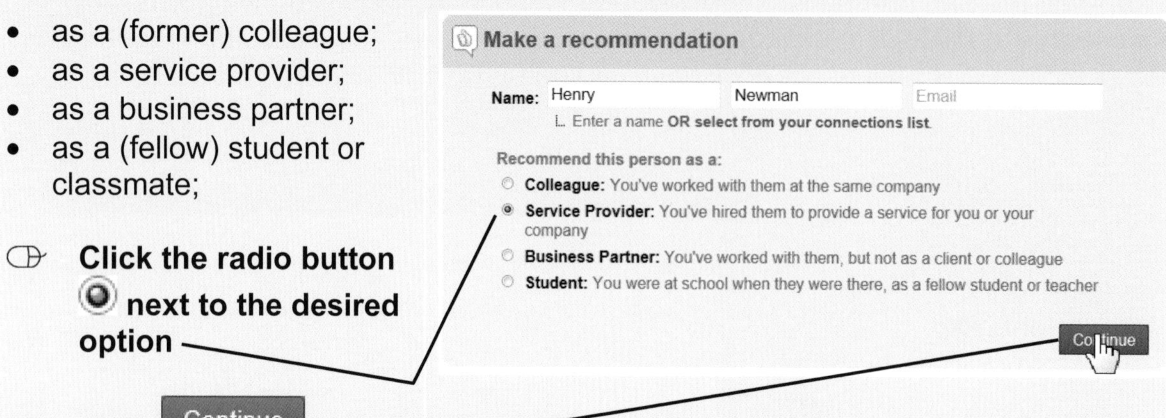

Click the radio button next to the desired option

Click Continue

Depending on the option you have chosen, you will see a new window with several additional options. In the example on the next page you will see the window that appears when you want to recommend someone as a service provider.

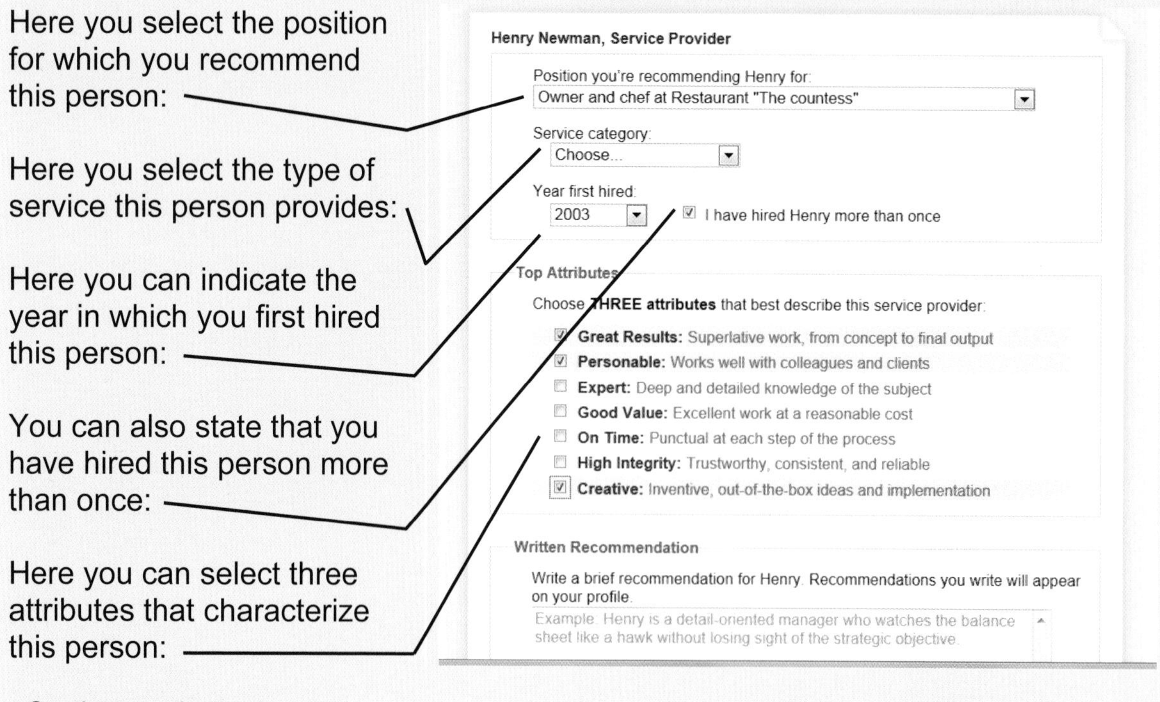

Here you select the position for which you recommend this person:

Here you select the type of service this person provides:

Here you can indicate the year in which you first hired this person:

You can also state that you have hired this person more than once:

Here you can select three attributes that characterize this person:

- Continue on the next page -

For example, you can state that this person delivers a great service, is easy to get along with, gives good value for money, etc.

In the text box by **Written Recommendation** you can write your recommendation. This recommendation will be added to your own profile as well as the profile of the person you recommend. If you want to send the recommendation:

Click Send

Tip

Status message

The white section beneath your professional headline is your *status update*:

Click Profile

Click Post an update

Type your status message in the text box

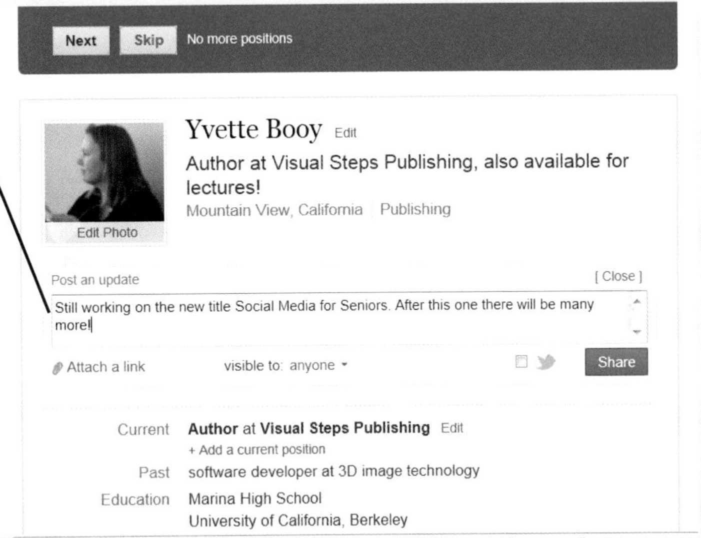

This function can be compared to *Twitter* or the *Facebook* status update. The text you write will appear in the news overview of all your connections' home pages. Here you can also ask a question. Try to be brief and very specific; a concrete question is likely to get you some useful answers.

You can also add a link:

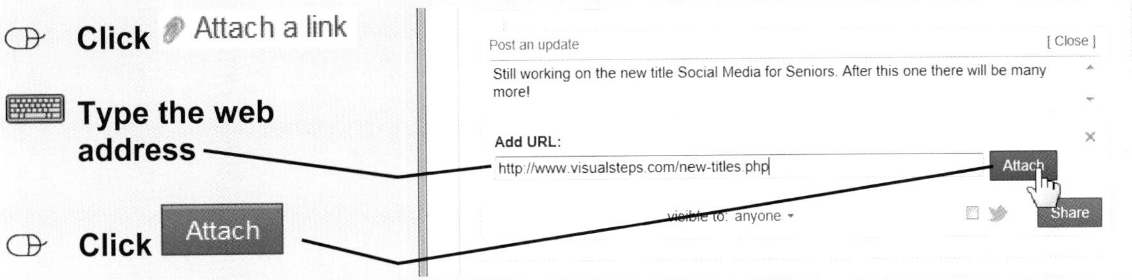

Click Attach a link

Type the web address

Click Attach

- Continue on the next page -

The website URL will be verified. You can now select an image which represents this website:

Click « or » to view the images

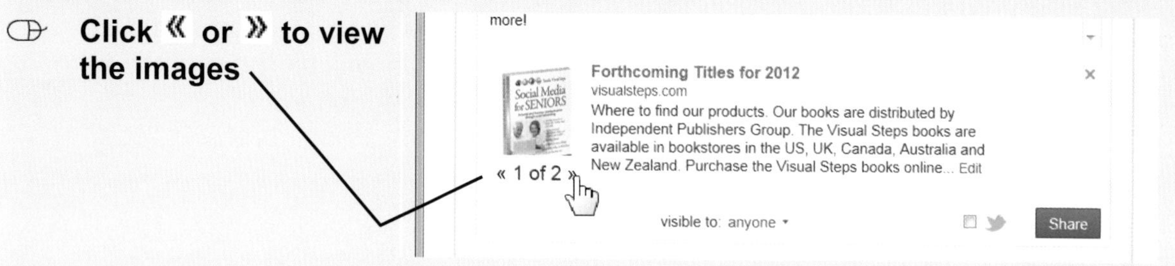

By visible to: anyone you can select who is allowed to view your status updates: *anyone* or just your connections. If you check the box ☑ by the Twitter icon, you can also display the status message on *Twitter*. Although you will need to link your *Twitter* account to your *LinkedIn* account first.

Click 

You will see the status update:

By clicking Like, your connections can indicate that they like the message:

With Comment they can write a comment:

With Share they can integrate your status update within their own status update:

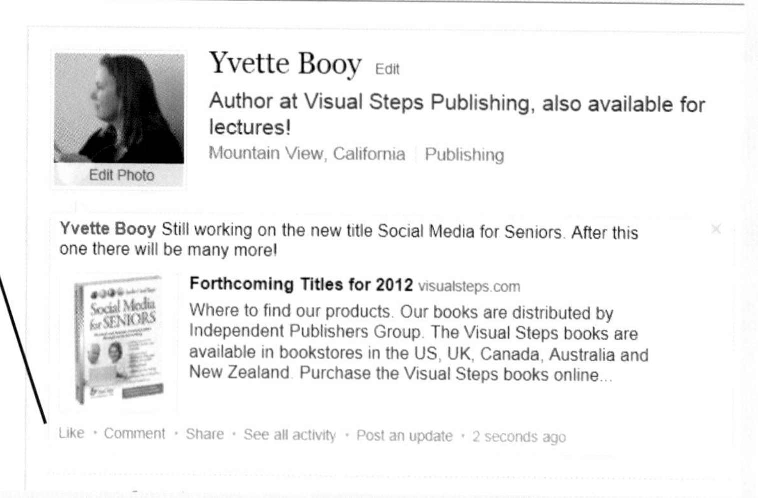

By using the link See all activity, people can view your recent activity on *LinkedIn*.

The link Post an update will not be visible to your connections. You can use this link to post a new status update.

Tip

Profile views

On your home page you can see how many people have visited your profile and how often your profile has shown up in search results:

Who's Viewed Your Profile?

2 Your profile has been viewed by 2 people in the past 90 days.

3 You have shown up in search results 3 times in the past 90 days.

This information is called the *profile stats*.

Click Your profile has been viev

Here you can see who has viewed your profile. Sometimes, you will see a name with a headline and a photo, but you can also tell if **Someone on LinkedIn** or **Someone in the Writing and Editing industry from United States** has viewed your profile.

You can determine what information is displayed when you have viewed somebody else's profile:

Open the *Settings* page 7

By PRIVACY CONTROLS**, click** Select what others see when you've viewed their profile

You can select these options:

What others see when you've viewed their profile

- your name and professional headline:
- your anonymous profile characteristics:
- nothing:

Your name and headline (Recommended)
Yvette Booy
Author at Visual Steps Publishing, also available for lectures!
San Francisco Bay Area

Anonymous profile characteristics such as industry and title
Note: Selecting this option will disable Profile Stats.
Someone on LinkedIn

You will be totally anonymous.
Note: Selecting this option will disable Profile Stats.

Please note: selecting the last two options will disable the *Profile Stats* function. You will no longer be able to see who has visited your profile.

- Continue on the next page -

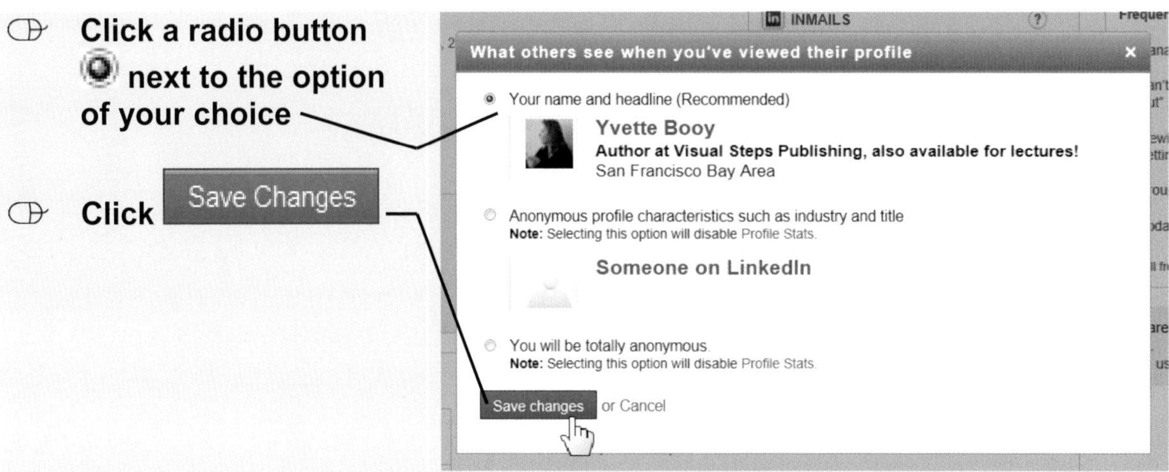

Please note: if the persons who have viewed your profile, have selected the second or third option themselves, you will still not be able to see who they are.

3. Twitter

Twitter is a social network site, developed around the answer to just one simple question: 'What are you doing?' Users, also called twitterers, can write messages consisting of 140 characters or less. Subjects can range from just about anything under the sun, from interesting to less interesting topics. Bits of news, tips and website links can be exchanged very rapidly. There is no need to spend a lot of time creating a long post. You just say what you are up to and leave it at that.

Twitter's goal is to build a network of followers and people whom you follow yourself. Followers read your messages (tweets) and you read the tweets of the people you follow.

This way, you can easily keep in touch with your friends and family, or your customers, if you use *Twitter* for business purposes or your fans if you are an artist, musician or celebrity. You can also use *Twitter* to react to current events in a simple way. For instance, during a TV news show or entertainment program, a radio program, or in regard to a website, newspaper or magazine.

This chapter will show you how to create an account, write a post, follow other people and respond to other people's messages. We also provide a number of tips for using *Twitter* for commercial purposes.

In this chapter you will learn how to:

- create an account;
- sign in with *Twitter*;
- find and follow other twitterers;
- post tweets;
- reply to messages, use @Mentions and direct messages;
- retweet messages;
- delete messages;
- add photos to a tweet;
- modify your profile;
- modify e-mail messages;
- invite followers;
- delete an account;
- use *Twitter* for commercial purposes.

Please note:

Twitter is subject to constant changes. The windows on your own screen may look different from the examples in this book. If you cannot find a specific button, it may be located somewhere else in the window.

3.1 Creating an Account

If you want to be able to use *Twitter* yourself (post messages) you will need to have an account. First, you go to the website, where you can create an account:

Open the www.twitter.com website [1]

You will see the *Twitter* home page. To create your own account:

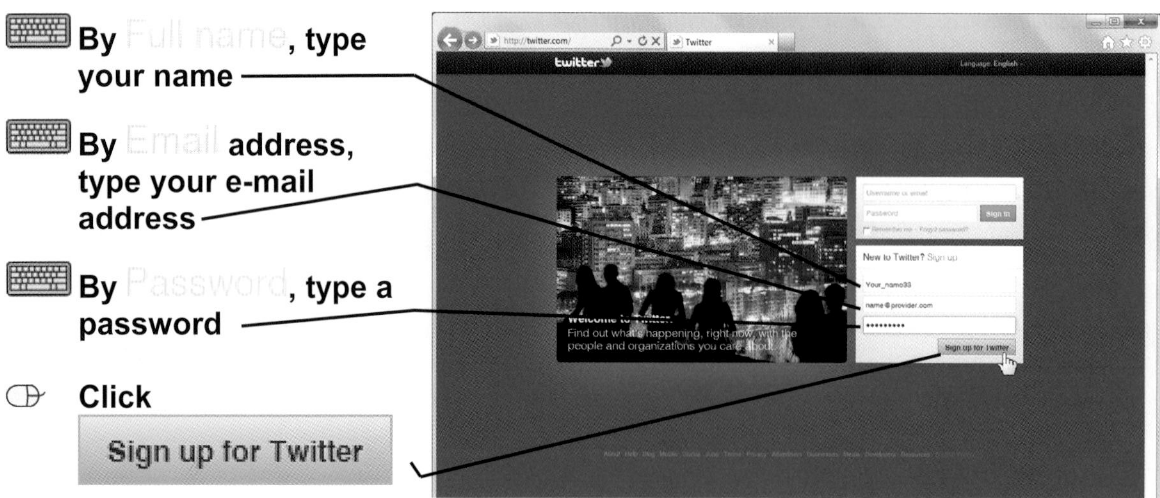

By Full name**, type your name**

By Email **address, type your e-mail address**

By Password**, type a password**

Click Sign up for Twitter

If you are using *Internet Explorer 8,* you may see a security warning message:

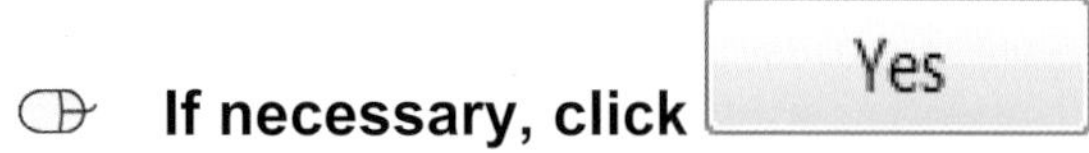

If necessary, click Yes

In the next window you will see the information you have just entered.

By Full name, type your name

Uncheck the box ☑ next to Keep me logged-in on t

Click **Create my account**

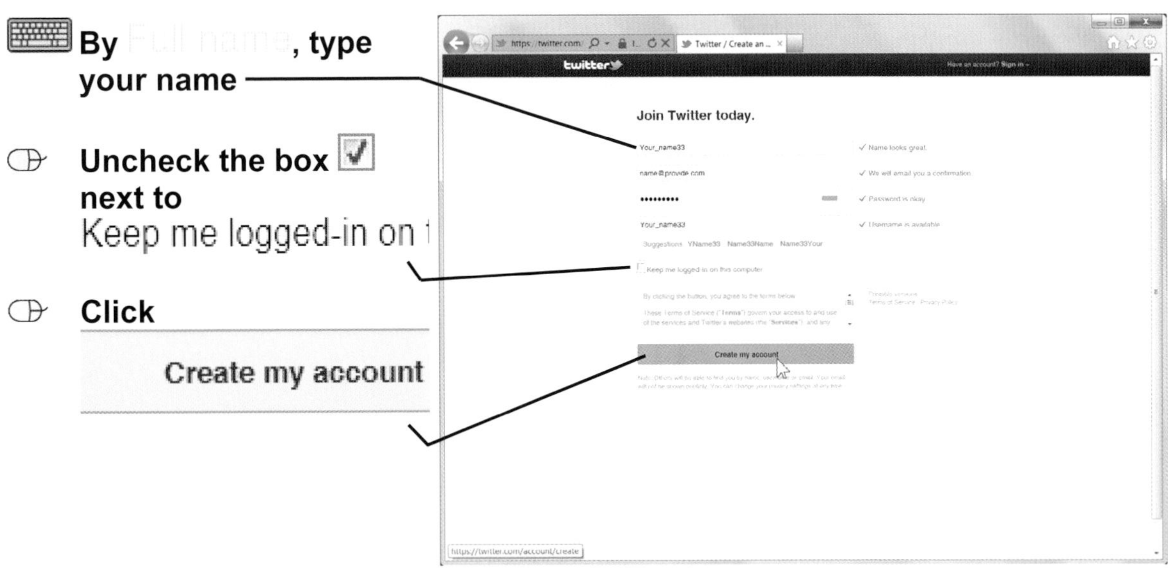

HELP! User name already exists

If the user name you have chosen is already in use, you will see the following message ✖ This username is already taken!. Then you will need to choose a different user name.

By , type a different user name

If you uncheck the box ☑ next to Keep me logged-in on this computer., you can make sure that other users of your computer cannot use your *Twitter*-account.

Write down your user name and password on paper and store it in a safe place

You will see this page:

Click **Next**

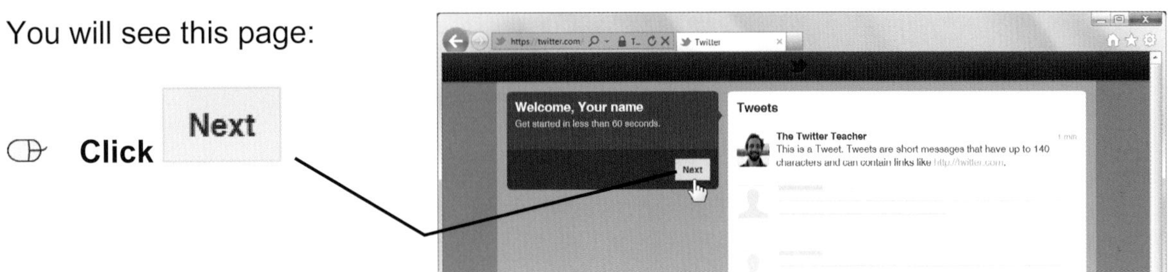

You will see a list of suggestions of other *Twitter* accounts to follow. For now, you do not need to do this:

Click 

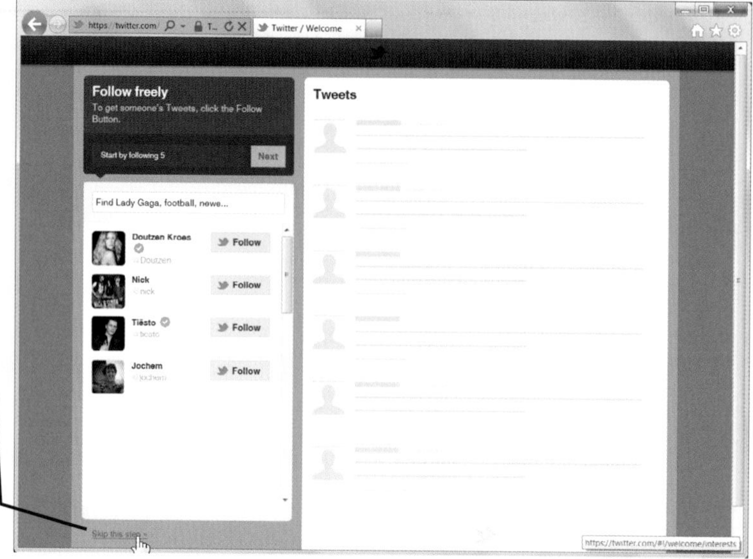

In the following windows you can select categories with various subjects you might be interested in and let the program search automatically for contacts. For now, this will not be necessary. In the bottom of the window:

Click Skip this step » twice

Your account has been created. You can now sign out. In the top right of the window:

HELP! I see a security window

If you are using *Internet Explorer 8,* you may see a security warning message once in a while. To display all the information in the windows, you need to click the No button.

You have created a *Twitter* account. A confirmation e-mail has been sent to your mail address. This e-mail contains a hyperlink with which you can activate your account.

Open the e-mail message from *Twitter* in your e-mail program

HELP! No e-mail message

It may take a while for you to receive the *Twitter* e-mail message. If you have not received a message after some time, you should check the folder with unwanted (junk) e-mail messages. Sometimes the confirmation e-mail message ends up in the junk bin.

Click the link

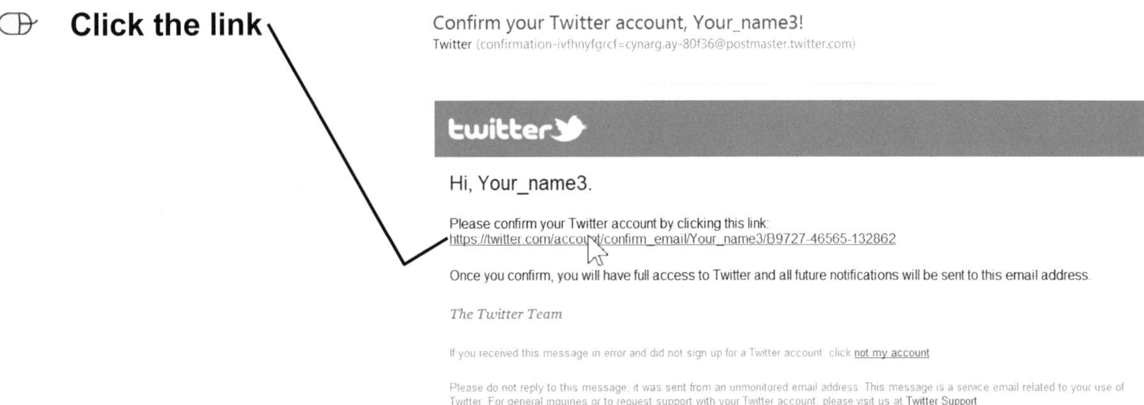

A new tab or window will be opened. You can close this:

If a new tab is opened:

Click

If a new window is opened:

Click

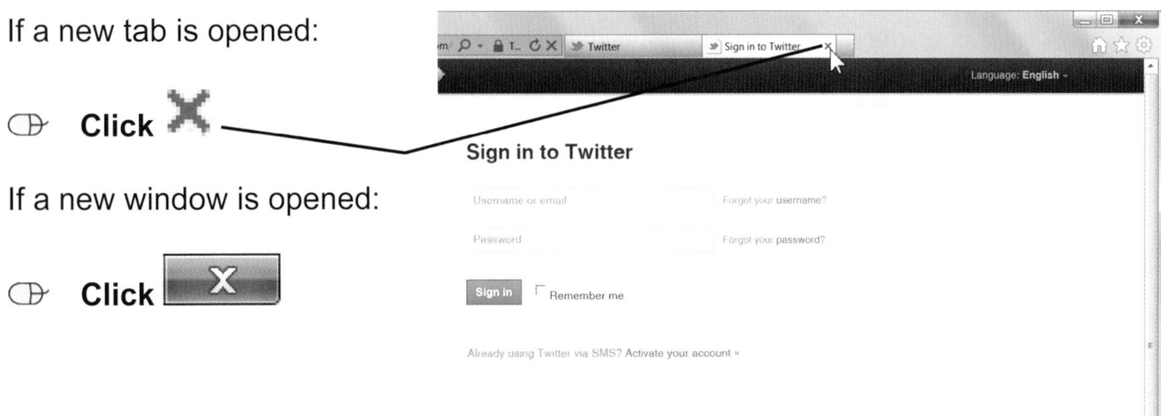

Close the windows of your e-mail program

In the next section you will sign in with *Twitter* and start using the social network.

3.2 Sign In

If you want to use *Twitter*, you will need to sign in with your account. You can do that in the *Twitter* window that is still open:

In the top right of the window:

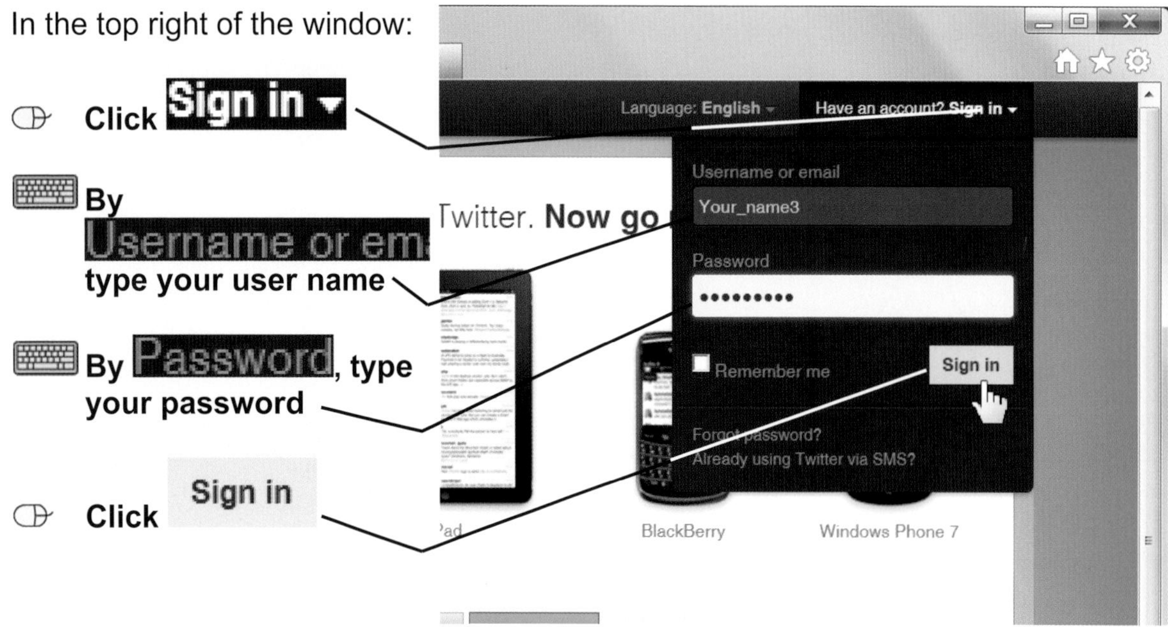

Click Sign in

By Username or em **type your user name**

By Password**, type your password**

Click Sign in

You may be asked whether you want *Internet Explorer* to remember the password. In this example we will choose not to let the program store the password. If you let the program store your data, other people who use your computer may be able to use your *Twitter* account without you knowing it.

In the message bar in *Internet Explorer 9*:

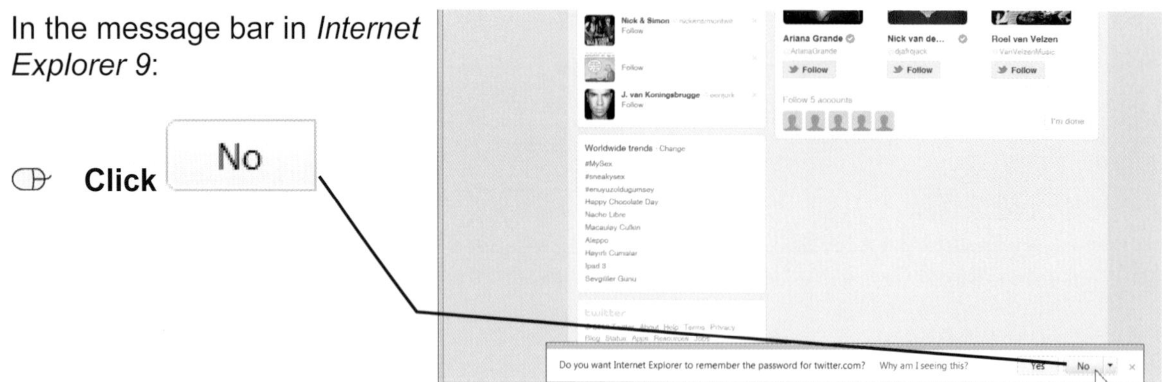

Click No

If you are using an earlier version of *Internet Explorer* you may see a small window:

Click No

You will see the following window:

You may also see a yellow bar at the top, where Twitter asks you to confirm your e-mail address. But you just did this:

This message will disappear by itself, as you use *Twitter* more often.

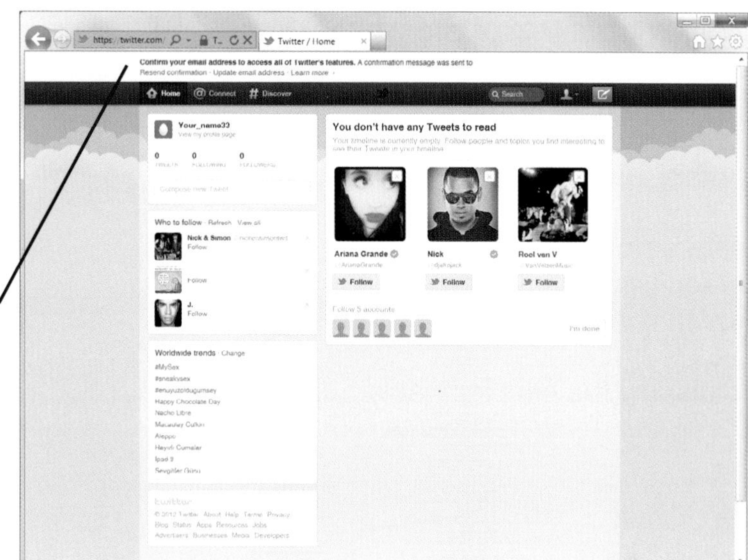

HELP! I see a security window

You may also see a security window now and then. To display all the information in every window, you can click the No button.

3.3 Deciding who to follow

Following people who post interesting messages on *Twitter* is a lot of fun. Visual Steps also has a *Twitter page*. By way of practice, you can follow Visual Steps:

In the top right of the window, in the search box:

Type: `visual steps`

Press Enter

Tip

Search box

In this example you are going to search for Visual Steps. But if you want, you can also search for family members, friends, movies stars, celebrities, artists, musicians, TV programs, journalists, sports stars, etc.

There are two lists of search results: tweets and people. On the right-hand side you will see the tweets that contain the keyword:

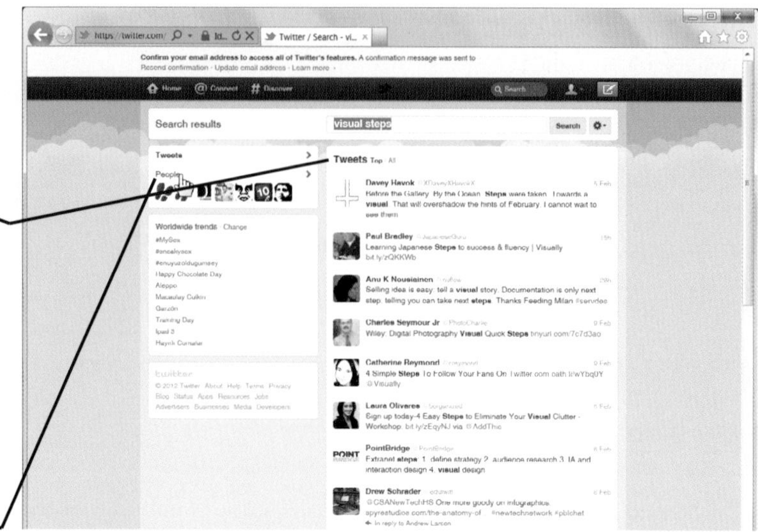

Please note: your own screen will display different search results.

To display the people, that is to say, the *Twitter* accounts:

Click People

On the right-hand side of the window, by

Click **Visual Steps**

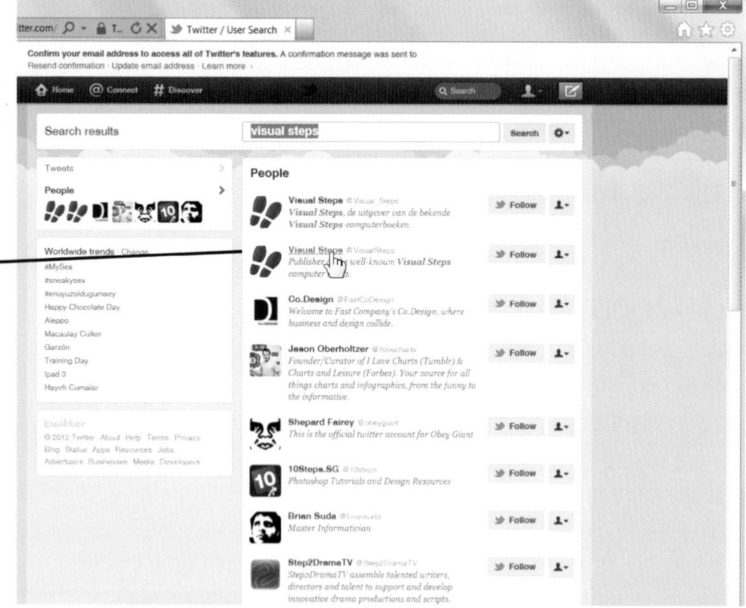

Please note: You can recognize Visual Steps by this image . There are two accounts, an English and a Dutch account. Select the English account **Visual Steps** @VisualSteps.

You will see a window overlaying the current page containing a summary of the most recent messages:

To follow Visual Steps:

Click 

Now you have become a Visual Steps follower. You can tell this because you see the **Following** button:

You can close this window:

🖱 **Click** ✖

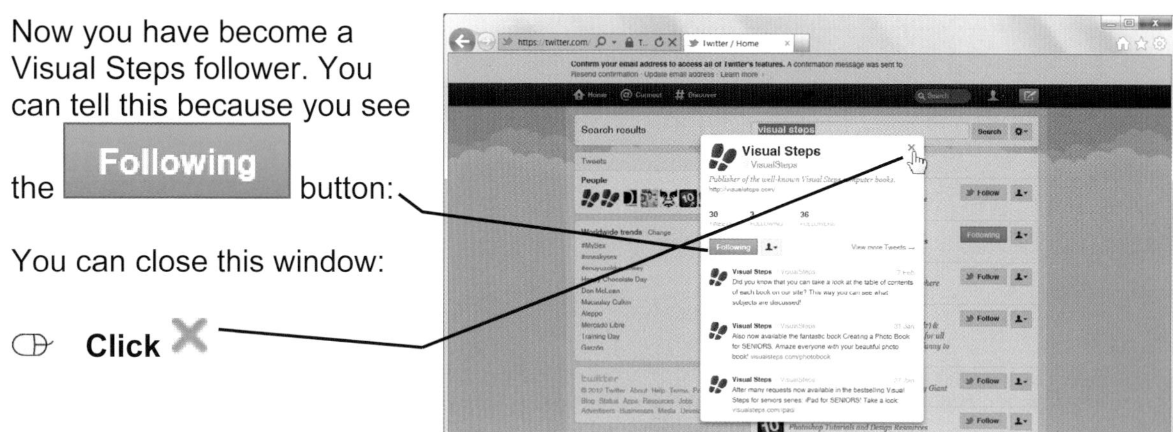

From now on, the home page will display the tweets sent by Visual Steps. This is how you open this page:

🖱 **Click** **Home**

Whenever Visual Steps publishes a new tweet, this tweet will be included in your timeline:

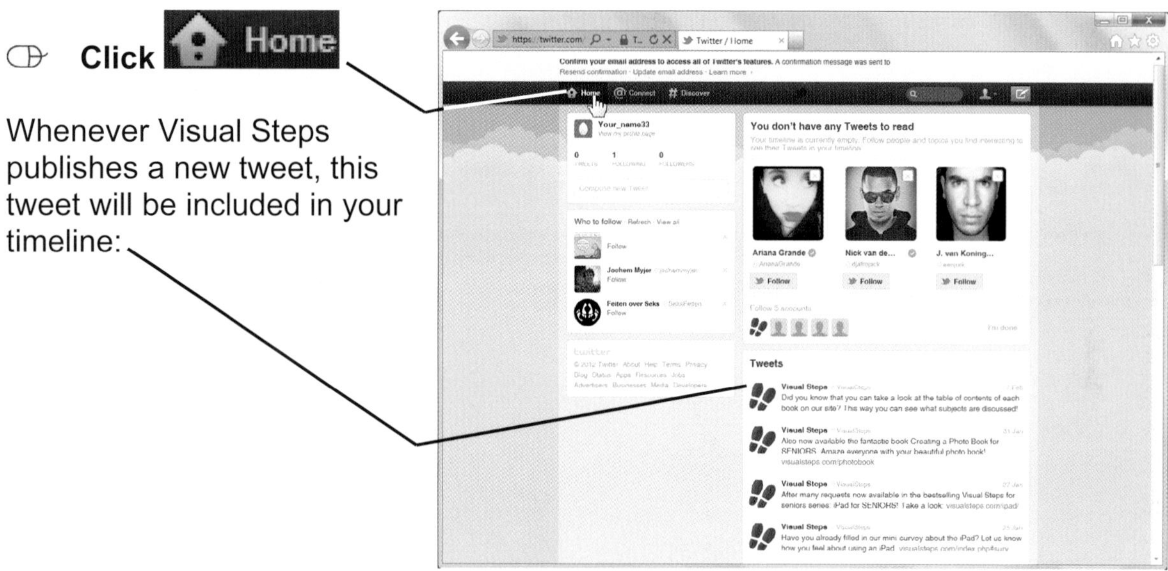

In this way you can follow several other people or topics. For instance, family members, friends, movie stars, artists, TV shows or a sports star. We recommend that you follow at least four other accounts. If you do this, your window will look similar to the examples shown in this book.

☞ **Follow at least four other *Twitter* accounts** 6

Pending
Other *Twitter* users may have determined that they need to approve a follower first.

In that case, you will not see **Following** on your screen, but **Pending**.
After such a user has accepted the request, the tweets will appear in your timeline.

Return to the home page 14

Now your timeline will also display the tweets of the other people you follow. In the next section you will learn how to publish your very first tweet.

3.4 Publish Your First Tweet

It is very simple to publish a message, also called *tweet*. Here is how to do that:

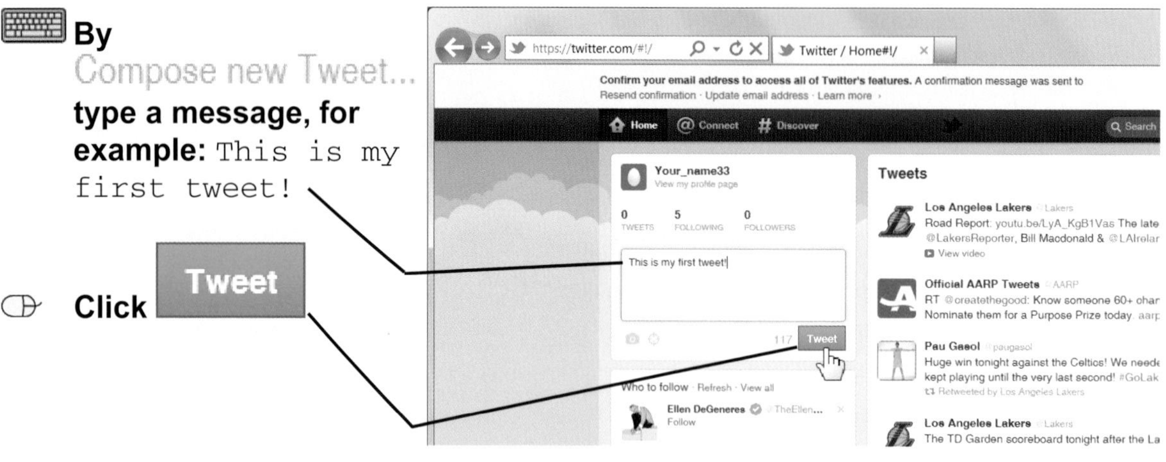

140 characters
A tweet cannot contain more than 140 characters.

You will see your tweet appear in the **Tweets** section:

The tweet may not appear at once. If necessary, try clicking the or button in the address bar to refresh the page.

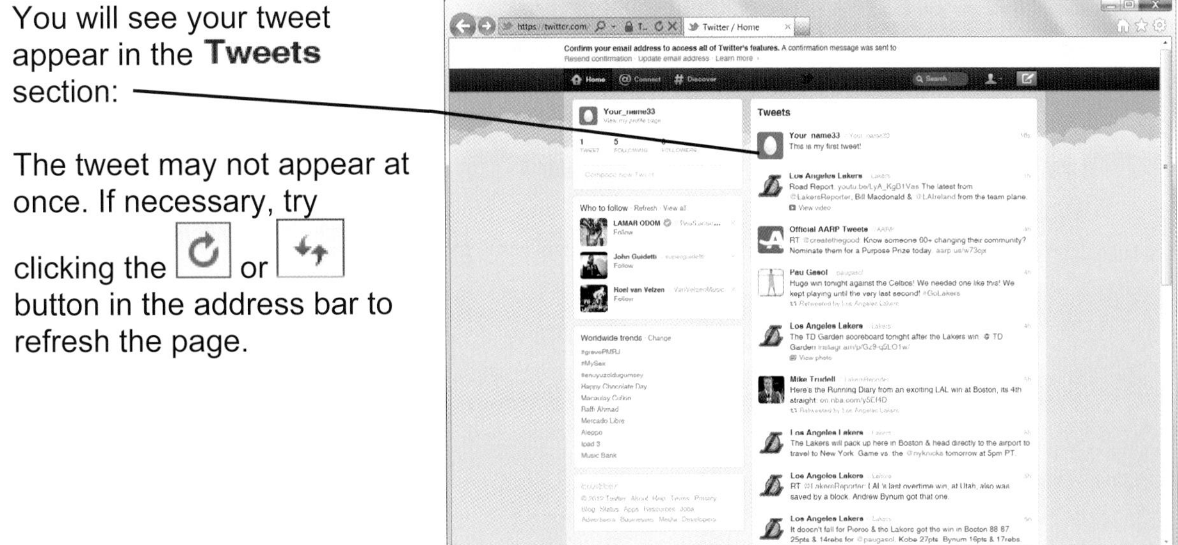

3.5 Reacting to Tweets by Replying to Messages

There are several ways in which you can react to other people's tweets.

- through a reply;
- through @Mentions;
- through a direct (private) message.

You can practice sending a message by sending one to Visual Steps with the Reply function. To do this, you will need to open the Visual Steps page:

Click FOLLOWING

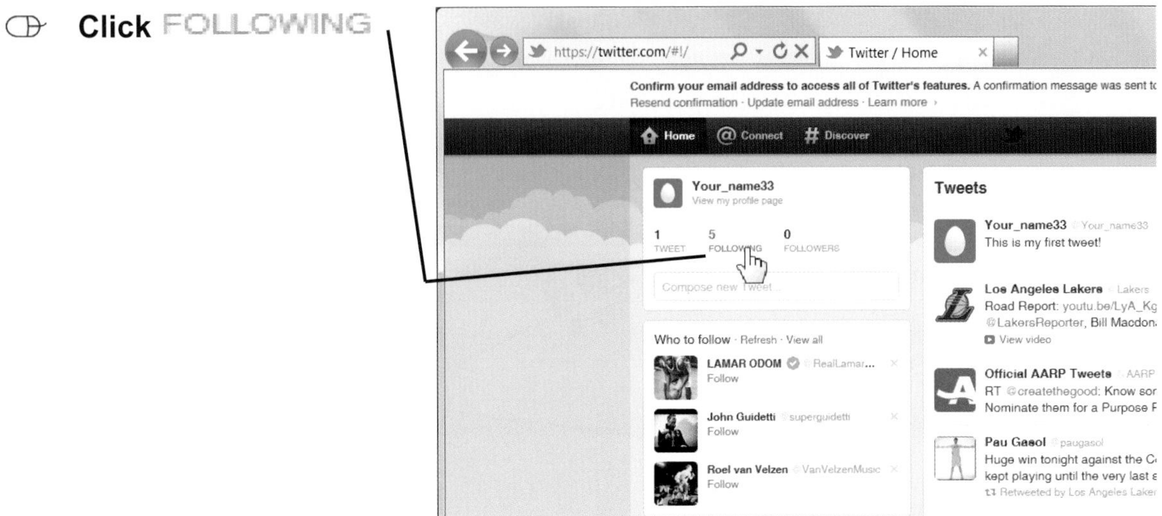

Click Visual Steps

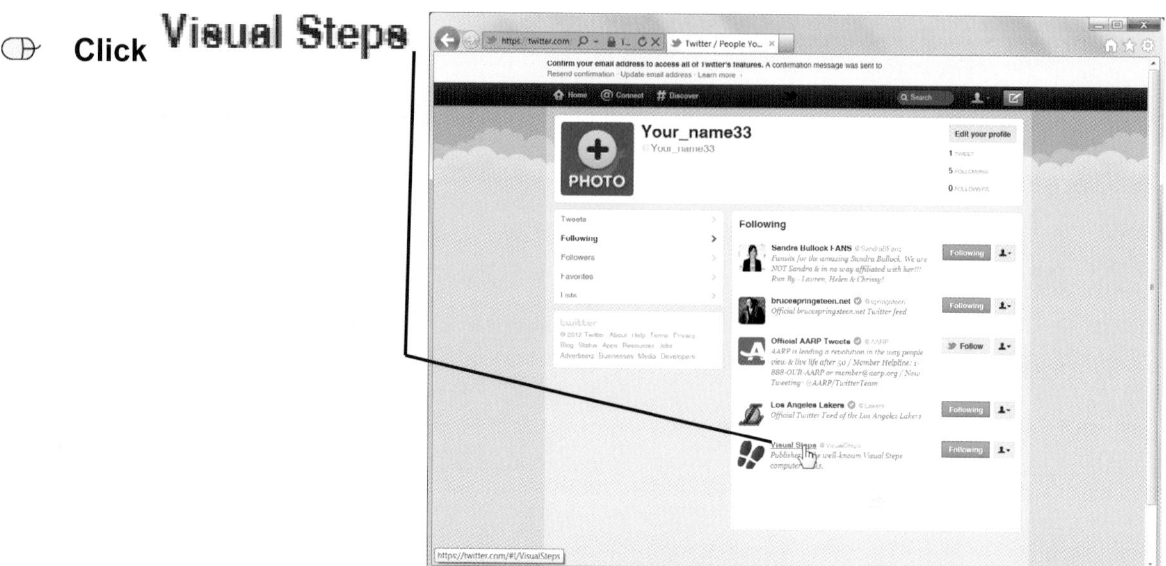

Click View more Tweets

Now the Visual Steps page will be opened:

Position the pointer on a tweet

You will see a small menu:

Click Reply

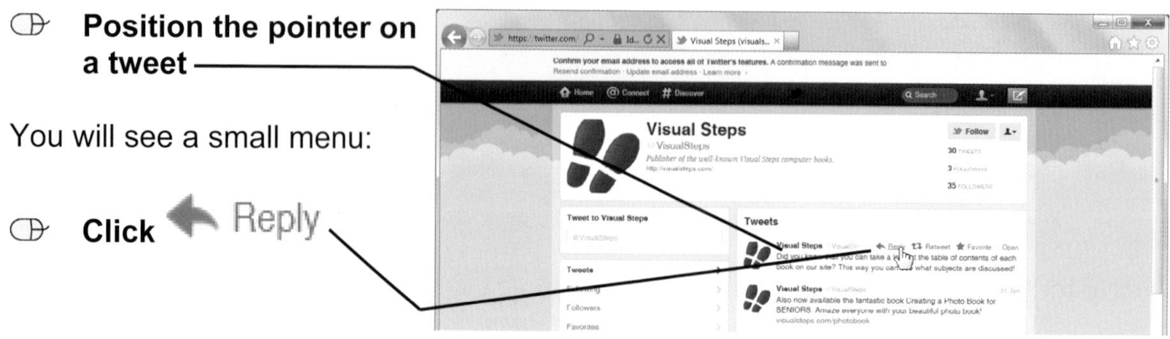

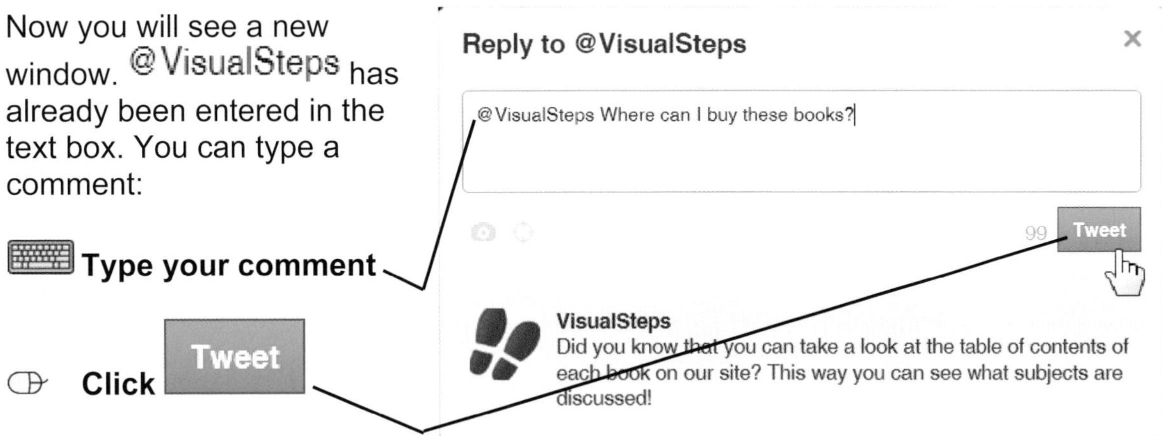

Now you will see a new window. @VisualSteps has already been entered in the text box. You can type a comment:

Type your comment

Click **Tweet**

Please note:

A reply always starts with the user name, in this example @VisualSteps. If you place the @VisualSteps user name in the middle of the message, it will turn into a @Mention. In the next section, you can read more about this type of tweet.

The message is sent to @VisualSteps. Now you can return to your own *Twitter* page:

Click **Home**

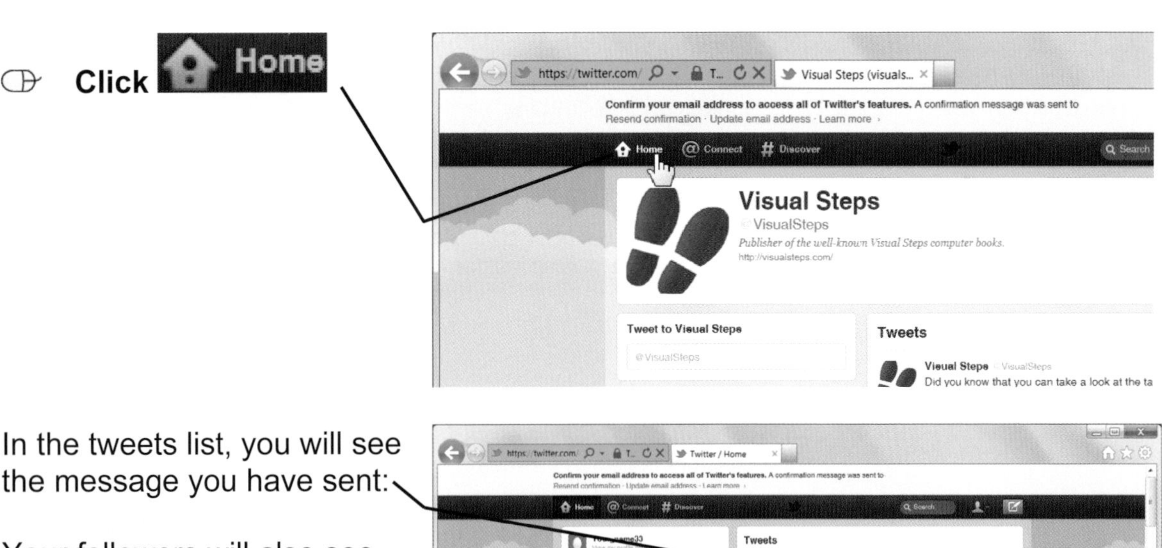

In the tweets list, you will see the message you have sent:

Your followers will also see this message appear in their timeline.

Please note:

A reply that is sent in this way is not just visible to Visual Steps. The tweet also appears in your timeline. The people who follow you on *Twitter* will see your reply in their timeline.

Tip

Private message

If you want to send a message that is only visible to one specific recipient, it is better to send a direct (private) message. See *section 3.7 Sending a Direct Message*.

Tip

Where can I find the message?

Visual Steps will only see this message appear in their timeline if they follow you. If they do not follow you, they will only see the replies to tweets in the Mentions section. In the next section you will learn more about what mentions are.

If you react to a tweet in the manner described above, you will get a reaction quite soon. Because this is just a practice tweet to Visual Steps, you will not receive a reaction.

3.6 Reacting to Tweets with @Mentions

Another way of replying to the tweets of another *Twitter* user is by using the @Mentions option anywhere in the body of the message. Not only can you use @Mentions when you reply to a tweet, but also when creating a new tweet yourself:

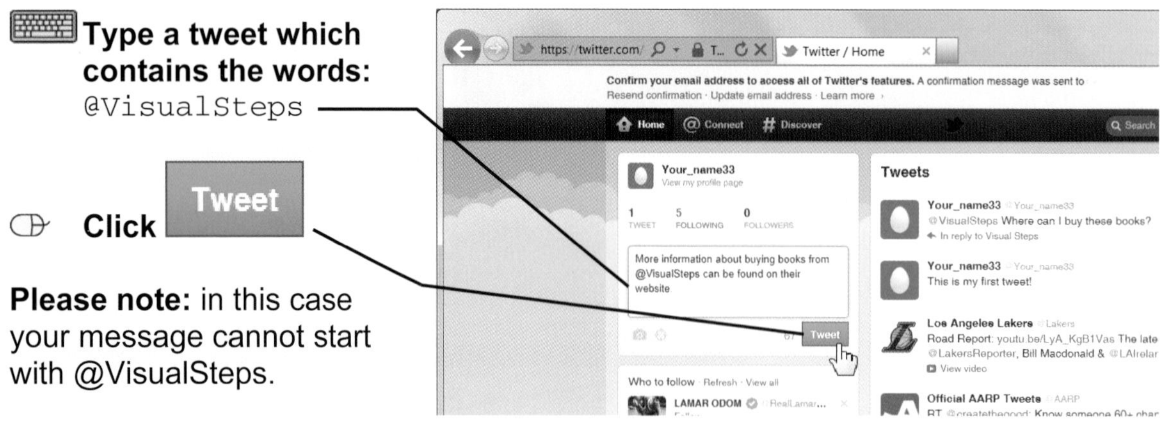

Type a tweet which contains the words:
`@VisualSteps`

Click Tweet

Please note: in this case your message cannot start with @VisualSteps.

The message will be sent and is included in your timeline. This means all your followers will also see this message in their timeline. If the person mentioned by you in your tweet with the @Mentions is not following you, he will be able to find the tweet through @ Connect, Mentions.

Tip

@Mentions

Are you wondering how to view the tweets that are addressed to you or mention your name by people you do not follow yourself?

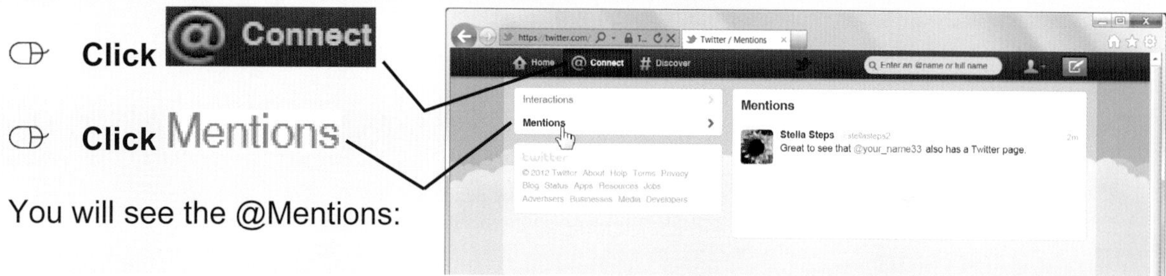

Click Connect

Click Mentions

You will see the @Mentions:

Please note:

A reply to a tweet and a @Mentions name will both be listed on the Mentions page. You will not get a message when a @Mentions or a reply to a tweet have been received. So you will need to regularly click Mentions to see whether you have received a reply or are mentioned in someone else's tweets.

3.7 Sending a Direct Message

You can also send a direct message to the people who are following you on *Twitter*. This is a type of message that can only be viewed by the recipient.

Please note:

If you have not yet acquired any followers, you can just read through this section.

This is how you send a direct message:

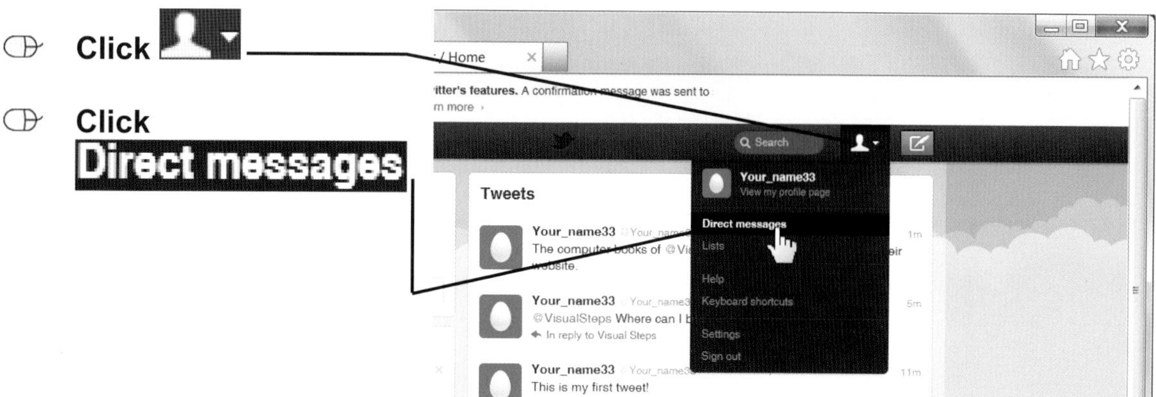

Click

Click Direct messages

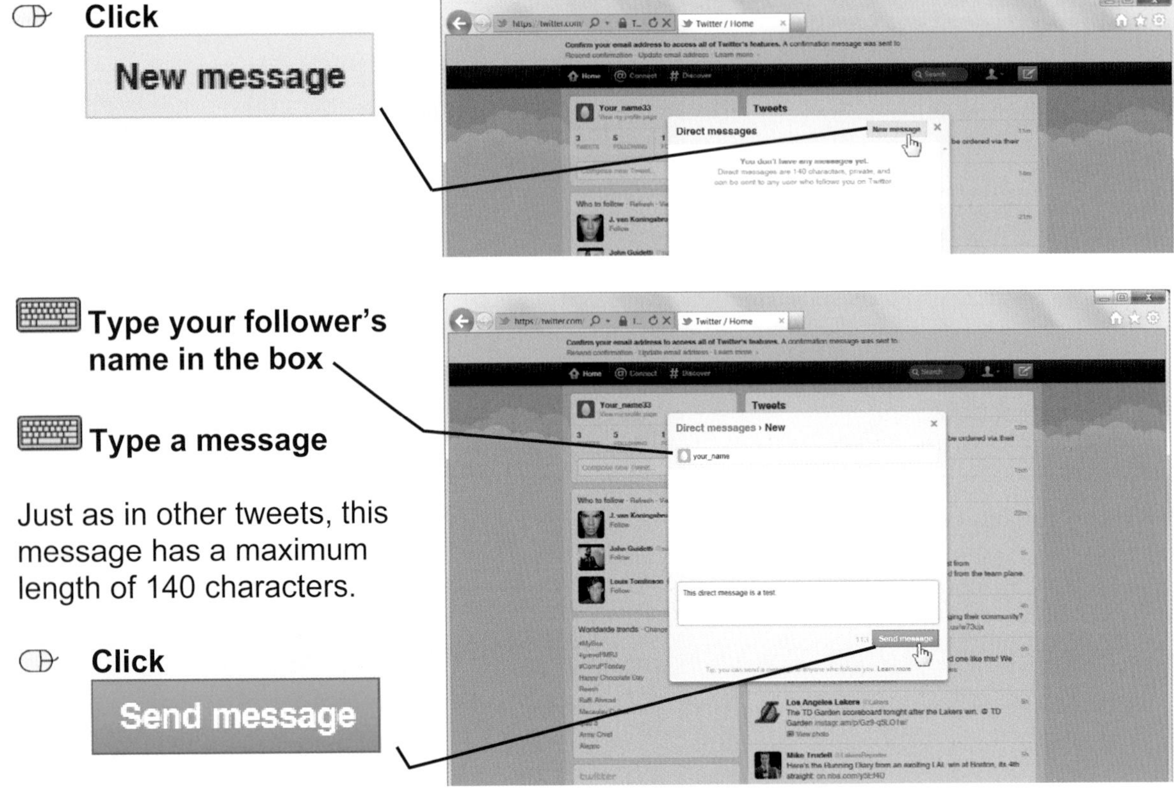

Click **New message**

Type your follower's name in the box

Type a message

Just as in other tweets, this message has a maximum length of 140 characters.

Click **Send message**

HELP! Error message

Do you see this message?

You can't send a message to a user who is not following you.

Then you have mistakenly selected someone you follow yourself, instead of a follower. You can only send a direct message to your own followers.

Now a conversation will be opened. This way, the follower will be able to react to your message right away:

You can close this window:

Click ✕

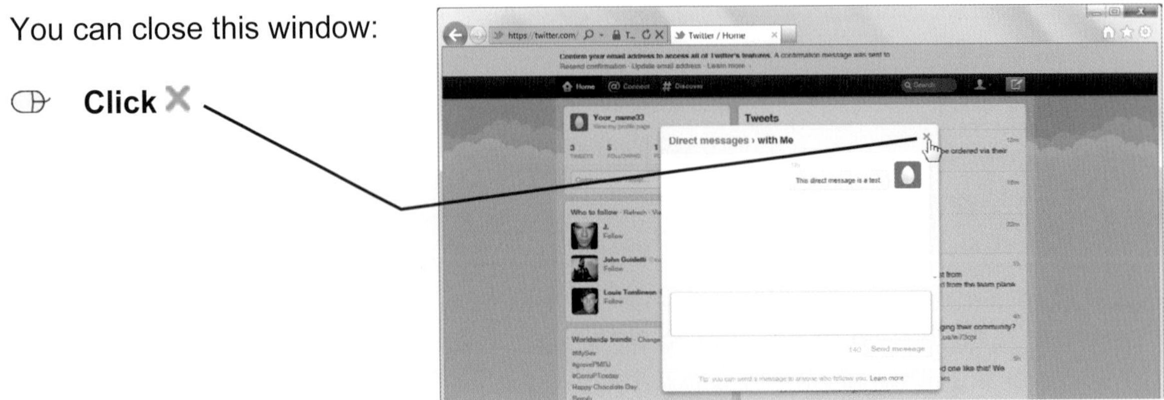

 **Tip**

View the Direct Messages you have received

Here is how to view the Direct Messages you have received:

- **Click** , **Direct messages**
- **Click the follower**

You will see the conversation. You can react to a message in the same way you learned earlier on in this section.

 **Tip**

Delete message

Both the sender and recipient will be able to delete the message. If the recipient deletes the message, this message will also disappear from the sender's inbox; and vice versa. This is how you delete a message:

- **Position the pointer on a direct message**
- **To the left of the direct message, click**
- **Click** Delete message

 **Tip**

Direct message through a tweet

You can also send a direct message to your followers by using the text box of your regular tweets. A direct message always has the following structure:

DM @name message or dm @name message

DM stands for *Direct Message*, or in other words, a private message.
If you start a tweet with 'DM @VisualSteps', the message will be delivered as a direct message to the Visual Steps address.

Please note: do not forget to type DM or dm, followed by a blank space. If you do, the message will be displayed as a regular message, in all the timelines.

3.8 Retweet

When you have stumbled upon an interesting or funny tweet, you may want all your followers to read this tweet too. You can do this by *retweeting* the message. This means you are going to forward the message as if it were your own tweet. Your followers will see this tweet appear in their timeline.

Here is how to retweet:

Open the www.twitter.com/visualsteps website 1

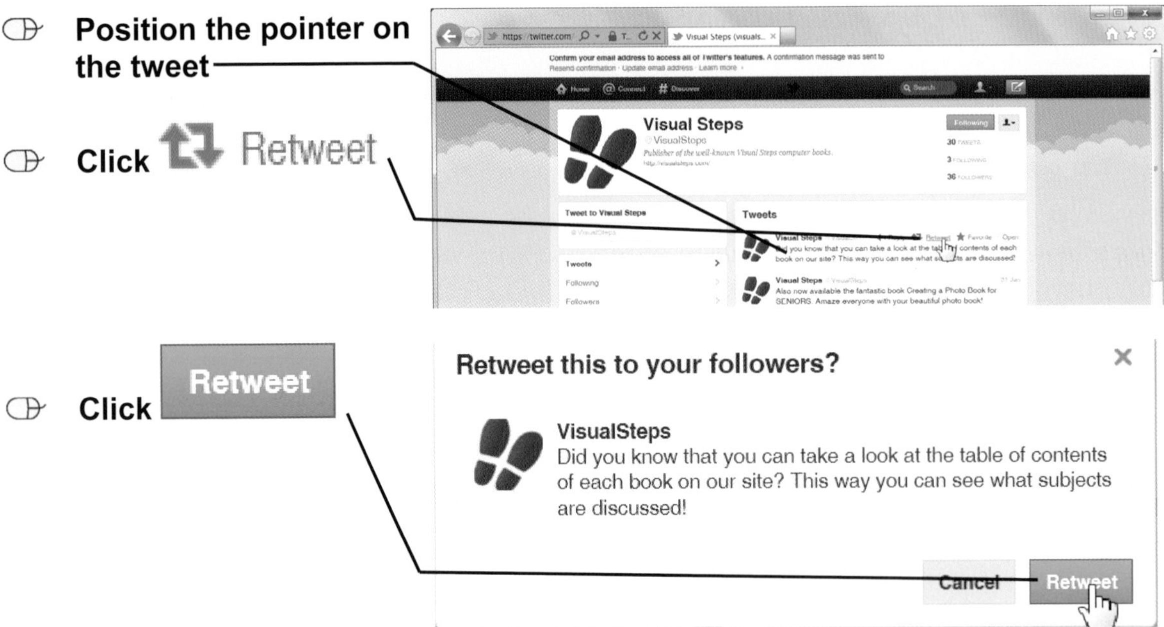

Now the message has been sent and can be viewed by all your followers. Next to the message you will see this symbol: .
You have now learned how to send messages in a variety of different ways. In the next section you will read about deleting messages.

3.9 Deleting a Message

Since many readers will be working through the current chapter, Visual Steps will receive lots of tweets. This is why you can use the practice tweet to learn how to delete a tweet. Here is how you do that:

You will be asked to confirm the deletion:

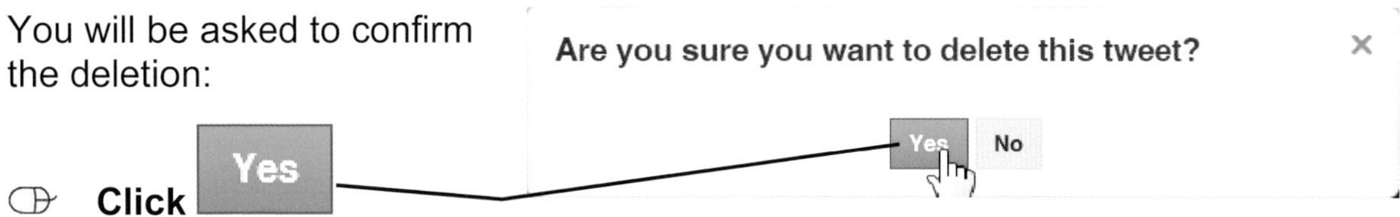

Click **Yes**

The message has been deleted and it will also be deleted by @VisualSteps.

Delete the @Mention too 12

Your retweet is also included in your timeline. But if you follow various *Twitter* users who post a lot of messages, you might find it difficult to retrieve this retweet among the multitude of tweets. You can quickly find this message among your own tweets:

Click TWEETS

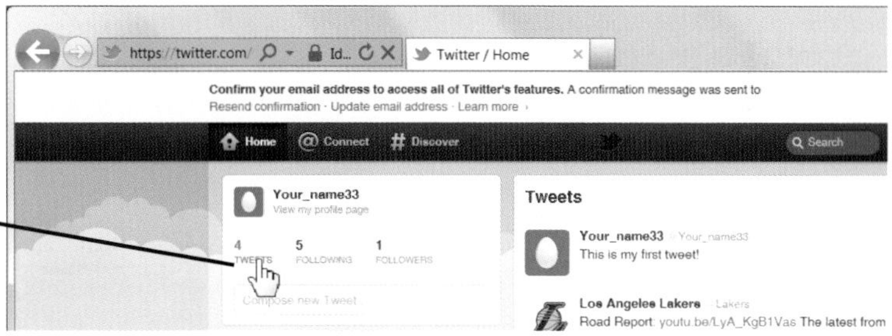

This is how you undo the retweet:

Position the pointer on the message

Click Retweeted

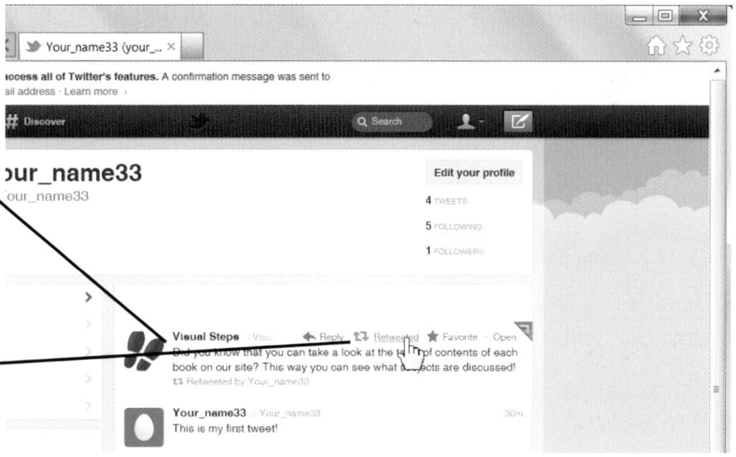

Now the retweet has been undone:

After a while, your retweet will disappear from the timeline of your followers.

Click Home

Tip

Other retweets

To view who has retweeted your tweets, you can visit the 

, Interactions page.

3.10 Add a Photo to Your Tweet

You can also include a link to a photo in your tweet:

By Compose new Tweet... **type a message, for instance:** `Here's another picture of our trip to New York!`

To add the photo:

Click

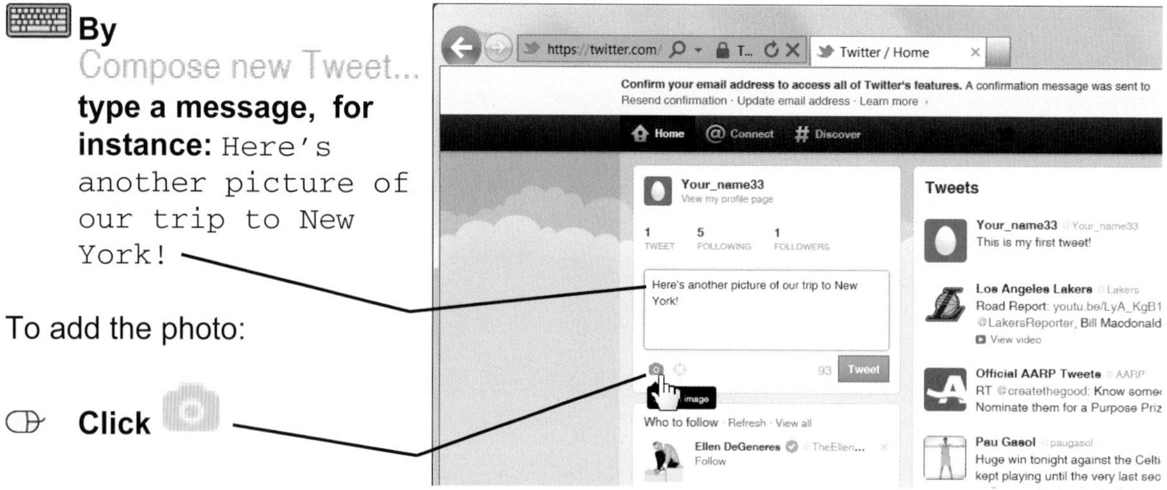

Add the desired picture 5

Now the photo has been added. You will see a message, telling you that the photo will be added as a link. The tweet can be sent:

Click Tweet

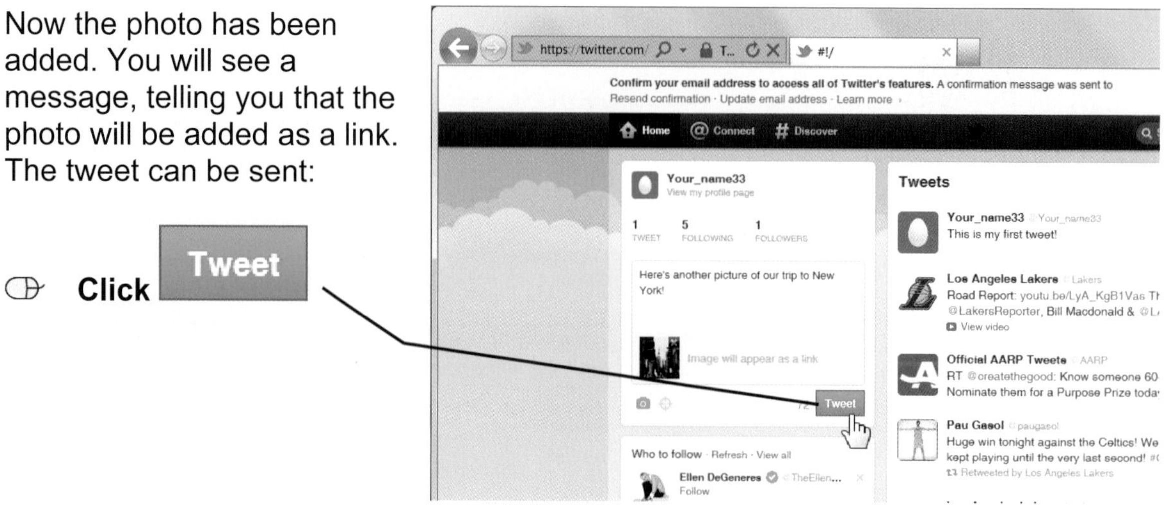

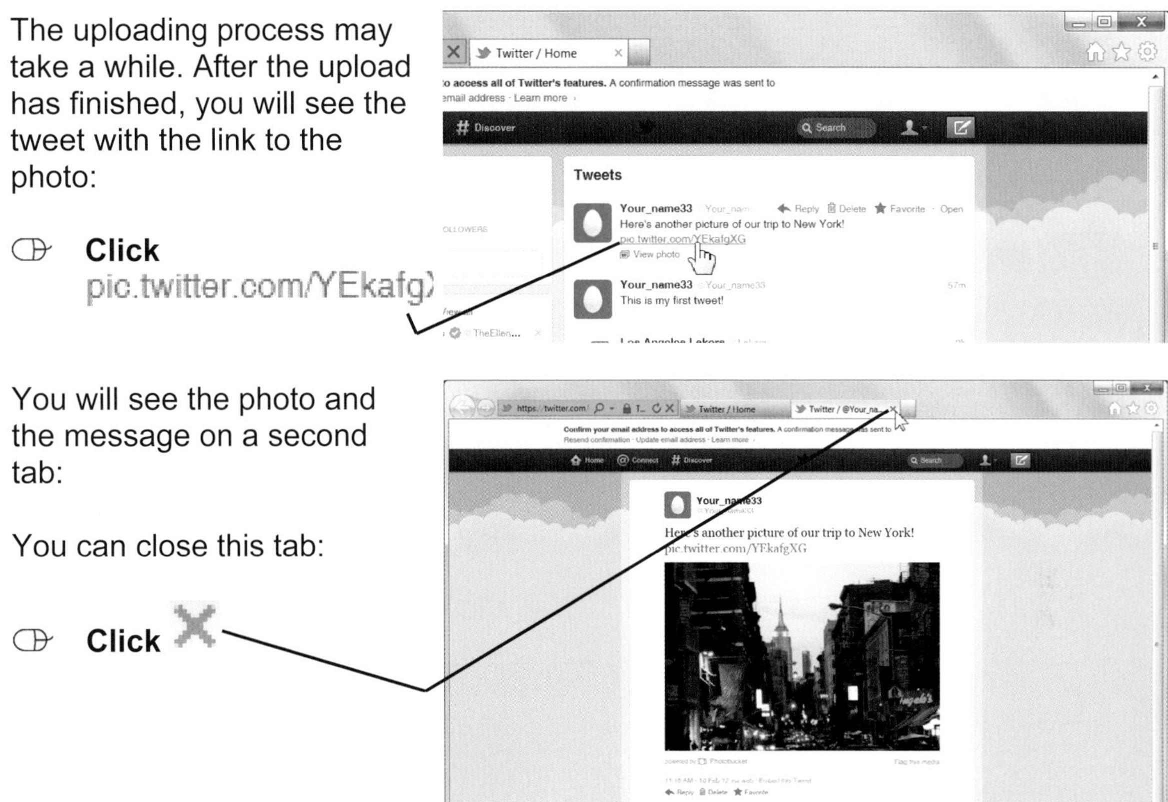

The uploading process may take a while. After the upload has finished, you will see the tweet with the link to the photo:

Click pic.twitter.com/YEkafg)

You will see the photo and the message on a second tab:

You can close this tab:

Click X

3.11 Modifying Your Profile

By now, you have mastered the basic operations in *Twitter*. Before you actually start twittering, you may want to personalize your account by adding a photo.
Please note: the size of the picture cannot be larger than 700 Kb.

Click

Click Settings

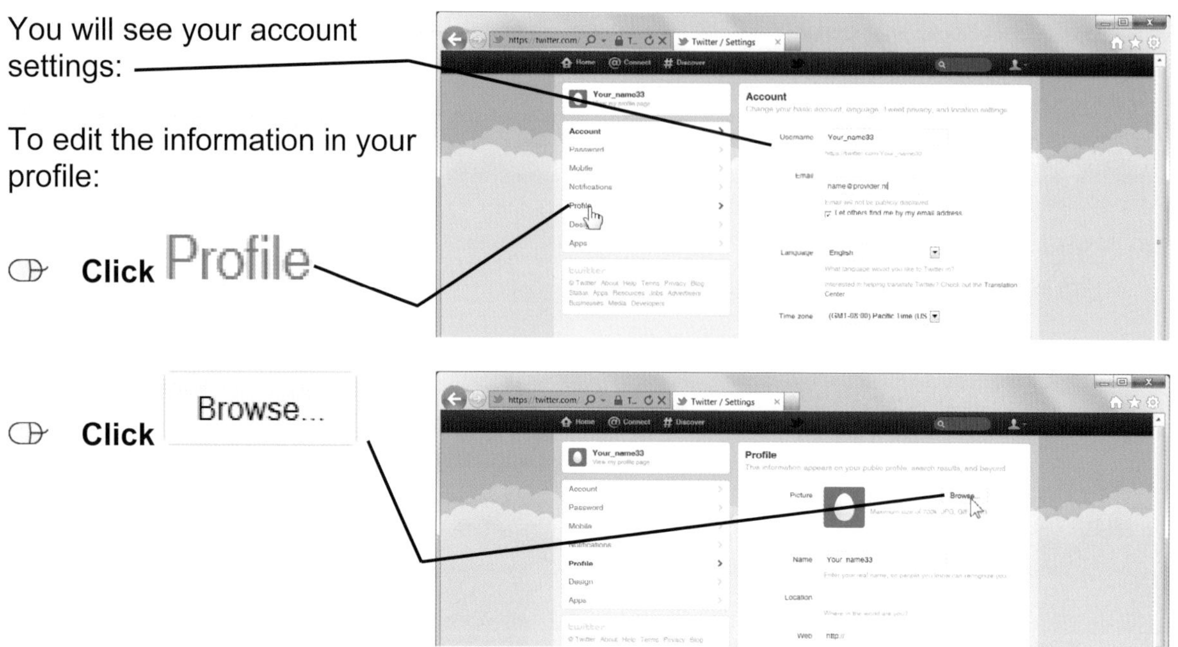

You will see your account settings:

To edit the information in your profile:

- Click **Profile**

- Click **Browse...**

Add the desired image 5

On this page you can add more information about yourself, if you wish. This information will be displayed on your profile page:

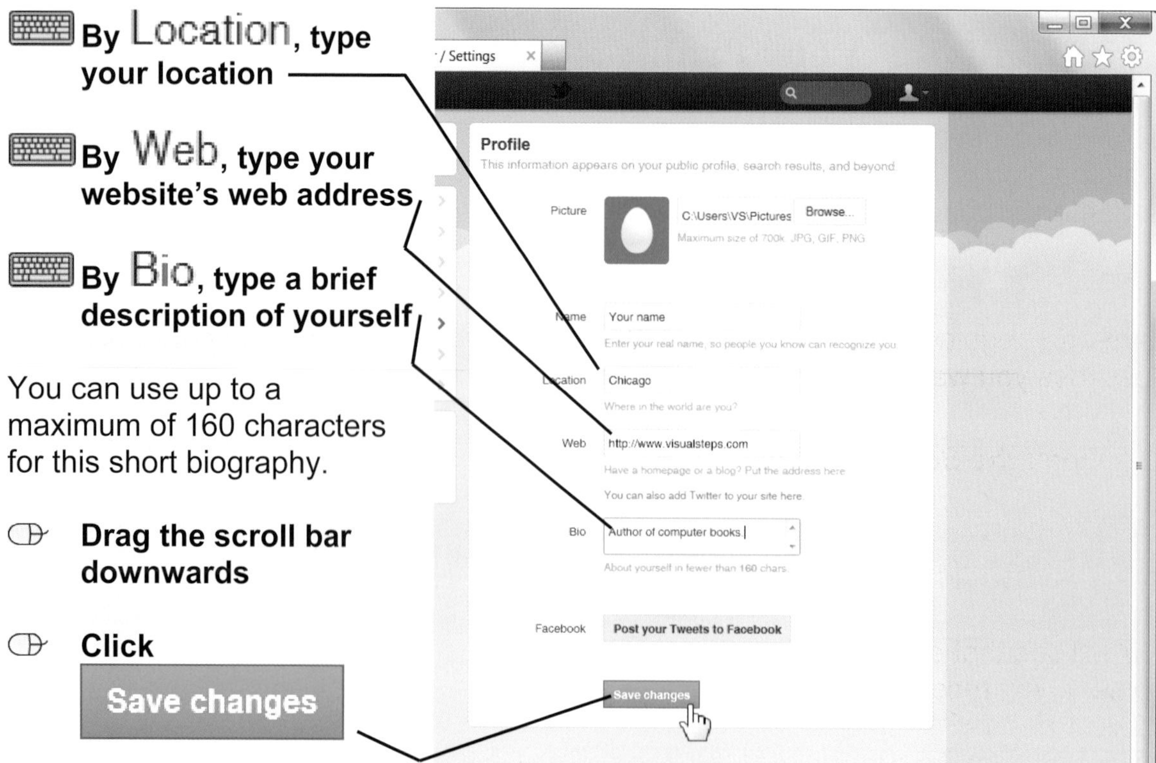

By Location, type your location

By Web, type your website's web address

By Bio, type a brief description of yourself

You can use up to a maximum of 160 characters for this short biography.

- **Drag the scroll bar downwards**

- **Click Save changes**

Tip

Bio

The kind of information you include in your biography will depend on the purpose for which you want to use *Twitter*. If you are just going to use *Twitter* for personal messages, you can add a few keywords to describe yourself and your hobbies. If you want to use *Twitter* for business purposes, it is better to keep the biographic text short and professional: who are you and how can you help your target group?

Now you can take a look at your current profile:

In the top left of the window:

Click

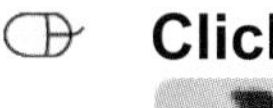

Your name
View my profile page

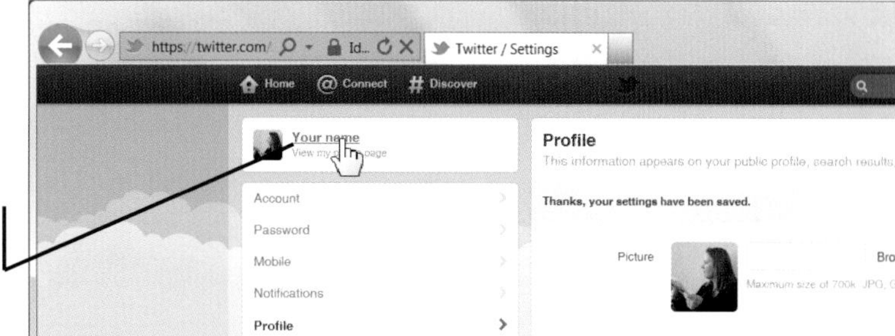

You will see your profile:

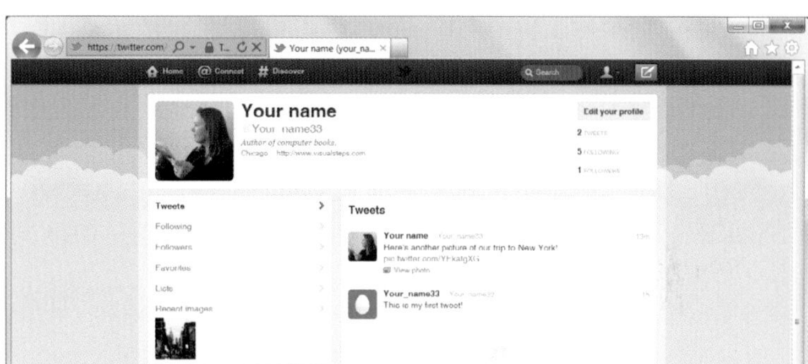

3.12 Modify E-mail Messages

Twitter will regularly send you e-mails. You can determine the number of e-mail messages you want to receive. Here is how to do that:

Open the *Settings* page 13

Click the

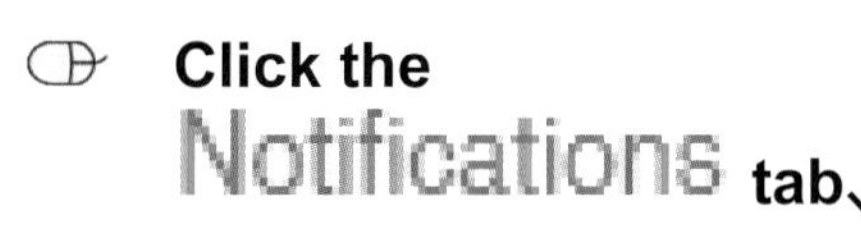

Notifications tab

You will see that at the moment, you receive three different kinds of e-mail messages from *Twitter*:

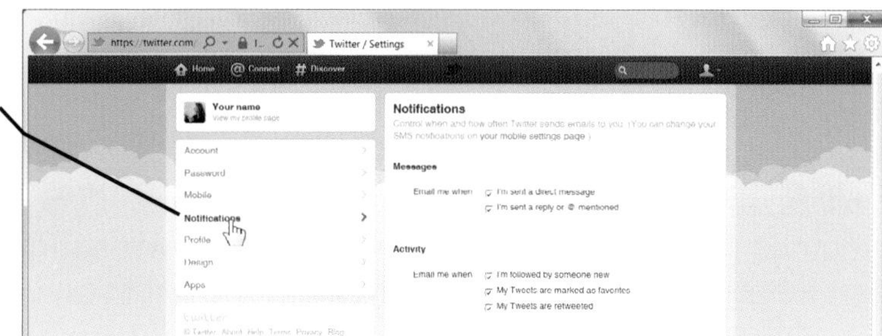

Messages: you receive an e-mail message whenever a direct message, reply or @Mentions message is received.
Activity: you receive an e-mail message when somebody is starting to follow you, when your tweets are selected as a favorite or when your tweet is retweeted.
Updates: you receive a *Twitter* e-mail message when new products, options and tips are available, or when there are product and service updates to be installed.

Uncheck the box ☑ next to the type of e-mails you do not wish to receive

Click Save changes

3.13 Inviting Followers

Meanwhile, your first messages have been published on *Twitter*. Naturally, you would like others to read your tweets, but how are you going to attract followers?

Send your contacts an e-mail with an invitation

Through an e-mail message you can let others know that you have a *Twitter*-account. Include the link to your *Twitter* page in this e-mail message, for example: http://www.twitter.com/Your_name
If the people who are going to follow you have a *Twitter* account themselves, all they need to do is click the Follow button.

Post a link to your *Twitter* page on your own website

On websites you often see the button, or a text such as Follow Visual Steps with Twitter with a link to the relevant *Twitter* page.

Publish a link to your *Twitter* page in your advertisement or newsletter

You can also publish a link to your *Twitter* page in a digital newsletter, whether personal or from you company or business.

It will take time to gather a network of followers. If you actively start using *Twitter*, it becomes more fun and easier to do and you will soon attract new followers. You will then be able to interact and share news, information or tips quite rapidly.

3.14 Deleting an Account

If you want, you can delete (deactivate) your account in the following way. If you do not want to do this, just read through this section.

Please note:

Once your account has been deleted, you will not be able to create a new account with the same e-mail address.

Open the *Settings* page 13

If necessary, drag the scroll bar downwards

Click Deactivate my account

You will be asked if you want to permanently delete your account.

Read the information

If you are sure:

Click Okay, fine, deactivate

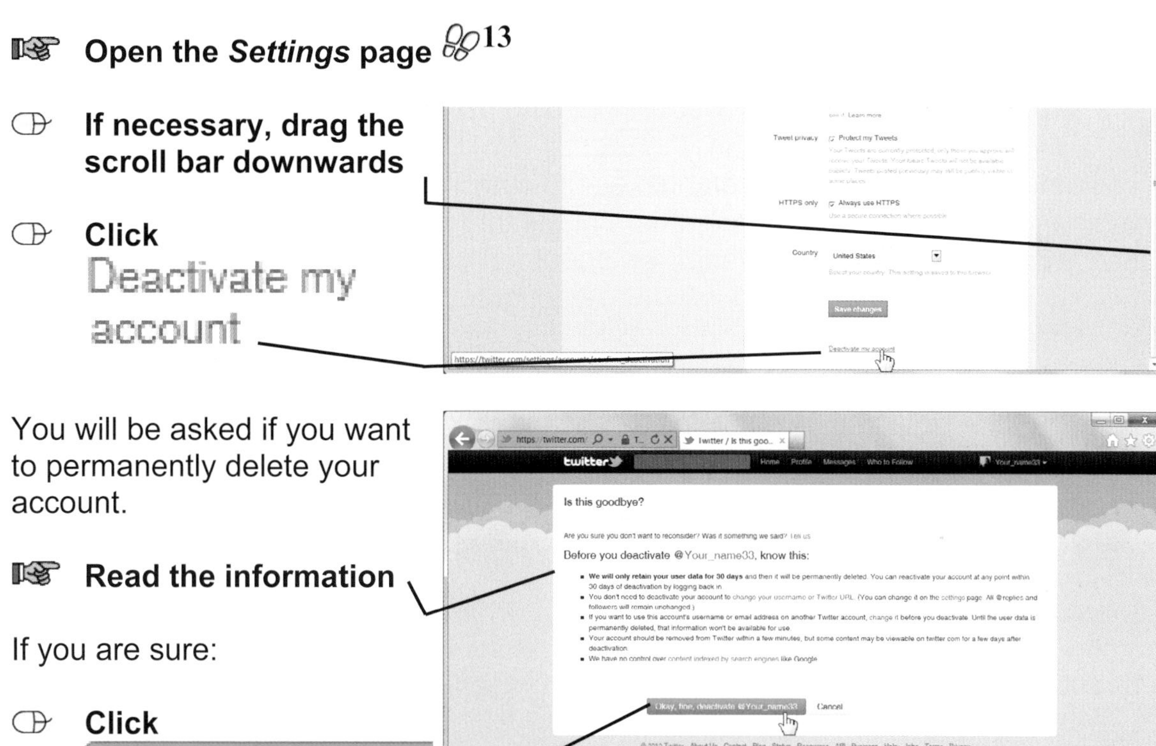

You will see this window:

By Password, **type your password**

Click Deactivate account

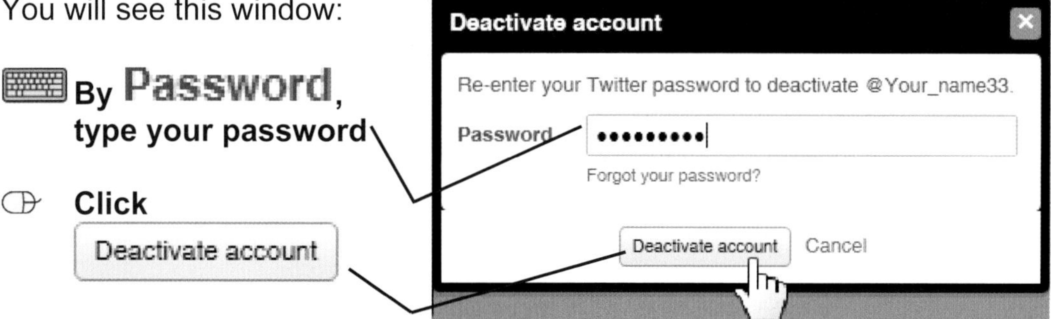

Your account has been deactivated.

Close all windows 4

3.15 Using Twitter for Commercial Purposes

Many companies, brands, organizations and clubs can be found already on *Twitter*. That is not surprising. Many active twitterers have already sent tweets regarding a certain product or business, even before the business itself starts to use *Twitter*.

A business or an organization can use the business' official *Twitter* account to:

- find out what kind of image the company has among the target group (customers or members) by following the tweets regarding this company.
- establishing a bond with the target group by directly engaging in conversation with customers or members (for instance, by the customer service).
- offer a meeting space for the members of the target group, a place where they can 'meet' and exchange experiences about a product or the organization.
- quickly share new information with the target group (customers or members).
- promote a special offer, a new product or an event.

Below you will find a number of tips on what to do and what not to do, if you start to use *Twitter* for your company, organization or club.

Tip

Do it!

1. Search

Search *Twitter* for the name of your company, product, service, organization or club, on a regular basis. You can do this on the *Twitter* home page with the Search button. In the *Tip* at the end of this section you can read how to save a search previously carried out. Also, keep an eye on your @Mentions. Make sure you know what people are saying about your company, product or organization. These messages and comments can provide important feedback for you.

2. Follow

Make sure you are always aware of the current news by following the right people. Follow your competitors, present customers, potential customers and other companies in the same line of business.

3. Answer questions

Try to answer questions within 24 hours, by replying to them or by using @Mentions. Do this in a professional and positive way.

- Continue on the next page -

4. React to compliments and feedback
React within 24 hours, to a compliment or other types of feedback, just with a thank you note, if necessary. Naturally you can also retweet an extremely favorable tweet. The more active you are in sending tweets and reactions, the more your followers will feel that you take them seriously. This will increase the chance of your followers becoming your ambassadors and letting others know about your product or service.

5. React to negative comments
You may also encounter negative comments from people who are not satisfied with a product or service you have provided. Make sure you react at once, be professional and friendly and try to find out why they are not satisfied. Otherwise, a negative tweet can spread like wildfire and lead to all sorts of unpleasant consequences.
Does it, for example, concern a tweet from someone who has not received proper assistance by the helpdesk (whether per e-mail or telephone)? Offer your help by letting people know that the people who work for your company are human and not automated robots. Does somebody have a negative experience with your company, product or service? Offer your apologies and ask whether he needs help in solving a specific problem. Or ask how you will be able to help him in a better way, in the future. Always keep in mind that many people will read these messages.

6. Share the latest news
Twitter is very useful for finding and sharing the most current news. Make sure your followers also get to know the news. Share a photo with a glimpse of your new product. Be the first one to share the information about a forthcoming project on *Twitter*. Are you going to organize an event? Let your followers know what is going on behind the screens.

7. Ask questions
Ask for your followers' opinions, for example, when you are developing a new product or a new service. This way, you will become visible in your followers' timelines, you let them know you appreciate their opinion and at the same time you will be able to gather valuable marketing information.

8. Reward your followers
Publish a tweet with an attractive offer for your followers, every once in a while. For example, a link to a discount coupon or a special code with which you can get a discount in a certain shop or restaurant. These types of tweets can spread rapidly and bring in many new followers.

Tip

Do not do this!

1. Send pointless tweets

Make sure your tweets provide added value for your readers. Find out who your followers are and determine what it is that you want to achieve with your tweets. Your readers will not be interested in your opinions on the current weather or in a description of what you had for lunch. But they will appreciate useful information on the activities of your company, organization or club.

2. Include too many links or send too many retweets

Only include links that are genuinely interesting to your followers and use the tweet to explain why the link is of interest. Do not just link to your own website. A retweet is a great tool for sharing a nice message with your followers but do not use it too often.

3. Send too many messages

If you send too many tweets on the same day, your followers may become irritated. They may decide to 'unfollow' you.

Some companies occasionally take a look at *Twitter* and then, suddenly, start to send an avalanche of tweets to make up for this. This is not a good idea.

4. Not send any messages or too few messages

A *Twitter* account from a company or organization where the most recent tweet is more than six months old does not come across as a professional account.

5. Shield your Tweets

People expect to be able to follow your company, organization or club on *Twitter*. If you shield your tweets by letting potential followers send a request to become a follower, it will look like you have got something to hide.

6. Only twitter commercial messages

Your followers do not want to see nothing but advertisements in their timeline. They will quickly lose interest. Alternate these commercial messages with entertaining news and information, links and photos.

7. Not register your company name on Twitter

Even if you do not intend to use *Twitter* yet, it is recommended that you create an account for your company, organization or club in advance. It has happened that a large company's name was 'hijacked' and could only be bought back for a large sum of money. It is also possible for an unauthorized user to post a fake message in the company's name, which may damage the company's reputation.

3.16 Background Information

Dictionary

Direct message A private message. When you click , Direct messages you will see a list of the direct messages you have sent and received.

Favorites Each tweet contains a small star at the bottom. If you want to save a tweet, you can do this by clicking the star. Your favorites will be visible to everyone. (See the *Tip* at the end of this chapter).

Followers By FOLLOWERS you will see a list of the twitterers who follow you.

Following By FOLLOWING you will see a list of the twitterers you follow.

Hashtag The # sign. This symbol is used to indicate the specific subject you have tweeted about.

Home page If you click Home, you will see the timeline containing the messages (tweets) from the twitterers you follow as well as your own tweets. This page is visible to you only, once you have signed in.

@Mentions @Mentions are all the retweets, replies and messages in which your user name is mentioned.

Profile If you click Your name View my profile page, your profile will appear, along with the timeline containing the tweets you have sent. This page is visible to everyone.

Retweets Retweets are messaged that have been forwarded by the people you follow, or they can be your own retweets and retweets of your messages.

- Continue on the next page -

Timeline	The timeline displays the messages (tweets) of the twitterers you follow as well as your own tweets.
Trends	By Worldwide trends you will see the current most popular topics being talked about in *Twitter*.
Tweet	A *Twitter* message.
Twitter	Post messages through the social network site *Twitter*.
Who to follow	By Who to follow, *Twitter* will offer suggestions of people you may want to follow.
Your tweets	By TWEETS you will see the last tweet you sent.

Source: Twitter

Hyperlinks in a tweet
You can also insert a hyperlink (URL) into your tweet. When you insert a URL into the tweet, *Twitter* will automatically shorten it to 19 characters, no matter how long or short the actual link is. *Twitter's* link service (http://t.co) makes this possible.

3.17 Tips

Tip

Search the list of contacts

You can let *Twitter* search your lists of contacts in the *LinkedIn*, *Gmail*, *Yahoo*, *Hotmail* and *Messenger* web services and see if some of your contacts have a *Twitter* account too.

This option is only available if you have an e-mail address with *Gmail*, *Yahoo* or *Hotmail*. If you use one of these e-mail services, you can do this:

- **Click** Connect
- **By** Who to follow, **click** View all 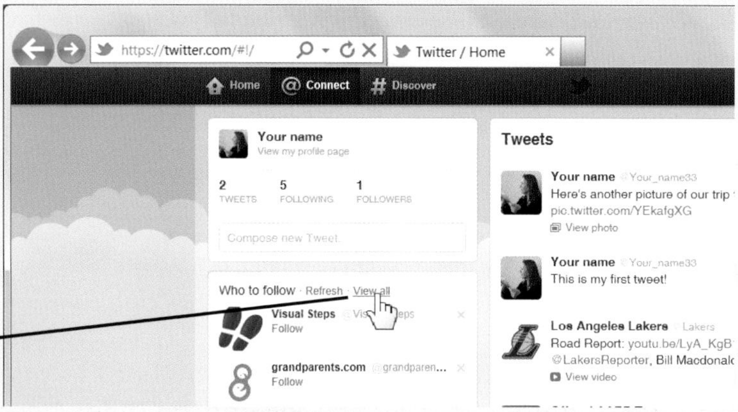
- **Click** Find friends
- **For example, by** Hotmail & M **click** Search contacts 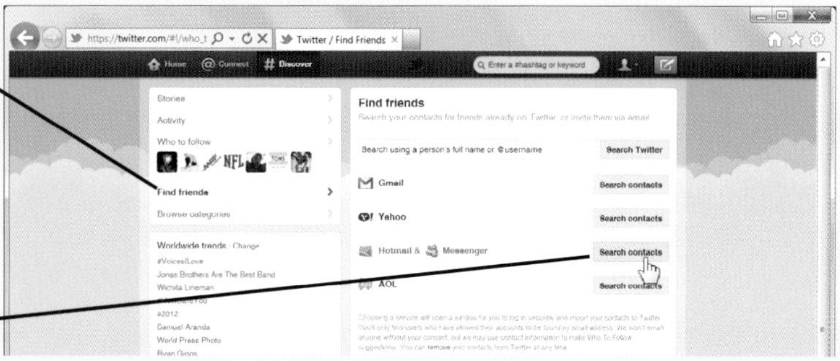
- **If necessary, type your e-mail address**
- **Type your password**
- **Click** Connect
- **Follow the instructions in the next few windows**

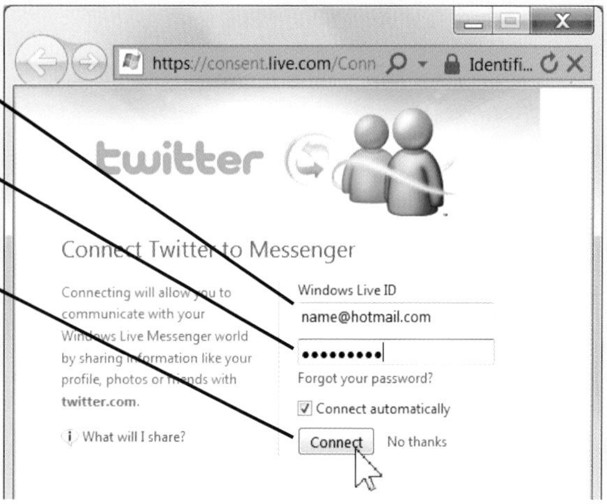

Tip

Longer tweets with XLTweet

If you think your story is too long to fit *Twitter's* 140 character limit, you can add a link to your tweet. This link will lead the viewer to a web page that contains the remainder of your tweet.

Open the www.xltweet.com website 1

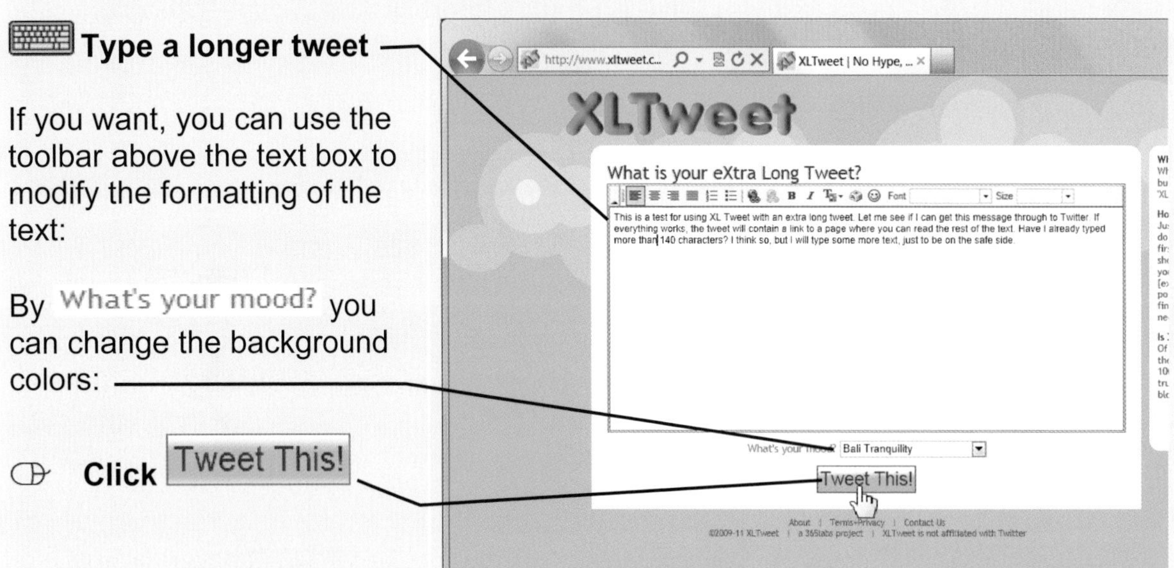

Type a longer tweet

If you want, you can use the toolbar above the text box to modify the formatting of the text:

By What's your mood? you can change the background colors:

Click Tweet This!

If you are still logged in with *Twitter* you will see a page with a message by *Twitter*, stating that an application (*XLTweet*) asks for permission to connect to your account. You will need to give permission to do this:

Click Authorize app

Now you will return to the *XLTweet* page.

By now, your tweet containing the link has been posted on *Twitter*:

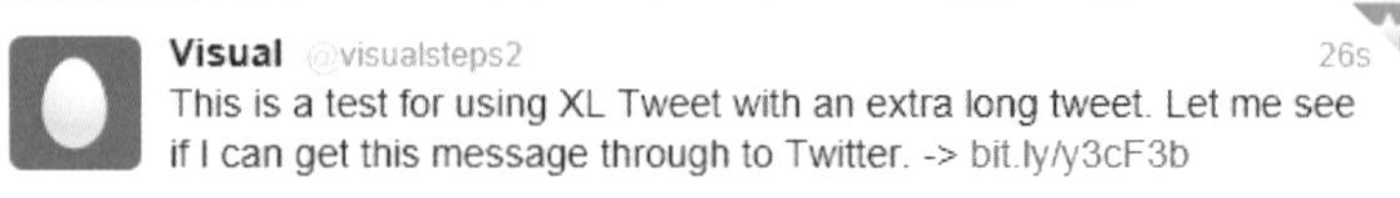

 **Tip**

Favorites

Below each tweet you will see a star. If you want to save a tweet, you can store it by clicking this star. Your favorites will be visible to everyone.

Position the pointer on the tweet

Click Favorite

The tweet will be marked with a  .

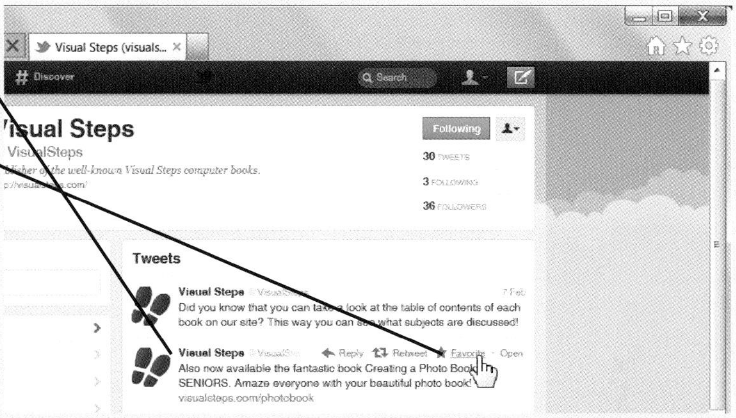

You can find your favorites on your profile page:

Open your profile page 15

Click Favorites

You will see your favorite tweets:

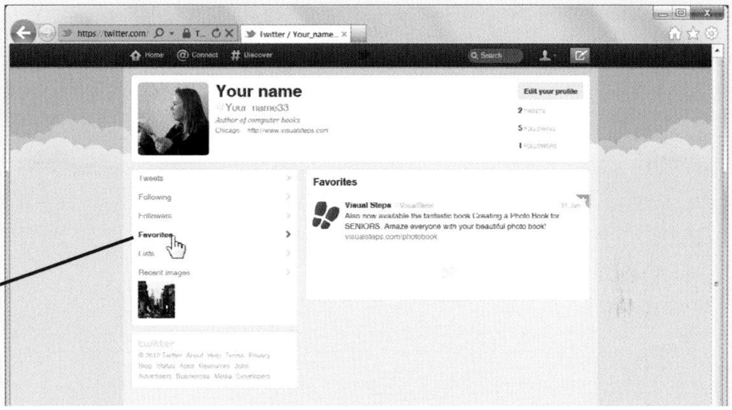

 **Tip**

Unfollow

Do you no longer wish to follow a certain person or company you have been following on *Twitter*? Then go to your home page and do this:

Click FOLLOWING

By the relevant twitterer:

Position the pointer on Following

Click Unfollow

- Continue on the next page -

You will also find several options regarding the people who follow you. This is how to view these options:

Click Followers

Click

You will see the options:

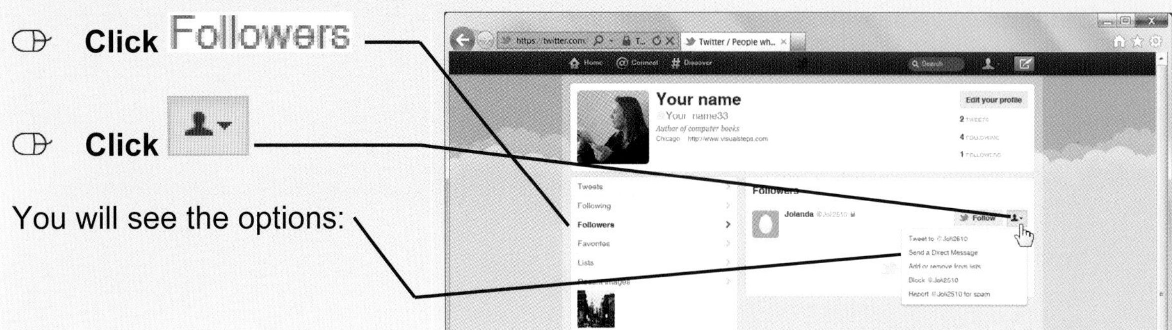

Tip

Hashtag

In tweets you often see the # symbol. This is called a *hashtag*. A hashtag is a simple way of marking a keyword or topic by appending a *tag* (label) to the message, so you can make sure that other *Twitter* users will find the message. For example, if you are going to organize an event and send tweets about this event, you can include the #bookfair hashtag in your tweets. If somebody is looking for #bookfair, he or she will find all the messages about this topic, including your tweets.

A well-known hashtag is #daretoask. If you search for #daretoask you will see all sorts of questions asked by other twitterers. You can react to these questions, if you know the answers.

Tip

Search tips

If you have searched for something on *Twitter* and found some useful results, you can save this search and use it again later on.

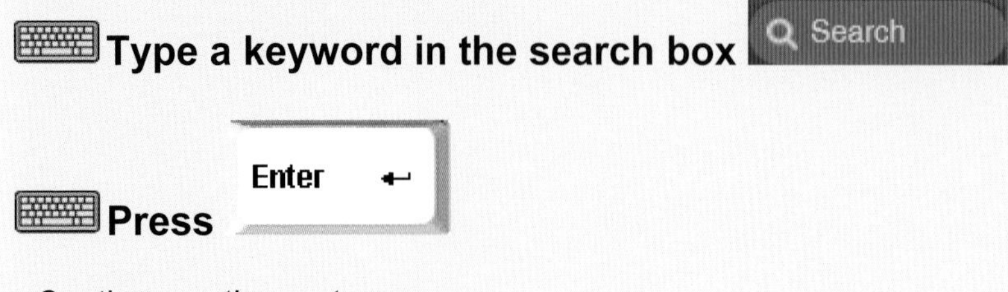

Type a keyword in the search box Search

Press Enter

- Continue on the next page -

You will see the search results for people and tweets:

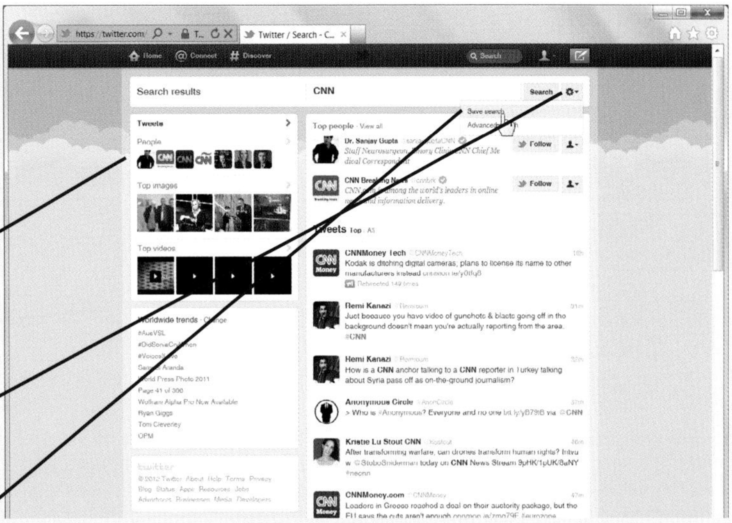

If you want, you can select just the people, images or videos:

To save this search:

- **Click** 
- **Click** Save search

With the search box you can view the search you just saved:

- **Click the search box**

You will see the name of your stored search. If you click it, the search will be carried out once more:

You can also look for Twitter messages which include hashtags #.

Tip

Change the visibility of your tweets

If you have a *Twitter* account, by default, anybody who visits your *Twitter* page can follow your tweets. If you only want people of whom you approve to read your tweets, you can change the default settings:

Open the *Settings* page 13

- Continue on the next page -

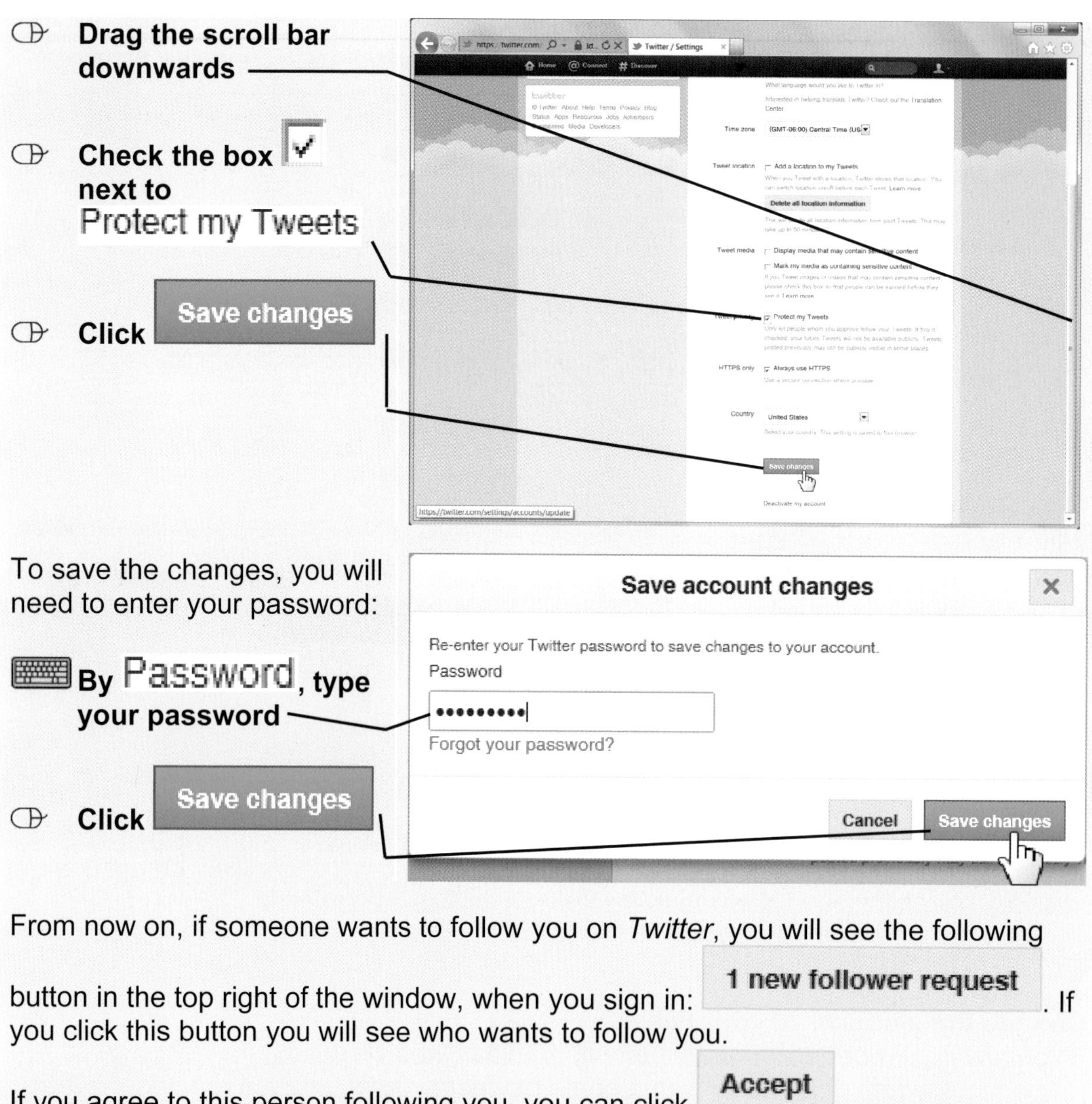

Drag the scroll bar downwards

Check the box ☑ **next to** Protect my Tweets

Click Save changes

To save the changes, you will need to enter your password:

By Password**, type your password**

Click Save changes

From now on, if someone wants to follow you on *Twitter*, you will see the following button in the top right of the window, when you sign in: 1 new follower request. If you click this button you will see who wants to follow you.

If you agree to this person following you, you can click Accept.

In turn, you can also start following this person by clicking Follow in the next window.

4. WordPress

WordPress is an Internet service that offers space for you to maintain a free blog. This is a kind of online diary. A blog is also called a *weblog*. That is why a person who maintains a blog is called a *blogger*.

If you start writing a blog, you should try to make sure that new messages are posted on a regular basis. As a rule, the most recent posts from the blog will be displayed as soon as the page with the blog is opened. The previous messages (known as *posts*) will be listed beneath the most recent post, or they may be accessed through a menu. Older editions are often stored in an archive. Apart from text, you can also add photos to your posts.

Visitors can read your blog and comment on individual posts. These comments will be displayed directly underneath the relevant post. In turn, other readers can react to these comments, which can lead to lively discussions.

In this chapter you will learn how to:

- create a *WordPress.com* blog;
- sign in;
- adjust the interface language along with other settings;
- edit your profile;
- create your first post on your blog;
- view your blog;
- delete a post;
- change the theme of your blog;
- edit a page;
- add a page with photos;
- change the privacy settings;
- change the settings for the visitors' comments;
- delete your blog;
- use your blog for commercial purposes.

Please note:

WordPress is subject to regular changes. The windows on your own screen may look a little different from the examples in this chapter. If you cannot find a specific button, try looking to see if it is located somewhere else in the window.

4.1 Creating a WordPress.com Blog

If you want to create a blog, you will need to register with *WordPress* first. The first thing to do is to visit the website and create an account:

Open the website at wordpress.com 1

You will see the *WordPress* home page. To the right you will see links to several topics. To create your own account:

Click

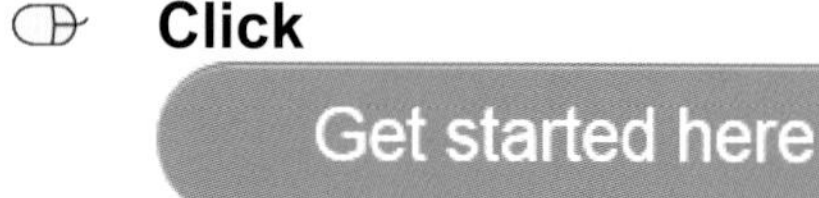

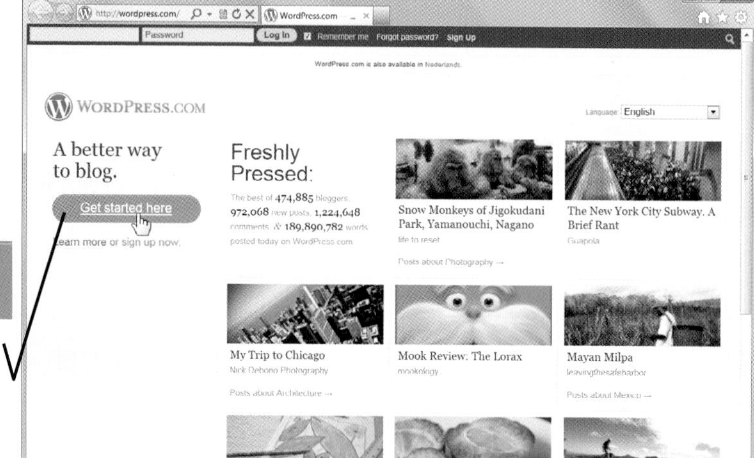

You just need to fill in a single form to get started with your own *WordPress* blog. First, you need to choose a web address for your blog. This web address will look like this: *yourname.wordpress.com*.

By Blog Address, **type the name of your blog**

Right away, you will find out if this name is still available.

By Username, **click the text box**

The name of the blog will also be entered automatically as the username. But you can choose a different username, if you like:

By Username, **type a username**

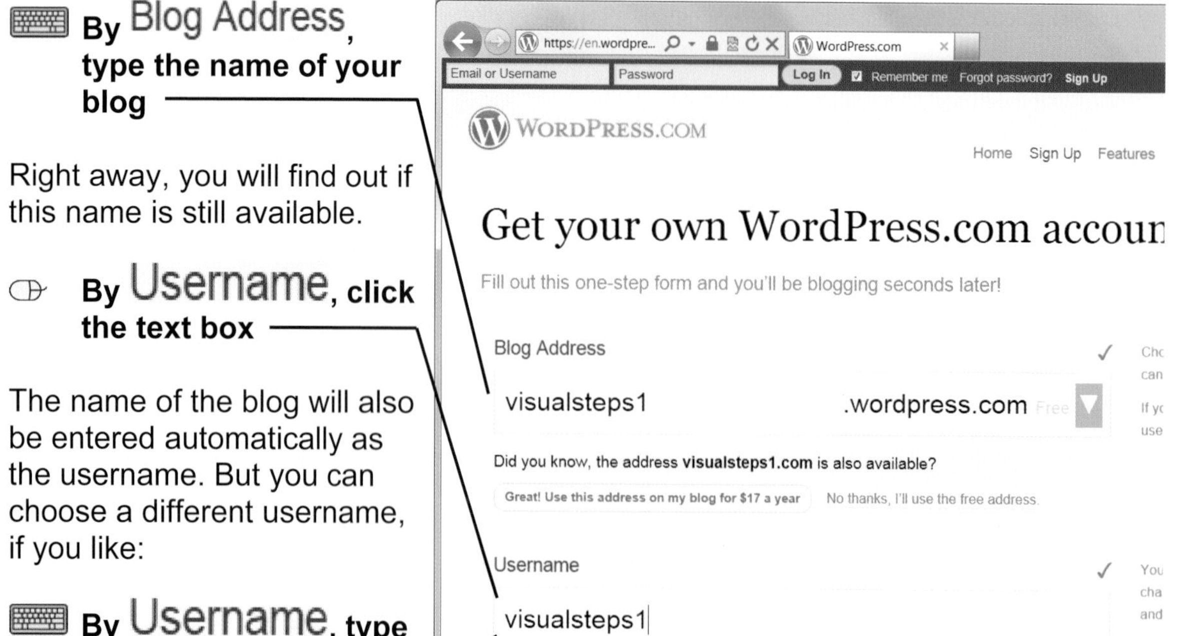

You can choose your own password. Make sure that your password is rated as a Strong password. The best way of doing this is to combine capital letters and lower case letters, numbers and symbols, such as ? or %.

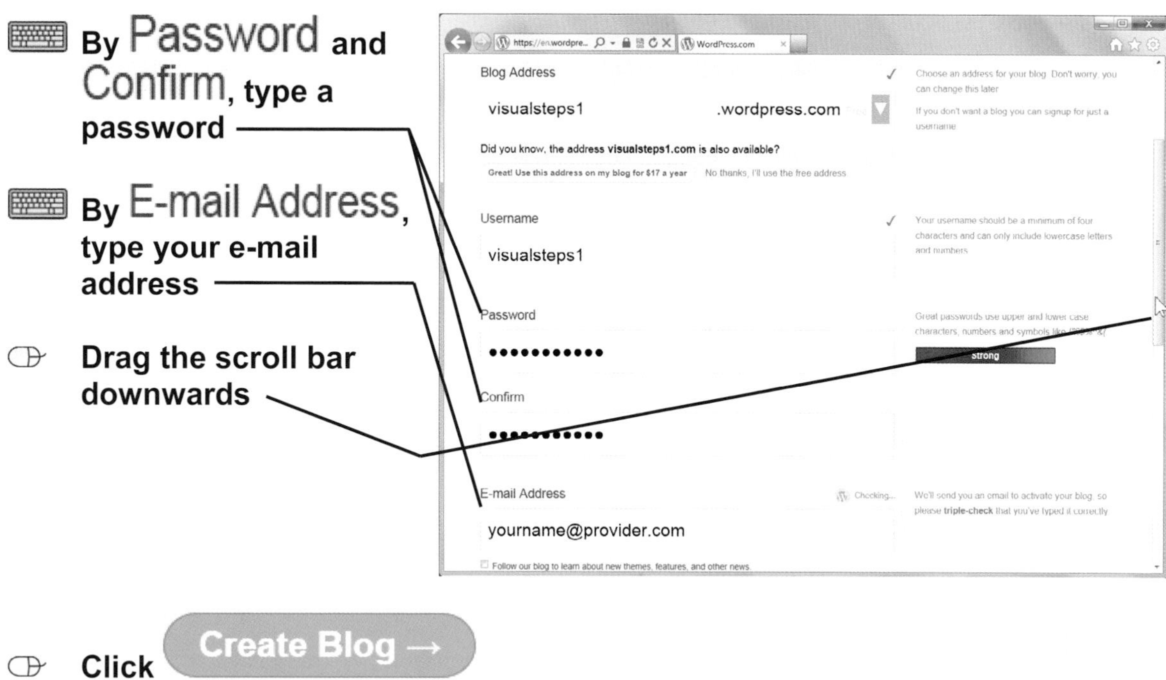

By Password and Confirm, type a password

By E-mail Address, type your e-mail address

Drag the scroll bar downwards

Click Create Blog →

You may see a warning message about security during these operations:

If necessary, click No

Write down your username and password on a piece of paper and save this in a safe location

Now you will see a message saying Check Your E-mail to Complete Registration. *WordPress* has sent a confirmation e-mail message to your e-mail address. You need to open this e-mail in order to complete your registration with *WordPress*.

Open the e-mail message sent by *WordPress* in your e-mail program

HELP! No e-mail message

It may take a while before you receive an e-mail message from *WordPress*. If you have not received anything after a longer period of time, you should check the folder with the unwanted (trash) messages. The conformation e-mail sometimes ends up in the trash bin.

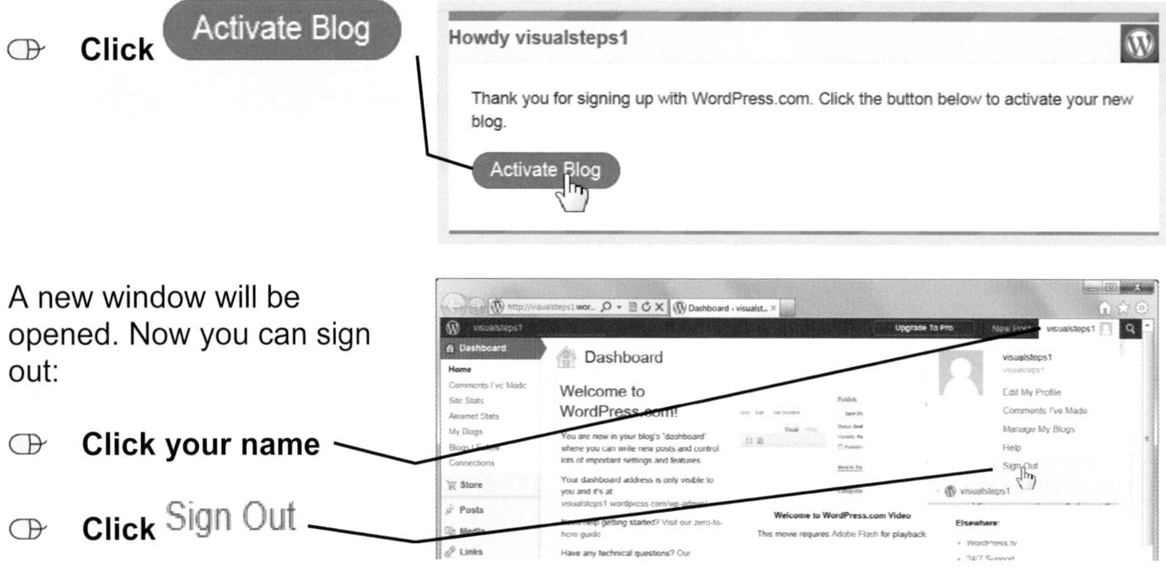

Click **Activate Blog**

A new window will be opened. Now you can sign out:

Click your name

Click **Sign Out**

In the following section you will use this same window.

Close all the windows of your e-mail program 4

Close the other tab, or the *Internet Explorer* window 4

In the next section you will sign in and start working with *WordPress*.

4.2 Sign In

If you want to use *WordPress*, you first need to sign in to your account. This is how you do that:

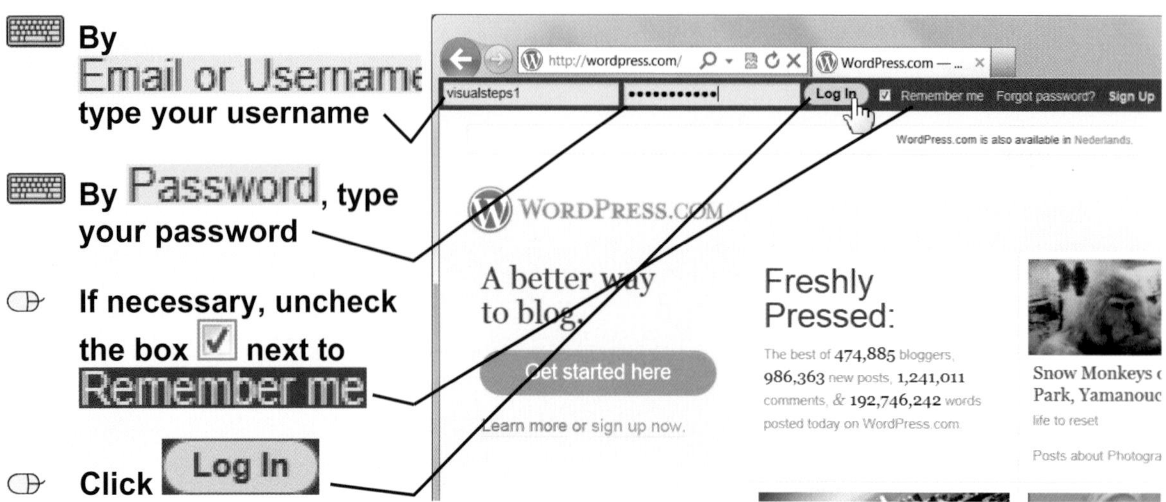

By Email or Username type your username

By Password, type your password

If necessary, uncheck the box ☑ next to Remember me

Click Log In

You will still see the same window. Only, the bar at the top has changed:

4.3 Changing General Settings

If you want you can change a number of general settings such as the tagline and the date and time format. Here is how you do that:

- **Click your name**
- **Click** Edit My Profile 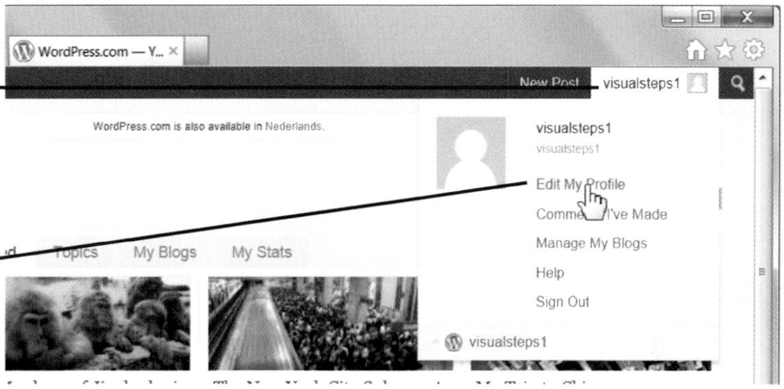
- **Click** **Settings**

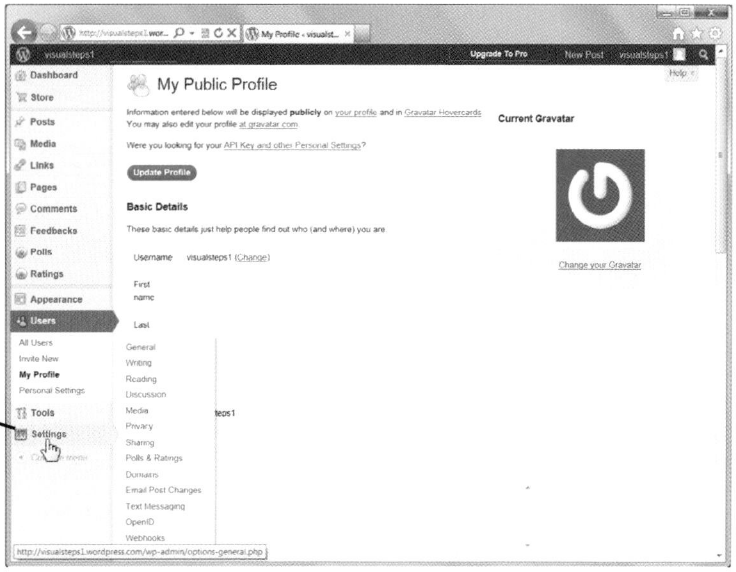

You can change a number of other settings:

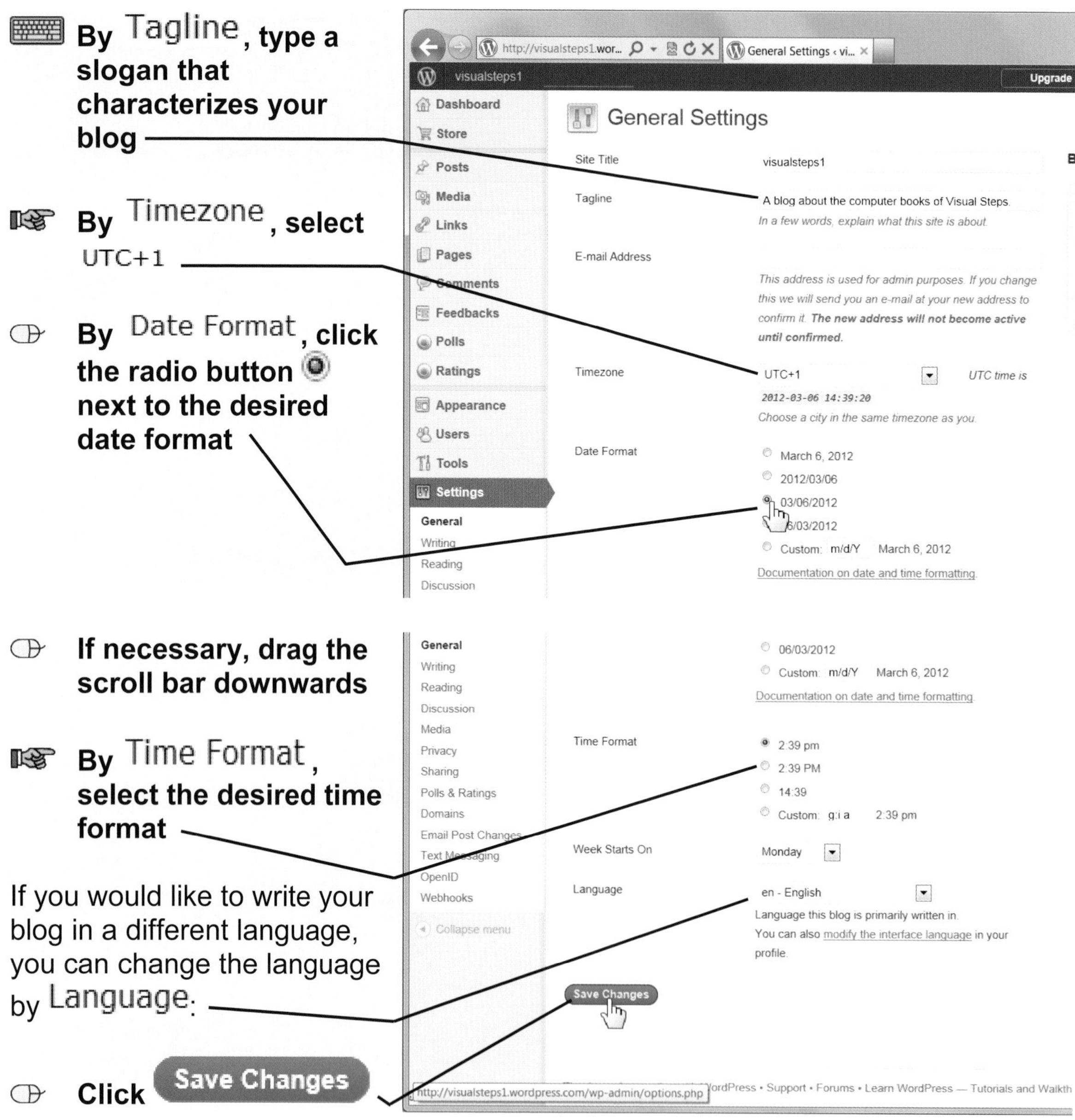

By Tagline, type a slogan that characterizes your blog

By Timezone, select UTC+1

By Date Format, click the radio button next to the desired date format

If necessary, drag the scroll bar downwards

By Time Format, select the desired time format

If you would like to write your blog in a different language, you can change the language by Language:

Click Save Changes

If you have changed the language, you will see that for the most part, the web page is immediately rendered in the language you chose.

4.4 Editing a Profile

Your public profile will display information visible to the people who read your blog. Now you will learn how to edit your profile:

Click your name

Click Edit My Profile

By First name**, type your first name**

By Last name**, type your last name**

By Full name**, type your first and last name**

By Display name publicly as**, type the name that will be displayed in your blog**

By Location**, type your home town**

By About you**, type some lines about yourself**

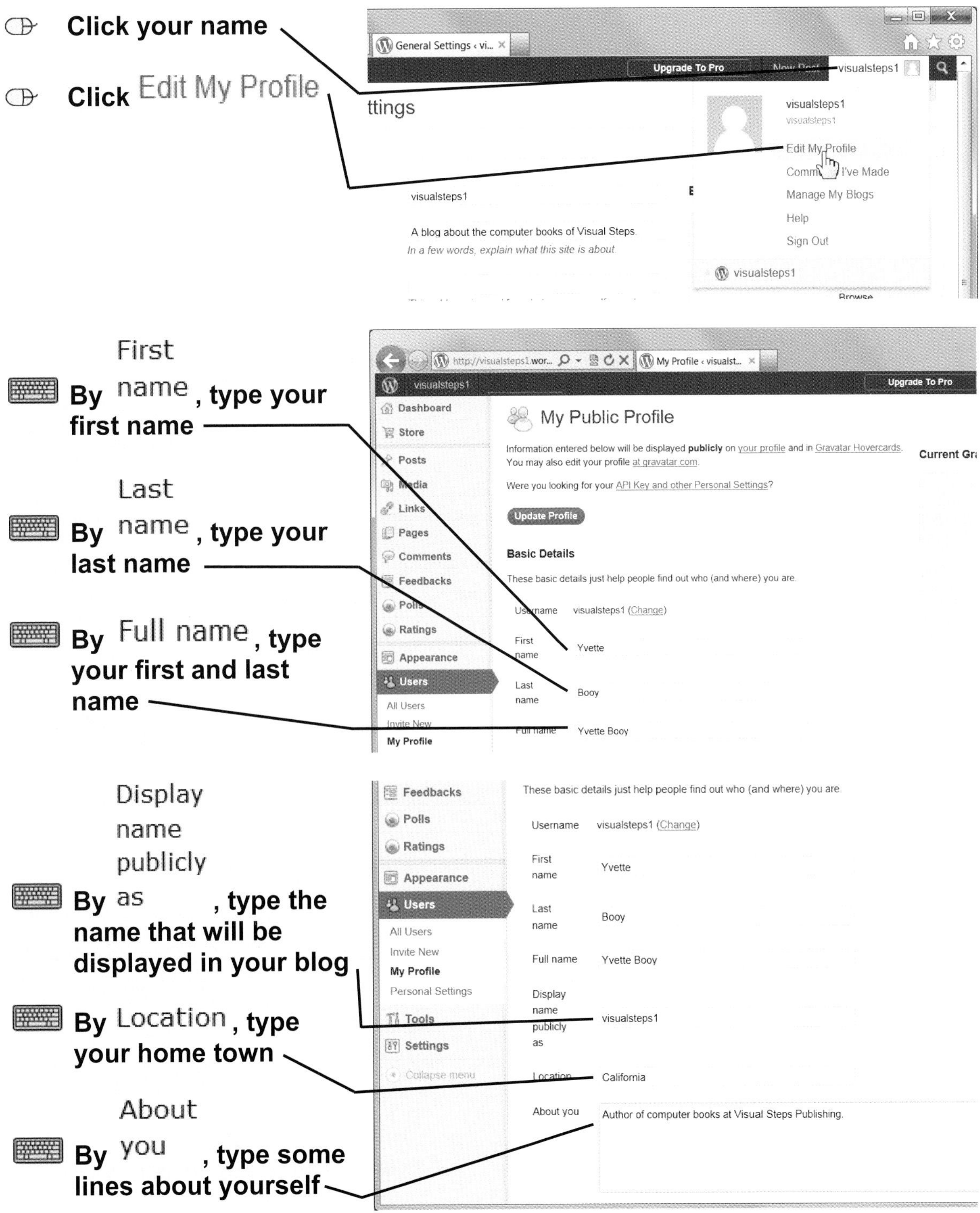

When you have finished entering this information:

Click **Update Profile**

You can also add a photo to your profile:

Click Change your Gravatar

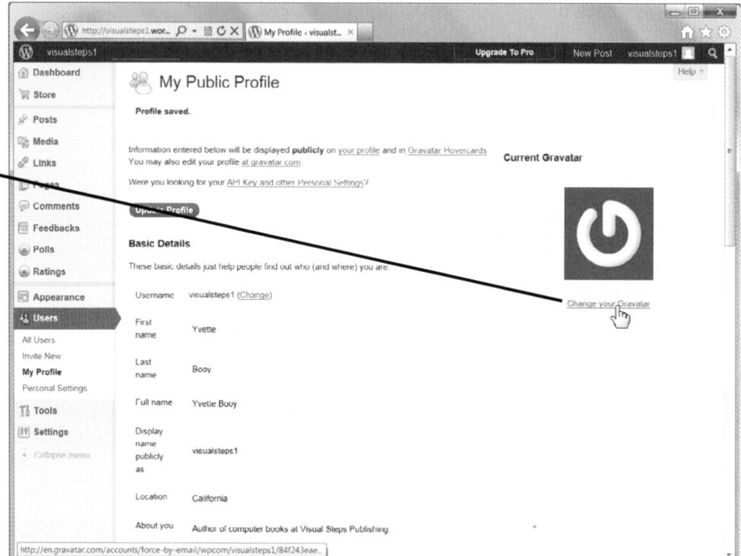

Gravatar stands for *Globally Recognized Avatar*, which is a small picture of the user of a service such as *WordPress*. Through Gravatar you can use the same picture for multiple online web services.

A new window will be opened. There you can choose whether to take a new picture with your webcam, select a picture from an online source or select a picture from your own computer (or tablet). In this example, we have selected a picture from the computer:

Click

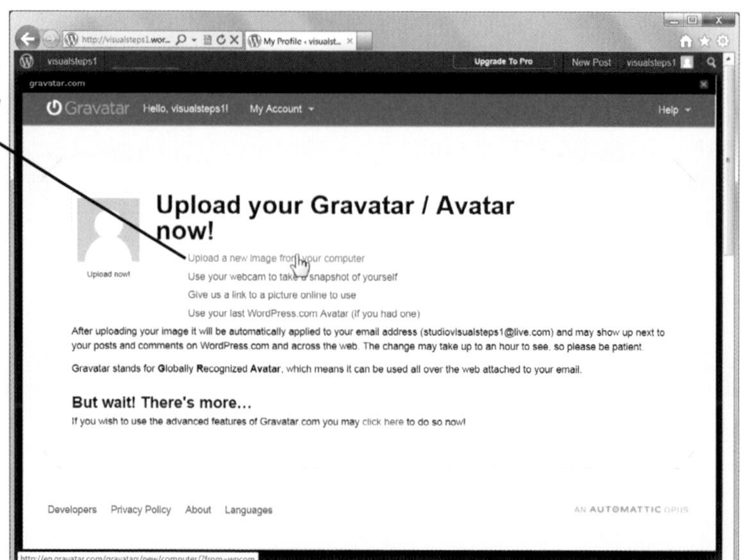

Click Browse...

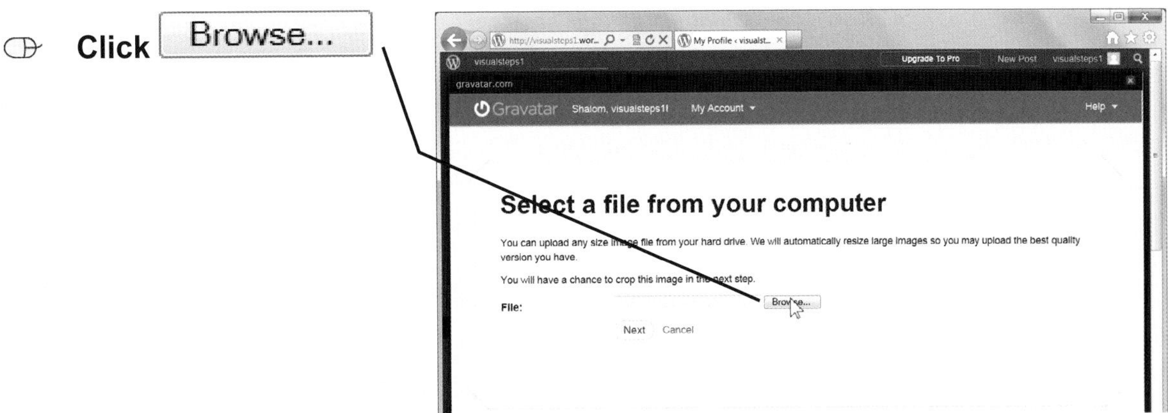

Select the desired photo and add it to the profile 5

Click Next

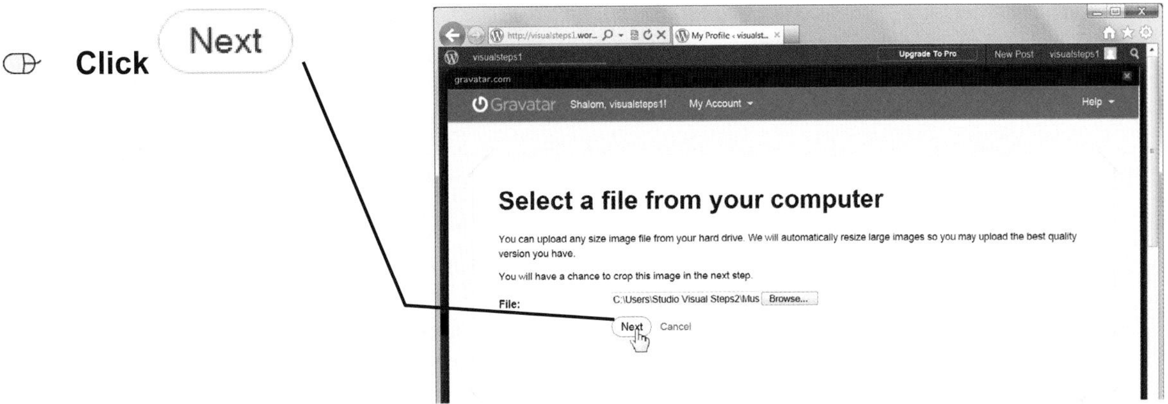

Now you can decide to crop the photo a bit further:

Use the ← ○ → or ↑ ○ ↓ buttons to move the frame with the dotted line:

If you are satisfied with the result:

Drag the scroll bar downwards

Click Crop and Finish!

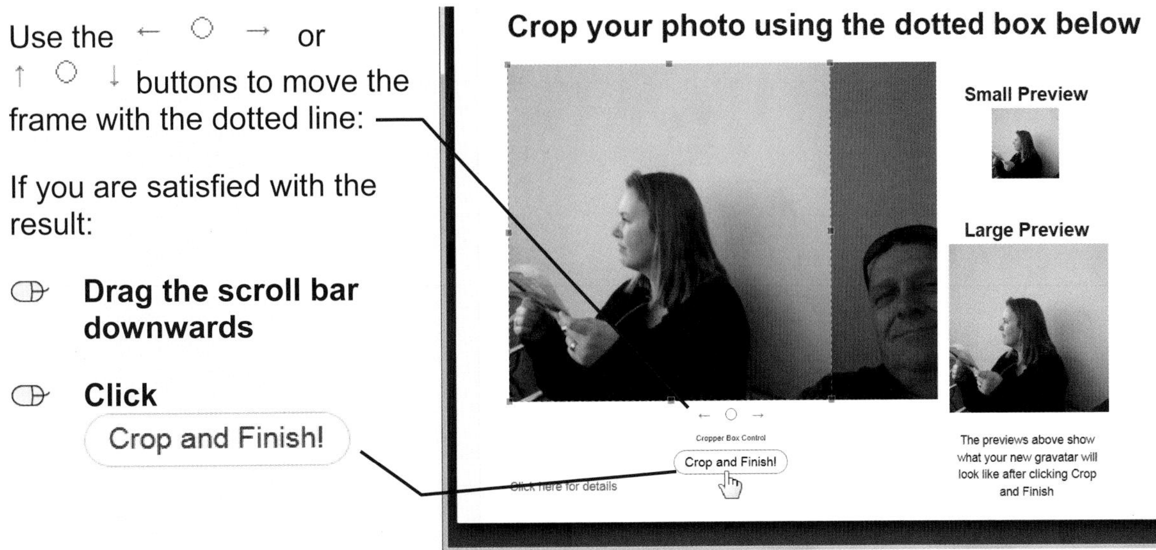

Finally, you will need to choose a 'rating' for your photo. If you have used a regular portrait image or holiday picture:

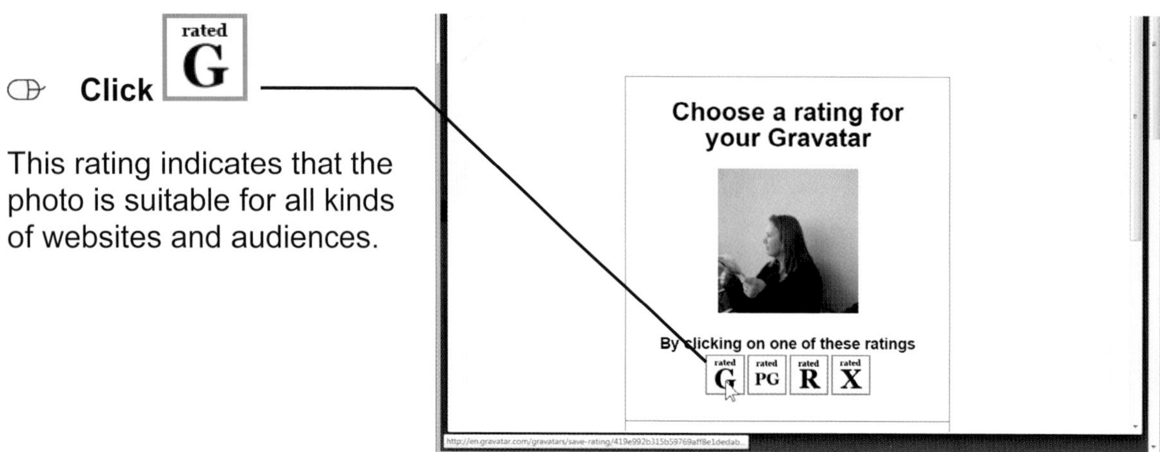

Click rated G

This rating indicates that the photo is suitable for all kinds of websites and audiences.

Now you can close the Gravatar window:

Click ✕

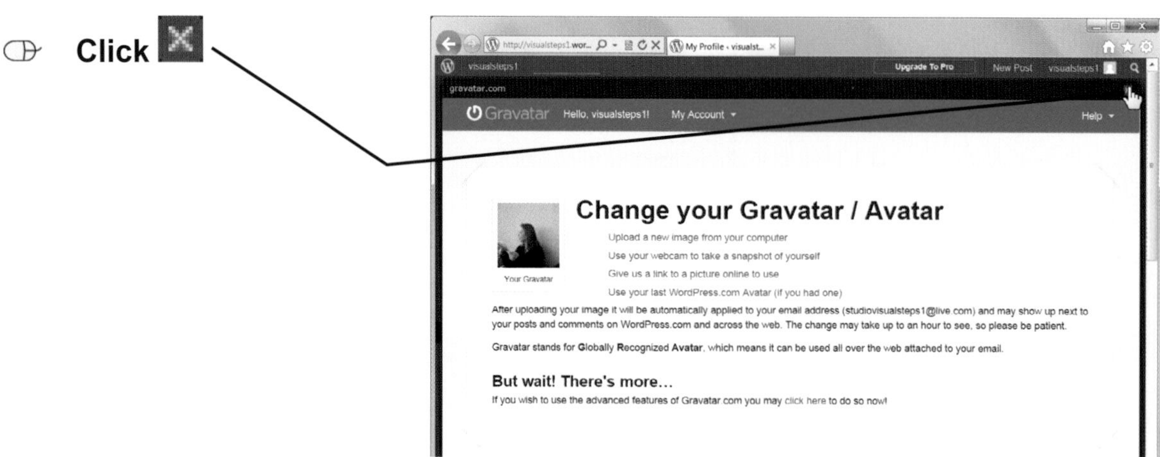

You will see your Gravatar:

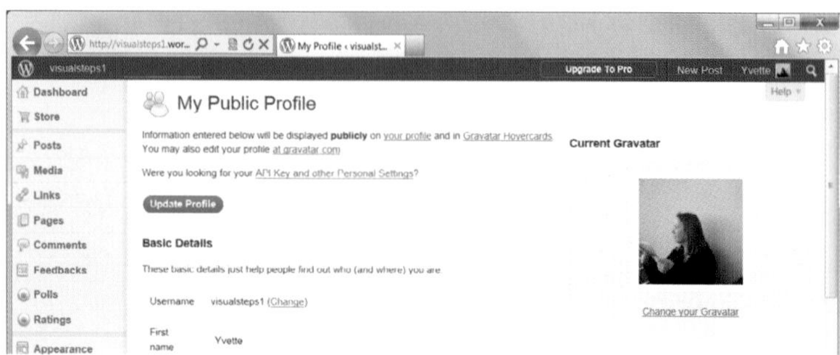

HELP! I do not yet see my Gravatar

Use the ⟳ or ↰↱ button to refresh the page.

4.5 The First Post on Your Blog

Now you are going to create your first post on your blog. You can write a post about any kind of subject, for example, your hobby, family, company, club or your recent travel experiences. This is how you create a new post:

In the top left of the window:

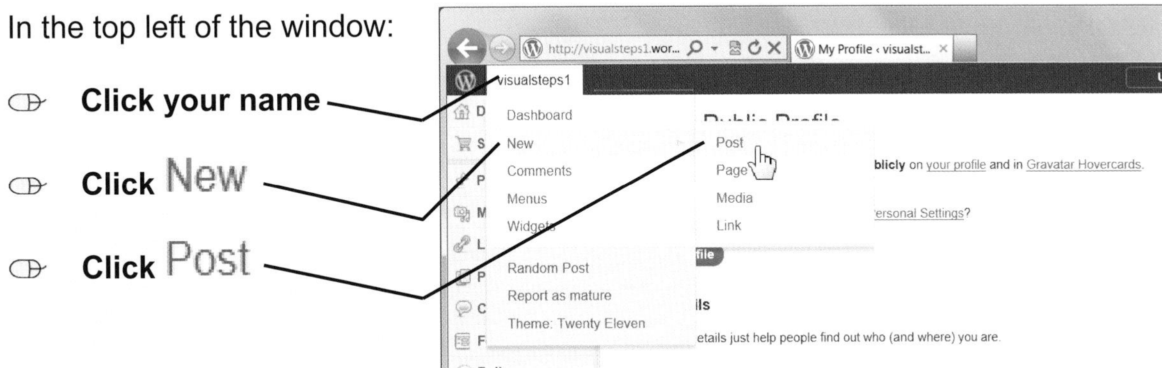

- **Click your name**
- **Click** New
- **Click** Post

You will see the page on which you can write the new message. You start by adding a title for this post:

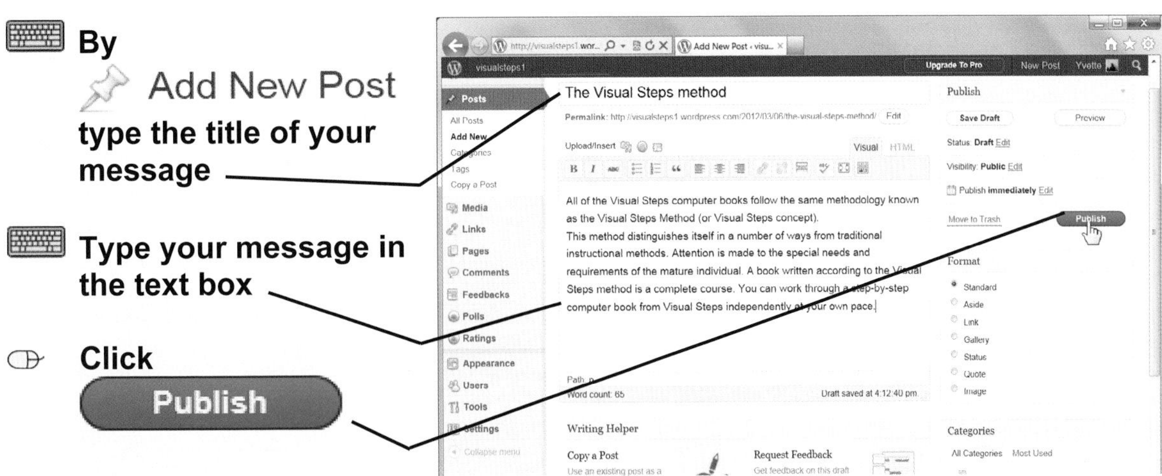

- **By** Add New Post **type the title of your message**
- **Type your message in the text box**
- **Click** Publish

Tip

Format a message

You can format your message with the same types of text editing tools that you use in your regular text editing program such as *Word*. This is how you display the extra text formatting toolbar:

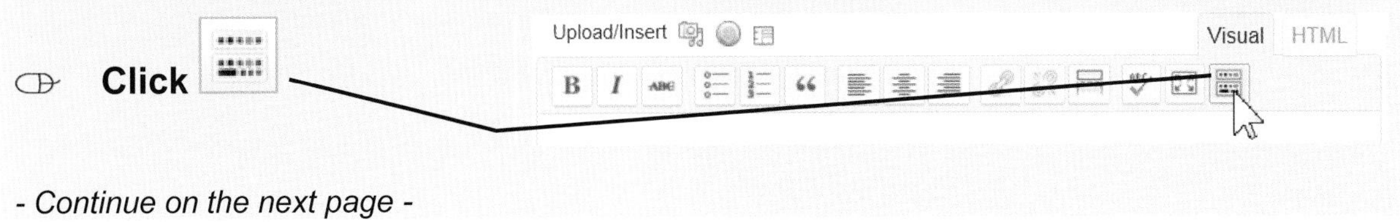

- **Click**

- Continue on the next page -

You will see the extra text formatting toolbar:

With the button you can paste text that you copied from *Word* into your message, including the formatting.

Now the message will be posted on your blog.

You will see your blog in the same way as your visitors will see it:

The message you just posted is not the only message on your blog:

- Click **Previous**

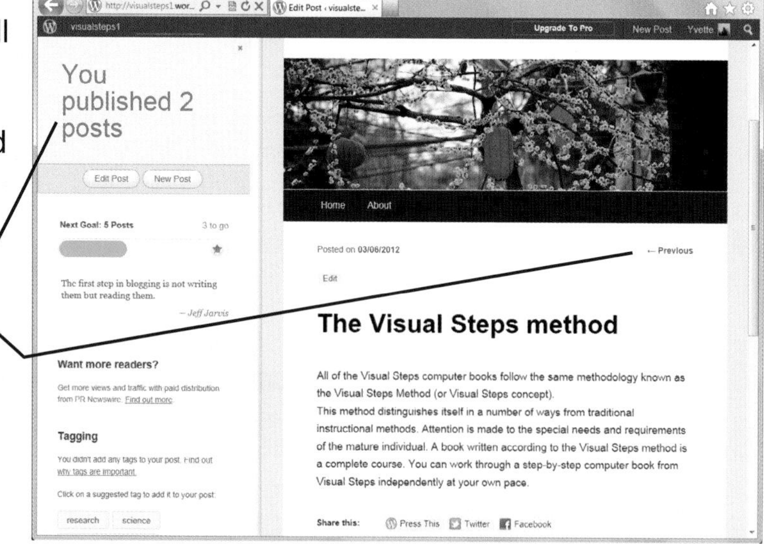

You will see a sample message, posted on your blog by *WordPress*:

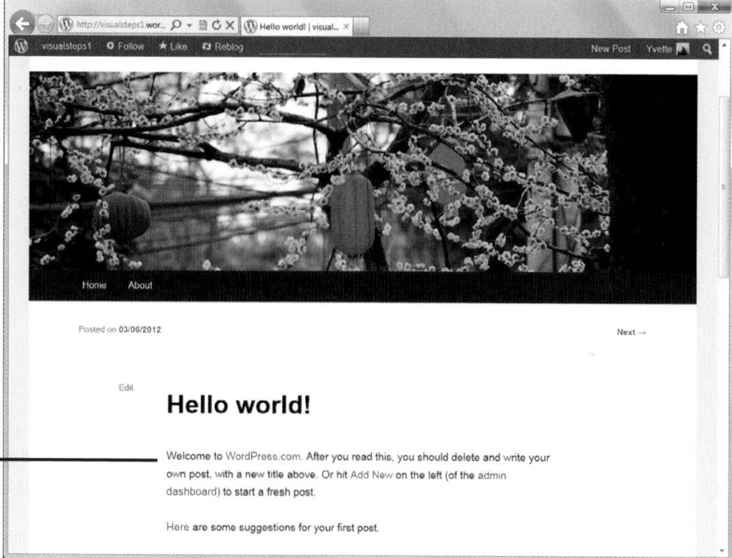

As an example, *WordPress* has also posted a reader's comment on the sample message:

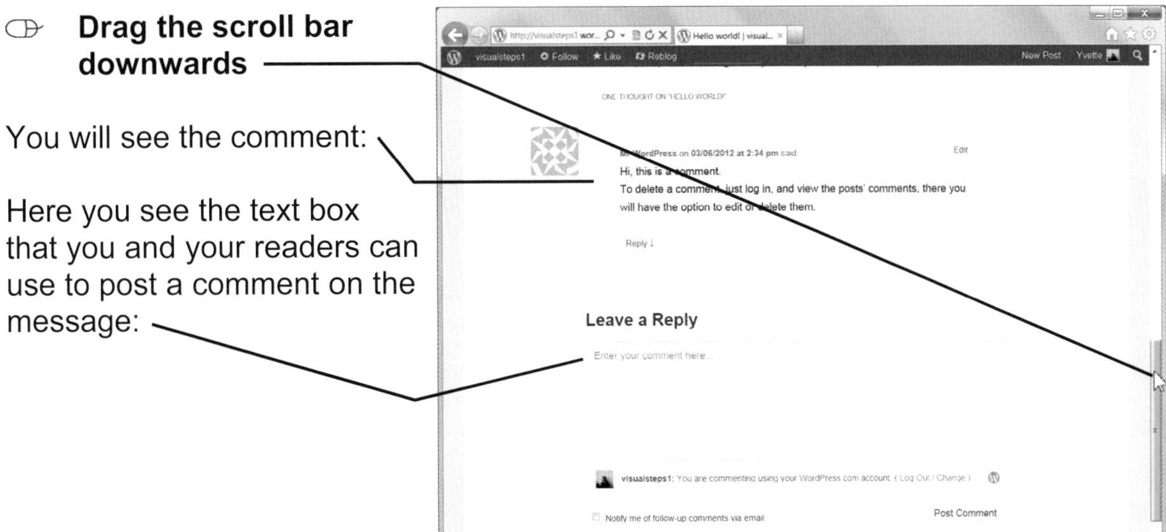

☞ **Drag the scroll bar downwards**

You will see the comment:

Here you see the text box that you and your readers can use to post a comment on the message:

In the next section you will learn how to delete the sample message from your blog.

4.6 Deleting a Message

The *Dashboard* is the central point from which you can manage and edit your blog. This is how you go to the Dashboard:

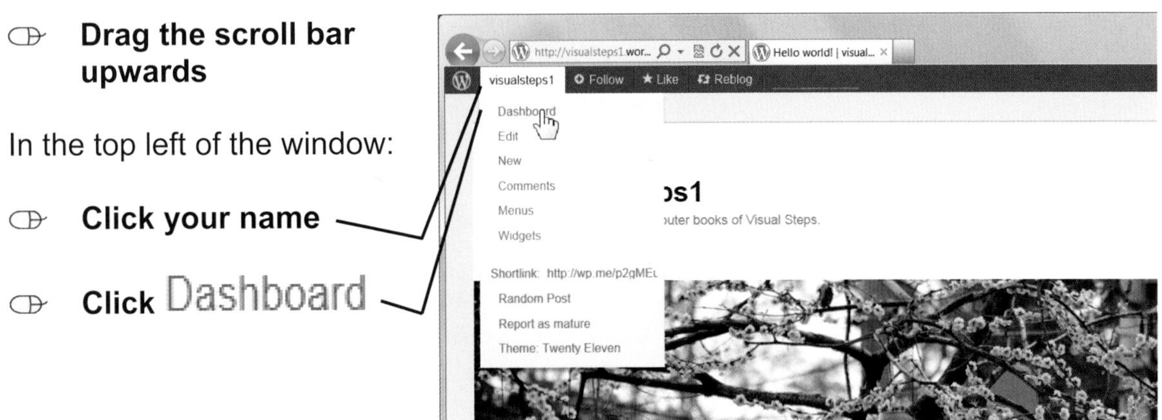

☞ **Drag the scroll bar upwards**

In the top left of the window:

☞ **Click your name**

☞ **Click** Dashboard

On the Dashboard you can see at a glance what is happening with your blog.

Here you see the number of messages you have posted, and the number of comments you have received:

- **Click** **Posts**

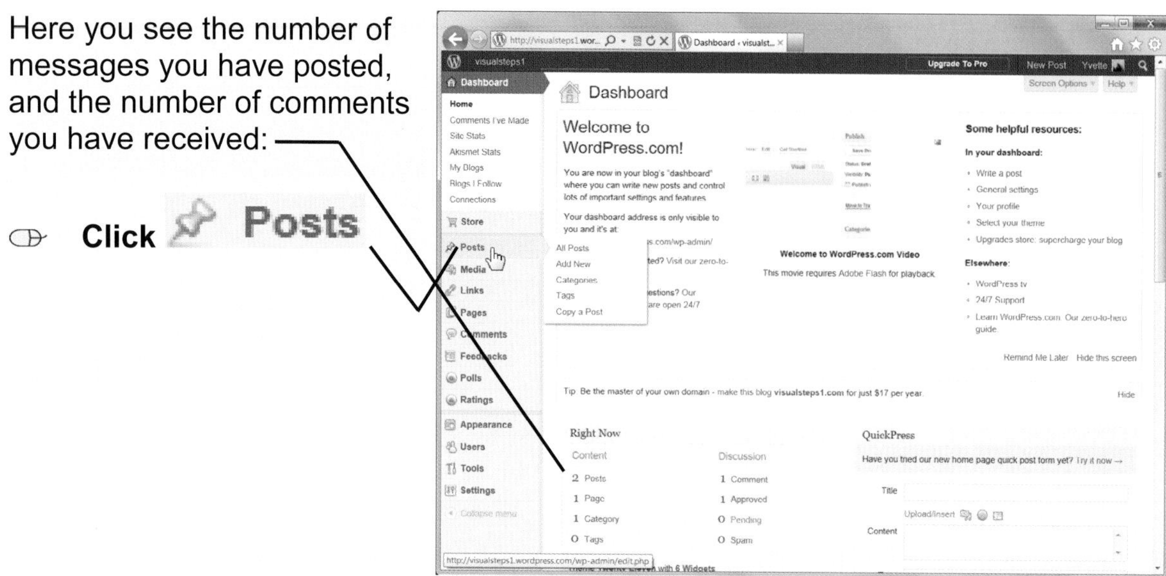

On the *Posts* page you will see which messages have been posted on your blog. This is how you delete the sample message:

- **Position the pointer on** **Hello world!**

You will see a menu:

- **Click** Trash

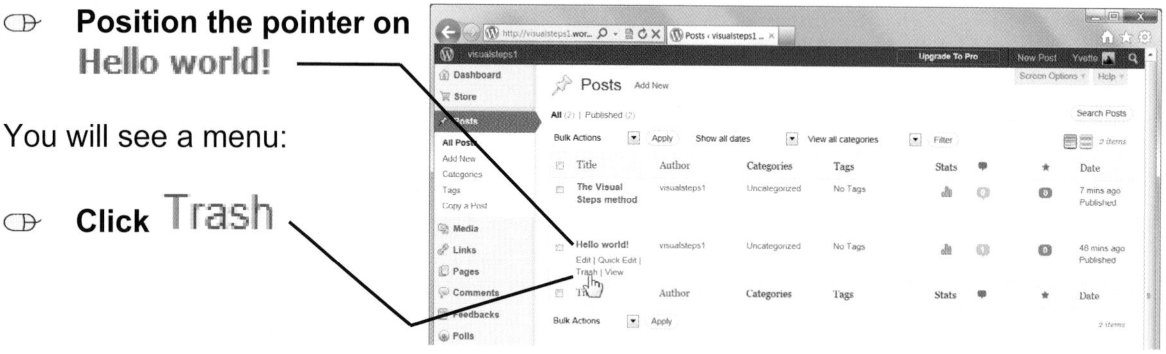

Now the post will be deleted. You will see the message Item moved to the Trash. Undo.

Tip

Retrieve a post from the recycle bin

Have you deleted a post accidentally? Here is how you can get it back:

- **Click** Trash
- **Position the pointer on the post**
- **Click** Restore

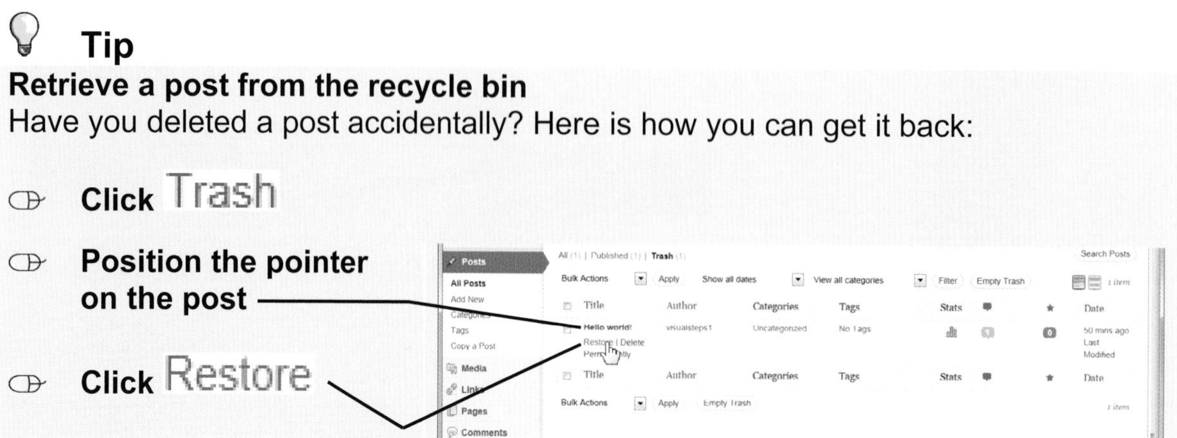

4.7 Changing the Theme

You can format your blog according to your own taste, by selecting or editing a theme.

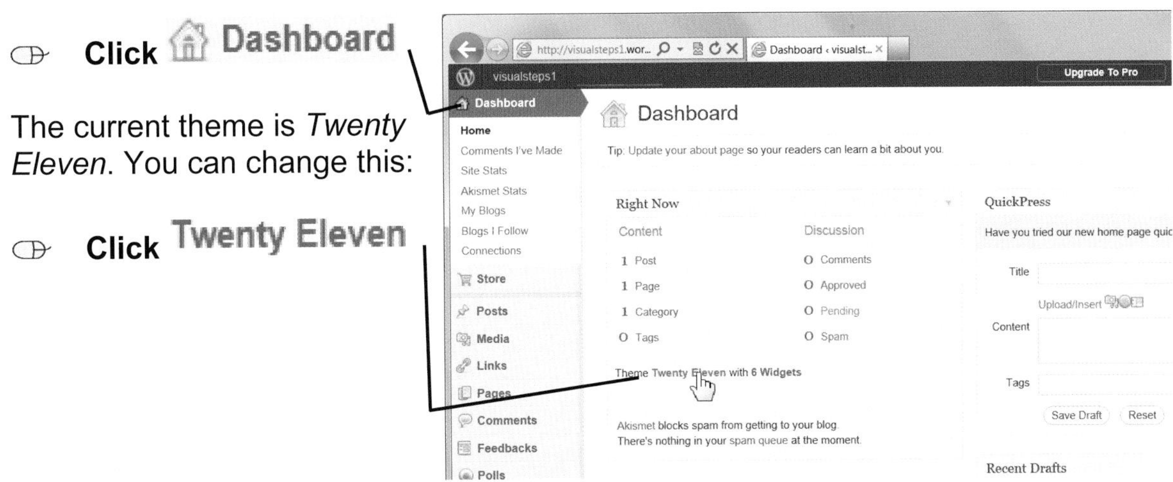

Click Dashboard

The current theme is *Twenty Eleven*. You can change this:

Click Twenty Eleven

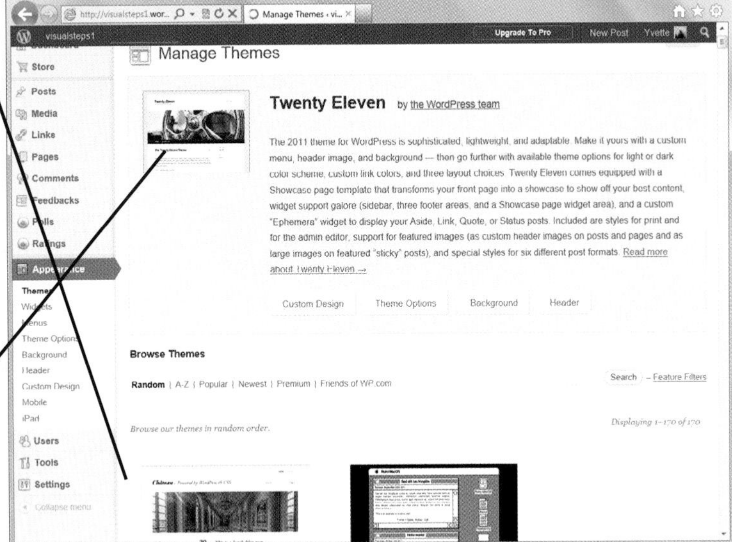

On the Manage Themes page you can choose from a large number of different themes:

New themes are added all the time. You will probably see different themes from the ones in this example.

At the top you will see the theme that is currently used for your blog:

Tip

View a theme

For each theme you can view a preview and see what your blog will look like:

- **By the theme, click** Preview

You will see a preview window, in which your blog will be displayed with the new theme. To close this preview:

- **Click next to the preview window**

If you have found a nice theme, you can easily apply it to your blog:

- **By the relevant theme, click** Activate

You can also adjust the current theme by simply changing the *header*:

- **Click** Header

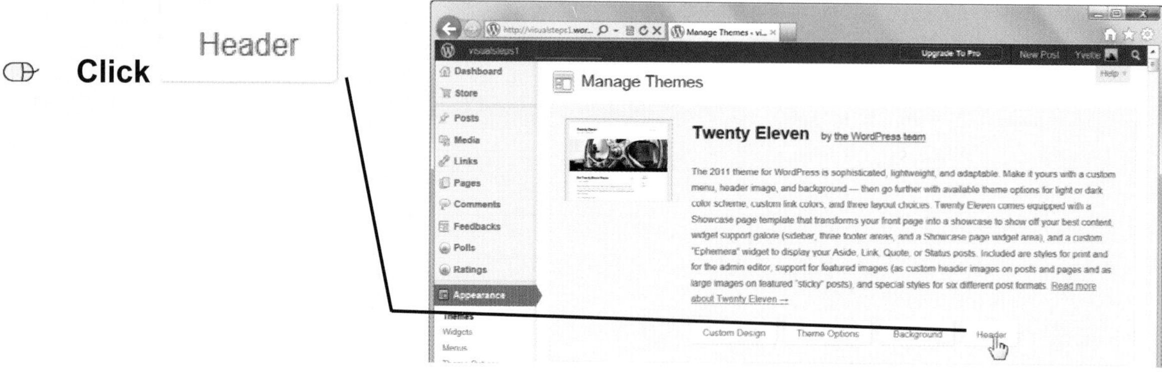

If you want to use one of your own photos:

- **Click** Browse...

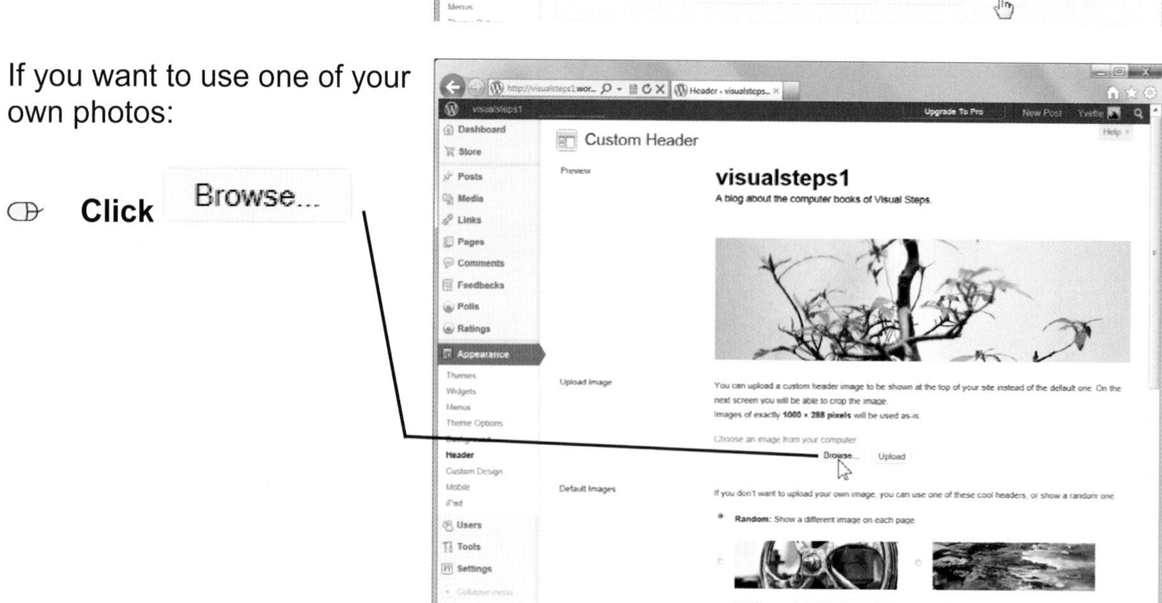

Select the desired photo and add it 5

Click Upload

The photo may need some adjustments to its size and placement:

Drag the frame with the dotted line to the desired position

Drag the scroll bar downwards

Click Crop and Publish

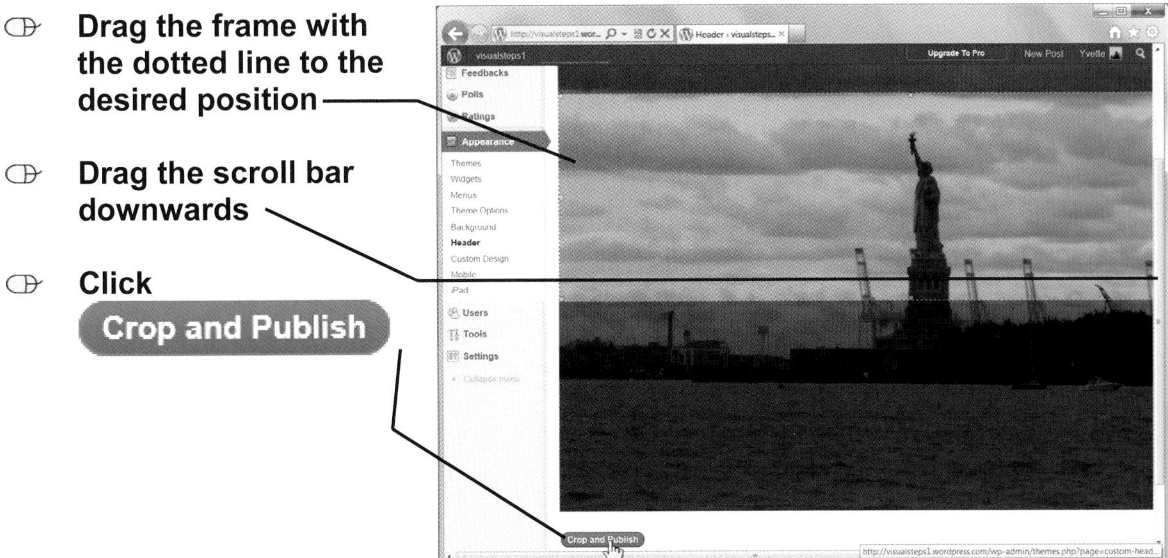

Drag the scroll bar downwards

Click Save Changes

The header will be edited.

4.8 Editing a Page

You can take a look now and see what your blog looks like:

Click Visit your site

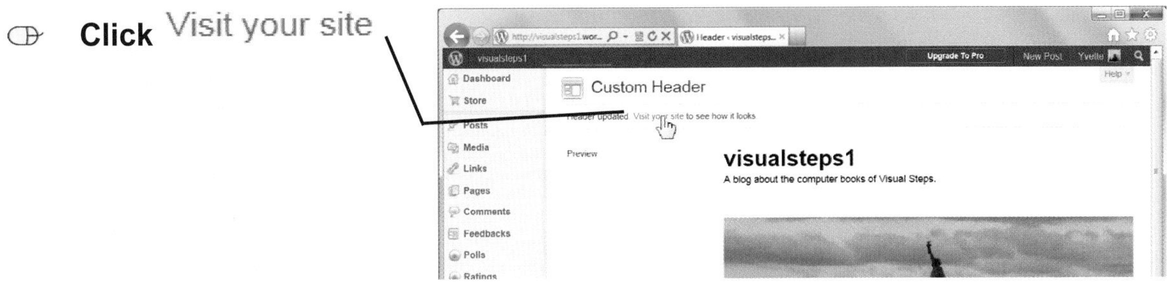

You will see the page with the new header:

Besides the **Home** page with your blog posts, your blog also contains one other page:

Click About

Now you will see a page where you can show information about yourself, your company or your organization:

Currently, this page contains nothing more than a sample message from *WordPress*:

Click Edit

Type a new title for the page

Type a new text

Click Update

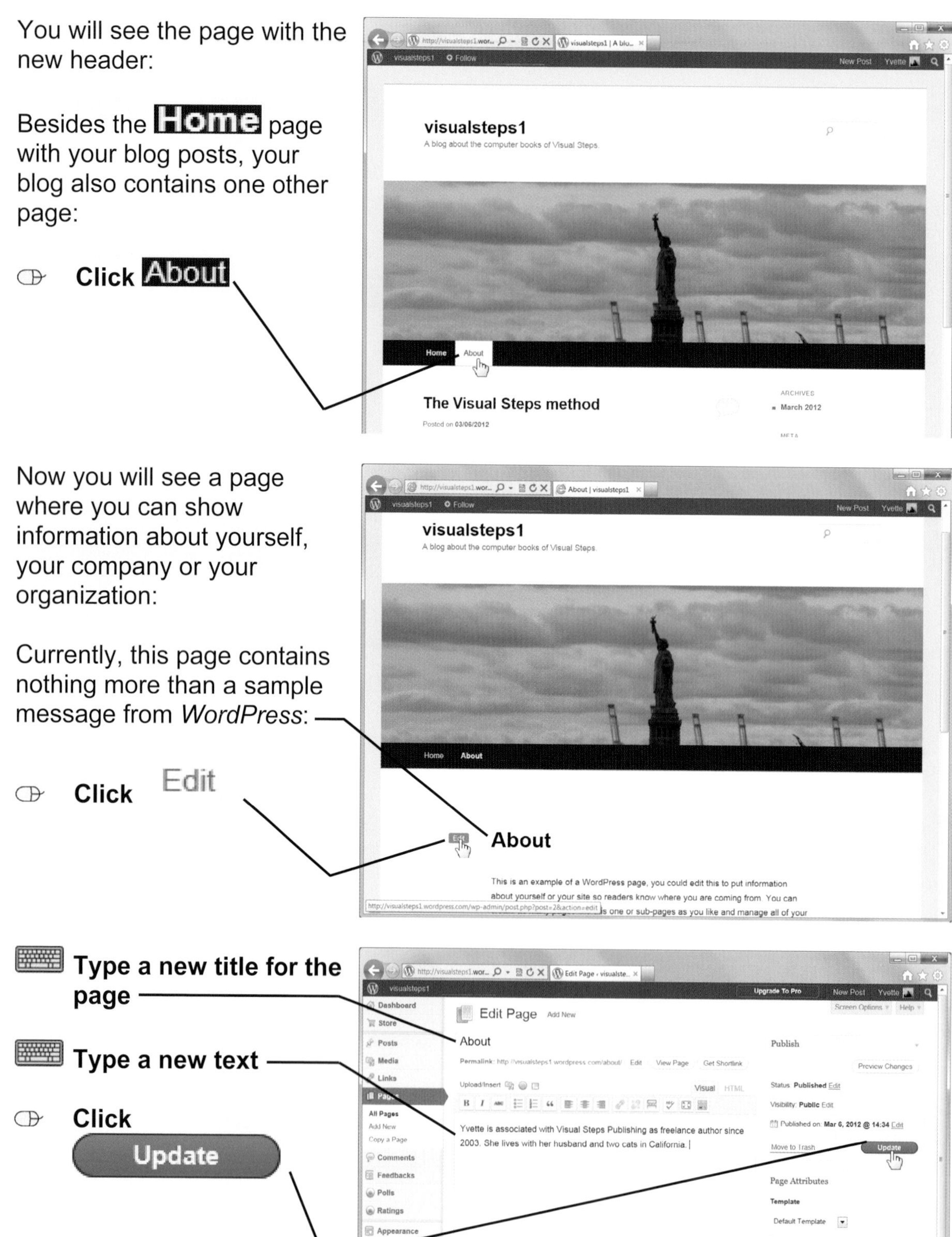

The page will be updated.

Tip

Profile

The type of information you publish on this page, will depend on the purpose for which you want to use your blog. If you only intend to use your blog for personal messages, you can tell something about yourself and your hobbies. If you want to use your blog for business purposes, it is better to keep the text more professional. Write about who you are and what you have to offer to your target group.

Please note:

On this page you cannot add blog posts. You can only do this on the **Home** page.

4.9 Adding a Photo Page

Your blog can consist of more than one page. This is how you add an extra page:

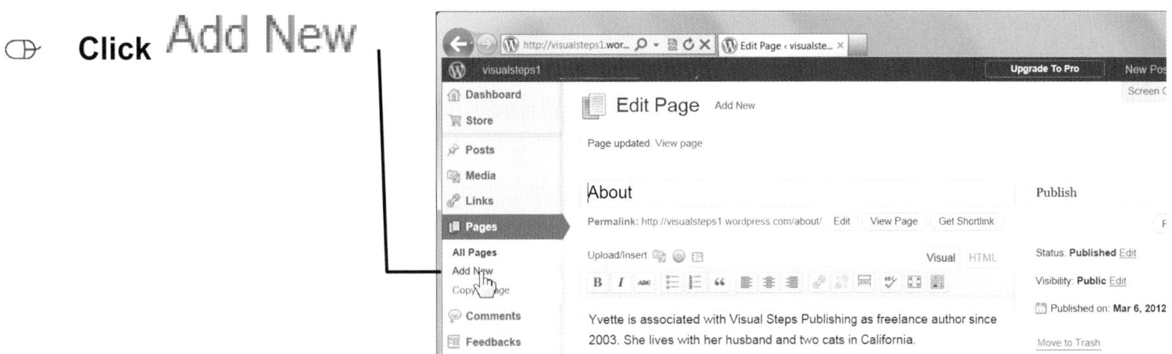

Instead of a page filled with text, you can also add a photo gallery. Here is how you do that:

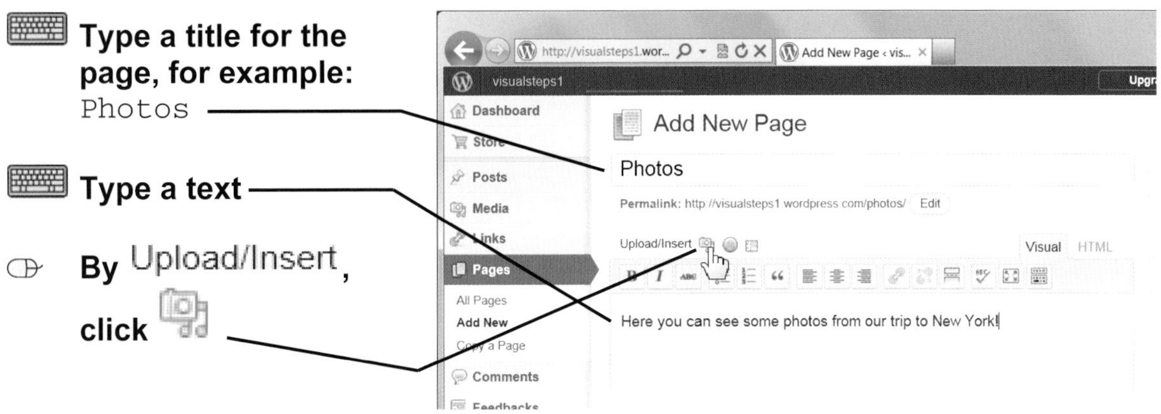

Click Select Files

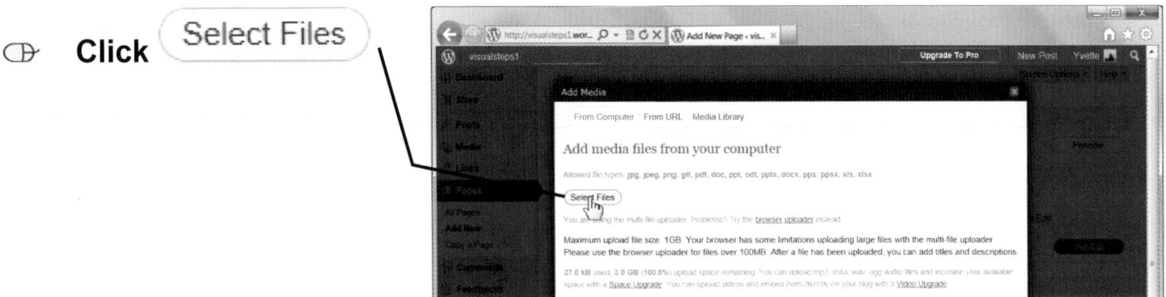

Select the folder that contains your photos

Now you can select the photos you want to upload:

Keep Ctrl depressed

Click the photos you want to upload

Release Ctrl

Click Open

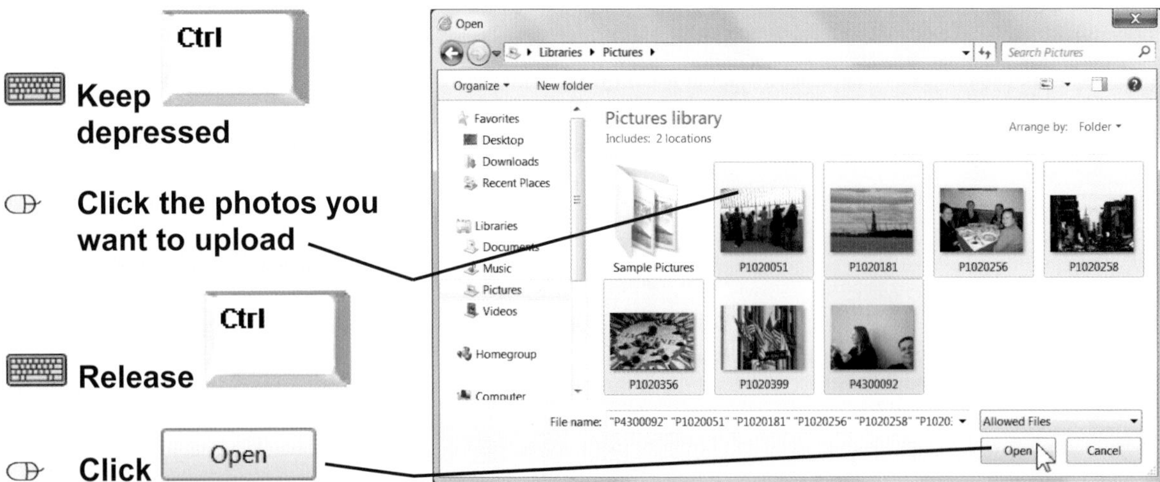

Now the photos will be uploaded. The progress of this operation will be displayed in the window. After all the photos have been uploaded:

Click Save all changes

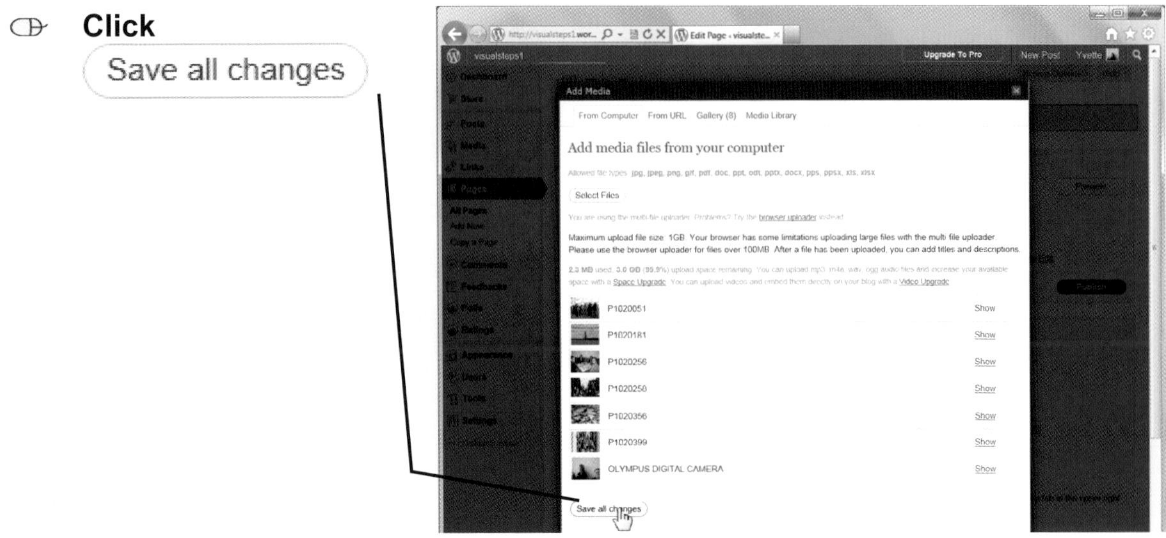

Now you can choose whether you want to add the photos as a photo gallery or as a slideshow. In this example we will add the photos as a photo gallery:

Drag the scroll bar downwards

By default, the photo gallery contains three columns:

Click Insert gallery

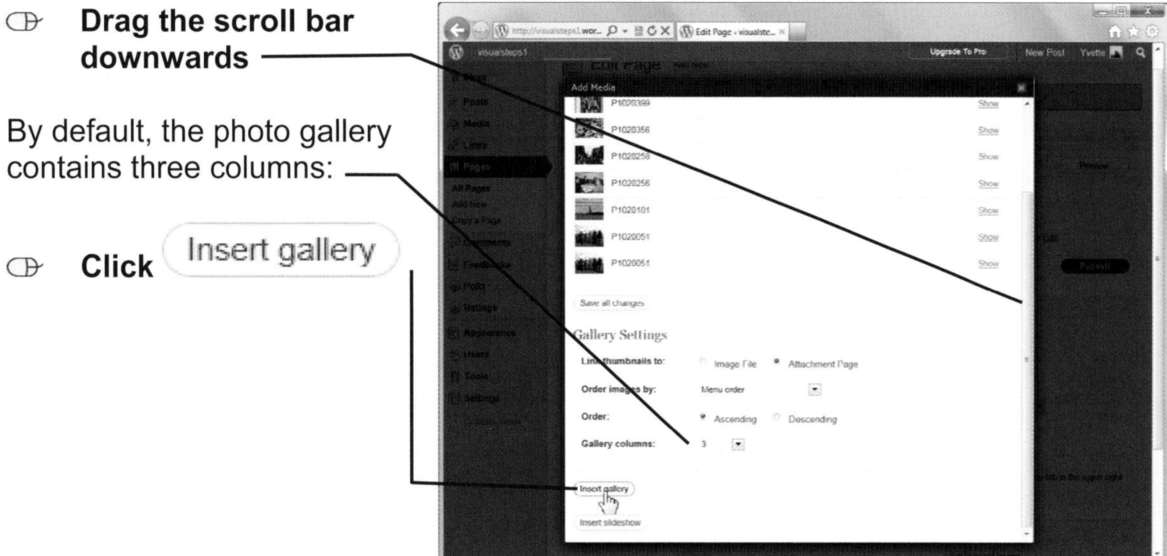

The photo gallery has been added to the page. Now you can publish the new page:

Click Publish

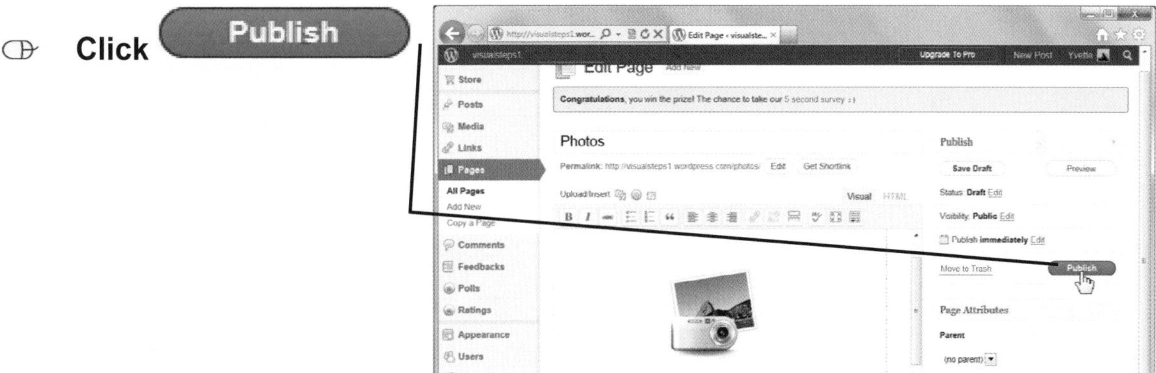

You can take a look now at the new page:

Click View page

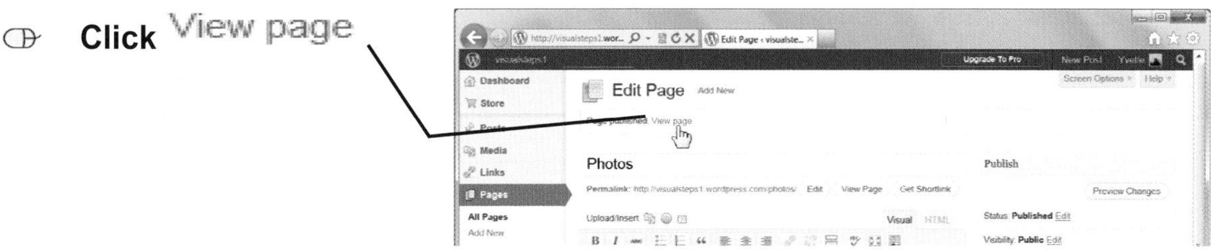

The page will be opened and you will see the photo gallery:

Click a photo

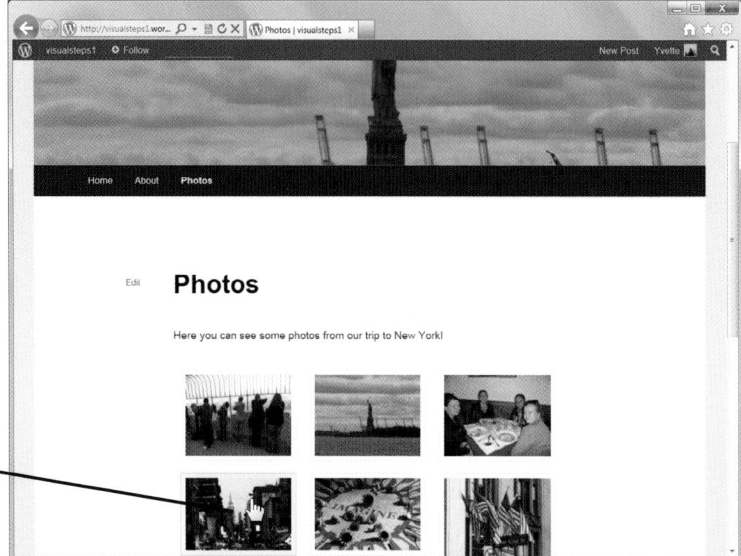

You will see a large display of the photo:

Click **Permalink**

Drag the scroll bar downwards

Click Edit

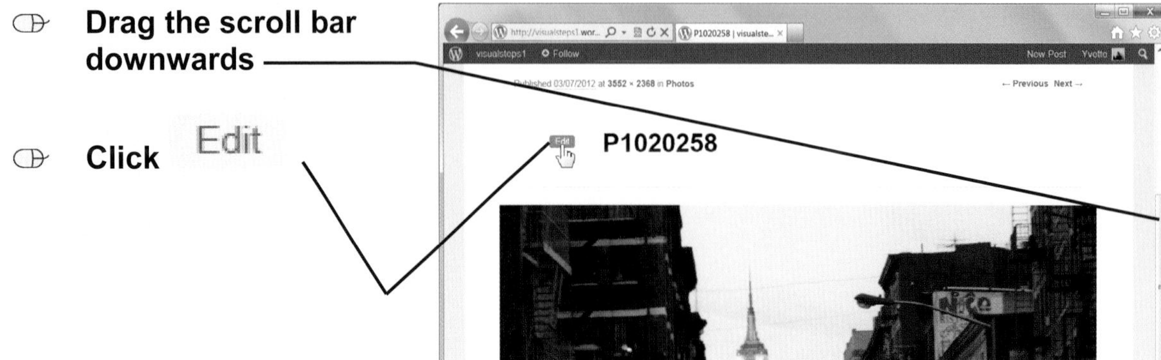

On the *Edit Media* page you can change the photo's title and add a caption:

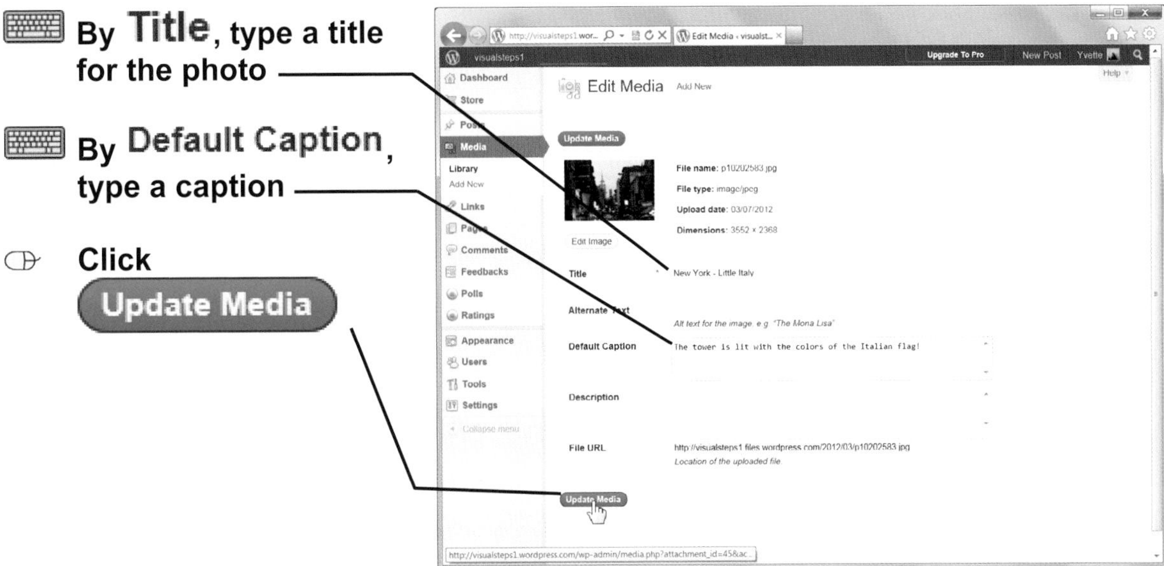

By Title, type a title for the photo

By Default Caption, type a caption

Click Update Media

You will see the photo once again, including the new title and caption. To return to the photo gallery:

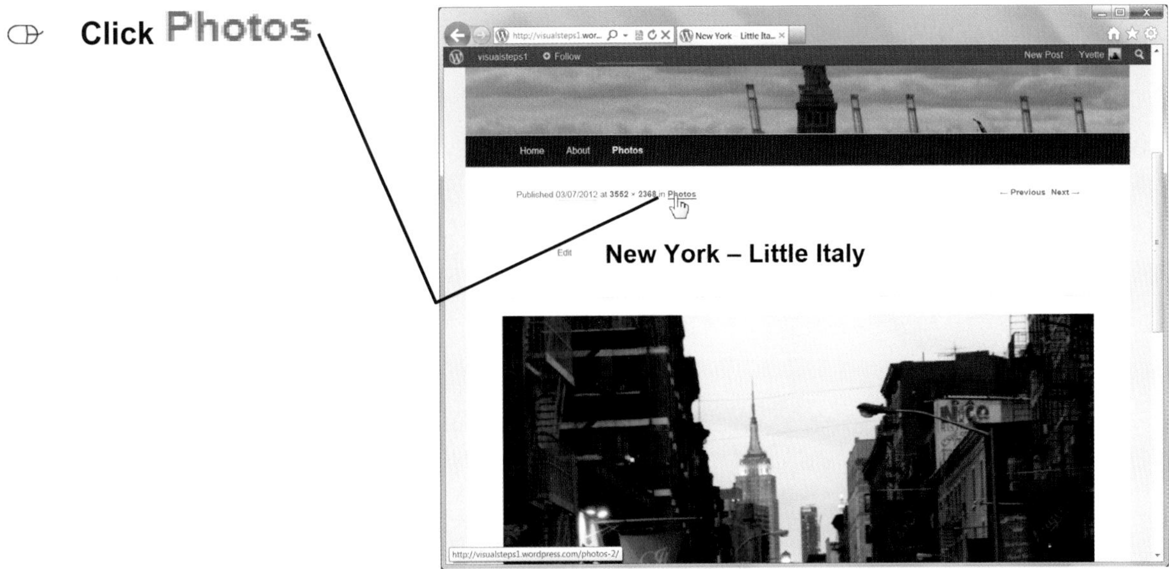

Click Photos

If you want, you can also edit the titles and captions of the other photos

4.10 Changing the Privacy Settings

You can decide who is allowed to view your blog by changing the privacy settings. To do this, you need to go to the settings page:

- **Click your name**
- **Click** Edit My Profile

- **If necessary, drag the scroll bar downwards**
- **Click** Settings
- **Click** Privacy

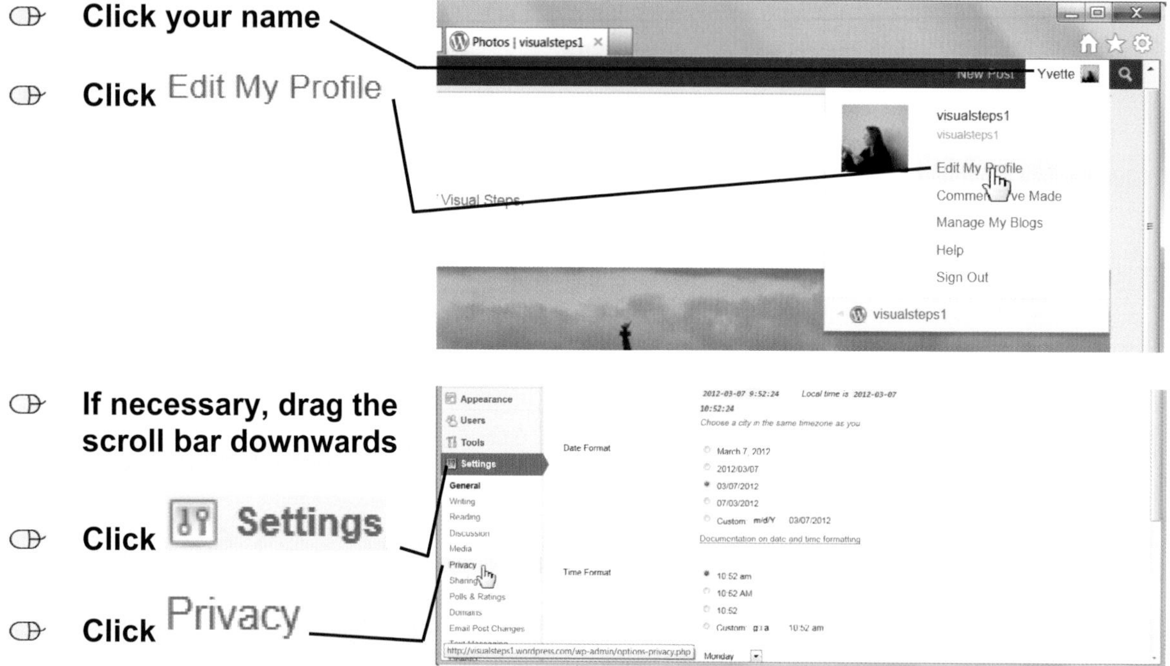

You can choose between three different settings. The first option, Allow search engines to index this site., means your site is visible to anyone, including all search engines. The Ask search engines not to index this site. option means anyone can view your site, except the search engines. Or you can decide to display your site only to your friends.

- **Click the radio button next to the option you want to use**
- **Click** Save Changes

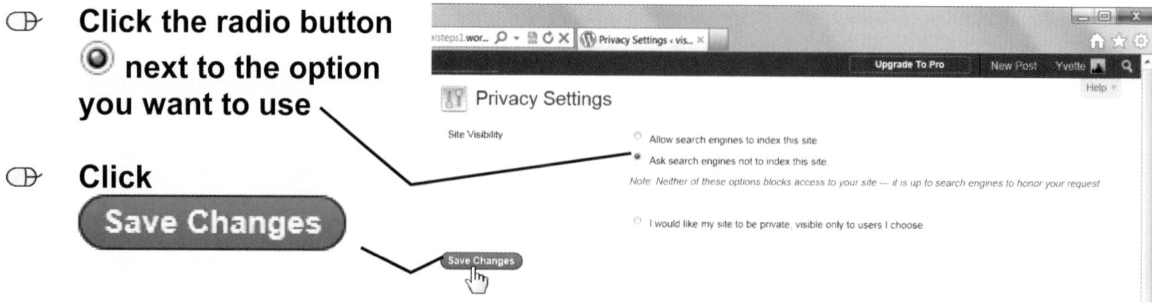

Tip

Private blog

If you decide to create a private blog, you can list up to 10 *WordPress* usernames of people who will be granted access to your blog. This is how you add the usernames:

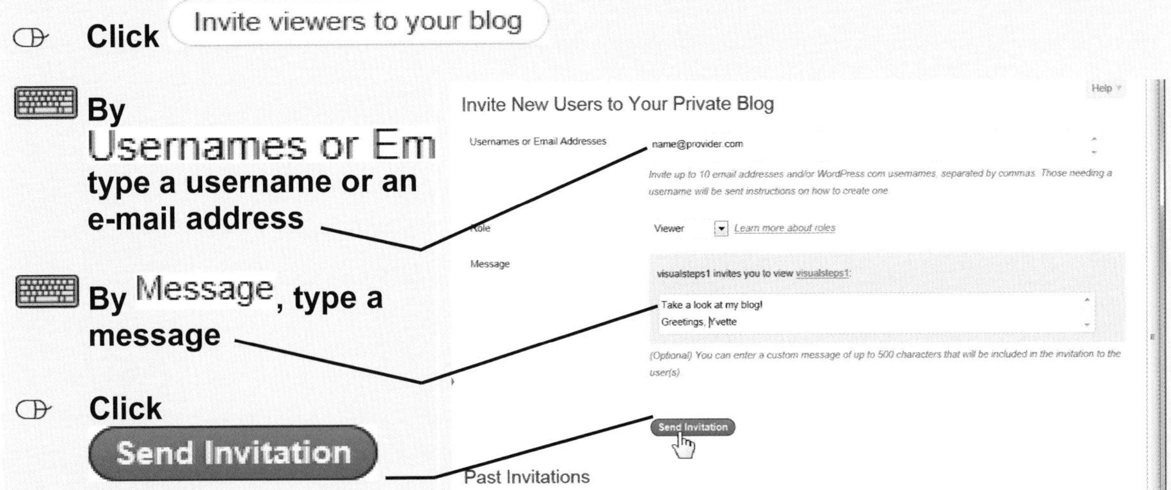

Click Invite viewers to your blog

By Usernames or Em **type a username or an e-mail address**

By Message**, type a message**

Click Send Invitation

Do you want to let more than 10 people view your site? That is possible, but you will need to pay a fee for this option. If you click Upgrade To Pro, you will be forwarded to a page where you can buy a license with which you can add an unlimited number of users to your private blog.

4.11 Changing the Comment Settings

You can also adjust the settings regarding the comments which will be posted on your blog:

By Settings**, click** Discussion

You will see the page with the comment settings:

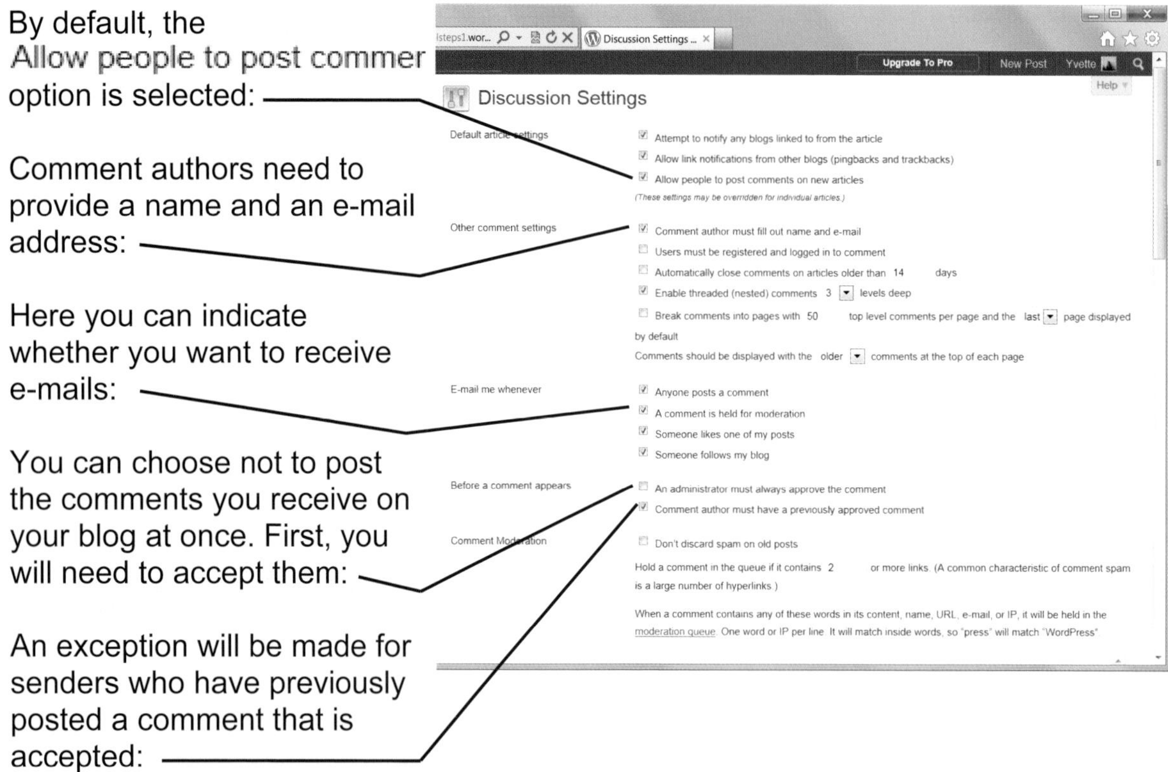

By default, the Allow people to post commer option is selected:

Comment authors need to provide a name and an e-mail address:

Here you can indicate whether you want to receive e-mails:

You can choose not to post the comments you receive on your blog at once. First, you will need to accept them:

An exception will be made for senders who have previously posted a comment that is accepted:

Take your time to read this page, because there are a lot of options to choose from. For instance, you can set up a blacklist, which will automatically categorize a comment as 'spam', if it contains a specific word or e-mail address.

Adjust the settings according to your wishes

Click 

Tip

Moderate comments

If you have decided that al comments need to be approved by the administrator (you), the Dashboard will tell you when new comments have been received:

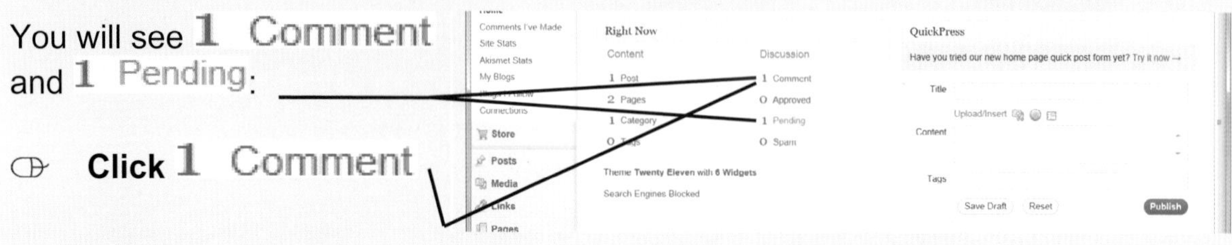

You will see 1 Comment and 1 Pending:

Click 1 Comment

- Continue on the next page -

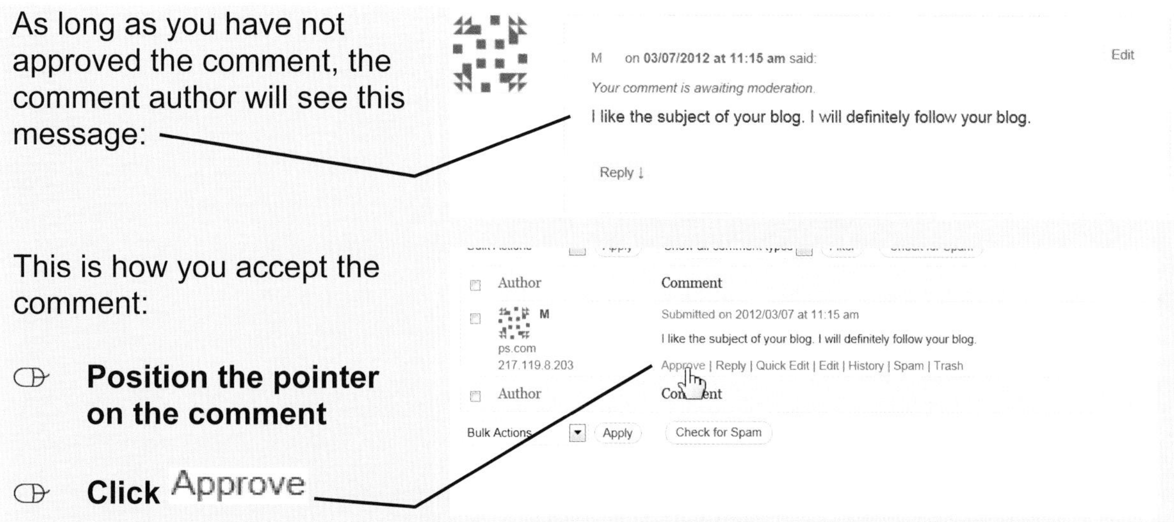

As long as you have not approved the comment, the comment author will see this message:

This is how you accept the comment:

- **Position the pointer on the comment**

- **Click** Approve

Now the comment will be displayed on your blog.

If you do not want to publish a comment on your blog, you can select either Trash or Spam (unwanted e-mail) and move the comment there. You can also Edit the comment.

4.12 Invite Readers

You have just created a blog and the blog is now online. Of course, you would like other people to read your messages. But how do you get in touch with your readers?

- **Send an e-mail message to your contacts and invite them to view your blog**

You can let everybody know you have a new blog by sending them an e-mail message. In this message you need to insert the hyperlink to your blog, for example: http:// visualsteps1.wordpress.com

- **Insert a link to your blog in your advertisement or your newsletter**

You can also publish a link to your blog in your digital company or family newsletter.

- **Post a link to your blog on your own website**

If you have your own website, you can also post a link to your blog on this website.

4.13 Deleting a Blog

If you want to delete your blog, follow these steps:

- **Click** Tools
- **Click** Delete Site

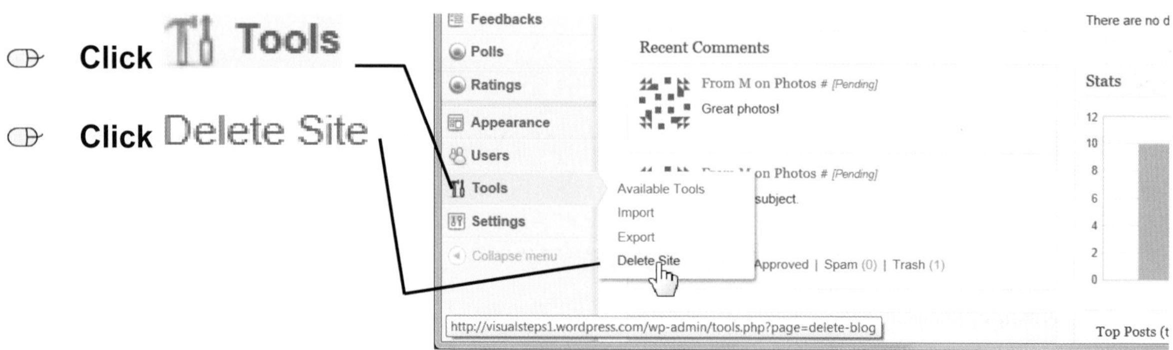

Please note:

Once you have deleted your blog, you will not be able to create a new blog using the same web address as in your previous blog.

You will be asked to confirm the delete operation.

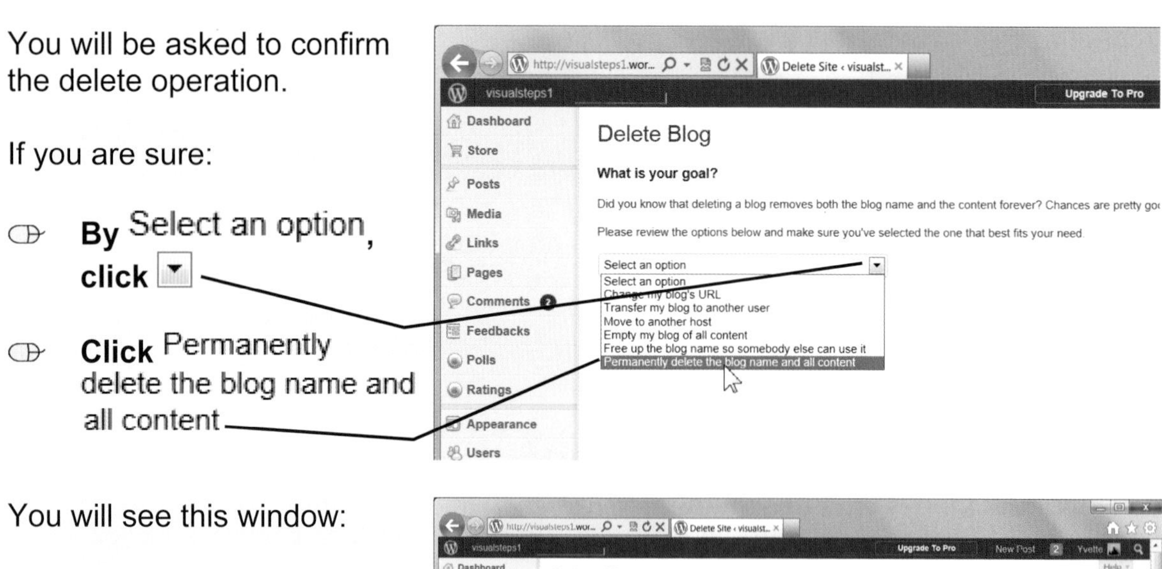

If you are sure:

- **By** Select an option, **click** ▼
- **Click** Permanently delete the blog name and all content

You will see this window:

- **Check the box** ☑ **next to** I want to **permanently remove** visualsteps1.wor
- **Click** Delete visualsteps1.wordpres Permanently »

Now you will see this window:

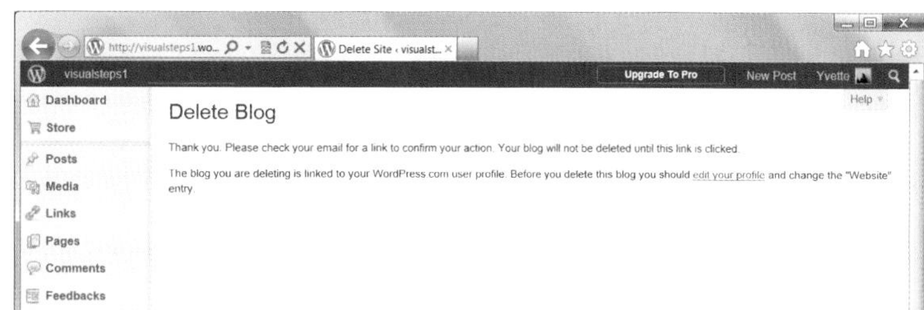

Your blog will be permanently deleted once you have clicked the link in the e-mail message sent to you by *WordPress*.

Open the *WordPress* e-mail message in your e-mail program

Click the link

Dear User,
You recently clicked the 'Delete Blog' link on your blog and filled in a form on that page.
If you really want to delete your blog, click the link below. You will not be asked to confirm again so only click this link if you are 100% certain:
http://visualsteps1.wordpress.com/wp-admin/tools.php?page=delete-blog&h=EDMa0MjFPkljmRFlghlw

If you delete your blog, please consider opening a new WordPress.com blog some time in the future! But remember your current blog is gone forever.

Thanks for using the site,
All at WordPress.com
http://wordpress.com/

Your blog has been deleted.

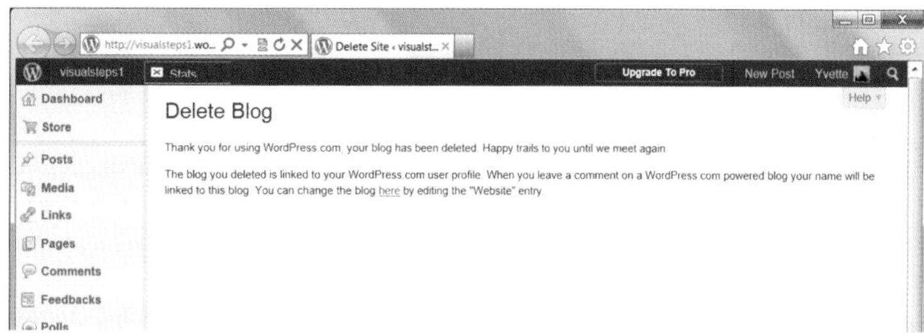

Your account and the public profile linked to this account will still exist at *WordPress*. *WordPress* accounts cannot be completely deleted. This policy will not pose a security or privacy threat to you. If you do not wish to use *WordPress* any longer, just stop using the account. *WordPress* itself will not make use of this account in any way.

Close all windows 4

In this chapter you have learned how to create and edit a *WordPress* blog. In the following section you will read about some useful ways of maintaining a blog for a company, organization or a club.

4.14 Using a WordPress Blog for Commercial Purposes

A *WordPress* blog is a very flexible medium that can easily be used for communicating with companies, organizations and clubs. For instance, a club can use a blog for publishing reports and photos on various events and, of course, for announcing new events. A blog post can also be used for introducing a new team or a team member.

A company can use a blog as a marketing and PR tool. You can post messages about new developments within the company (new products, services, employees or locations) and alternate these messages with tips regarding the use or maintenance of your products. Also, you can discuss a frequently asked question, or frequently occurring problems and present answers and solutions. Have you just completed an interesting project? Show some pictures and ask your customers to comment on the project. But remember; always ask the customers for permission if you want to post their comments on your blog.

Usually, the articles published on a blog are written by private persons in their own personal style. The topics often revolve round your own personal opinions and knowledge. Because readers are allowed to comment on the posts in the blog, you have actually opened an informal communication channel. Other readers can react to the comments, which may lead to a lively discussion on your blog. With a blog, your company or organization has a new tool for communicating with customers or members and it can allow you to forge a better bond with a specific target group.

Below you will find a number of tips regarding the do's and don'ts of maintaining a blog for a company, organization or club.

 **Tip**

Do it!

1. Search

It is a good idea to search for the name of your company, brand, product, service, organization or club in other people's blogs, on a regular basis. Make sure you know what people are saying about your company or organization. In this way, you will find messages and comments you can use for your own blog, and you can react to general comments you find on the Internet. At the http://wordpress.com website you can use the button to start a search.

2.Follow

Make sure you know what is going on, by following the right people and reading their blogs. Follow your competitors' blogs, as well as the blogs of potential customers and companies in the same line of business as you.

- Continue on the next page -

3. Quickly allow comments
If you have determined that comments need to be reviewed first, before they are posted, make sure you do this very swiftly. If it takes several days for a comment to be posted, the readers will not be inclined to react to your future posts in a hurry, or will not react at all.

4. Answer questions
Try to answer questions on your blog within 24 hours. Post your answer in the form of a reaction, so others will also be able to read your answer. Answer any questions in a professional and positive manner.

5. React to compliments and feedback
React within 24 hours, to compliments and other types of feedback. If necessary just send a thank you message. The faster you post and react to messages, the more your followers will feel that you appreciate them and you will come across as someone who takes his customers or members seriously. This will increase the chance of your followers acting as your ambassadors, because they will start telling others about your product or service.

6. React to negative comments
Of course, you may also receive some negative comments on your blog, if people are not satisfied with a product or service. Do not hesitate to engage in a conversation with such people, be friendly and professional and try to find out why they are not happy with the product. If you do not do this, a negative comment can spread like wildfire, and possibly damage your business.
Could it be that someone has not received adequate assistance from the (telephonic) helpdesk? Offer your help, which will make it clear that your company employs people, not robots. Did somebody have a negative experience with your company, product or service? Offer your apologies and ask if this person needs assistance regarding a specific problem. Or ask him how you can provide more adequate help in the future. Keep in mind that a lot of people will read your messages.

7. Share the latest news
Provide your readers with useful information. Use your blog for sharing the latest news. Share a photo which offers a preview of your new product. Are you going to organize an event? Let your readers look behind the screen.

8. Ask questions
Ask your readers for their opinion; for instance, when you write about a new product or a new service you are developing. This will generate 'traffic' to your blog and people will start to react. This way, you can let people know that you appreciate their opinion, but you will also be able to collect valuable marketing information.

- Continue on the next page -

9. Post useful information on the About page
The About page is primarily intended for information about yourself, because you are the one writing the blog. If you are maintaining a blog for your company or association, you will also need to add information about this company or association, of course. But do not be too cool and businesslike; give your message a personal touch.

10. Carefully select the categories and tags for your messages
This will make your blog easier to find. In the *Tip* that follows this section you can read more about categories and tags.

11. Invite a guest blogger, once in a while
For a change, you can also invite a colleague or employee to write a post now and then, and let them express their opinion on the company and their job. Let them tell about their daily lives and experiences. Only ask them to do this if they really like to write, do not force them. And do not re-write their posts, just correct the typos and leave it at that.

Tip

Do not do this!
1. Post pointless messages
Make sure your posts contain added value for your readers. Find out who are the readers of your blog and establish the goal you want to achieve with your blog. If you are maintaining a professional blog, your readers will not be very interested in stories about your leisure activities in the weekend. But they will appreciate useful and pertinent information about the activities of your company, organization or club.

2. Post too many messages
Remember that your readers will usually view your blog just once a day. If a reader has subscribed to your blog, he or she may also receive your new posts per e-mail. Sending multiple messages a day may start to annoy them. It is better to post one message a day and think carefully about what you are going to say.

3. Post too few messages, or no messages at all
A company blog or an organization's blog where the most recent post is older than six months does not come across as a professional blog.

4. Only use the blog for advertising purposes
You readers expect more from your blog than just a bunch of advertisements. Of course you are allowed to pay some discreet attention to new products and services. But be sure to alternate these posts with information on other useful subjects, tips, news, links or photos.

- Continue on the next page -

5. Refuse comments
If you have determined that you want to accept the comments first, before posting them on your blog, it is not wise to delete negative messages right away. Of course, you can delete messages that contain foul language and unwanted merchandising. But if you delete a negative comment, the writer of that comment may start looking for publicity somewhere else on the Internet. It is better to publish the comment and react to it in a professional manner.

6. Edit comments
It is not recommended to edit comments before publishing them. Even if you think a comment contains false information, it is wiser to post the comment and react to it in a friendly and professional manner.

Tip

Categories and tags
You can use *categories* to group related messages. This makes it more clear what the posts are about. Categories will also make it easier for your readers to find your messages.
Categories are a lot like *tags* (keywords). You can use tags to give more detailed information on the subject of your post. For instance, if you post a message with a recipe for making apple pie, you could use the categories 'recipe' and 'pie' for this post. But you can also add tags, such as 'apple', 'raisins' and 'cinnamon'.

This is how you add a category to your message:

By Categories**, click** + Add New Category

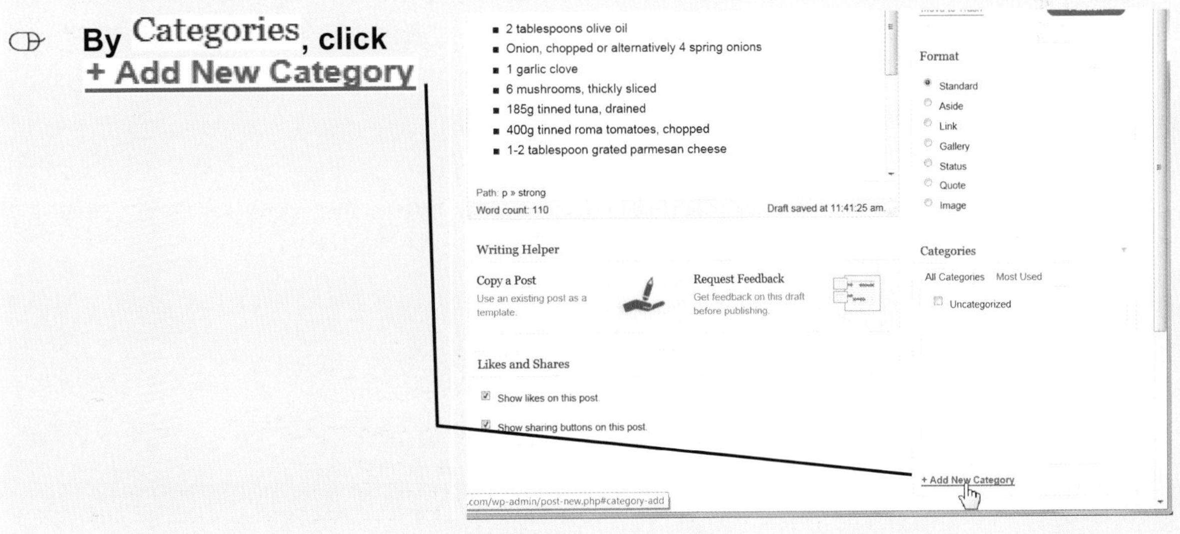

- Continue on the next page -

For example, type:
`recipe`

Click Add New Category

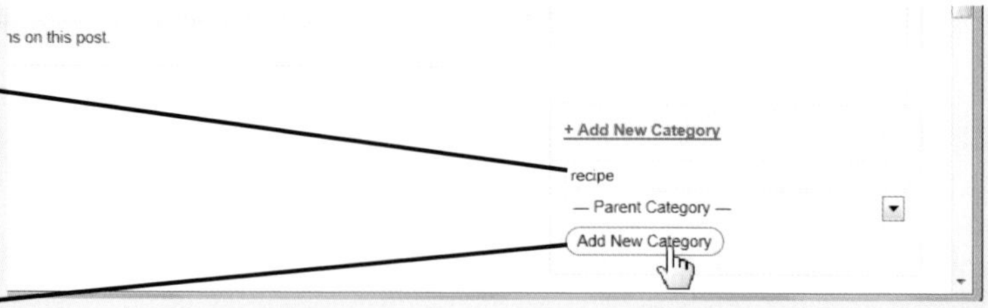

Now the category will be added:

The box ☑ next to the category has been checked right away. This means that the category is used for the current message:

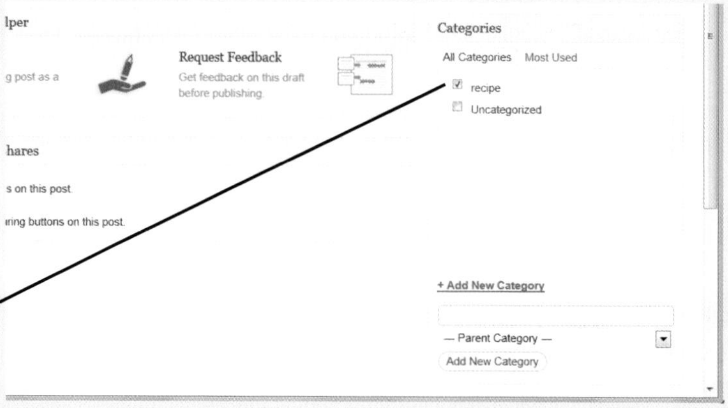

In the same way, you can add a single tag or multiple tags to your message:

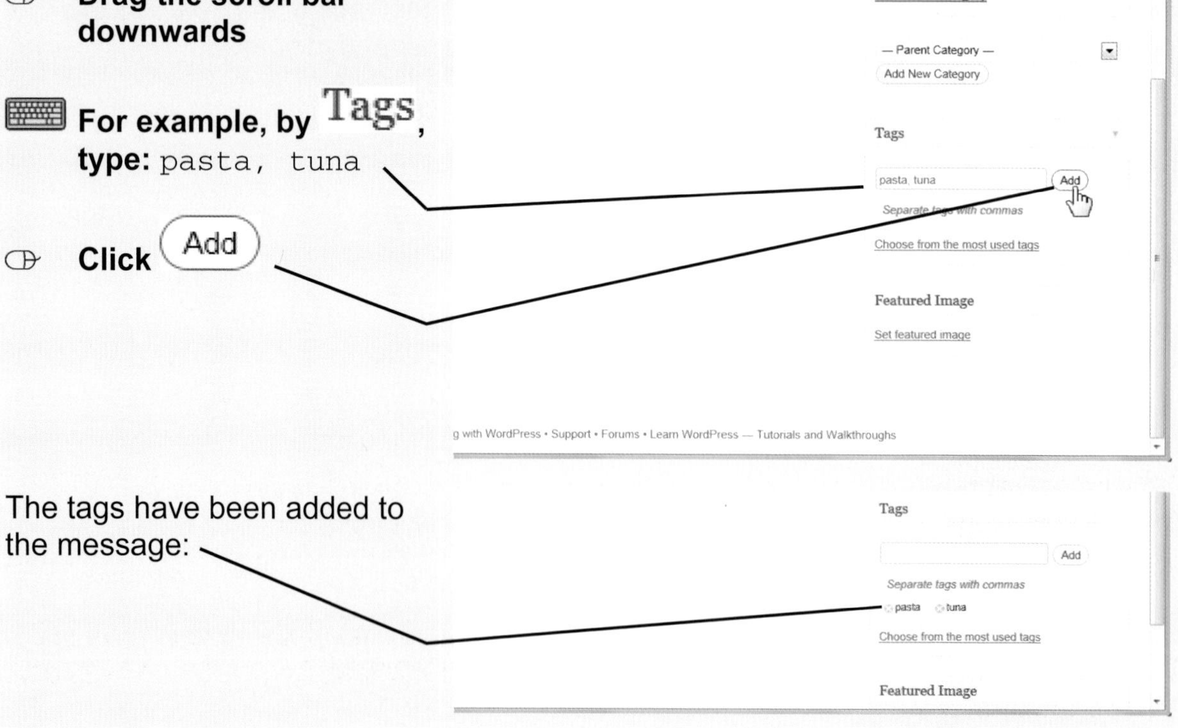

Drag the scroll bar downwards

For example, by Tags, **type:** `pasta, tuna`

Click Add

The tags have been added to the message:

- Continue on the next page -

The category and the tags will be displayed together with the message you posted:

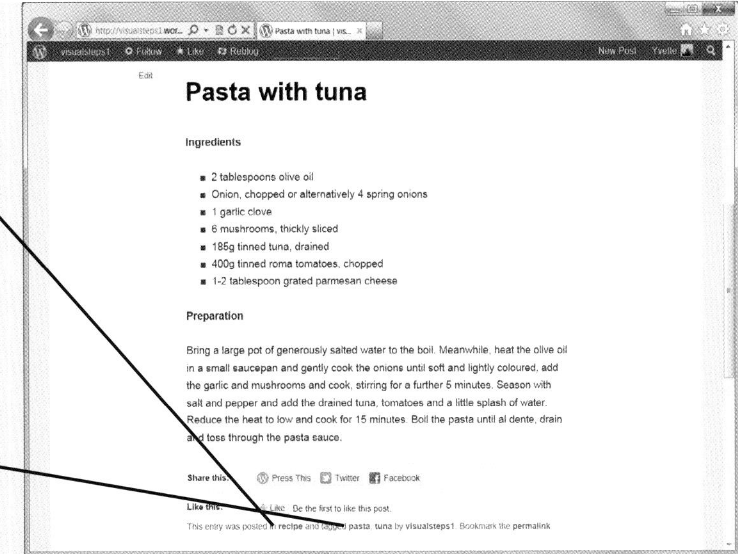

Here you see the categories that are used in this blog:

When the reader clicks a category, all messages in this category will be displayed.

The tags will also be displayed beneath the message:

When the reader clicks a tag, all messages with this tag will be displayed.

By using categories and tags, you will increase the chance of other *WordPress* users noticing your blog.
Then, your post can be included in the *global tag listing* on the http://wordpress.com/tags website:

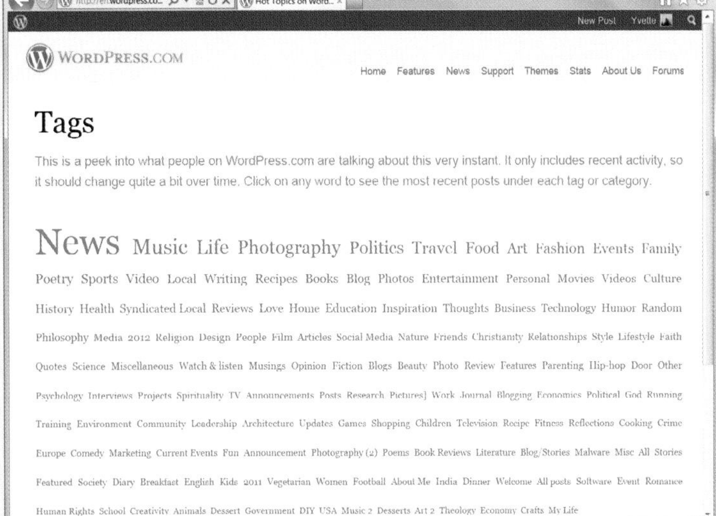

This listing represents a current overview of the most frequently used tags in *WordPress* blogs. If you click a tag, the most recent posts with this tag or category will be displayed.

The more tags and categories you use, the smaller the chance for you to end up in the global tag listing. So do not overdo it: do not use more than five up to ten tags or categories or a combination of both.

4.15 Visual Steps Website and Newsletter

So you have noticed that the Visual Steps-method is a great method to gather knowledge quickly and efficiently. All the books published by Visual Steps have been written according to this method. There are quite a lot of books available, on different subjects. For instance about *Windows*, *Mac*, iPad, photo editing, and about free programs, such as *Google Earth* and *Skype*.

Website
Use the blue *Catalog* button on the **www.visualsteps.com** website to read an extensive description of all available Visual Steps titles, including the full table of contents and part of a chapter (as a PDF file). In this way you can find out if the book is what you expected.

This instructive website also contains:

- free computer booklets and informative guides (PDF files) on a range of subjects;
- a large number of frequently asked questions and their answers;
- information on the free *Computer certificate* you can obtain on the online test website **www.ccforseniors.com**;
- free 'Notify me' e-mail service: receive an e-mail when book of interest are published.

Visual Steps Newsletter
Do you want to keep yourself informed of all Visual Steps publications? Then subscribe (no strings attached) to the free Visual Steps Newsletter, which is sent by e-mail.

This Newsletter is issued once a month and provides you with information on:

- the latest titles, as well as older books;
- special offers;
- new, free computer booklets and guides.

As a subscriber to the Visual Steps Newsletter you have direct access to the free booklets and guides, at **www.visualsteps.com/info_downloads**

4.16 Background Information

Dictionary

About	A page on your blog that contains information about yourself.
Administrator	The administrator or moderator of a blog.
Blog	Online diary, or journal also known as a *weblog*.
Blogger	Someone who maintains a blog.
Category	A method for grouping related messages on your blog.
Crop	Cut out an image, make it smaller.
Dashboard	The central page where you can manage and edit your blog.
Gallery	A rendering of photos on a page in your blog.
Gravatar	Short for *Globally Recognized Avatar*. A small image which represents the user of a service. If you move the pointer over the Gravatar, you will see brief profile information.
Header	The photo that is displayed at the top of your blog.
Home	The main page of your blog, where your messages are posted.
Moderate	View the comments to a post and evaluate whether you want to publish them on your blog.
Privacy settings	The settings you can use to determine whether your blog can be found (or not) by search engines. You can also decide to create a private blog.
Private blog	A blog that can only be viewed by a maximum of 10 people whom you have registered with their user name.
Publish	Post your message on your blog.
Spam	Unwanted messages, usually advertisements.

- Continue on the next page -

Tag	A keyword you can add to your messages, so the readers can find the message more easily.
Tagline	A slogan that defines your blog.
Theme	The appearance of your blog. *WordPress* contains a large number of themes you can choose from.
Videopress	A paid extension of your *WordPress* account, which enables you to add video files to your blog.
Weblog	A different word for blog.
WordPress	A website where you can create and maintain a free blog.

Source: WordPress Help

Access account via an iPad
If you have an iPad you can also access your accounts via your iPad. You can use *Safari* to open the websites or use the app that belongs with the program. You can download these apps in the App Store.
Please note: the screens of the apps might look different than the screens on your computer.

4.17 Tips

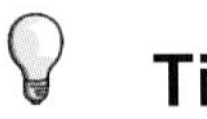

Tip

Message with a photo

You can very easily add a photo to a post on your blog. On the left-hand side of the window:

Click your name

Click New, Post

Type a title

Type the message

By Upload/Insert,

click

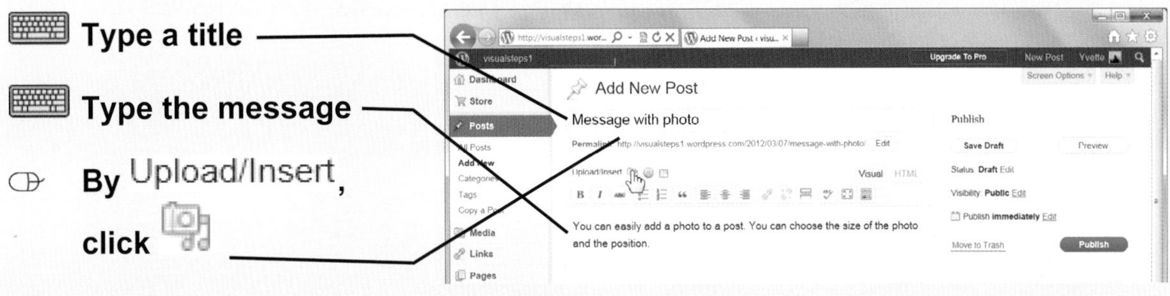

Click Select Files

Select the desired image and add this image 5

After the photo has been uploaded:

Drag the scroll bar downwards

Type a title and a caption for the photo

By Alignment**, select the desired alignment for the photo within the text**

By Size**, select the desired photo size**

Click Insert into Post

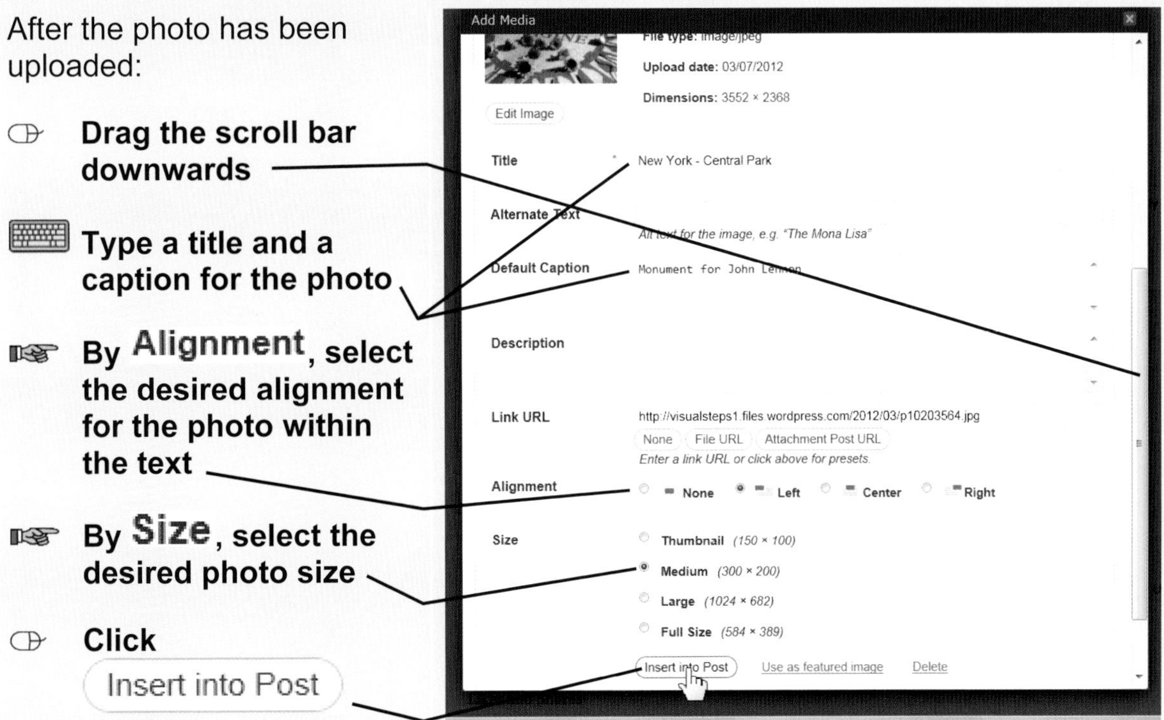

- Continue on the next page -

You will see the photo appear in the text. Now you can post the message on your blog:

- **Click** Publish

You can view the message right away on your blog:

- **Click, if necessary,** View page

You will see the message, with an average-sized photo that is aligned to the left:

Tip

Add audio and video

It is also possible to add audio or video files to a message on your blog. For adding video files you will need to purchase a paid extension for your account.

- **Click** Store

To upload a video, you will need VideoPress:

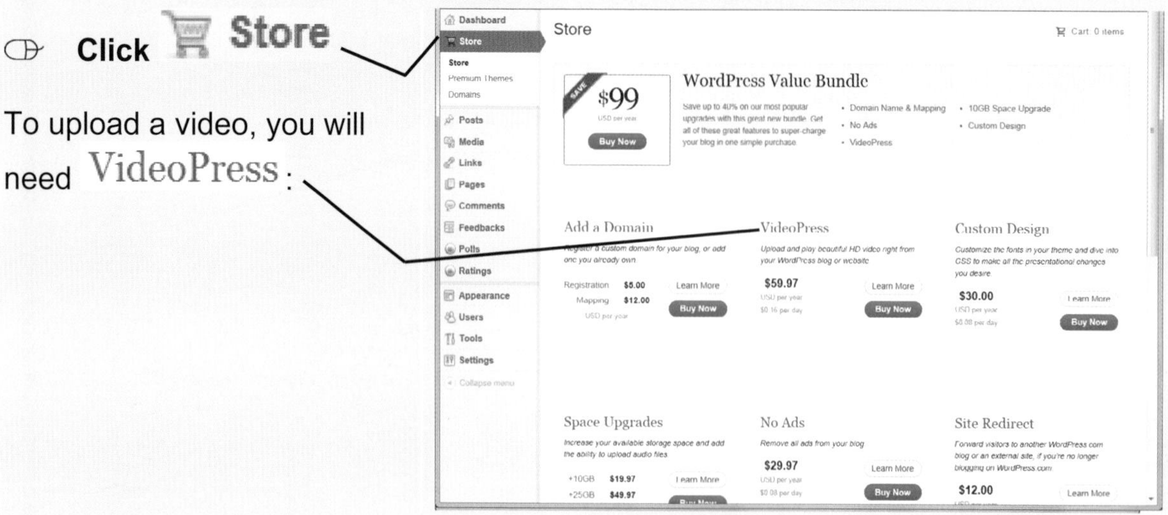

- Continue on the next page -

If you want to buy an extension:

- **By the desired extension, click** Buy Now
- **Follow the instructions in the window**

After you have purchased an extension, you can use the button by Upload/Insert to add a video clip to your message. For adding audio files directly from your computer, you will need to purchase the Space Upgrade before you can upload the audio files.

Tip

Create messages with *Writer*

You can use the free *Writer* program from the *Windows Live Essentials* suite of applications to compose and publish messages directly to your blog.
You can find more information about *Windows Live* at explore.live.com, or in **Windows Live Essentials for SENIORS** (ISBN 978 90 5905 356 4).

Tip

Add a link to a Word, Excel, PowerPoint or PDF document

You can also add a document to a message on your blog. This document will not be posted directly on the blog, but you will see a hyperlink with which the reader can open the document. In order to use *Word*, *Excel* or *PowerPoint* files, the reader will need to have the *Microsoft Office* program suite installed. For PDF files the reader will need to use the *Adobe Reader* program.

Adding a link to a document is very similar to adding a link to a photo:

- **Position the cursor on the spot in the text where you want to insert the link**
- **By** Upload/Insert, **click**

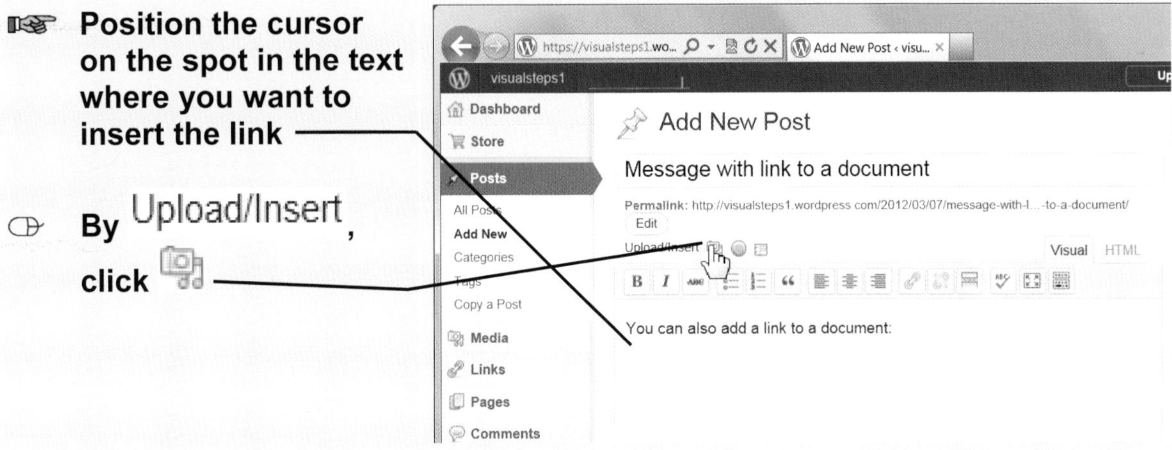

- *Continue on the next page* -

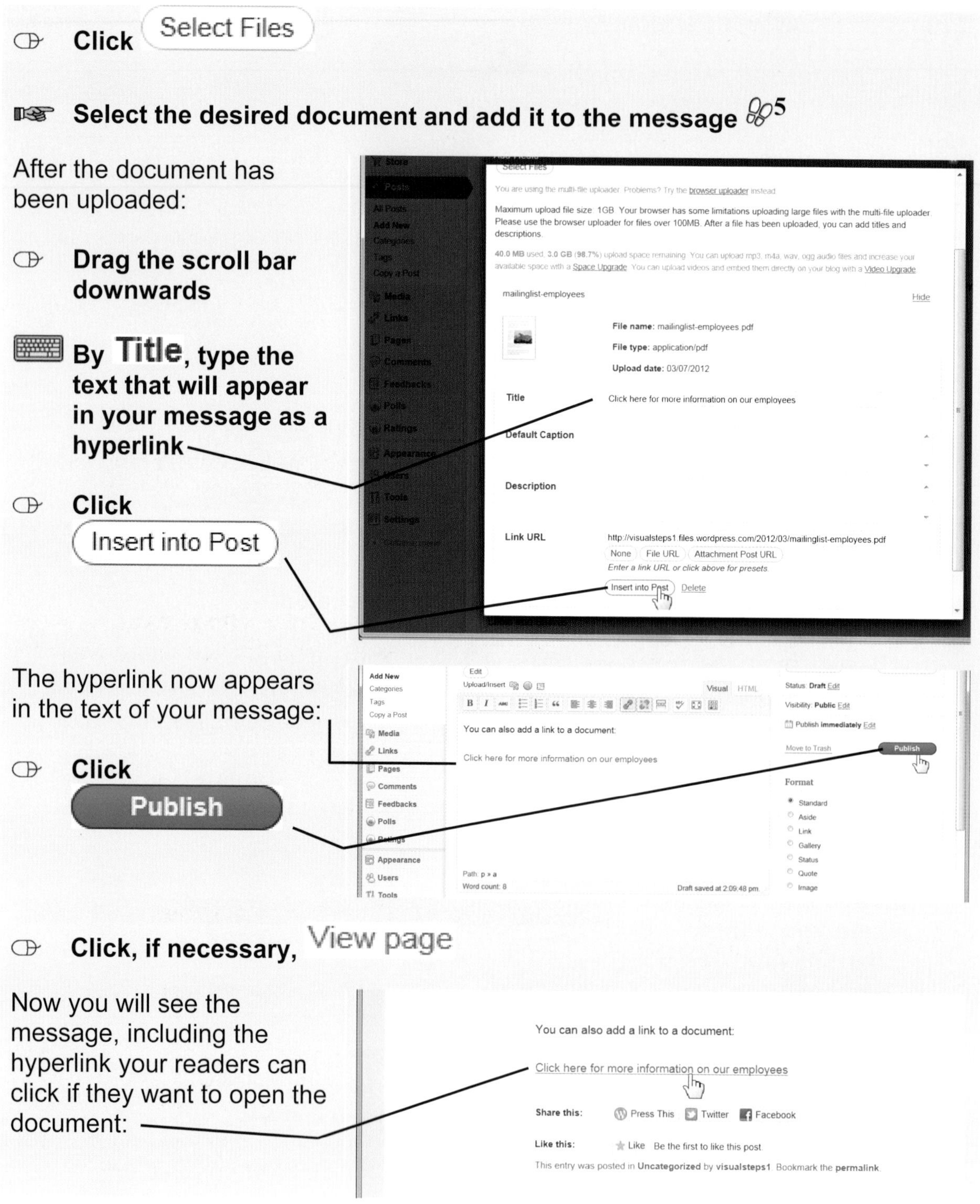

Click Select Files

Select the desired document and add it to the message 5

After the document has been uploaded:

Drag the scroll bar downwards

By Title, type the text that will appear in your message as a hyperlink

Click Insert into Post

The hyperlink now appears in the text of your message:

Click Publish

Click, if necessary, View page

Now you will see the message, including the hyperlink your readers can click if they want to open the document:

Appendix A How Do I Do That Again?

Many of the actions in this book are marked with footsteps: 1
In this appendix you can look up the numbers of the footsteps and read how to carry out a certain action once more.

1 **Open a website**
In Windows 7 and Windows Vista:

- Click
- Position the pointer on All Programs
- Click Internet Explorer

In Windows XP:

- Click 

- Click 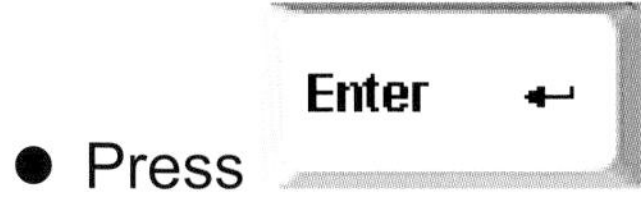

In the web browser:

- Click the address bar
- Type the web address
- Press Enter

2 **Open the home page**
- Click Home

3 **Open the profile page**
- Click your name

4 **Close window or tab**
- Click X or ×

5 **Select image or document and add**
- Select the folder with the images or documents
- Click the desired image or document
- Click Open

6 **Follow a *Twitter* account**
- Click the desired *Twitter* account
- Click Follow

7 **Open the *Settings* page**
- Position the pointer on your name
- Click Settings

8 **Open the home page**
- Click Home

9 **Copy a web address**
- Select the web address
- Right-click the web address
- Click Copy

10 **Paste a web address**
- Right-click the spot where the link should be inserted
- Click Paste

11 **Open your own *Twitter* page**

- Click Home

12 **Delete a tweet**

- Position the pointer on the message
- Click Delete
- Click Yes

13 **Open the *Settings* page**

- Click
- Click Settings

14 **Open home page**

- Click Home

15 **Open profile page**

- Click Your name View my profile page

Appendix B. Index

G

H

I

L

iPad for SENIORS

iPad for SENIORS
Get started quickly with the user friendly iPad

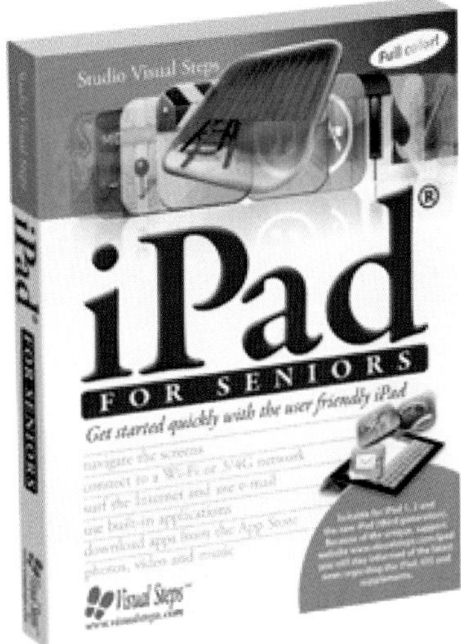

Author: Studio Visual Steps
ISBN: 978 90 5905 108 9
Book type: Paperback, full color
Number of pages: 296
Accompanying website:
www.visualsteps.com/ipad

This comprehensive and invaluable guide will show you how to get the most out of your iPad. The iPad is a very user friendly, portable multimedia device with endless capabilities. Use it to surf the Internet, write e-mails, jot down notes and maintain your calendar.
But that is not all you can do with the iPad by far. With the Apple App Store you can choose from hundreds of thousands of applications (apps). Many apps can be downloaded for free or cost practically nothing. This practical tablet computer offers apps to allow you to listen to music, take and view photos and make video calls. Perhaps you are interested in new recipes, horoscopes, fitness exercises, news from around the world or podcasts? You can even use it to view the place where you live in Google Street View. There is literally an app to do almost anything.
With *iPAD FOR SENIORS* you can learn how to take complete advantage of this technology. Before you know it, you won't believe you ever lived without an iPad and your world will open up and become a lot bigger!

You will learn how to:

- navigate the screens
- connect to a Wi-Fi or 3G network
- surf the Internet and use e-mail
- use built-in applications
- download apps from the App Store
- work with photos, video and music

Creating a Photo Book for SENIORS

Creating a Photo Book for SENIORS
Everything you need to create a professionally printed photo book

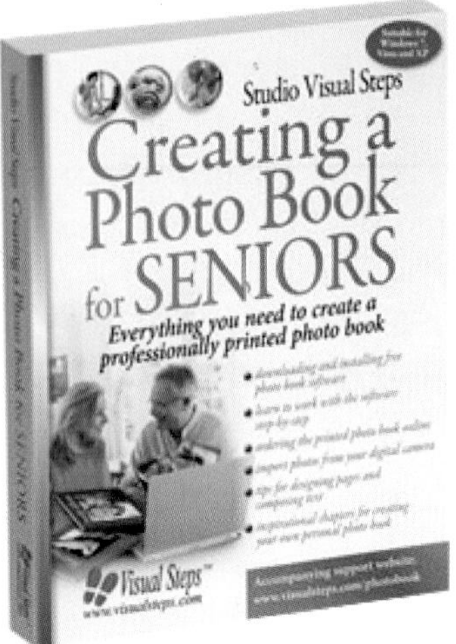

Author: Studio Visual Steps
ISBN 978 90 5905 247 5
Book type: Paperback, full color
Nr of pages: 240
Accompanying website:
www.visualsteps.com/ photobook

Creating your own illustrated book of memories has never been easier! This book will give you easy to understand step-by-step instructions with clear illustrations to guide you through the entire process.

Using free photo book software, this computer book will show you how to lay out your story with text, photos and other graphical elements. This step-by-step book offers lots of original ideas and practical tips for composing your text. For instance, the story of your childhood, your son or daughter's wedding, your family history, a travelogue, a chronicle of a baby's first year, even your own autobiography.

You will also learn how to transfer photos from your digital camera to your computer and incorporate them into your book and how to scan photos or other historical documents so that you can use them to further embellish your special photo book. And, finally, take advantage of the printing services offered by the photo book provider to insure that you will get a beautifully-crafted and professionally-bound photo book at the end of the process.
Creating a photo book has never been so easy!

You will learn how to:

- download and install the photo book software
- work with photo book software
- get your photo book printed
- transfer photos from a camera to the PC, scan photos
- use practical and creative tips for writing and layout
- view inspirational chapters to help you compile your own photo book